EDUCATION

Science and Religious Belief
A Selection of Recent Historical Studies

Science and Religious Belief
A Selection of Recent
Historical Studies

Readings edited by C. A. Russell

for the Open University Course
Science and Belief: from Copernicus to Darwin

HODDER AND STOUGHTON
in association with
The Open University Press

ISBN 0 340 18171 0 Paper

First published 1973: second impression 1979

Printed in Great Britain for
Hodder and Stoughton Educational,
a division of Hodder and Stoughton Ltd,
Mill Road, Dunton Green, Sevenoaks, Kent,
by Biddles Ltd, Guildford, Surrey.

Contents

Acknowledgments

The editor and publisher wish to thank the following for permission to reprint the articles included in this book: Professor Danton B. Sailor and The Journal of the History of Ideas Inc for 'Moses and Atomism' by Danton B. Sailor (reprinted from *Journal of the History of Ideas*, volume 25 (1964), pp. 3–16); the Editorial Board of the *Sociological Review* for 'Puritanism, Pietism and Science' by Robert K. Merton (reprinted from *Sociological Review* (old series), volume 28, part I (January 1936); Professor A. Rupert Hall and the Editorial Board of Science History Publications Ltd for 'Merton Revisited, or Science in the Seventeenth Century' (reprinted from *History of Science*, 1963, volume 2, pp. 1–16); Messrs Taylor and Francis Ltd for 'Religious Influences in the Rise of Modern Science' (reprinted from *Annals of Science*, volume 24, number 3 (September 1968), pp. 199–226); Messrs Heinemann Educational Books Ltd for 'The Grand Design – a New Physics' (reprinted from *The Birth of a New Physics* by I. B. Cohen, chapter 7, pp. 152–90); Messrs Routledge and Kegan Paul Ltd for 'The Metaphysics of Newton' (reprinted from *The Metaphysical Foundations of Modern Physical Science* by E. A. Burtt, second revised edition 1932, pp. 283–302); Professor David Kubrin and The Journal of the History of Ideas Inc for 'Newton and the Cyclical Cosmos: Providence and the Mechanical Philosophy' (reprinted from *Journal of the History of Ideas*, volume 28 (1967), pp. 325–46); Messrs Doubleday and Company Inc for 'The Apologetic Defence of Christianity' (reprinted from *Protestant Thought and Natural Science* by John Dillenberger, copyright © 1960 John Dillenberger, pp. 133–62); The Rev David Cairns and Cambridge University Press for 'Thomas Chalmers's Astronomical Discourses; A Study in Natural Theology' (reprinted from *The Scottish Journal of Theology*, 1956, volume 9, pp. 410–21); Dr M. J. S. Rudwick and the Editorial Board of Science History Publications Ltd for 'The Principle of Uniformity' (reprinted from *History of Science*, 1962, volume 1, pp. 82–6); The MIT Press for 'Diluvialism and Its Critics' (reprinted from *Towards a History of Geology*, edited by Cecil J. Schneer, 1969, pp. 259–71); Harvard University Press for 'Cuvier and Evolution' (reprinted from *Georges Cuvier, Zoologist* by William Cole-

52120

man, copyright 1964 the President and Fellows of Harvard College, pp. 170–86); Dr J. S. Wilkie and Cambridge University Press for 'Buffon, Lamarck and Darwin: The Originality of Darwin's Theory of Evolution' (reprinted from *Darwin's Biological Work*, edited by P. R. Bell, 1954, pp. 262–307, 340–3); Professor Owen Chadwick and Messrs A. & C. Black Ltd for 'Evolution and the Churches' (reprinted from *The Victorian Church*, Part II, 1966, chapter 1, pp. 23–35); Messrs Basil Blackwell and Mott Ltd for 'The Christian Doctrine of Creation and the Rise of Modern Natural Science' (reprinted from *Mind*, 1934, volume 43, pp. 446–68).

Introduction

This anthology is a collection of fairly recent scholarly articles brought together for the Open University course, 'Science and Belief: from Copernicus to Darwin'. It is intended to be complete in itself, though a complementary collection of primary source material[1] has been compiled to be used with it in that course, together with two other set books[2] and the Open University correspondence and broadcasting material. The intention has been to make available something of the wealth of modern scholarship to readers who do not have access to the great university libraries with their holdings of books and periodicals.

A curious reader who happens to see this book may well be puzzled by several of its features. In the first place it deals with one of those issues considered by many to be now stone dead, the interaction between Science and Belief, the latter being chiefly of the religious variety. Indeed, its subject-matter to all intents and purposes runs out at least a century ago, with the rise of Darwinism; this reinforces the impression that the controversies are now only distant echoes from the Victorian past, and before. Then, secondly, even granted that the subject-matter is treated from a basically historical point of view, there is relatively little on the great crises in which religious belief seemed likely to be engulfed in the advancing tides of science. Finally, an inordinate amount of attention appears to have been paid to events in the eighteenth century.

Whether the science and religion controversy really is quite as dead as some would wish to make it appear is a matter for debate. But the Course Team responsible for this Open University course are in no doubt that a serious historical study can often illustrate contemporary issues in a significant way, and that it is often highly relevant to enquire how a given situation in the present arose from complex combinations of circumstances in

[1] *Science and Religious Belief: A Selection of Primary Sources*, edited by D. C. Goodman, John Wright & Sons, 1973.
[2] R. Hooykaas, *Religion and the Rise of Modern Science*, Scottish Academic Press, 1972; C. C. Gillispie, *Genesis and Geology*, Harper and Row, 1959.

the past. Hence we make no apology for attempting a historical analysis of the interaction between scientific and non-scientific belief systems. Once such an enquiry is begun one of the first things to become clear is that the great 'confrontations' between organised religion and science associated with the names of Galileo and Darwin are mere episodes in the much larger historical development of modern science. For this reason the matter becomes a proper subject of enquiry in the History of Science, though that is not to say that it finds no place on the even larger canvas of general intellectual history. So instead of concentrating on polemics for or against the claims of Christian theology in the light of modern science the course, and therefore this anthology also, is attempting to place such polemics in their true historical context. This is not to deny the relevance of theological and philosophical debate; it might even be to assert it by providing a historical analysis of the underlying issues. The simple fact that emerges is that science has been affected by religious and other non-scientific belief at least as much as the converse may be true.

That there is a strong interest in such matters amongst professional historians of science may be evident from this collection, most of which derives from their writings. It is in fact an extremely rich area from which to draw, and the problem of selection has been an acute one. There is so much worthwhile material of a high order of scholarship that has simply had to be omitted on the grounds of space. To some extent selection has been conditioned by the recent publication of Hooykaas's *Religion and the Rise of Modern Science*, and the desirability to avoid too much overlap with that and with Gillispie's *Genesis and Geology*. There are contributions from a sociologist and several philosophers and theologians, though most come from the pens of historians of science. (The importance attached to this theme by such scholars is reflected in the subject chosen for the annual summer meeting of the British Society for the History of Science, held at Lancaster in 1973: 'Science and Faith'.)

The collection opens with an account by Danton B. Sailor of a seventeenth-century tendency to ascribe atomism to Moses (rather than the Greeks) in order to divest it of materialistic implications! The next three articles are more sociological in tone, and concern particularly the association between puritanism and science in seventeenth-century England. They include the crucial paper of 1936 in which the so-called 'Merton thesis' was first expounded. Since then much scholarship has gone into an examination of this thesis and its ramifications, and we reprint two more recent essays by A. Rupert Hall and Douglas S. Kemsley.

Another trio of articles is concerned with Sir Isaac Newton. A chapter from I. B. Cohen's *The Birth of a New Physics* is a remarkably lucid exposition of the scientific background to the unparalleled achievement that was Newtonian dynamics. Although this is the most scientifically technical extract in the book non-scientists will read it without much difficulty. If ever science and theology were inextricably bound up in the mind of one man, that man was Newton. The chapter by Burtt on his metaphysics is followed by a paper from Kubrin on the implication of Newton's cosmology for the concept of Providence.

The mechanical philosophy of the eighteenth century was far from always being a thorn in the side of religious belief generally, but it did create some difficulties. One consequence was the new emphasis on the revelation of God in nature and the popularisation of natural theology. John Dillenberger gives a wide-ranging survey of events, while David Cairns gives a sensitive account of one particular discourse in natural theology from the point of view of a mid-twentieth-century theologian.

There are two essays in geological history, to complement the fuller account given by Gillispie. A book review by Martin Rudwick and a chapter on Diluvialism by Leroy Page underline the essential issues. These, together with the preceding articles, may help to explain why the eighteenth century was considered sufficiently important to be well represented in the collection.

Clearly no book of this kind could afford to ignore Darwin, and three extracts deal at some length with his work, that of his predecessors and the impact made on the Victorian Church by his theory of evolution. Finally we have included a crucial paper by M. B. Foster which argues from the view-point of a philosopher the underlying relationships between Christian theology and modern science. This is one of the oldest essays in the book (it dates from 1934) but because of its depth of insight and profound influence on later thinking it forms a fitting conclusion to the anthology.

In assembling this collection I am glad to acknowledge helpful discussions with colleagues on the Course Team, particularly Dr John Brooke and Dr David Goodman. I am grateful to my wife, Shirley, for preparing the indexes.

The Open University   *C. A. Russell*
March 1973

Footnote—In several of the articles a few obvious and minor misprints have been corrected.

1   Moses and Atomism[*]

Danton B. Sailor

Science in the seventeenth century seemed to have materialistic
and even atheistic implications not only for religious thinkers but
for many of the scientists themselves. Accordingly, a considerable effort was made, especially in England, to show that science
as a method could only reveal the same truths as religion. In the
most significant instance, the attempt was made to show that
the dominant materialistic hypothesis, i.e. the atomic, had
theistic rather than atheistic implications. There were two basic
approaches to the latter problem. The first advanced the argument that since, by the admission of the materialists themselves,
matter is inert and incapable of self-creation, then there must
exist non-matter, which is self-creative and the source of all
material existence, i.e. God. This argument hinges on the classical
formula of *de nihilo nihil* and can be associated broadly with the
interests and methods of scholasticism.

A second approach is perhaps even more significant for the
history of ideas in that it can illuminate the sources of certain
key elements in the metaphysical thought of seventeenth-century
scientists. It was the special product of Renaissance humanism
and sought to show that the atomic hypothesis was not atheistic,
through a kind of historical scholarship as well as through logic.
Specifically, it came to assert that that hypothesis originated not
with the Greek materialistic philosophers but much earlier in the
Hebraic tradition, namely with Moses the prophet.

The attempt to broaden the acceptance of all manner of pagan
ideas by this means characterized humanism in the Italian quat-
trocento. Marsilio Ficino not only asserted repeatedly the parallelism of Platonism with the Mosaic and Christian doctrines but absorbed the idea, chiefly from Pletho, of an ancient succession
through which certain truths came down from the Hebraic to
the Hellenic culture.[1] But it was Pico della Mirandola who was

*Danton B. Sailor, 'Moses and Atomism', *Journal of the History of Ideas*,
1964, 25, 3–16.
[1] P. O. Kristeller, *The Philosophy of Marsilio Ficino* (New York, 1943), 15.

most influential in disseminating this doctrine. Notably in his *Heptaplus* he focused attention on Moses as the source of the truth attributed to the Greeks, his judgment being summarized in his famous statement: 'Was not Plato rightly called by Numenius *Moses Atticus?*'[2] Walter Mönch writes:

> With Pico, not Zoroaster but Moses was the beginning of that long chain, the members of which rank wonderfully in the generations of mankind. Plato is only one of the most illustrious members following after the Hebrews and the Egyptians and is in no way the originator of the significant philosophy. It is assumed much more by Pico that the deepest and most correct views upon the mysteries of God, the world and men, might have been contained in the Old Testament story of creation, indeed that the writings of the prophets had immediate divine origins. Moses was to Pico the most profound, the wisest and greatest writer of all time and people, the father of the original unified philosophy.[3]

The building materials for this curious but influential viewpoint were found by the thinkers of the Florentine Academy in the Neo-platonic writings of the first centuries A.D., writings which had been produced originally for much the same purposes. The Hermetic writings and the Jewish Cabala were also important. Ficino reintroduced the Hermetic books to Europe with his Latin translation of 1463. This was published without his supervision in 1471 and then went through twenty-four editions under the title *Mercurii Trismegisti Liber de Sapientia et Potestate Dei.* Following his lead, Turnebus produced a first edition of some of the Hermetic writings in Greek in 1554, then Flussas in 1574, and Patrizi in 1591, culminating in the critical edition published by Isaac Casaubon in 1614.[4] Pico's intense interest in the Cabala virtually produced a cult in Renaissance scholarship; indeed, Joseph L. Blau treats Pico as the seed of this significant phase of Renaissance thought.[5] An interfused – or perhaps confused – Neoplatonism, Hermeticism, and Cabalism was given ever wider currency by such important sixteenth-century thinkers as John

---

[2] J. M. Rigg, ed., in the Preface to *Giovanni Pico della Mirandola: His Life by his Nephew Giovanni Francesco Pico: ...* (etc.), tr. Sir Thomas More (London, 1890), xiv.

[3] Walter Mönch, *Die italienische Platonrenaissance und ihre Bedeutung für Franksreichs Literatur- und Geistesgeschichte (1450–1550)* (Romanische Studien, XL, 1936), xix.

[4] Karl H. Dannenfeldt, 'Hermetica philosophica' in *Catalogus Translationum et Commentariorum,* ed. P. O. Kristeller (Washington, D.C., 1960), *passim.*

[5] Joseph L. Blau, *The Christian Interpretation of the Cabala in the Renaissance* (New York, 1944).

Reuchlin, Henry Cornelius Agrippa von Nettesheim, Jean Thenaud, Guillaume Postel, and Peter Bongus.[6]

A *philosophia mosaica*, based on a rather special technique of scholarship and its arcane sources, was emerging then in the fifteenth and sixteenth centuries when the dredging process of the Renaissance brought to the surface one of the most important and troublesome hypotheses in Western thought, i.e. atomism. The late Middle Ages had known something of ancient atomism from Aristotle's criticisms, but in a formal sense the doctrine had its renaissance when Poggio Bracciolini sent back to Italy in 1417 a manuscript of Lucretius's *De Rerum Natura* which he had discovered in Germany. This manuscript was lost, but from a copy the first printed edition of this work appeared in Brescia in 1473;[7] there were about thirty editions of the work before 1600. The Renaissance also learned of Greek atomism from Diogenes Laertius's *Lives of the Philosophers* in which appeared Epicurus's letter to Herodotus, purported to be the original Epicurean statement on the subject. Sometime before 1439 Ambrogio Traversaei made a Latin translation of it which was widely circulated and a first edition was published by Hieronymus Froben and Nicolas Episcopius in Basel in 1533. Another edition was published by H. Estienne in Paris in 1570 but the rather definitive edition was published by Casaubon in 1583.[8]

During the sixteenth century scattered allusions to Epicureanism appeared increasingly in popular literature,[9] and traces of atomistic thought entered into the philosophical work of such writers as Julius Caesar Scaliger[10] (1484–1558), Giordano Bruno[11] (1548–1600), and Eilard Lubin,[12] each of whom represented to some degree the growing discontent with Aristotelian meta-

---

[6] *Ibid.*, *passim*. See also André M. J. Festugière, *La révélation d'Hermès Trismégiste* (4 vols, Paris, 1944–54).

[7] George D. Hadzsits, *Lucretius and His Influence* (New York, 1935), xi.

[8] J. E. Sandys, *A History of Classical Scholarship* (3 vols, Cambridge, 1908), II, 102–6.

[9] In addition to Hadzsits, *op. cit.*, see also Max Lehnerdt, *Lucretius in der Renaissance* (Königsberg, 1904) and George Buckley, *Atheism in the English Renaissance* (Chicago, 1932).

[10] Scaliger's atomism appears in his *Exotericarum Exercitationum Libri XV de subtilitate ad Hieronymum Cardanum* (Paris, 1557). See A. G. Melsen, *From Atomos to Atom* (Pittsburgh, 1952), 73–7.

[11] Dorothea W. Singer states in her work, *Giordano Bruno: His Life and Thought* (New York, 1950), 50, that paradoxically the two writers who most influenced Bruno's thought were Lucretius and Nicholas of Cusa. Hadzsits, *op. cit.*, 279–80, asserts that the 'first startling illustration of Lucretius's influence, as a thinker, appears in the works of Giordano Bruno ...' Lucretius's influence on Bruno is emphasized also by Irving L. Horowitz, *The Renaissance Philosophy of Giordano Bruno* (New York, 1952), 35. However, Bruno's monads were spiritual mirrors of the One, Infinite God.

[12] Melsen, 78.

physics in that era. But there was no adoption or advocacy of classical atomism and the impact of the revival of the theory was felt much more in physics than in metaphysics. Indeed, atomism became an essential factor first in the field of iatrochemistry where, with due acknowledgment to the ancient atomists, it was used to oppose the influence of Galen, the Pergamene who had attempted to apply Aristotle's physical theories to medicine. Paracelsus is frequently regarded as the founder of this movement and undoubtedly influenced many of those who showed an early interest in atomism, such as Fracastoro, Jean Fernel, Jean Bodin, David Gorlaeus, Sebastian Basso, Berigard, J. C. Magnenus, Angelo Sala, and Jean Beguin.[13]

One of the most important of the early iatrochemists was Daniel Sennert who has been credited, perhaps erroneously,[14] by Lasswitz and others as the founder of modern scientific atomism. Born in Silesia in 1572, Sennert spent most of his career in Wittenberg University where he took his Master of Arts degree in 1597, and his M.D. in 1601. From 1602 he was professor and is credited with introducing the study of chemistry in that school.[15] His influence was considerable in the seventeenth century; Robert Boyle, for example, almost invariably referred to him as 'the learned Sennert'.

It was in the writings of Sennert that an important step was

[13] The iatrochemical beginnings of modern atomism are discussed in such works as Melsen; Walter Pagel, Paracelsus: An Introduction to Philosophical Medicine in the Era of the Renaissance (New York, 1958); Kurd Lasswitz, Geschichte der Atomistik vom Mittelalter bis Newton (2 vols. Hamburg, 1890), I; Léopold Mabilleau, Histoire de la Philosophie Atomistique (Paris, 1895); G. B. Stones, 'The Atomic View of Matter in the Fifteenth, Sixteenth, and Seventeenth Centuries', Isis, X (1928), 454–7; J. R. Partington, 'The Origins of the Atomic Theory', Annals of Science, IV (1939) 245 et seq.; R. Hooykaas, 'The Experimental Origin of Chemical Atomic and Molecular Theory before Boyle', Chymia, II (1949), 65–80. Much of what has been presented here concerning the renaissance of atomism is discussed in greater detail in Marie Boas Hall, 'The Establishment of the Mechanical Philosophy', Osiris, X (1952).

[14] The validity of this assertion is discussed by Thorndike, VII, 206–8. He quotes Lasswitz's reference to Sennert's work De Chymicorum, etc, in which Lasswitz states: 'In diesen Ausführungen ist die Korpuskular-theorie so bewusst ausgesprochen, dass wir von Jahre 1619 ab die Erneuerung der physikalischen Atomistik datieren müssen.' Thorndike, on the other hand, argues that '... Only a small part of a single chapter in that work is devoted to the subject and even in Sennert's later works it occupies relatively little space. Moreover, in the earliest passage Sennert gave credit for the idea to Scaliger saying: "I, to use the words of Scaliger in Exercise 101, if I am forced to speak, confess that I am now won over by the opinion of Scaliger, who defines mixture as "the motion of very small bodies to mutual contact in order to achieve union".' Thorndike suggests subsequently that Isaac Beeckman 'would seem to have a superior claim to that of Sennert to be regarded as founder of the corpuscular theory, ...'

[15] Daniel Sennert, Thirteen Books of Natural Philosophy, ed. and tr. Peter Cole (London, 1659) pref.; a close translation of Sennert's Hypomnemata.

taken toward the assertion of Moses as the originator of atomism. In at least two of his works, *Tractatus de consensu et dissensu Galenicorum et peripateticorum cum Chymicis* (1619) and the *Hypomnematum Physicorum* (1636), he attempted to present a kind of history of atomism. In the latter work he tried to protect Democritus from undeserved notoriety and then delved into the sources of the classical atomists:[16]

> Now amongst other Opinions ascribed to Democritus, Empedocles, and other most noble ancient Philosophers, is this; That they held Atomes or individual Bodikies to be the Principles of Natural things, from the various mixture whereof other Bodies have their Original. And this Opinion was a most ancient Opinion, and is now being attributed to one Mochus a Phoenician, who is reputed to have flourished before the destruction of Troy; yea, and that it was the common Opinion of Philosophers before Aristotle, is apparent from the beginning of his Second Book de Generat. & Corrupt.

In the years that followed, the writings of the ancient atomists received increasing attention and the theory itself was to be offered by the mid-seventeenth century without direct acknowledgment to antiquity. Grant McColley has written that Nicholas Hill's *Philosophia Epicurea, Democritiana, Theophrastica, proposita simpliciter, non edocta* (Paris, 1601) was '... apparently the first modern work to urge actively the atomic theories of Leucippus, Democritus, and Epicurus', and that Hill '... seemingly was the first to provide this atomism with a theistic interpretation'.[17] This judgment still stands. Pierre Gassendi (1592–1665) built a whole philosophic position largely on the inspiration and example of Epicurus; according to Bernard Rochot, Gassendi's life work 'has for its center the work and the personality of Epicurus'.[18] Francis Bacon and Kenelm Digby were consciously influenced by the ideas of the ancient atomists and the same was believed true of Thomas Hobbes to a much greater degree.[19] In his book, *Epicurus in England*, T. F. Mayo showed

[16] *Ibid.*, 446.
[17] Grant McColley, 'Nicholas Hill and the Philosophia Epicurea', *Annals of Science*, IV (1939–40), 390–2.
[18] Bernard Rochot, in *Tricentenaire de Pierre Gassendi, 1655–1955* (Paris, 1957), v.
[19] See Charles T. Harrison, 'Bacon, Hobbes, Boyle, and the Ancient Atomists', *Harvard Studies in Classical Philology*, XV (1933), 191–218. Harrison explains there that, ironically, whereas Bacon and Boyle made extensive and favorable reference to Epicurus and some of the other ancient atomists, it is doubtful that the ideas of the ancient atomists 'had any influence at all on Hobbes' (p. 200). See also Harrison's later article, 'The Ancient Atomists and English Literature of the Seventeenth Century', *Harvard Studies in Classical Philology*, XLV (1934), 1–79.

that whereas before 1650 the English press produced remarkably
few works dealing in any way with Epicurus, a number of such
works appeared in the following seventy-five years after which
there was a definite ebbing of interest. Thus, he concluded, '... it
would seem safe to assert that the seventy-five years from 1650
to 1725 witnessed an Epicurean vogue, modest but distinct in
English bookmaking'.[20] He went on to explain that much of
Epicurean publication was redemptive in purpose; the attempt
was made usually to assert the Christian uses of the atomic
hypothesis and to emphasize the purity, even the austerity of the
Epicurean ethic.[21]

Nevertheless, it is conspicuous throughout the seventeenth
century that even among those who translated or interpreted
Epicurus or Lucretius there was rather strong feeling ranging
from anxiety to intense fear and hostility.[22] The response, fully
in the Renaissance tradition, was to pursue ever more earnestly
the fundamental humanistic assumption that the origins of good
and useful ideas, even of such fearful ideas as Epicurean atomism,
could be found in the Hebraic tradition which pre-existed their
perversion by Greek pagans. The resort to the *philosophia mosaica*
was strongly reinforced by the spread of radical Protestantism
with its emphasis on the all-sufficing authority of the Bible. The
key materials for the restitution of atomism had been emerging
steadily. Sennert, for example, must have been indebted to the
work of the Friesian philologist, Johann Arcerius Theodoretus,
whose translation of Iamblichus's *Life of Pythagoras* appeared as
a first edition in 1598. In his editorial notes, Arcerius was perhaps the first to suggest that the Phoenician Mochus was the

---

[20] T. F. Mayo, *Epicurus in England* (College Station, Texas, 1934), xi.

[21] Mayo describes, for example, the anxious efforts of Lucy Hutchinson,
Walter Charleton, John Evelyn, and Thomas Creech to accomplish this
purpose. Marjorie Hope Nicolson has noted this phenomenon in her
Mountain Gloom and Mountain Glory (Ithaca, 1959). After quoting Evelyn
to the effect that prior to the mid-seventeenth century 'little of the
Epicurean philosophy was then known amongst us', she herself goes on to
assert that 'For nearly a century Epicureanism had been more powerful in
France than in England, where no complete translation of the *De Rerum
Natura* appeared before 1675'. Interest developed rapidly in England during
the Restoration era due to the contacts with French Epicureanism by
Englishmen in exile. Miss Nicolson then refers to the '*annus mirabilis* of
English Lucretianism, 1685, during which Dryden and Sir William Temple
in England and Saint-Evremond in France published translation, letters and
essays that caused a literary vogue' (pp. 120–1).

[22] Harrison lists some of those who, in addition to the Cambridge Platonists,
denounced the ancient atomists and their teachings: Barrow, Howe,
Pearson, Parker, Wilkins, Stillingfleet, Tenison, Eachard, Tillotson, Cumber-
land, Beveridge, and Leighton ('Bacon, Hobbes, Boyle and the Ancient
Atomists', *op. cit.*, 191). Isaac Barrow gave the characteristic Restoration
lament: 'Of all the Sects and factions which divide the world, that of
Epicurean scorners is become the most formidable.' *The Theological
Works of Isaac Barrow* (8 vols, Oxford, 1830), IV, 232.

same as Moses. Isaac Casaubon was making important philological contributions in his critical editions of the works of
Diogenes Laertius (1583), Strabo (1587), and Athenaeus (1597), all
of which carried some reference to the Phoenician atomist.
Mochus was mentioned also in Eusebius's *Praeparatio Evangelica*,
translated into Latin in the fifteenth century by Georgius Trapez-
untius and published by R. Estienne in 1544–6, and in Sextus
Empiricus's *Adversus Mathematicos* which was published with
the rest of his works by H. Stephen in Paris in 1562.

The application of the *philosophia mosaica* to the problem of
atomism was pressed more urgently in Great Britain since the
shift of scientific leadership there seemed to make such humanistic rescue-work especially imperative. This was personified by
John Comenius, the great Czech philologist who made his way to
England in 1641. His discussion of Moses and atomism appeared
in his work originally published on the continent under the title
of *Synopsis Physicae ad lumen divinum reformatae* and republished in English as *Naturall Philosophie Reformed by Divine
Light: or a Synopsis of Physicks* (London, 1651). Paradoxically,
he did not avail himself of the philological pattern which had
been developing but simply asserted that all cosmological knowledge was to be derived from Moses's account in the first book
of Genesis, '... For thus, says he, God, by his secretary Moses.
Gen. I ...'.[23] On that basis, Comenius proceeded to elaborate
that book of the Bible, virtually sentence by sentence, implying
strongly Moses's authorship of the atomic hypothesis. In the
second chapter he discussed the 'visible principles of the World,
matter, spirit, and light', and drew from Moses's account the
postulate that 'the first matter of the world, was a Chaos of dispersed Atomes, cohering in no part thereof'.[24] He went on shortly
to explain that in Proverbs it is stated that 'the beginning of the
World was dust' and then, in Genesis, iii, 14, 'dust thou art, and
into dust thou shalt return'. Dust is identified with atoms, and
everything, organic and inorganic, is 'at last scattered into very
Atomes. Read and understand, what is said (Job, iv, 19; item xix,
19; Essay, xxvi, 19; Psal. civ, 29) therefore, Democritus erred,
not altogether, in making Atomes the matter of the World ...'[25]

John Selden, however, took up the question of the authenticity of the record concerning Mochus, the Phoenician, in his
work, *De Jure Naturali et Gentium Juxta Disciplinam Ebraeorum*
(1665). He questioned Arcerius' identification of Mochus with
Moschus and came to the conclusion that there were really two
individuals involved, an historian by the name of Mochus and a

[23] Johan Comenius, *Naturall Philosophie Reformed by Divine Light: or a
Synopsis of Physics* (London, 1651), 10.
[24] *Ibid.*, 28.
[25] *Ibid.*, 30.

physiologer by the name of Moschus who was the true author of the atomistic idea.[26]

This problem of double identity was taken up in a much more erudite way by Theophilus Gale in his *The Court of the Gentiles* (1669–77) in which he was able finally to extend the credit for atomism to Moses the prophet. After reviewing the various writings which had dealt with the Phoenician – or Phoenicians – he suggested that 'this seeming Contradiction' is easily resolved because physiology and natural history are ultimately the same thing. In any case, he had been assured by the geographer, Bochart,[27] that the natural philosophy which Thales brought back from Phoenicia was really '... no other, than a Natural Historie, or some broken fragments of the Historie of the Creation, delivered by Moses, Gen. i, etc. ....' Bochart further insisted that Thales's predecessor, Mochus, was mistakenly called Moschus '... and that his philosophie was nothing else, but the Historie of the Creation, the same with that of Sanchoniathon'.[28]

Yet, Gale did not identify Mochus with the Moses of the Old Testament but asserted instead that the former borrowed directly from the latter: 'That Mochus did really traduce his Physiologie, or natural Historie, from the Historie of the Creation, written by Moses, will be farther evident, if we consider the main principle, for which he was renowned amongst the Ancients, viz the doctrine of Atomes'. He cited Strabo (lib. 16) and then returned to Bochart:

> Bochart, Phaleg, lib. 4 cap. 35, having made mention of Arithmetic, and Astronomie, being derived from the Phenicians to the Grecians, addes thus: 'that I may be silent as to later Philosophers, *Mochus* began to philosophise of *Atomes* at Sidon, before the Trojan War, etc. Hence Democritus borrowed his notions of Atomes, as Epicurus from him. And that the whole doctrine of Atomes to be the first principles of the Universe came from Moses's Historie of the Creation, is asserted by some late Authors.'[29]

Much the same approach was implied in George Horn's *Arcis Moses, sive Historia* (1668). But, in general, the *philosophia mosaica* was most strongly espoused in England by the Cambridge Platonists. One of the more famous of the group, Henry More, dwelt on this theme in his *Conjectura Cabbalistica* (1653).

[26] John Selden, *De Jure Naturali et Gentium Juxta Disciplinam Ebraeorum* (Strasburg, 1665), 22–3.

[27] Samuel Bochart (1599–1667) published his *Phaleg and Chanaan* (Caen, 1646 and 1651) as two parts of his *Geographia Sacra*. His *Sam. Bochart Opera Omnia*, 2 vols fol. appeared in 1675.

[28] Gale, *The Court of the Gentiles* (4 vols, Oxford, 1669–77), II, 62.

[29] *Ibid.*

After dealing with the 'Literal' and then the 'Moral', he turned to the 'Philosophical' Cabbala, where he explained: 'Nor is he [Moses] to fall short in Philosophy; and therefore the Philosophical Cabbala contains the noblest Truths, as well Theological as Natural, that the minds of man can entertain her self with; insomuch that Moses seems to have been aforehand, and prevented the subtilest and abstrusest inventions of the choicest Philosophers that ever appeared after him to this very day.'[30] In the time of his greatest enthusiasm for Cartesianism, More implied strongly Moses's authorship of the atomism which was being revived in the seventeenth century in his *Defence of the Philosophick Cabbala*. He cited references in Casaubon, Selden, and Vossius concerning Moschus–Mochus and then summarized the Sidonian's philosophy in a sentence. 'Whence', he concluded, 'there must be no small affinity betwixt this ancient Moschical or rather Mosaical Physiologie and the Cartesian Philosophy which has so often and so naturally born a part in this Philosophick Cabbala.'[31] He goes on[32] to explain:

> The Cartesian philosophy being in a manner the same with that of Democritus, and that of Democritus the same with the physiological part of Pythagoras's philosophy, and Pythagoras's philosophy the same with the Sidonian, as also the Sidonian with the Mosaical; it will necessarily follow that the Mosaical philosophy, in the physiological part thereof, is the same with the Cartesian. And how fitly the Cartesian Philosophy sutes [sic] with Moses his text I have again and again taken notice.

The final synthesis in which Moschus was identified with Moses as the originator of atomism came in the work of Ralph Cudworth. Cudworth, who was perhaps the most erudite of the Cambridge group, personified the last stages of Renaissance humanism in England. He not only had a mastery of Greek and Latin but of Hebrew as well, being appointed to the Regius Professorship of Hebrew in Cambridge in 1645. In his *magnum opus*, *The True Intellectual System of the Universe*, and in his voluminous manuscripts, his main purpose was to oppose Thomas Hobbes whom he labelled an atheistic atomist. He rang all the changes on the ancient argument based on *de nihilo nihil* but depended at least as much on the tradition which has been described. For Cudworth, truth lay in antiquity so that the current struggle over the atomic hypothesis was only a reenactment.

[30] Henry More, *Conjectura Cabbalistica* in *A Collection of Several Philosophical Writings of Dr Henry More* (London, 1662), 3.
[31] *Ibid.*, 102–3: *Appendix to the Defence of the Philosophical Cabbala*.
[32] *Ibid.*, 104.

Just as Hobbes was trying to do in the seventeenth century, there had been those in antiquity who had tried to claim and pervert the true atomistic philosophy. But, the Greek materialistic atomists could not have originated it, Cudworth insisted, because

> ... We have also good historical probability for this Opinion, that this Philosophy was a thing of much greater Antiquity than either Democritus or Leucippus; and first, because Posidonius, an ancient and learned philosopher, did (as both Empiricus and Strabo tell us) avouch it for an old tradition, that the first Inventor of this Atomical Philosophy was one Moschus, a Phoenician, who, as Strabo also notes, lived before the Trojan Wars. Moreover, it seems not altogether Improbable, but that his Moschus a Phoenician Philosopher, mentioned by Posidonius, might be the same with that Mochus a Phoenician Physiologer in Jamblichus, with whose successors, Priests and Prophets, he affirms that Pythagoras, sometimes sojourning at Sidon (which was his native city) had converst: which may be taken for an intimation, as if he had been by them instructed in that atomical physiology which Moschus or Mochus, the Phoenician, is said to have been the inventor of. Mochus or Moschus is plainly a Phoenician name, and there is one Mochus a Phoenician writer cited in Athenaeus, whom the Latin translator calls Mochus; and Mr Selden approves of the conjecture of Arcerius, the publisher of Iamblichus, that this Mochus was no other than the celebrated Moses of the Jews, with whose successors, the Jewish philosophers, priests, and prophets, Pythagoras conversed at Sidon.[33]

As a rationalist, however, Cudworth was anxious lest such an argument appear to undermine his logical arguments against atheistic atomism.

> Some Phantastick Atomists perhaps would here catch at this, to make their Philosophy to stand by Divine Right, as owing its Original to Revelation; whereas philosophy being not a matter of faith but reason, men ought not to affect (as I conceive) to derive its pedigree from revelation, and by that very pretence seek to impose it tyrannically upon the minds of men, which God hath here purposely left free to the use of their own faculties, that so finding out truth by them, they might enjoy that pleasure and satisfaction, which arises from thence.[34]

[33] Ralph Cudworth, *The True Intellectual System of the Universe, wherein all the Reason and Philosophy of Atheism is Confuted, and its impossibility Demonstrated* (London, 1678), 12–13.
[34] *Ibid.*

Nonetheless, Cudworth attributed the invention of atomism to Moses repeatedly, saying in another place in the *True Intellectual System*, for example, that '... there were two several forms of atomical philosophy; first, the most ancient and genuine, that was religious, called Moschical (or if you will Mosaical) and Pythagorical; secondly, the adulterated atheistic atomology, called Leucippean or Democritical'.[35] In one of his manuscripts he referred to the old 'atomicall or mechanicall physiologie ... which is reported by Strabo and S. Empiricus to have derived its originall from our Moschus, a Phoenician that liv'd before the Trojan Wars, who can scarcely be thought to be other than Moses ...'[36]

The humanist arsenal of arguments was adopted even to this extreme by the scientists of the Royal Society. One of its spokesmen, Bishop Sprat, relied heavily on the humanist example and developed the characteristic humanistic historiography for ancient science in his quasi-official *History of the Royal Society*, a work which was more of an apologetic than a history. The scientists themselves, in many impressive instances, echoed the argument from design, the argument from *de nihilo* in its almost infinite variations, and advanced the humanistic conception of the relationship of matter to non-matter in close detail. The very lack of originality in these matters is an accurate measure of their dependence on non-scientific sources for their philosophical ideas. The substance of their extensive and intensive writings under this category really did not require scientific experience; the experiments and observations with which they occasionally illustrated their metaphysical points appear to have provided only a kind of pious window-dressing. The ultimate revelation of their dependence is in their obvious acceptance, in key instances, of the humanistic Moses-theory.

From the seventeenth century to the present, the piety of Robert Boyle has been emphasized by his biographers; he was indeed the Christian Virtuoso. His contribution to science in that era was second only to that of Isaac Newton. But his defense of Christian metaphysics was about as original in his many writings on the subject as his defense of Christian ethics was in his earnest essay on customary swearing. His personal ties with the Cambridge Platonists were considerable and their influence on him inescapable. Thus, he reiterated Cudworth's history of ancient atomism fairly closely.

In his work entitled 'Some Specimens of an attempt to make Chymical Experiments useful to illustrate the notions of Corpuscular Philosophy', for example, he made reference to his early reading of Diogenes Laertius's *Lives of the Philosophers*, explaining a little later that he calls atomism the 'corpuscular philo-

[35] *Ibid.,* 74.
[36] British Museum, *Additional Manuscript* 4979, fol. 139.

sophy ... though I sometimes style it the Phaenician [sic] philosophy, because some antient writers inform us that not only
before Epicurus and Democritus, but even before Leucippus
taught in Greece, a Phaenician naturalist was wont to give an
account of the Phaenomena of nature by the motion and other
affections of the minute particles of matter'.[37] In one of his most
famous works, his *Sceptical Chymist*, he went further to imply
the Moses thesis:

> The devising of the atomical hypothesis commonly ascribed
> to Leucippus and his disciple Democritus is by learned men
> attributed to one Moschus a Phaenician. And possibly the
> opinion is yet ancienter than so; for it is known, that the
> Phenicians borrowed most of their learning from the Hebrew.
> And among those, that acknowledge the books of Moses,
> many have inclined to think water to have been the primi-
> tive and universal matter, by perusing the beginnings of
> Genesis....[38]

A little later, Boyle seems to have developed a sudden awareness
of the direction of his thinking for he says to his reader, 'But you,
I presume, expect, that I should discourse of this matter like a
naturalist, not a philologer'.[39]

Similarly, echoes of the *philosophia mosaica* are to be found
in the thought of Isaac Newton. His contacts with the Cambridge
Platonists,[40] his absorption of humanistic learning, his growing

[37] Robert Boyle, *The Works of the Honourable Robert Boyle*, ed. Thomas
Birch (6 vols, London, 1772), I, 356.
[38] *Ibid.*, 497.
[39] *Ibid.*, 498. See also his 'The Excellency of Theology', *Works*, IV, 48,
where he parallels Cudworth even to the description of Descartes as having
improved on atomism in the seventeenth century: 'Whatever may be
said to excuse pride (if there were any) in Moschus the Phoenician, who is
affirmed to have first invented the atomical hypothesis, and in Democritus
and Leucippus (for Epicurus scarce deserves to be named with them) that
highly advanced that philosophy; and in Monsieur Des Cartes, who either
improved, or at least much innovated the corpuscularian hypothesis....'
[40] Newton knew More, and though there is no direct evidence, he probably
knew Cudworth or at least read his works. The three were at Cambridge
for nearly thirty years, and it can be assumed that Newton's appreciation
of More's ideas establishes the strong probability that he sympathized as
well with those of Cudworth. The biographer of both Newton and Boyle,
Louis Trenchard More, asserts that '... Newton became an intimate as-
sociate of Henry More, who exerted on him a profound influence in both
philosophy and religion'. *Isaac Newton: A Biography* (New York, 1934),
II. Rupert Hall finds evidence in one of Newton's manuscript notebooks
that Newton was studying More's works as early as the period 1661–5
(Rupert Hall, 'Sir Isaac Newton's Notebook', *Cambridge Historical Journal*,
IX, 2 (1948), 243. The notebook itself is to be found in the Cambridge
University Library as *Additional Manuscript* 4000). A peculiarly impressive
bit of evidence lies in a letter which More wrote to a Dr Sharp, who had

preoccupation with alchemy are all well known. R. J. Forbes notes Newton's relationship to the Platonists and gives the following rough tabulation of the contents of Newton's library:[41]

Theology and philosophy	515 titles	32%
History and chronology	215	14
Classical authors	182	11
Chemistry, mineralogy	165	10
Mathematics, physics and astronomy	268	16

The preponderance of the non-scientific is at least as great in Newton's own manuscript writings, judging from those listed in the *Catalogue of the Portsmouth Papers* (Cambridge, 1888) and other sources.

That Newton took seriously the idea that Moses had understood the true scientific cosmology is apparent from his widely-cited correspondence with Thomas Burnet. In his *Telluris Theoria Sacra* (1681), Burnet had tried to carry out the popular turn-of-the-century purpose of reconciling the Mosaic account with Newtonian science, and he sought Newton's judgment of his work. Newton was able to concur, not only with its purpose (which Newton shared enthusiastically) but with most of its content. In his response to Burnet, Newton made a number of suggestions but explained that '... All this I write not to oppose you, for I think the main part of your hypothesis as probable, as that I have here written, if not in some respects more probable'.[42] He assured Burnet that Moses's mode of presentation was necessarily allegorical.

As to Moses [he wrote] I do not think his description of the creation either philosophical or feigned, but that he described realities in a language artificially adapted to the sense of the vulgar.... For Moses, accommodating his words to the gross conceptions of the vulgar, describes things much after the manner as one of the vulgar would have been inclined to do had he lived & seen the whole series of what Moses describes.[43]

---

inquired about Newton's ideas on the Apocalypse. More replied: 'I remember I told you how well we agreed. For after his reading of the *Exposition of the Apocalypse*, which I gave him, he came to my chamber, where he seemed to me not only to approve my *Exposition* as coherent and perspicuous throughout from the beginning to the end, but (by the manner of his countenance which is ordinarily melancholy and thoughtful, but then mightily lightsome and cheerful, and by the free profession of what satisfaction he took therein) to be in a manner transported' (More, *Newton*, 629–30). Newton also seems to have proposed More for membership in the early days of the Royal Society (More, *Newton*, 245).

[41] R. J. Forbes, 'Was Newton an Alchemist?' *Chymia*, II (1949), 28–8.
[42] *The Correspondence of Isaac Newton*, ed. H. W. Turnbull (3 vols, Cambridge, 1959–61), II, 331.
[43] *Ibid.*, 333.

Newton was fundamentally an atomist, and he showed his familiarity with the humanistic theory of the origins of atomism in his argument against the idea of a cosmological fluid, the *plenum* of Descartes. 'For rejecting such a medium,' he argued, 'we have the authority of those oldest and most celebrated philosophers of Greece and Phoenicia, who made a vacuum, and atoms, and the gravity of atoms, the first principles of their philosophy....'[44]

By the early eighteenth century the issue represented in humanistic historiography was being perpetuated in the debate between the Ancients and the Moderns in the Battle of the Books and, more relevantly, in the flurry of writings, like Burnet's, designed to show at least the agreement between Moses and contemporary science if not always to show Moses's priority in such ideas. Katherine Brownell Collier's *Cosmogonies of Our Fathers* surveys these efforts, including such interesting titles as Edmund Dickinson's *Physica Vetus et Vera* (1703) which attributed the origin of atomism to Moses, John Witty's *An Essay towards the Vindication of the Vulgar Exposition of the Mosaic History of the Creation of the World* (1705), and John Hutchinson's *Moses's Principia* (1724).[45]

But the humanist enterprise was doomed. In his abridgement of Cudworth's *True Intellectual System* entitled *A Confutation of the Reason and Philosophy of Atheism* (1706), Thomas Wise had to acknowledge that Cudworth had stretched the point with respect to Moses. He explained that

> Some critics would here put in and say, that tho it was indeed usual with the Greeks to confound the Phoenicians with the Jews, and there be also a great resemblance between Moschus and Moscheh (as the Jews write Moses) and they were both of 'em very ancient names; yet one would not think this Moschus or Mochus to be really Moses, when one considers that in the writings of Moses and his successors the Prophets, there are not only no Footsteps or signs of the Atomical Hypothesis, nor even of any part whatsoever of the speculative Physicks, which searches into the Reasons of natural effects.[46]

He argued further that the Egyptians and Phoenicians had flourished long before the Jews and that the borrowing was in

[44] Isaac Newton, *Opticks, or a Treatise of the Reflections, Refractions, Inflections & Colours of Light*, ed. E. T. Whittaker (New York, 1931), 3, i, Quaery 28.
[45] Some further aspects of this controversy have been presented in Nicolson, *op. cit.*, ch. 6.
[46] Thomas Wise, *A Confutation of the Reason and Philosophy of Atheism, Being, In a great measure either an Abridgment or an Improvement of what Dr Cudworth offer'd to that Purpose in his True Intellectual System of the Universe* (2 vols, London, 1706), I, 132–3.

reverse. He concluded the discussion by saying that '... the Mochus of Josephus and Athenaeus was not, according to the Jewish historian, the same with Moses'. Finally, there was Tatian's account that there had been an '... antient Tyrian Philosopher call'd Moschus, and it may be an Historian too call'd Mochus, quite different from the Moses of the Jews'.[47]

The Moses theory was demolished further by J. L. Mosheim, a continental scholar who published a Latin translation of Cudworth's work with elaborate notes in 1733. After a detailed discussion of the scholarship involving Mochus, or Moschus, running to thirty-seven lines in a footnote, he concluded that '... The fact that this Phoenician is said by ancient authors to have written a physical work consisting of many books and is therefore called by them φυσιόλογος is, I conceive, a sufficient argument to refute those, who make Moschus to be the same with Moses'.[48]

By the mid-eighteenth century, the attempt to sanctify scientific ideas by ascribing their origins to the ancient religious tradition not only succumbed to new scholarship but, more realistically, became irrelevant. This is to be seen, finally, in the complaint of Bishop Warburton regarding the fate of Cudworth's writings. Writing to Thomas Birch who was preparing another edition of the *True Intellectual System* to be published in 1742, he stated:

> The fate of the volume was odd enough, you know, at first and more so in the progress: about 30 years ago it might have been bought for a crown. Besides the clamour of Bigots, that kind of learning was not in vogue when the book was first published. But the principal reason of its after-neglect was, the voluminous way of treating every head of his subject, and the rough, unpleasing, unpolished, unspirited style of his English. The book is in English words, it is true; but it is as impossible a mere English reader should understand him, as if he had wrote in Latin.[49]

The resort to the *philosophia mosaica* in the late seventeenth century showed that the Natural Theology which was used as a defense by members of the Royal Society was really derived from humanism more than from science, and thus shared the fate of Renaissance humanism.

---

[47] *Ibid.*

[48] Ralph Cudworth, *The True Intellectual System of the Universe ... with a Treatise concerning Eternal and Immutable Morality*, to which are added, the notes and dissertations of Dr J. L. Mosheim, translated by John Harrison, 3 vols, I (London, 1843), 21.

[49] Quoted in John Nichols, *Illustrations of the Literary History of the Eighteenth Century. Consisting of Authentic Memoirs and Original Letters of Eminent Persons: ...* (2 vols, London, 1817), II, 127-9.

2 Puritanism, Pietism and Science*

Robert K. Merton

In his prolegomena to a cultural sociology Alfred Weber has discriminated between the processes of society, culture, and civilization.[1] Since his primary interest lay in differentiating these categories of sociological phenomena, Weber in large measure ignored their specific inter-relationships, a field of study which is fundamental for the sociologist. It is precisely this interaction between certain elements of culture and civilization, with especial reference to seventeenth-century England, which constitutes the object-matter of the present essay.

THE PURITAN ETHOS

The first section of this paper outlines the Puritan value-complex in so far as it was related to the notable increase of interest in science during the latter part of the seventeenth century, while the second presents the relevant empirical materials concerning the differential cultivation of natural science by Protestants and other religious affiliates.

It is the thesis of this study that the Puritan ethic, as an ideal-typical expression of the value-attitudes basic to ascetic Protestantism generally, so canalized the interests of seventeenth-century Englishmen as to constitute one important *element* in the enhanced cultivation of science. The deep-rooted religious *interests*[2] of the day demanded in their forceful implications the

*Robert K. Merton, 'Puritanism, Pietism and Science', *Sociological Review* (old series), 28, part I (January 1936). Reprinted in Robert K. Merton, *Social Theory and Social Structure* (New York: Free Press of Glencoe, 1957, revised edition), pp. 574–606
[1] Alfred Weber, 'Prinzipielles zur Kultursoziologie: Gesellschaftsprozess, Zivilisationsprozess und Kulturbewegung', *Archiv für Sozialwissenschaft und Sozialpolitik*, xlvii, 1920, 47, 1–49. See the similar classification by R. M. MacIver, *Society: Its Structure and Changes*, chap. xii; and the discussion of these studies by Morris Ginsberg, *Sociology* (London, 1934), 45–52.
[2] 'Nicht die ethische Theorie theologischer Kompendien, die nur als ein (unter Umständen allerdings wichtiges) Erkenntnismittel dient, sondern

systematic, rational, and empirical study of Nature for the glorification of God in His works and for the control of the corrupt
world.

It is possible to determine the extent to which the values of
the Puritan ethic stimulated interest in science by surveying the
attitudes of the contemporary scientists. Of course, there is a
marked possibility that in studying the avowed motives of scientists we are dealing with rationalizations, with derivations, rather
than with accurate statements of the actual motives. In such instances, although they may refer to isolated specific cases, the
value of our study is by no means vitiated, for these conceivable
rationalizations themselves are evidence (Weber's *Erkenntnis-
mitteln*) of the motives which were regarded as socially acceptable, since, as Kenneth Burke puts it, 'a terminology of motives is
moulded to fit our general orientation as to purposes, instru-
mentalities, the good life, etc.'.

Robert Boyle was one of the scientists who attempted explicitly to link the place of science in social life with other
cultural values, particularly in his *Usefulness of Experimental
Natural Philosophy*. Such attempts were likewise made by John
Ray, whose work in natural history was path-breaking and who
was characterized by Haller as the greatest botanist in the history
of man; Francis Willughby, who was perhaps as eminent in
zoology as was Ray in botany; John Wilkins, one of the leading
spirits in the 'invisible College' which developed into the Royal
Society; Oughtred, Wallis, and others. For additional evidence
we can turn to the scientific body which, arising about the
middle of the century, provoked and stimulated scientific advance
more than any other immediate agency: the Royal Society. In
this instance we are particularly fortunate in possessing a contemporary account written under the constant supervision of
the members of the Society so that it might be representative of
their views of the motives and aims of that association. This is
Thomas Sprat's widely read *History of the Royal Society of London*, published in 1667, after it had been examined by Wilkins
and other representatives of the Society.[3]

---

die in den psychologischen und pragmatischen Zusammenhängen der
Religionen gegründeten praktischen Antriebe zum Handeln sind das, was
in Beracht kommt [unter "Wirtschaftsethik" einer Religion].' Max Weber,
Gesammelte Aufsätze zur Religionssoziologie (Tübingen, 1920), I, 238. As
Weber justly indicates, one freely recognizes the fact that religion is but
one element in the determination of the religious ethic, but none the less it
is at present an insuperable, and for our purposes, unnecessary task to
determine *all* the component elements of this ethic. That problem awaits
further analysis and falls outside the scope of this study.
[3] *Cf.* C. L. Sonnichsen, *The Life and Works of Thomas Sprat* (Harvard
University, unpublished doctoral dissertation, 1931), 131 ff., where substantial evidence of the fact that the *Historian's* representative of the views of

Even a cursory examination of these writings suffices to disclose one outstanding fact: certain elements of the Protestant ethic had pervaded the realm of scientific endeavour and had left their indelible stamp upon the attitudes of scientists toward their work. Discussions of the why and wherefore of science bore a point-to-point correlation with the Puritan teachings on the same subject. Such a dominant force as was religion in those days was not and perhaps could not be compartmentalized and delimited. Thus, in Boyle's highly commended apologia for science it is maintained that the study of Nature is to the greater glory of God and the Good of Man.[4] This is the motif which recurs in constant measure. The juxtaposition of the spiritual and the material is characteristic. This culture rested securely on a substratum of utilitarian norms which constituted the measuring-rod of the desirability of various activities. The definition of action designed for the greater glory of God was tenuous and vague, but utilitarian standards could easily be applied.

Earlier in the century, this keynote had been sounded in the resonant eloquence of that 'veritable apostle of the learned societies', Francis Bacon. Himself the initiator of no scientific discoveries, unable to appreciate the importance of his great contemporaries, Gilbert, Kepler, and Galileo, naïvely believing in the possibility of a scientific method which 'places all wits and understandings nearly on a level', a radical empiricist holding mathematics to be of no use in science, he was, nevertheless, highly successful as one of the principal protagonists of a positive social evaluation of science and of the disclaim of a sterile scholasticism. As one would expect from the son of a 'learned, eloquent, and religious woman, full of puritanic fervour' who was admittedly influenced by his mother's attitudes, he speaks in the *Advancement of Learning* of the true end of scientific activity as the 'glory of the Creator and the relief of man's estate'. Since, as is quite clear from many official and private documents, the Baconian teachings constituted the basic principles on which the Royal Society was patterned, it is not strange that the same sentiment is expressed in the charter of the Society.

In his last will and testament, Boyle echoes the same attitude,

---

the Society is presented. It is of further interest that the statements in Sprat's book concerning the aims of the Society bear a distinct similarity on every score to Boyle's characterizations of the motives and aims of scientists in general. This similarity is evidence of the dominance of the ethos which included these attitudes.

[4] Robert Boyle, *Some Considerations Touching the Usefulness of Experimental Natural Philosophy* (Oxford, 1664), 22ff. See, also, the letters of William Oughtred in *Correspondence of Scientific Men of the Seventeenth Century*, edited by S. J. Rigaud (Oxford, 1841), xxxiv *et passim*; or the letters of John Ray in the *Correspondence of John Ray*, edited by Edwin Lankester (London, 1848), 389, 395, 402 *et passim*.

petitioning the Fellows of the Society in this wise : 'Wishing them also a happy success in their laudable attempts, to discover the true Nature of the Works of God; and praying that they and all other Searchers into Physical Truths, may cordially refer their Attainments to the Glory of the Great Author of Nature, and to the Comfort of Mankind'.[5] John Wilkins proclaimed the experimental study of Nature to be a most effective means of begetting in men a veneration for God.[6] Francis Willughby was prevailed upon to publish his works – which he had deemed unworthy of publication – only when Ray insisted that it was a means of glorifying God.[7] Ray's *Wisdom of God*, which was so well received that five large editions were issued in some twenty years, is a panegyric of those who glorify Him by studying His works.[8]

To a modern, comparatively untouched by religious forces, and noting the almost complete separation, if not opposition, between science and religion today, the recurrence of these pious phrases is apt to signify merely customary usage, and nothing of deep-rooted motivating convictions. To him these excerpts would seem to be a case of *qui nimium probat nihil probat*. But such an interpretation is possible only if one neglects to translate oneself within the framework of seventeenth-century values. Surely such a man as Boyle, who spent considerable sums to have the Bible translated into foreign tongues, was not simply rendering lip service. As G. N. Clark very properly notes in this connection :

> There is ... always a difficulty in estimating the degree to which what we call religion enters into anything which was said in the seventeenth century in religious language. It is not solved by discounting all theological terms and treating them merely as common form. On the contrary, it is more often necessary to remind ourselves that these words were then seldom used without their accompaniment of meaning, and that their use did generally imply a heightened intensity of feeling.[9]

The second dominant tenet in the Puritan ethos designated social welfare, the good of the many, as a goal ever to be held in mind. Here again the contemporary scientists adopted an objective prescribed by the current values. Science was to be fostered and nurtured as leading to the domination of Nature by tech-

[5] Quoted by Gilbert, Lord Bishop of Sarum, *A Sermon Preached at the Funeral of the Hon. Robert Boyle* (London, 1692), 25.
[6] *Principles and Duties of Natural Religion* (London, 1710 – 6th edn), 236 *et passim*.
[7] *Memorials of John Ray*, 14 f.
[8] *Wisdom of God* (London, 1691), 126–9 *et passim*.
[9] G. N. Clark, *The Seventeenth Century* (Oxford, 1929), 323.

nological invention. The Royal Society, we are told by its worthy historian, 'does not intend to stop at some particular benefit, but goes to the root of all noble inventions'.[10] But those experiments which do not bring with them immediate gain are not to be condemned, for as the noble Bacon has declared, experiments of Light ultimately conduce to a whole troop of inventions useful to the life and state of man. This power of science to better the material condition of man, he continues, is, apart from its purely mundane value, a good in the light of the Evangelical Doctrine of Salvation by Jesus Christ.

And so on through the principles of Puritanism there was the same point-to-point correlation between them and the attributes, goals, and results of science. Such was the contention of the protagonists of science at that time. Puritanism simply made articulate the basic values of the period. If Puritanism demands systematic, methodic labour, constant diligence in one's calling, what, asks Sprat, more active and industrious and systematic than the Art of Experiment, which 'can never be finish'd by the perpetual labours of any one man, nay, scarce by the successive forces of the greatest Assembly?'[11] Here is employment enough for the most indefatigable industry, since even those hidden treasures of Nature which are farthest from view may be uncovered by pains and patience.[12]

Does the Puritan eschew idleness because it conduces to sinful thoughts (or interferes with the pursuit of one's vocation)? 'What room can there be for low, and little things in a mind so usefully and successfully employ'd [as in natural philosophy]?'[13] Are plays and playbooks pernicious and flesh-pleasing (and subversive of more serious pursuits)?[14] Then it is the 'fittest season for experiments to arise, to teach us a Wisdome, which springs from the depths of Knowledge, to shake off the shadows, and to scatter the mists [of the spiritual distractions brought on by the Theatre]'.[15] And finally, is a life of earnest activity within the world to be preferred to monastic asceticism? Then recognize the fact that the study of natural philosophy 'fits us not so well for the secrecy of a Closet: It makes us serviceable to the World'.[16]

[10] Thomas Sprat, *History of the Royal Society*, 78–9.

[11] *Ibid.*, 341–2.

[12] Ray, *Wisdom of God*, 125.

[13] Sprat, *op. cit.*, 344–5.

[14] Richard Baxter, *Christian Directory* (London, 1825 – first published in 1664), I, 152; II, 167. Cf. Robert Barclay, the Quaker apologist, who specifically suggests 'geometrical and mathematical experiments' as innocent divertisements to be sought instead of pernicious plays. *An Apology for the True Christian Divinity* (Phila., 1805 – first written in 1675), 554–5.

[15] Sprat, *op. cit.*, 362.

[16] *Ibid.*, 365–6. Sprat perspicaciously suggests that monastic asceticism induced by religious scruples was partially responsible for the lack of empiricism of the Schoolmen. 'But what sorry kinds of Philosophy must

In short, science embodies two highly prized values: utilitarianism and empiricism.

In a sense this explicit coincidence between Puritan tenets and the qualities of science as a calling is casuistry. It is an express attempt to fit the scientist *qua* pious layman into the framework of the prevailing social values. It is a bid for religious and social sanction, since both the constitutional position and the personal authority of the clergy were much more important then than now. But this is not the entire explanation. The justificatory efforts of Sprat, Wilkins, Boyle, or Ray do not simply present opportunistic obsequiousness, but rather an earnest attempt to justify the ways of science to God. The Reformation had transferred the burden of individual salvation from the Church to the individual, and it is this 'overwhelming and crushing sense of the responsibility for his own soul' which explains the acute religious interest. If science were not demonstrably a lawful and desirable calling, it dare not claim the attention of those who felt themselves 'ever in the Great Task-master's eye'. It is to this intensity of feeling that such apologias were due.

The exaltation of the faculty of reason in the Puritan ethos – based partly on the conception of rationality as a curbing device of the passions – inevitably led to a sympathetic attitude toward those activities which demand the constant application of rigorous reasoning. But again, in contrast to medieval rationalism, reason is deemed subservient and auxiliary to empiricism. Sprat is quick to indicate the pre-eminent adequacy of science in this respect.[17] It is on this point probably that Puritanism and the scientific temper are in most salient agreement, for the combination of *rationalism and empiricism* which is so pronounced in the Puritan ethic forms the essence of the spirit of modern science. Puritanism was suffused with the rationalism of neo-Platonism, derived largely through an appropriate modification of Augustine's teachings. But it did not stop there. Associated with the designated necessity of dealing successfully with the practical affairs of life within this world – a derivation from the peculiar twist afforded largely by the Calvinist doctrine of predestination and *certitudo salutis* through successful worldly activity – was

---

the Schoolmen needs produce, when it was part of their Religion, to separate themselves, as much as they could, from the converse of mankind? When they were so far from being able to discover the secrets of Nature, that they scarce had opportunity to behold enough of its common works.' *Ibid.*, 19.

[17] Sprat, *op. cit.*, 361. Baxter in a fashion representative of the Puritans decried the invasion of 'enthusiasm' into religion. Reason must 'maintain its authority in the command and government of your thoughts'. *C.D.*, ii, 199. In like spirit, those who at Wilkins's lodgings laid the foundation of the Royal Society 'were invincibly arm'd against all the inchantments of Enthusiasm'. Sprat, *op. cit.*, 53.

an emphasis upon empiricism. These two currents brought to convergence through the logic of an inherently consistent system of values were so associated with the other values of the time as to prepare the way for the acceptance of a similar coalesence in natural science.

Empiricism and rationalism were canonized, beatified, so to speak. It may very well be that the Puritan ethos did not directly influence the method of science and that this was simply a parallel development in the internal history of science, but it is evident that through the psychological compulsion toward certain modes of thought and conduct this value-complex made an empirically-founded science commendable rather than, as in the medieval period, reprehensible or at least acceptable on sufferance. This could not but have directed some talents into scientific fields which otherwise would have engaged in more highly esteemed professions. The fact that science today is largely if not completely divorced from religious sanctions is itself of interest as an example of the process of secularization.

The beginnings of such secularization, faintly perceptible in the latter Middle Ages, are manifest in the Puritan ethos. It was in this system of values that reason and experience were first markedly considered as independent means of ascertaining even religious truths. Faith which is unquestioning and not 'rationally weighed', says Baxter, is not faith, but a dream or fancy or opinion. In effect, this grants to science a power which may ultimately limit that of theology.

Thus, once these processes are clearly understood, it is not surprising or inconsistent that Luther particularly, and Melanchthon less strongly, execrated the cosmology of Copernicus and that Calvin frowned upon the acceptance of many scientific discoveries of his day, while the religious ethic which stemmed from these leaders invited the pursuit of natural science.[18] In so far as the attitudes of the theologians dominate over the,

[18] On the basis of this analysis, it is surprising to note the statement *accredited* to Max Weber that the opposition of the Reformers is sufficient reason for not coupling Protestantism with scientific interests. See *Wirtschaftsgeschichte* (München, 1924), 314. This remark is especially unanticipated since it does not at all accord with Weber's discussion of the same point in his other works. Cf. *Religionssoziologie*, I, 141, 564; *Wissenschaft als Beruf* (München, 1921), 19–20. The probable explanation is that the first is not Weber's statement, since the *Wirtschaftsgeschichte* was compiled from classroom notes by two of his students who may have neglected to make the requisite distinctions. It is unlikely that Weber would have made the elementary error of confusing the Reformers' opposition to certain scientific discoveries with the unforeseen consequences of the Protestant ethic, particularly since he expressly warns against the failure to make such discriminations in his *Religionssoziologie*. For perceptive but vague adumbrations of Weber's hypothesis, see Auguste Comte, *Cours de philosophie positive* (Paris, 1864), IV, 127–30.

in effect, subversive religious ethic – as did Calvin's authority in Geneva until the early eighteenth century – science may be greatly impeded. But with the relaxation of this hostile influence and with the development of an ethic, stemming from it and yet differing significantly, science takes on a new life, as was indeed the case in Geneva.

Perhaps the most directly effective element of the Protestant ethic for the sanction of natural science was that which held that the study of nature enables a fuller appreciation of His works and thus leads us to admire the Power, Wisdom, and Goodness of God manifested in His creation. Though this conception was not unknown to medieval thought, the consequences deduced from it were entirely different. Thus Arnaldus of Villanova, in studying the products of the Divine Workshop, adheres strictly to the medieval ideal of determining properties of phenomena from *tables* (in which all combinations are set forth according to the canons of logic). But in the seventeenth century, the contemporary emphasis upon empiricism led to investigating nature primarily through observation.[19] This difference in interpretation of substantially the same doctrine can only be understood in the light of the different values permeating the two cultures.

For a Barrow, Boyle, or Wilkins, a Ray or Grew, science found its rationale in the end of all existence: glorification of God. Thus, from Boyle:[20]

> ... God loving, as He deserves, to be honour'd in all our Faculties, and consequently to be glorified and acknowledg'd by the acts of Reason, as well as by those of Faith, there must be sure a great Disparity betwixt that general, confus'd and lazy Idea we commonly have of His Power and Wisdom, and the Distinct, rational and affecting notions of those Attributes which are form'd by an attentive Inspection of those Creatures in which they are most legible, and which were made chiefly for that very end.

Ray carries this conception to its logical conclusion, for if Nature is the manifestation of His power, then nothing in Nature is too mean for scientific study.[21] The universe and the insect, the

---

[19] Walter Pagel, 'Religious motives in the medical biology of the seventeenth century', *Bulletin of the Institute of the History of Medicine*, 1935, 3, 214–15.
[20] *Usefulness of Experimental Natural Philosophy*, 53; cf. Ray, *Wisdom of God*, 132; Wilkins, *Natural Religion*, 236 ff.; Isaac Barrow, *Opuscula*, iv, 88 ff.; Nehemiah Grew, *Cosmologia sacra* (London, 1701), who points out that 'God is the original End', and that 'we are *bound* to study His works'.
[21] Ray, *Wisdom of God*, 130 ff. Max Weber quotes Swammerdam as saying: 'ich bringe Ihnen hier den Nachweis der Vorschung Gottes in der Anatomie einer Laus'. *Wissenschaft als Beruf*, 19.

macrocosm and microcosm alike, are indications of 'divine Reason, running like a Golden Vein, through the whole leaden Mine of Brutal Nature'.

Up to this point we have been concerned in the main with the directly felt sanction of science through Puritan values. While this was of great influence, there was another type of relationship which, subtle and difficult of apprehension though it be, was perhaps of paramount significance. It has to do with the preparation of a set of largely implicit assumptions which made for the ready acceptance of the scientific temper characteristic of the seventeenth and subsequent centuries. It is not simply that Protestantism implicitly involved free inquiry, *libre examen*, or decried monastic asectism. These are important but not exhaustive.

It has become manifest that in each age there is a system of science which rests upon a set of assumptions, usually implicit and seldom questioned by the scientists of the time.[22] The *basic* assumption in modern science 'is a widespread, instinctive conviction in the existence of an *Order of Things*, and, in particular, of an Order of Nature'.[23] This belief, this faith, for at least since Hume it must be recognized as such, is simply 'impervious to the demand for a consistent rationality'. In the systems of scientific thought of Galileo, Newton, and of their successors, the testimony of experiment is the ultimate criterion of truth, but the very notion of experiment is ruled out without the prior assumption that Nature constitutes an intelligible order, so that when appropriate questions are asked, she will answer, so to speak. Hence this assumption is final and absolute.[24] As Professor Whitehead indicated, this 'faith in the possibility of science, generated antecedently to the development of modern scientific theory, is an unconscious derivative from medieval theology'. But this conviction, prerequisite of modern science though it be, was not sufficient to induce its development. What was needed was a constant interest in searching for this order in nature in an empirico-rational fashion, that is, an active interest in this world and its occurrences plus a specific frame of mind. With Protestantism, religion provided this interest: it actually imposed obligations of intense concentration upon secular activity with an emphasis upon experience and reason as bases for action and belief.

Even the Bible as final and complete authority was subject to

22 A. E. Heath, in *Isaac Newton: A Memorial Volume*, ed. by W. J. Greenstreet (London, 1927), 133 ff.; E. A. Burtt, *The Metaphysical Foundations of Modern Physical Science* (London, 1925).
23 A. N. Whitehead, *Science and the Modern World* (New York, 1931), 5 ff.
24 Cf. E. A. Burtt in *Isaac Newton: A Memorial Volume*, 139. For the classic exposition of this scientific faith, see Newton's 'Rules of Reasoning in Philosophy', in his *Principia* (London, 1729 edn), II, 160 ff.

the interpretation of the individual upon these bases. The similarity in approach and intellectual attitude of this system to
that of the contemporary science is of more than passing interest.
It could not but mould an attitude of looking at the world of
sensuous phenomena which was highly conducive to the willing
acceptance, and indeed, preparation for, the same attitude in
science. That the similarity is deep-rooted and not superficial
may be gathered from the following comment upon Calvin's
theology:[25]

> Die Gedanken werden objektiviert und zu einem objektiven
> Lehrsystem aufgebaut und abgerundet. Es bekommt geradezu
> ein naturwissenschaftliches Gepräge; es ist klar, leicht fassbar
> und formulierbar, wie alles, was der äusseren Welt angehört,
> klarer zu gestalten ist als das, was im Tiefsten sich abspielt.

The conviction in immutable law is as pronounced in the
theory of predestination as in scientific investigation: 'the immutable law is there and must be acknowledged'.[26] The similarity
between this conception and the scientific assumption is clearly
drawn by Hermann Weber:[27]

> ... die Lehre von der Prädestination in ihrem tiefsten Kerne
> getroffen zu sein, wenn mann sie als Faktum im Sinne eines
> naturwissenschaftlichen Faktums begreift, nur dass, das
> oberste Prinzip, das auch jedem naturwissenschaftlichen
> Erscheinungskomplex zugrunde liegt, die im tiefsten erlebte
> gloria dei ist.

The cultural environment was permeated with this attitude
toward natural phenomena which was derived from both science
and religion and which enhanced the continued prevalence of
conceptions characteristic of the new science.

There remains a supremely important part of this study to be
completed. It is not sufficient verification of our hypothesis that
the cultural attitudes induced by the Protestant ethic were favourable to science. Nor, yet again, that the consciously expressed
motivation of many eminent scientists was provided by this
ethic. Nor, still further, that the cast of thought which is characteristic of modern science, namely, the combination of empiricism and rationalism and the faith in the validity of one basic
postulate, an apprehensible order in Nature, bears any other than

[25] Hermann Weber, *Die Theologie Calvins* (Berlin, 1930), 23.
[26] *Ibid.*, 31. The significance of the doctrine of God's foreknowledge for the
re-enforcement of the belief in natural law is remarked by H. T. Buckle,
History of Civilization in England (New York, 1925), 482.
[27] *Op. cit.*, 31.

fortuitous congruency with the values involved in Protestantism. All this can but provide some evidence of a certain probability of the connection we are arguing. The most significant test of the hypothesis is to be found in the confrontation of the results *deduced* from the hypothesis with relevant empirical data. If the Protestant ethic involved an attitudinal set favourable to science and technology in so many ways, then we should find amongst Protestants a greater propensity for these fields of endeavour than one would expect simply on the basis of their representation in the total population. Moreover, if, as has been frequently suggested,[28] the impression made by this ethic has lasted long after much of its theological basis has been largely disavowed, then even in periods subsequent to the seventeenth century, this connection of Protestantism and science should persist to some degree. The following section, then, will be devoted to this further test of the hypothesis.

THE PURITAN IMPETUS TO SCIENCE

In the beginnings of the Royal Society there is found a closely wrought nexus between science and society. The Society itself arose from an antecedent interest in science and the subsequent activities of its members provided an appreciable impetus to further scientific advance. The inception of this group is found in the occasional meetings of devotees of science in 1645 and following. Among the leading spirits were John Wilkins, John Wallis, and soon afterwards Robert Boyle and Sir William Petty, upon all of whom religious forces seem to have had a singularly strong influence.

Wilkins, later an Anglican bishop, was raised at the home of his maternal grandfather, John Dod, an outstanding Non-conformist theologian, and 'his early education had given him a strong bias toward Puritanical principles'.[29] Wilkins's influence as Warden of Wadham College was profound; under it came Ward, Rooke, Wren, Sprat, and Walter Pope (his half-brother), all of whom were original members of the Royal Society.[30] John

---

[28] As Troeltsch puts it: 'The present day world does not live by logical consistency, any more than any other; spiritual forces can exercise a dominant influence even where they are avowedly repudiated.' *Die Bedeutung des Protestantismus für die Entstehung der modernen Welt* (München, 1911), 22: cf. Georgia Harkness, *John Calvin: The Man and his Ethics* (New York, 1931), 7 ff.

[29] Memorials of John Ray, 18–19; P. A. W. Henderson, *The Life and Times of John Wilkins* (London, 1910), 36. Moreover, after Wilkins took holy orders, he became chaplain to Lord Viscount Saye and Sele, a resolute and effective Puritan.

[30] Henderson, *op. cit.*, 72–3.

Wallis, to whose *Arithmetica Infinitorum* Newton was avowedly indebted for many of his leading mathematical conceptions, was a clergyman with strong leanings toward Puritan principles. The piety of Boyle has already been remarked; the only reason he did not take holy orders, as he said, was because of the 'absence of an inner call'.[31]

Theodore Haak, the German virtuoso who played so prominent a part in the formation of the Royal Society, was a pronounced Calvinist. Denis Papin, who during his prolonged stay in England contributed notably to science and technology, was a French Calvinist compelled to leave his country to avoid religious persecution. Thomas Sydenham, sometimes called 'the English Hippocrates', was an ardent Puritan who fought as one of Cromwell's men. Sir William Petty was a latitudinarian; he had been a follower of Cromwell, and in his writings he evinced clearly the influences of Puritanism. Of Sir Robert Moray, described by Huyghens as the 'Soul of the Royal Society', it could be said that 'religion was the mainspring of his life, and amidst courts and camps he spent many hours a day in devotion'.[32]

It is hardly a fortuitous circumstance that the leading figures of this nuclear group of the Royal Society were divines or eminently religious men, though it is not quite accurate to maintain, as did Dr Richardson, that the beginnings of the Society occurred in a small group of learned men among whom Puritan *divines* predominated.[33] But it is quite clearly true that the originative spirits of the Society were markedly influenced by Puritan conceptions.

Dean Dorothy Stimson, in a recently published paper, has independently arrived at this same conclusion.[34] She points out that of the ten men who constituted the 'invisible college', in 1645, only one, Scarbrough, was clearly non-Puritan. About two of the others there is some uncertainty, though Merret had a Puritan training. The others were all definitely Puritan. Moreover, among the original list of members of the Society of 1663, forty-two of the sixty-eight concerning whom information about their religious orientation is available were clearly Puritan. Considering that

---

[31] *Dictionary of National Biography*, II, 1028. This reason, effective also for Sir Samuel Morland's turning to mathematics rather than to the ministry, is an example of the direct working of the Protestant ethic which, as exposited by Baxter for example, held that only those who felt an 'inner call' should enter the clergy, and that others could better serve society by adopting other accredited secular activities. On Morland, see the 'Autobiography of Sir Samuel Morland', in J. O. Halliwell-Phillipps's *Letters Illustrative of the Progress of Science in England* (London, 1841), 116 ff.

[32] *Dictionary of National Biography*, xiii, 1299.

[33] C. F. Richardson, *English Preachers and Preaching* (New York, 1928), 177.

[34] Dorothy Stimson, 'Puritanism and the new philosophy in seventeenth-century England', *Bulletin of the Institute of the History of Medicine*, 1935, 3, 321–34.

the Puritans constituted a relatively small minority in the English population, the fact that they constituted sixty-two per cent of the initial membership of the Society becomes even more striking. Dean Stimson concludes: 'that experimental science spread as rapidly as it did in seventeenth-century England seems to me to be in part at least because the moderate Puritans encouraged it'.

THE PURITAN INFLUENCE ON SCIENTIFIC EDUCATION

Nor was this relationship only evidenced among the members of the Royal Society. The emphasis of the Puritans upon utilitarianism and empiricism was likewise manifested in the type of education which they introduced and fostered. The 'formal grammar grind' of the schools was criticized by them as much as the formalism of the Church.

Prominent among the Puritans who so consistently sought to introduce the new realistic, utilitarian, and empirical education into England was Samuel Hartlib. He formed the connecting link between the various Protestant educators in England and in Europe who were earnestly seeking to spread the academic study of science. It was to Hartlib that Milton addressed his tractate on education and Sir William Petty dedicated his 'Advice ... for the Advancement of some particular Parts of Learning', namely, science, technology, and handicraft. Moreover, it was Hartlib who was instrumental in broadcasting the educational ideas of Comenius and in bringing him to England.

The Bohemian Reformist, John Amos Comenius, was one of the most influential educators of this period. Basic to the system of education which he promulgated were the norms of utilitarianism and empiricism: values which could only lead to an emphasis upon the study of science and technology, of *Realia*.[35] In his most influential work, *Didactica Magna*, he summarizes his views:[36]

> The task of the pupil will be made easier, if the master, when he teaches him everything, shows him at the same time its practical application in everyday life. This rule must be carefully observed in teaching languages, dialectic, arithmetic, geometry, physics, etc. ... the truth and certainty of science depend more on the witness of the senses than on anything else. For things impress themselves directly on the senses, but

[35] Wilhelm Dilthey, 'Pädagogik: Geschichte und Grundlinien des Systems', *Gesammelte Schriften* (Leipzig and Berlin, 1934), 163 ff.
[36] J. A. Comenius, *The Great Didactic*, translated by M. W. Keatinge (London, 1896), 292, 337; see also 195, 302, 329, 341.

on the understanding only mediately and through the senses.
... Science, then, increases in certainty in proportion as it
depends on sensuous perception.

Comenius found welcome among Protestant educators in England who subscribed to the same values; individuals such as Hartlib, John Dury, Wilkins, and Haak.[37] At the request of Hartlib, he
came to England for the express purpose of making Bacon's
Solomon's House a reality. As Comenius himself remarked:
'nothing seemed more certain than that the scheme of the great
Verulam, of opening in some part of the world a universal college,
whose one object should be the advancement of the sciences,
would be carried into effect'.[38] But this aim was frustrated by the
social disorder attendant upon the rebellion in Ireland. However,
the Puritan design of advancing science was not entirely without
fruit. Cromwell founded the only new English university instituted between the Middle Ages and the nineteenth century, Durham
University, 'for all the sciences'.[39] And in Cambridge, during the
height of the Puritan influence there, the study of science was
considerably augmented.[40]

In the same vein, the Puritan Hezekiah Woodward, a friend
of Hartlib, emphasized realism (things, not words) and the teachings of science.[41] In order to initiate the study of the new science
on a much more widespread scale than had hitherto obtained, the
Puritans instituted a number of Dissenting Academies. These were
schools of university standing opened in various parts of the kingdom. One of the earliest of these was Morton's Academy wherein
there was pronounced stress laid upon scientific studies. Charles
Morton later went to New England, where he was chosen vice-
president of Harvard College, in which 'he introduced the system
of science that he used in England'.[42] At the influential Northampton Academy, another of the Puritan educational centres,
mechanics, hydrostatics, physics, anatomy, and astronomy had
an important place in the time-table. These studies were pursued
largely with the aid of actual experiments and observations.

But the marked emphasis placed by the Puritans upon science
and technology may perhaps best be appreciated by a comparison
between the Puritan academies and the universities. The latter,
even after they had introduced scientific subjects, continued to
give an essentially classical education; the truly cultural studies

[37] Robert F. Young, *Comenius in England* (Oxford, 1932), 5–9.
[38] *Opera Didactica Omnia* (Amsterdam, 1657), Book II, preface.
[39] F. H. Hayward, *The Unknown Cromwell* (London, 1934), 206–30, 315.
[40] James B. Mullinger, *Cambridge Characteristics in the Seventeenth Century* (London, 1867), 180–1 *et passim*.
[41] Irene Parker, *Dissenting Academies in England* (Cambridge, 1914), 24.
[42] *Ibid.*, 62.

were those which, if not entirely useless, were at least definitely nonutilitarian in purpose. The academies, in contrast, held that a truly liberal education was one which was 'in touch with life' and which should therefore include as many utilitarian subjects as possible. As Dr Parker puts it:[43]

> ... the difference between the two educational systems is seen not so much in the introduction into the academies of 'modern' subjects and methods as in the fact that among the Nonconformists there was a totally different system at work from that found in the universities. The spirit animating the Dissenters was that which had moved Ramus and Comenius in France and Germany and which in England had actuated Bacon and later Hartlib and his circle.

This comparison of the Puritan academies in England and Protestant educational developments on the Continent is well warranted. The Protestant academies in France devoted much more attention to scientific and utilitarian subjects than did the Catholic institutions.[44] When the Catholics took over many of the Protestant academies, the study of science was considerably diminished.[45] Moreover, as we shall see, even in the predominantly Catholic France, much of the scientific work was being done by Protestants. Protestant exiles from France included a large number of important scientists and inventors.[46]

VALUE-INTEGRATION OF PURITANISM AND SCIENCE

Of course, the mere fact that an individual is *nominally* a Catholic or Protestant has no bearing upon his attitudes toward science. It is only as he adopts the tenets and implications of the teachings that his religious affiliation becomes significant. For example, it was only when Pascal became thoroughly converted to the teachings of Jansenius that he perceived the 'vanity of science'. For Jansenius characteristically maintained that above all we must beware of that vain love of science, which though seemingly innocent, is actually a snare 'leading men away from the contemplation of eternal truths to rest in the satisfaction of the finite intelligence'.[47] Once Pascal was converted to such beliefs, he

---

[43] *Ibid.*, 133–4.
[44] P. D. Bourchenin, *Étude sur les académies protestantes en France au XVIième et au XVIIième siècle* (Paris, 1882), 445 ff.
[45] M. Nicolas, 'Les académies protestantes de Montauban et de Nimes', *Bulletin de la société de l'histoire du protestantisme française*, 1858, 4, 35–48.
[46] D. C. A. Agnew, *Protestant Exiles from France* (Edinburgh, 1866), 210 ff.
[47] Émile Boutroux, *Pascal*, trans. by E. M. Creak (Manchester, 1902), 16.

resolved 'to make an end of all those scientific researches to which he had hitherto applied himself'.[48] It is the firm acceptance of the values basic to the two creeds which accounts for the difference in the respective scientific contributions of Catholics and Protestants.

The same association of Protestantism and science was marked in the New World. The correspondents and members of the Royal Society who lived in New England were 'all trained in Calvinistic thinking'.[49] The founders of Harvard sprang from this Calvinistic culture, not from the literary era of the Renaissance or from the scientific movement of the seventeenth century, and their minds were more easily led into the latter than the former channel of thought.[50] This predilection of the Puritans for science is also noted by Professor Morison, who states: 'the Puritan clergy, instead of opposing the acceptance of the Copernican theory, were the chief patrons and promoters of the new astronomy, and of other scientific discoveries, in New England'.[51] It is significant that the younger John Winthrop, of Massachusetts, later a member of the Royal Society, came to London in 1641 and probably spent some time with Hartlib, Drury, and Comenius in London. Apparently, he suggested to Comenius that he come to New England and found a scientific college there.[52] Some years later, Increase Mather (President of Harvard College from 1684–1701) did found a 'Philosophical Society' at Boston.[53]

The scientific content of Harvard's educational programme derived greatly from the Protestant Peter Ramus.[54] Ramus had formulated an educational curriculum which in contrast to that of the Catholic universities laid great stress on the study of the sciences.[55] His ideas were welcomed in the Protestant universities on the Continent, at Cambridge (which had a greater Puritan

[48] *Ibid.*, 17; cf. Jacques Chevalier, *Pascal* (New York, 1930), 143; Pascal's *Pensées*, trans. by O. W. Wright (Boston, 1884), 224, No. xxvii. '*Vanity of the Sciences*. The science of external things will not console me for ignorance of ethics in times of affliction; but the science of morals will always console me for ignorance of external sciences.'

[49] Stimson, *op. cit.*, 332.

[50] Porter G. Perrin, 'Possible sources of *Technologia* at early Harvard', *New England Quarterly*, 1934, 7, 724.

[51] Samuel E. Morison, 'Astronomy at colonial Harvard', *New England Quarterly*, 1934, 7, 3–24; also Clifford K. Shipton, 'A plea for Puritanism', *The American Historical Review*, 1935, 40, 463–4.

[52] R. F. Young, *Comenius in England*, 7–8.

[53] *Ibid.*, 95.

[54] Perrin, *op. cit.*, 723–4.

[55] Theobald Ziegler, *Geschichte der Pädagogik* (München, 1895), I, 108. Ziegler indicates that while the contemporary French Catholic institutions only devoted one-sixth of the curriculum to science, Ramus dedicated fully one-half to scientific studies.

and scientific element than Oxford),[56] and later at Harvard, but were firmly denounced in the various Catholic institutions.[57] The Reformation spirit of utilitarianism and 'realism' probably accounts largely for the favorable reception of Ramus's views.

VALUE-INTEGRATION OF PIETISM AND SCIENCE

Dr Parker notes that the Puritan academies in England 'may be compared with the schools of the Pietists in Germany, which under Francke and his followers prepared the way for the *Realschulen*, for there can be no doubt that just as the Pietists carried on the work of Comenius in Germany, so the Dissenters put into practice the theories of Comenius's English followers, Hartlib, Milton, and Petty'.[58] The significance of this comparison is profound for, as has been frequently observed, the values and principles of Puritanism and Pietism are almost identical. Cotton Mather had recognized the close resemblance of these two Protestant movements, saying that 'ye American puritanism is so much of a piece with ye Frederician pietism' that they may be considered as virtually identical.[59] Pietism, except for its greater 'enthusiasm', might almost be termed the Continental counterpart of Puritanism. Hence, if our hypothesis of the association between Puritanism and interest in science and technology is warranted, one would expect to find the same correlation among the Pietists. And such was markedly the case.

The Pietists in Germany and elsewhere entered into a close alliance with the 'new education': the study of science and technology of *Realia*.[60] The two movements had in common the realistic and practical point of view, combined with an intense aversion to the speculation of Aristotelian philosophers. Fundamental to the educational views of the Pietists were the same deep-rooted utilitarian and empirical values which actuated the

[56] David Masson properly calls Cambridge the alma mater of the Puritans. In listing twenty leading Puritan clergymen in New England, Masson found that seventeen of them were alumni of Cambridge, while only three came from Oxford. See his *Life of Milton* (London, 1875), II, 563; cited by Stimson, *op. cit.*, 332. See also *A History of the University of Oxford*, by Charles E. Mallet (London, 1924), II, 147.
[57] Heinrich Schreiber, *Geschichte der Albert-Ludwigs Universität zu Freiburg* (Freiburg, 1857–68), II, 135. For example, at the Jesuit university of Freiburg, Ramus could only be referred to if he were refuted, and 'no copies of his books are to be found in the hands of a student'.
[58] Parker, *op. cit.*, 135.
[59] Kuno Francke, 'Cotton Mather and August Hermann Francke', *Harvard Studies and Notes*, 1896, 5, 63. See also the cogent discussion of this point by Max Weber, *Protestant Ethic*, 132–5.
[60] Friedrich Paulsen, *German Education: Past and Present*, trans. by T. Lorenz (London, 1908), 104 ff.

Puritans.[61] It was on the basis of these values that the Pietist leaders, August Hermann Francke, Comenius, and their followers emphasized the new science.

Francke repeatedly noted the desirability of acquainting students with practical scientific knowledge.[62] Both Francke and his colleague, Christian Thomasius, set themselves in opposition to the strong educational movement developed by Christian Weise, which advocated primarily training in oratory and classics, and sought rather 'to introduce the neglected modern disciplines, which served their purposes more adequately; such studies as biology, physics, astronomy, and the like'.[63]

Wherever Pietism spread its influence upon the educational system there followed the large-scale introduction of scientific and technical subjects.[64] Thus, Francke and Thomasius built the foundations of the University of Halle, which was the first German university to introduce a thorough training in the sciences.[65] The leading professors, such as Friedrich Hoffman, Ernst Stahl (professor of chemistry and famous for his influential phlogiston theory), Samuel Stryk, and, of course, Francke, all stood in the closest relations with the Pietistic movement. All of them characteristically sought to develop the teaching of science and to ally science with practical applications.

Not only Halle, but other Pietistic universities manifested the same emphases. Königsberg, having come under the Pietistic influence of the University of Halle through the activities of Francke's disciple, Gehr, early adopted the natural and physical sciences in the modern sense of the seventeenth century.[66] The University of Göttingen, an offshoot of Halle, was famous essentially for the great progress which it effected in the cultivation of the sciences.[67] The Calvinistic university of Heidelberg was like-

---

[61] Alfred Heubaum, *Geschichte des deutschen Bildungswesens seit der Mitte des siebzehnten Jahrunderts* (Berlin, 1905), I, 90. 'Ziel der Erziehung [among Pietists] ist praktische Verwendbarkeit des Zöglings im Gemeinwohl. Der starke Einfluss des utilitaristichen Moments ... vermindert die Gefaher der Uebertreibung des religiösen Moments und sichert der Bewegung für die nächste Zukunft ihre Bedeutung'.

[62] During walks in the field, says Francke, the instructor should 'nützliche und erbauliche Geschichten erzählen oder etwas aus der Physik von den Geschöpfen und Werken Gottes vorsagen'. '... im Naturalienkabinet diente dazu, die Zöglinge in ihren Friestunden durch den Anstaltarzt mit naturwissenschaftlichen Erscheinungen, mit Mineralien, Bergarten, hier und da mit Experimenten bekannt zu machen'. Quoted by Heubaum, *op. cit.*, I, 89, 94.

[63] *Ibid.*, I, 136.   [64] *Ibid.*, I, 176 ff.

[65] Koppel S. Pinson, *Pietism as a Factor in the Rise of German Nationalism* (New York, 1934), 18; Heubaum, *op. cit.*, I, 118. 'Halle war die erste deutsche Universität von ganz eigenartigem wissenschaftlichen und nationalen Gepräge ...'

[66] Heubaum, *op. cit.*, I, 153.

[67] Paulsen, *op. cit.*, 120–1.

wise prominent for instituting a large measure of scientific study.[68] Finally, the University of Altdorf, which was at that time the most conspicuous for its interest in science, was a Protestant University subject to Pietistic influence.[69] Heubaum summarizes these developments by asserting that the essential progress in the teaching of science and technology occurred in Protestant, and more precisely, in Pietistic universities.[70]

RELIGIOUS AFFILIATION OF RECRUITS TO SCIENCE

This association of Pietism and science, which we have been led to anticipate from our hypothesis, did not confine itself to the universities. The same Pietist predilection for science and technology was evidenced in secondary school education. The *Pädagogium* of Halle introduced the subjects of mathematics and natural science; stress being laid, in all cases, on the use of object lessons and on practical applications.[71] Johann Georg Lieb, Bernhard von Rohr, and Johann Peter Ludwig (Chancellor of Halle University), all of whom had come under the direct influence of Francke and Pietism, advocated schools of manufacture, physics, mathematics, and economics, in order to study how 'manufacture might be ever more and more improved and excelled'.[72] They hoped that the outcome of these suggestions might be a so-called *Collegium physicum-mechanicum* and *Werkschulen*.

It is a significant fact, and one which lends additional weight to our hypothesis, that the *ökonomisch-mathematische Realschule* was completely a Pietist product. This school, which centered on the study of mathematics, the natural sciences, and economics, and which was avowedly utilitarian and realistic in temper, was planned by Francke.[73] Moreover, it was a Pietist and

[68] Heubaum, *op. cit.*, I, 60.

[69] S. Günther, 'Die mathematischen Studien und Naturwissenschaften an der nürnbergischen Universität Altdorf', *Mitteilungen des Vereins für Gesichichte der Stadt Nürnberg*, Heft. III, 9.

[70] Heubaum, *op. cit.*, I, 241; see also Paulsen, *op. cit.*, 122; J. D. Michaelis, *Raisonnement über die protestantischen Universitäten in Deutschland* (Frankfurt, 1768), I, section 36.

[71] Paulsen, *op. cit.*, 127.

[72] Heubaum, *op. cit.*, I, 184.

[73] Alfred Heubaum, 'Christoph Semlers Realschule und seine Beziehung zu A. H. Francke', *Neue Jahrbücher für Philologie und Pädagogik*, 1893, 2, 65–77; see also Ziegler, *Geschichte der Pädagogik*, I, 197, who observes: 'einem inneren Zusammenhang zwischen der auf das Praktische gerichteten Realschule und der aufdas Praktische gerichteten Frömmigkeit der Pietisten fehlte es ja auch nicht, nur éine ganz einseitig religiöse und theologische Auffassung des Pietismus kann das verkennen: im Geist der praktischen Nützlichkeit und Gemeinnützigkeit ist dieser dem Rationalismus vorangegangen und mit ihm eins gewesen, und aus diesem Geist heraus ist zu Franckes Zeiten in Halle die Realschule entstanden'.

a former student of Francke, Johann Julius Hecker, who first actually organized a *Realschule*.[74] Semler, Silberschlag, and Hähn, the directors and co-organizers of this first school, were all Pietists and former students of Francke.[75]

All available evidence points in the same direction. Protestants, without exception, form a progressively larger proportion of the student body in those schools which emphasize scientific and technologic training,[76] while Catholics concentrate their interests on classical and theological training. For example, in Prussia, the distribution shown in Table 1 was found.[77]

TABLE 1 *Attendance at secondary schools differentiated by religious affiliations of the students, Prussia, 1875–6*

Religious Affiliation	Pro-gym-nasium	Gymna-sium	Real-schule	Ober-realsch	Höheren Bürger	Total	General Population
Protestants	49·1	69·7	79·8	75·8	80·7	73·1	64·9
Catholics	39·1	20·2	11·4	6·7	14·2	17·3	33·6
Jews	11·2	10·1	8·8	17·5	5·1	9·6	1·3

This greater propensity of Protestants for scientific and technical studies accords with the implications of our hypothesis. That this distribution is typical may be gathered from the fact that other investigators have noted the same tendency in other instances.[78] Furthermore, these distributions do not represent a spurious correlation resulting from differences in rural-urban

[74] Paulsen, *op. cit.*, 133.

[75] Upon the basis of this and other facts, Ziegler proceeds to trace a close 'Kausalzusammenhang' between Pietism and the study of science. See his *Geschichte*, I, 1960 ff.

[76] The characteristic feature of the *gymnasien* is the classical basis of their curricula. Demarcated from these schools are the *Realschulen*, where the sciences predominate and where modern languages are substituted for the classical tongues. The *Real-gymnasium* is a compromise between these two types, having less classical instruction than the *gymnasium* with more attention paid to science and mathematics. The *Ober-realschulen und höheren Bürgerschulen* are both *Realschulen*; the first with a nine-year course, the second with a six-year course. Cf. Paulsen, *German Education*, 46 *et passim*.

[77] Alwin Petersilie, 'Zur Statistik der höheren Lehranstalten in Preussen', *Zeitschrift des königlich Preussischen Statischen Bureaus*, 1877, *17*, 109.

[78] Edouard Borel, *Religion und Beruf* (Basel, 1930), 93 ff., who remarks the unusually high proportion of Protestants in the technical professions in Basel; Julius Wolf, 'Die deutschen Katholiken in Staat und Wirtschaft', *Zeitschrift für Sozialwissenschaft*, 1913, *4*, 199, notes that 'die Protestanten ihren "naturgemässen" Anteil überschreiten gilt für die wissenschaftliche und sonstige intellektuelle Betätigung (mit Ausnahme des geistlichen Berufs) ...'. In 1860, Ad. Frantz had already noted the same fact. See his 'Bedeutung der Religionunterschiede für das physische Leben der Bevölkerungen', *Jahrbücher für Nationalökonomie und Statistik*, 1868, *11*, 51. Cf. also similar results for Berlin in *Statistisches Jahrbuch der Stadt Berlin*, 1897, *22*, 468–72. Buckle, *op. cit.*, 482, notes that 'Calvinism is favourable to science'. Cf. also Weber, *Protestant Ethic*, *38*, 189; and Troeltsch, *Social Teachings* ..., II, 894.

distribution of the two religions, as may be seen from the pertinent data for the Swiss canton, Basel-Stadt. As is well known, the urban population tends to contribute more in the fields of science and technology than the rural. Yet for 1910 and following – the period to which Edouard Borel's study, with results similar to those just presented for Prussia, refers – Protestants constituted 63·4 per cent of the total population of the canton, but only 57·1 per cent of the population of Basel (the city proper) and 84·7 per cent of the rural population.[79]

Martin Offenbacher's careful study includes an analysis of the association between religious affiliation and the allocation of educational interests in Baden, Bavaria, Württemberg, Prussia, Alsace-Lorraine, and Hungary. The statistical results in these various places are of the same nature : Protestants, proportionately to their representation in the population at large, have a much higher attendance at the various secondary schools, with the difference becoming especially marked in the schools primarily devoted to the sciences and technology. In Baden,[80] for example, taking an average of the figures for the years 1885–95, we have Table 2.

TABLE 2

	Protestants, per cent	Catholics, per cent	Jews, per cent
Gymnasien	43	46	9·5
Realgymnasien	69	31	9
Oberrealschulen	52	41	7
Realschulen	49	40	11
Höheren Bürgerschulen	51	37	12
Average for the five types of schools	48	42	10
Distribution in the general population, 1895	37	61·5	1·5

However, it must be noted that although the *Realschulen* curricula are primarily characterized by their stress on the sciences and mathematics as contrasted with the relatively little attention paid these studies in the *gymnasien*, yet the latter type of school also prepares for scientific and scholarly careers. But, in general, the attendance of Protestants and Catholics at the *gymnasien* represents different interests. The relatively large number of Catholics at the *gymnasien* is due to the fact that these schools prepare for theology as well, while the Protestants generally use the *gymnasien* as a preparation for the other learned professions. Thus, in the three academic years 1891–4, 226, or over 42 per cent of the 533 Catholic graduates of the Baden *gymnasien* subsequently studied theology, while of the 375 Protestant graduates,

[79] See 'Die Bevölkerung des Kantons Basel-Stadt', *Mitteilungen des Statistischen Amtes des Kantons Basel-Stadt*, 1932, 48–9; and the same publication for the years 1910 and 1921.
[80] Martin Offenbacher, *Konfession und soziale Schichtung* (Tübingen, 1900), 16. The slight errors of the original are here unavoidably reproduced.

only 53 (14 per cent) turned to theology, while 86 per cent went into the other learned professions.[81]

Similarly, the Catholic apologist, Hans Rost, though he wishes to establish the thesis that 'the Catholic Church has been at all times a warm friend of science', is forced to admit, on the basis of his data, that the Catholics avoid the *Realschulen*, that they show 'eine gewisse Gleichgültigkeit und Abneigung gegen diese Anstalten'. The reason for this, he goes on to say, is 'das die Oberrealschule und das Realgymnasium nicht zum Studium der Theologie berechtigen : denn diese ist häufig die Tribfeder bei den Katholiken zum höheren Studium überhaupt'.[82]

Thus, statistical data point to a marked tendency for Protestants, as contrasted with Catholics, to pursue scientific and technical studies. This can also be seen in the statistics for Württemberg, where an average of the years 1872–9 and 1883–98 gives the figures[83] in Table 3.

TABLE 3

	Protestants, per cent	Catholics, per cent	Jews, per cent
Gymnasien	68·2	28·2	3·4
Lateinschulen	73·2	22·3	3·9
Realschulen	79·7	14·8	4·2
Total population, 1880	69·1	30·0	0·7

Nor do the Protestants evidence these foci of interest only in education. Various studies have found an unduly large representation of Protestants among outstanding scientists.[84] If the foregoing data simply provide slight probabilities that the connection we have traced does in fact obtain, Candolle's well known *Histoire des sciences et des savants* increases these probabilities consider-

[81] H. Gemss, *Statistik der Gymnasialabiturienten im deutschen Reich* (Berlin, 1895), 14–20.
[82] Hans Rost, *Die wirtschaftliche und kulturelle Lage der deutschen Katholiken* (Köln, 1911), 167 ff.
[83] Offenbacher, *op. cit.*, 18. These data are corroborated by the study of Ludwig Cron pertaining to Germany for the years 1869–93; *Glaubenbekenntnis und höheres Studium* (Heidelberg, 1900). Ernst Engel also found that in Prussia, Posen, Brandenburg, Pomerania, Saxony, Westphalia, and the Rhine Provinces, there is a higher incidence of Evangelical students in those schools which provide a maximum of natural science and technical subjects. See his 'Beiträge zur Geschichte und Statistik des Unterrichts', *Zeitschrift des königlich Preusischen statistichen Bureaus*, 1869, 9, 99–116, 153–212.
[84] For example, Havelock Ellis's *Study of British Genius*, 66 ff., finds that Protestant Scotland produced twenty-one of the outstanding scientists on his list as against one for Catholic Ireland. Alfred Odin finds that among the littérateurs on his list, the predominant emphasis of Protestants is on scientific and technical matters, rather than on literature, properly so called. See his *Genèse des grands hommes* (Paris, 1895), I, 477 ff.; II, Tables xx–xxi.

ably. Candolle finds that although in Europe, excluding France, there were 107 million Catholics and 68 million Protestants, yet on the list of scientists named foreign associates by the Academy of Paris from 1666–1883, there were only eighteen Catholics as against eighty Protestants.[85] But as Candolle himself suggests, this comparison is not conclusive since it omits French scientists who may have been Catholic. To correct this error, he takes the list of foreign members of the Royal Society of London at two periods when there were more French scientists included than at any other time: 1829 and 1869. In the former year, the total number of Protestant and Catholic scientists (who are foreign members of the Society) is about equal, while in 1869, the number of Protestants actually exceeds that of Catholics. But, outside the kingdom of Great Britain and Ireland, there were in Europe 139½ million Catholics and only 44 million Protestants.[86] In other words, though in the general population there were more than three times as many Catholics as Protestants, there were actually more Protestant than Catholic scientists.

However, there are yet more significant data than these which are based on different populations, where influence of economy, political regime, and other non-religious factors may be suspected to prevail over the actual influence of religion. A comparison of closely allied populations serves largely to eliminate these 'extraneous' factors, but the results are the same. Thus, on the list of foreign associates of the Academy of Paris, there is not a single Irish or English Catholic, although their proportion in the population of the three kingdoms exceeded a fifth. Likewise, Catholic Austria is not at all represented, while in general Catholic Germany is similarly lacking in the production of scientists of note relative to Protestant Germany. Finally, in Switzerland, where the two religions are largely differentiated by cantons, or mixed in some of them, and where the Protestants are to the Catholics as three to two there have been fourteen foreign Associates, of whom not one was Catholic. The same differentiation exists for the Swiss and for the English and Irish of the two religions in the lists of the Royal Society of London and the Royal Academy of Berlin.[87]

With the presentation of these data we close the empirical testing of our hypothesis. In every instance, the association of Protestantism with scientific and technologic interests and achievements is pronounced, even when extra-religious influences

[85] Alphonse de Candolle, *Histoire des sciences et des savants* (Geneva-Basel, 1885), 329.
[86] *Ibid.*, 330. Cf. J. Facaoaru, *Soziale Auslese* (Klausenberg, 1933), 138–9. 'Die Konfession hat einen grossen Einfluss auf die Entwicklung der Wissenschaft gehabt. Die Protestanten wiesen überall eine grössere Zahl hervorragender Männer auf.'
[87] Candolle, *op. cit.*, 330 ff.

are as far as possible eliminated. The association is largely understandable in terms of the norms embodied in both systems. The positive estimation by Protestants of a hardly disguised utilitarianism, of intra-mundane interests, of a thorough-going empiricism, of the right and even the duty of *libre examen*, and of the explicit individual questioning of authority were congenial to the same values found in modern science. And perhaps above all is the significance of the active ascetic drive which necessitated the study of Nature that it might be controlled. Hence, these two fields were well integrated and, in essentials, mutually supporting, not only in seventeenth-century England but in other times and places.

BIBLIOGRAPHICAL POSTSCRIPT

Max Weber's hypothesis of the role of ascetic Protestantism in the furtherance of modern capitalism has given rise to a substantial library of scholarly and polemical works on the subject. By the mid-thirties, for example, Amintore Fanfani could draw upon several hundred publications in his appraisal of the evidence; *Catholicism, Protestantism and Capitalism* (New York: Sheed & Ward, 1935). Weber did not himself conduct a similar inquiry into the relations between ascetic Protestantism and the development of science but concluded his classic essay by describing one of 'the next tasks' as that of searching out 'the significance of ascetic rationalism, which has only been touched in the foregoing sketch ... [for] the development of philosophical and scientific empiricism, [and for] ... technical development' (*The Protestant Ethic*, 182–3). First published in 1936, the preceding chapter was conceived as an effort to follow this mandate to extend the line of inquiry which Weber had opened up.

The books and papers cited in this chapter have since been supplemented by others bearing on one or another part of the hypothesis connecting Puritanism, Pietism and science. Numerous works have greatly clarified the varieties and shadings of doctrine and values comprised in Puritanism; among these, I have found the following most useful: John Thomas McNeill, *The History and Character of Calvinism* (New York: Oxford University Press, 1954) which shows Calvinism to have formed the core of English Puritanism and traces its varied consequences for society and thought; William Haller, *The Rise of Puritanism* (New York: Columbia University Press, 1939) which describes in rich and convincing detail how Puritan propaganda in press and pulpit helped prepare the way for the parliamentary rebellion, the radicalism of the Levellers, numerous sectarian fissions, an incipient bourgeois ethic and experimental science; Charles H.

George, 'A social interpretation of English Puritanism', *The Journal of Modern History*, 1953, 25, 327–42, which tries to identify the major components and the major types of Puritanism; G. R. Cragg, *From Puritanism to the Age of Reason* (Cambridge University Press, 1950), a 'study of changes in religious thought within the Church of England, 1660–1700'.

These and similar works have shown anew that Puritanism, like most religio-social creeds, was not of a piece. Practically all the scholars who have made intensive studies of the matter are agreed that most of the numerous sects comprising ascetic Protestantism provided a value-orientation encouraging work in science. (See also the note by Jean Pelseneer, 'L'origine Protestante de la science moderne', *Lychnos*, 1946–7, 246–8.) But there the near-unanimity ends. Some have concluded that it was the more radical sectarians among the Puritans who did most to develop an enlarged interest in science; see, for example, George Rosen, 'Left-wing Puritanism and science', *Bulletin of the Institute of the History of Medicine*, 1944, 15, 375–80. The biochemist and historian of science, Joseph Needham, comments on the close connections between the Diggers, the civilian wing of the Levellers, and the new and growing interest in experimental science, in his collection of essays, *Time: The Refreshing River* (New York: The Macmillan Company, 1943), 84–103. Others hold that the climate of values most conducive to an interest in science was found among the *moderate* Puritans, as exemplified by Robert Boyle. See James B. Conant, 'The advancement of learning during the Puritan Commonwealth', *Proceedings of the Massachusetts Historical Society*, 1942, 66, 3–31; and for a more generally accessible though less detailed discussion, the same author's *On Understanding Science* (New Haven: Yale University Press, 1947), 60–2. R. Hooykaas, the distinguished Dutch historian of science, reports that his biography of Boyle's scientific and religious orientations confirms the principal findings set out in the foregoing chapter: R. Hooykaas, *Robert Boyle: een studie over Natuurwetenschap en Christendom* (Loosduinen: Kleijwegt, 1943), Chapters 3–4 which analyse Boyle's convictions that the study of natural philosophy is a religiously founded moral obligation (especially as these are developed in Boyle's *The Christian Virtuoso, shewing, that by being addicted to experimental philosophy a man is rather assisted than indisposed to be a good Christian*, 1690), that empiricism and not merely rationality is required to comprehend God's works, and that tolerance, not persecution, is the policy appropriately governing relations with even the most fanatic sects.

The evidence in support of both the competing premises – that the chief locus of interest is to be found among the radical or the moderate Puritans – is still insufficient to justify a firm conclusion. Detailed distinctions among the various Puritan sects of course serve to specify the hypothesis more rigorously but the data in hand do not yet allow one to say, with any confidence, which of these were most disposed to advance the science of the day.

A recent group of studies provides substantial documentation of the ways in which the ethos of one of these Puritan sects – the Quakers – helped crystallize a distinct interest in science. Frederick B. Tolles, *Meeting House and Counting House* (Chapel Hill: University of North Carolina Press, 1948), 205–13, derives the marked interest of Quakers in science from their religious ethos. Less analytically and, at times, even tendentiously, Arthur Raistrick, *Quakers in Science and Industry, being an account of the Quaker contributions to science and industry during the 17th and 18th centuries* (London: The Bannisdale Press, 1950) emphasizes the *fact* of the large proportion of Quaker members of the Royal Society and the *fact* of their extensive work in science. But as Professor Hooykaas properly notes, these unanalysed facts do not themselves indicate that the distinctive participation of Quakers in scientific activity stemmed from their religious ethic; it might well be that it reflected the widespread tendency of well-to-do Englishmen, who included a disproportionately large number of Quakers, to turn their interest to matters of natural philosophy (R. Hooykaas, in *Archives Internationales d'Histoire des Sciences*, January, 1951). In a compact and instructive paper, however, Brooke Hindle goes on to show that the religious ethic did play this role among the Quakers of one colonial area; cf. his 'Quaker background and science in colonial Philadelphia', *Isis*, 1955, 46, 243–50; and his excellent monograph, *The Pursuit of Science in Revolutionary America, 1735–89* (Chapel Hill: University of North Carolina Press, 1956).

It may be remembered that one of the principal hypotheses of Chapter XVII[88] held that it was the *unintended and largely unforeseen consequences* of the religious ethic formulated by the great Reformist leaders which progressively developed into a system of values favorable to the pursuit of science (cf. S. F. Mason, 'The scientific revolution and the Protestant Reformation. I. Calvin and Servetus in relation to the new astronomy and the theory of the circulation of the blood. II. Lutheranism in relation to iatrochemistry and German nature philosophy', *Annals of Science*, 1953, 9, 64–87, 154–75). The historical shaping of this ethic was doubtless partly in response to changing social, cultural and economic contexts but partly also, it was an immanent development of the religious ideas and values themselves (as Wesley, above all other Protestant leaders, clearly perceived). This is only to say again that the rôle of ascetic Protestantism in

[88] Cf. *Social Theory and Social Structure*, New York, 1957.

encouraging the development of science did not remain fixed and unchanging. What was only implicit in the sixteenth and early seventeenth centuries became explicit and visible to many in the later seventeenth and eighteenth centuries. Several recent studies confirm this interpretation.

Based upon a close scrutiny of primary sources and present-day research, Paul H. Kocher's *Science and Religion in Elizabethan England* (San Marino, California: The Huntington Library, 1953) testifies to the long distance scholars have come since the day when they considered only the sources of conflict between science and religion as though conflict were plainly the *only* relation which could, and historically did, subsist between these social institutions. In contrast, this monograph shows that there was ample room for the science of Elizabethan England to develop within the bounds set by the religious doctrine of the time. Nor was this simply a matter of religion *tolerating* science. For the period before 1610, Kocher can find no convincing evidence 'for or against' the hypothesis that Puritanism provided a more 'fertile soil for natural science than ... its rival religions in England'. (17)[89] The data for this early period are inadequate to reach a sound conclusion. But, he goes on to say,

> We can see from our vantage point in the twentieth century that Puritan worldliness was ultimately to aid science more than Puritan otherworldliness was to inhibit it, in proportion more perhaps (though this much less certain) than could Anglican doctrine or practice. But the effects of such impetus were to become visible only gradually as Puritanism developed. The Elizabethan age came too early to afford concrete evidence for distinguishing and weighing against each other the contributions of Puritans and Anglicans to science. (19)

Considered in terms of the immanent dynamic of the religious ethos, however, Kocher's contrast between the 'worldliness' and 'otherworldliness' of successive generations of Puritans is more seeming than real. For, as Weber was able to show in detail, 'worldliness' was historically generated by the originally 'otherworldly' values of Puritanism, which called for active and sustained effort in this world and so subverted the initial value-orientation (this process being an example of what he called the *Paradoxie der Folgen*). Manifest conformity to these values produced latent consequences which were far removed in character from the values which released them.

By the eighteenth century, this process of change had resulted in what has been described by Basil Willey as 'the holy alliance between science and religion'. (*The Eighteenth-Century Back-*

[89] Numbers in parentheses refer to pages in the work cited.

ground, New York: Columbia University Press, 1941). Just as Robert Boyle in the seventeenth century, so Joseph Priestley, the scientist and apostle of Unitarianism, in the eighteenth, symbolized and actualized this alliance.

The later connections between science and religion in England from the late eighteenth to the mid-nineteenth century have been painstakingly examined in the monograph by Charles C. Gillispie, *Genesis and Geology: a study in the relations of scientific thought, natural theology and social opinion in Great Britain, 1790–1850* (Cambridge: Harvard University Press, 1951). Concerned less with the role of religion in the recruitment and motivation of scientists than with the grounds on which the findings of geology were regarded as consistent with religious teachings, Gillispie traces the process through which these tended to become culturally integrated.

When this paper was written in 1936, I relied almost entirely on Irene Parker's pioneering study (1914) of the role of the Dissenting Academies in advancing the new scientific education of the eighteenth century.[90] The import of her study is not basically changed but is substantially developed and somewhat modified in the remarkable study by Nicholas Hans, *New Trends in Education in the Eighteenth Century* (London: Routledge & Kegan Paul, 1951). Hans bases part of his study upon a statistical analysis of the social origins, formal education and subsequent careers of some 3,500 individuals who formed the intellectual élite of that century, the basic data having been systematically assembled from the individual biographies in that almost inexhaustible mine of materials for historical sociology, the *Dictionary of National Biography*.[91] Only a few of his numerous pertinent findings will

[90] Should it be asked why I did not make use of the later and amply documented book, M. McLachlan's *English Education under the Test Acts* (1931), I could only reply, in the words of another 'harmless drudge', 'Ignorance, Madam, pure ignorance'. It should be added, however, that McLachlan is in fundamental agreement with the major conclusions of Irene Parker.

[91] Studies in historical sociology have only begun to quarry the rich ore available in comprehensive collections of biography and other historical evidence. Although statistical analyses of such materials cannot stand in place of detailed qualitative analyses of the historical evidence, they afford a *systematic* basis for new findings and, often, for correction of received assumptions. At least, this has been my own experience in undertaking statistical analyses of some 6,000 biographies (in the D.N.B.) of those who comprised the élite of seventeenth-century England; of the lists of important discoveries and inventions listed in Darmstädter's *Handbuch zur Geschichte der Naturwissenschaften und der Technik*, and of 2,000 articles published in the *Philosophical Transactions* during the last third of the seventeenth century. (Cf. Merton, *Science, Technology and Society in Seventeenth-Century England*, 1938, Chapters II–III.) The most extensive use of such statistical analyses is found in P. A. Sorokin, *Social and Cultural Dynamics* (New York: American Book Co., 1937). Of course,

be summarized here. He finds, for example, that the Dissenting Schools and Academies produced about 10 per cent of the élite which, as Hans observes, 'was far above their relative strength in the total population of England in the eighteenth century'. (20) Nevertheless, he notes, as we have seen to be the case, that religious 'motives' were not alone in making for the emergence of modern education (and specifically, of scientific education) in this period; with religion were joined 'intellectual' and 'utilitarian' motives. Thus, while 'the Puritans promoted science as an additional support of Christian faith based on revelation, the deists looked upon science as the foundation of any belief in God'. (12) The three types of motivation tended to reinforce one another: 'The Dissenters, as well as many Puritans within the Church, represented the religious motive for educational reform. The idea of *propagatio fidei per scientia* found many adherents among the Dissenters. The intellectual and utilitarian reasons were put into full motion by secular bodies and teachers before the Dissenting Academies accepted them wholeheartedly.' (54)

It is in this last respect that Hans finds it necessary to dissent from the thesis put forward by Irene Parker (which I adopted in my own paper), holding that she attributes almost exclusive influence to the Academies in advancing modern education in the eighteenth century. His corrective modification appears, on the ample evidence, to be thoroughly justified. Furthermore, it serves to clarify a problem which, at least one student of the matter can report, has long been troublesome and unresolved. This is the well-recognized fact that certain extreme forms of Calvinist dissent were for a long time inimical to the advancement of science, rather than conducive to it. As Hans now points out, 'although the Calvinist tradition was essentially progressive it easily degenerated into narrow and intolerant dogmatism'. (55) The Baptists, for example, were thoroughly 'averse to the new learning from conviction and only late in the century joined other Dissenters [particularly the Presbyterians and Independents] in promoting the reform'. (55) One wing of nonconformity, in short, adhered literally to certain restrictive tenets of Calvinism and it

the preparation of statistical summaries of this kind have their hazards; routinized compilations unrestrained by knowledge of the historical contexts of the data can lead to unfounded conclusions. For a discussion of some of these hazards, see P. A. Sorokin and R. K. Merton. 'The course of Arabian intellectual development: a study in method', *Isis*, 1935, 22, 516–24; Merton, *op. cit.*, 367 ff.; and for a more thorough review of the problems of procedure, Bernard Berelson, *Content Analysis* (New York: The Free Press, 1951). Numerous recent studies of the social origins of business élites in the historical past have utilized materials of this sort: see the studies by William Miller, C. W. Mills, and Suzanne Keller instructively summarized by Bernard Barber, *Social Stratification* (New York: Harcourt, Brace & World, 1957).

was this subgroup that manifested the hostility to science which has for so long been found in certain fundamentalist sects of Protestantism. Figuratively, it can be said that 'Calvinism contained a seed of modern liberal education but it required a suitable environment to germinate and grow'. (57) And, as we have seen, this social and cultural context was progressively provided in England of the time.

Supplementing these studies of the changing relations between Puritanism and science in England is the remarkable study by Perry Miller of these relations under the special conditions afforded by New England. (*The New England Mind: The Seventeenth Century*. Reissue. *The New England Mind: From Colony to Province*. Cambridge: Harvard University Press, 1954.) This comprehensive work demonstrates the notable receptivity to science among the theocratic leaders of the colony and the ensuing process of secularization, with its emphasis on utilitarianism.

From the data assembled by Alphonse de Candolle the connections of ascetic Protestantism and interest in science evidently persisted to some extent through the nineteenth century. Candolle's data have lately been examined again, with the same conclusion. See Isidor Thorner, 'Ascetic Protestantism and the development of science and technology', *American Journal of Sociology*, 1952, 58, 25–33, esp. at 31–2. Thorner has also analysed the data presented by P. A. Sorokin as a basis for questioning this hypothesis and finds that the data are actually in accord with it; *ibid.*, 28–30. For Sorokin's critique, see his *Social and Cultural Dynamics*, II, 150–2.

In another, searching review of Candolle's materials, Lilley has indicated their limitations as well as their uses. S. Lilley, 'Social aspects of the history of science', *Archives Internationales d'Histoire des Sciences*, 1949, 28, 376–443, esp. 333 ff. He observes that the correlations between Protestantism and science may be spurious since 'on the average the commercial and industrial classes [who have a greater interest in science] have tended to be Protestant in persuasion and the peasantry and more feudal types of landowners to be Catholic'. We have taken note of this limitation and have accordingly compared the interest in scientific subjects of Protestants and Catholics drawn from the same areas. Lilley also criticizes Candolle's work for failing to take account of historical change in these relationships by lumping together, 'without distinction, the whole period from 1666 to 1868'. Presumably, religious affiliations in the latter and more secularized period would represent less by way of doctrinal and value commitments than in the earlier period; purely nominal memberships would tend to become more frequent. This criticism also has force, as we have seen. But as Lilley goes on to observe, further evidence in hand nevertheless confirms the underlying relationship between ascetic Protestantism and science, although this relationship may be masked or accentuated by other interdependent social and economic changes.

That the relationship persists to the present day in the United States is indicated by a recent thorough-going study of the social antecedents of American scientists, from 1880 to 1940. R. H. Knapp and H. B. Goodrich, *Origins of American Scientists* (Chicago: University of Chicago Press, 1952). Their evidence on this point is summarized as follows:

> Our data have shown the marked inferiority of Catholic [academic] institutions in the production of scientists [but not of other professionals; for example, lawyers] and, on the other hand, the fact that some of our most productive smaller institutions are closely connected with Protestant denominations and serve a preponderantly Protestant clientele. Moreover, the data presented by Lehman and Visher on the 'starred' scientists [i.e. the scientists listed in *American Men of Science* who are judged to be of outstanding merit], although limited, indicate very clearly that the proportion of Catholics in this group is excessively low – that, indeed, some Protestant denominations are proportionately several hundred times more strongly represented. These statistics, taken together with other evidence, leave little doubt that scientists have been drawn disproportionately from American Protestant stock. (274)

Much the same impression, but without systematic supporting data, has been reported by Catholic scientists. 'Father Cooper says he "would be loath to have to defend the thesis that 5 per cent or even 3 per cent of the leadership in American science and scholarship is Catholic. Yet we Catholics constitute something like 20 per cent of the total population".' J. M. Cooper, 'Catholics and scientific research', *Commonweal*, 1945, 42, 147–9, as quoted by Bernard Barber, *Science and the Social Order*, 136. Barber also cites a similar observation by James A. Reyniers, Director of the Lobund Laboratories of Notre Dame University and by Joseph P. Fitzpatrick, S.J.; *ibid.*, 271.

This review of the more recent literature on the subject rather uniformly confirms the hypothesis of an observable positive relationship between ascetic Protestantism and science. The data provided by any one of these studies is typically far from rigorous. But this is, after all, the condition of most evidence bearing upon historically changing relations between social institutions. Considering not this study or that, but the entire array, based upon materials drawn from varied sources, we would seem to have some reasonable assurance that the empirical relationship, supposed in the foregoing study, does in fact exist.

But, of course, the gross empirical relationship is only the beginning, not the end, of the intellectual problem. As Weber noted, early in his celebrated essay on *The Protestant Ethic*, 'a glance at the occupational statistics of any country of mixed religious composition brings to light with remarkable frequency a situation which has several times provoked discussion in the Catholic press and literature, and in Catholic congresses in Germany, namely, the fact that business leaders and owners of capital, as well as the higher grades of skilled labor, and even more the higher technically and commercially trained personnel of modern enterprises, are overwhelmingly Protestant'. (35) The fortuity that comparable statistics on the religious composition of scientists are not ready to hand but must be laboriously assembled for the present and partially pieced together for the past does not make the empirical finding any more significant in itself (though it may commend to our respectful attention the arduous labors of those doing the spadework). For, as we have seen in examining the status of empirical generalizations (in Chapter II[92]), this only sets the problem of analysing and interpreting the observed uniformity, and it is to this problem that the foregoing essay has addressed itself.

The principal components of the interpretation advanced in this essay presumably do not require repetition. However, a recent critique of the study provides an occasion for reviewing certain empirical and theoretical elements of the interpretation which can, apparently, be lost to sight. In this critique – 'Merton's thesis on English science', *American Journal of Economics and Sociology*, 1954, *13*, 427–32 – James W. Carroll reports what he takes to be several oversights in the formulation. It is suggested that the heterogeneity of the beliefs included in Protestantism generally and in Puritanism specifically has been overlooked or imperfectly recognized. Were the charge true, it would plainly have merit. Yet it should be observed that the hypothesis in question is introduced by a chapter which begins by noting 'the diversity of theological doctrines among the Protestant groups of seventeenth-century England' and continues by considering the values, beliefs and interests which are common to the numerous sects deriving from Calvinism (Merton, *Science, Technology and Society in Seventeenth-Century England*, Chapter IV, 415 ff.). And, as may be seen from this bibliographical postscript, historical scholarship has more thoroughly established the similarities, and not only the differences, among the Puritan sects stemming from ascetic Calvinism.

Carroll goes on to say that the evidence for the connection be-

[92] See *Social Theory and Social Structure*.

tween the norms of Puritanism and of science provides only an empirical similarity between the two (or what is described as a Comtean 'correlation of assertions'). But this is to ignore the demonstrated fact that English scientists themselves repeatedly invoked these Puritan values and expressly translated them into practice (cf. *ibid.*, Chapter V).

That the Puritan values were indeed expressed by scientists is in fact implied in Carroll's next suggestion that no basis is provided in the study for discriminating between the 'rationalizations' and the 'motives' of these scientists. This touches upon a theoretical problem of such general import, and widespread misunderstanding, that it is appropriate to repeat part of what was said about it in the earlier study. 'Present-day discussions of "rationalization" and "derivations" have been wont to becloud certain fundamental issues. It is true that the "reasons" adduced to justify one's actions often do not account satisfactorily for this behavior. It is also an acceptable hypothesis that ideologies [alone] seldom *give rise* to action and that both the ideology and the action are rather the product of common sentiments and values upon which they in turn react. But these ideas can not be ignored for two reasons. They provide clues for detecting the basic values which motivate conduct. Such signposts can not be profitably neglected. Of even greater importance is the rôle of ideas in directing action into *particular* channels. *It is the dominating system of ideas which determines the choice between alternative modes of action which are equally compatible with the underlying sentiments*' (*ibid.*, 450).

As for distinguishing between the expression of reasons which are merely accommodative lip-service and those which express basic orientations, the test is here, as elsewhere, to be found in the behavior which accords with these reasons, even when there is little or no prospect of self-interested mundane reward. As the clearest and best-documented case, Robert Boyle can here represent the other Puritans among his scientific colleagues who, in varying degree, expressed their religious sentiments in their private lives as in their lives as scientists. It would seem unlikely that Boyle was 'merely rationalizing' in saying 'that those who labour to deter men from sedulous Enquiries into Nature do (though I grant, designlessly) take a course which tends to defeat God ...' (Robert Boyle, *Some Considerations Touching the Usefulness of Experimental Natural Philosophy*, Oxford, 1664; 2nd edn, 27). For this is the same Boyle who had written religious essays by the age of twenty-one; had, despite his distaste for the study of language, expressed his veneration for the Scriptures by learning Hebrew, Greek, Chaldee and Syriac that he might read them in their early versions; had provided a pension for Robert Sanderson to enable him to continue writing books on casuistry; had largely paid for the costs of printing the Indian, Irish and Welsh Bibles and, as if this were not enough, for the Turkish New Testament and the Malayan version of the Gospels and Acts; had become Governor of the Corporation for the Spread of the Gospel in New England and as a director of the East India Company had devoted himself and his resources to the diffusion of Christianity in these areas; had contributed substantially to the fund for printing Burnet's *History of the Reformation*; had published his profession of faith in *The Christian Virtuoso* and, quite finally, had provided in his will for endowment of the 'Boyle lectures' for the purpose of defending Christianity against unbelievers. (This is the compact record set forth in A. M. Clerke's biography of Boyle in the *Dictionary of National Biography*.) Although Boyle was foremost in piety among Puritan scientists, he was still only first among equals, as witness Wilkins, Willughby and Ray among many others. So far as any historical record of words and action can permit us to say, it would appear that scientists like Boyle were not simply 'rationalizing'.

Carroll's final criticism, if intended conscientiously and not frivolously, exhibits a melancholy degree of immunity to commonplace and inconvenient facts of history. He observes that in showing the original membership of the Royal Society to have been preponderantly Protestant, the essay under review does not examine the possibility that the 'invisible college', from which the Society stemmed was part of a widespread Protestant movement of reform and that known Catholics were consequently banned from membership. That *Protestants* comprised the original membership of the Royal Society goes, one would suppose, without saying; in that day and age of the 1660s, in spite of the later political traffic of Charles II with the Catholicism of Louis XIV, Catholics would scarcely have been granted the prerogative of founding an association under the auspices of the Crown. The fact which is of more than passing interest is not, of course, that the Society was preponderantly *Protestant*, but that it was preponderantly *Puritan*. As for the observation that avowed Catholics were banned from academic posts, it evidently needs to be recalled that the Test Act of 1673, though later occasionally nullified in particular instances, excluded Nonconformists and not only Catholics and Jews from the universities. Yet, although this remained in force into the nineteenth century, Nonconformists continued to provide a large fraction of the men of science.

This short review of the most recently accumulated evidence suggests that, however contrary this may have been to the intentions of the Great Reformers, the ascetic Protestant sects developed a distinct predilection for working the field of science. In view of the powerful cross-currents of other historical forces, which might have deflected this early orientation toward science, it is notable that the association between ascetic Protestantism and science has persisted to the present day. Profound commitments to the values of ascetic Protestantism have presumably become less common, yet the orientation, deprived of its theological meanings, evidently remains. As with any hypothesis, particularly in historical sociology, this one must be regarded as provisional, subject to review as more of the evidence comes in. But as the evidence now stands, the fact is reasonably well established and has definite implications for the broader problem of the connections between science and other social institutions.

The first of these implications is that, in this case at least, the emerging connections between science and religion were indirect and unintended. For, as has been repeatedly said, the reformers were not enthusiastic about science. Luther was at best indifferent; at worst, hostile. In his *Institutes* and his *Commentarie upon Genesis*, Calvin was ambivalent, granting some virtue to the practical intellect but far less than that owing to revealed knowledge. Nevertheless, the religious ethic which stemmed from Calvin promoted a state of mind and a value-orientation which invited the pursuit of natural science.

Second, it appears that once a value-orientation of this kind becomes established, it develops some degree of functional autonomy, so that the predilection for science could remain long after it has cut away from its original theological moorings.

Third, this pattern of orientation, which can even now be detected statistically, may be unwitting and below the threshold of awareness of many of those involved in it.

Fourth and finally, the highly visible interaction of the institutions of science and religion – as in the so-called war between the two in the nineteenth century – may obscure the less visible, indirect and perhaps more significant relationship between the two.

3   Merton Revisited, *or* Science and Society in the Seventeenth Century*

A. Rupert Hall

A quarter of a century ago a brilliant young scholar, who has recently been dignified by the *New Yorker* as 'Mr Sociology', published a monograph with the title 'Science, technology and society in seventeenth-century England'.[1] In this thorough, well-argued and closely written study Robert K. Merton presented with a wealth of documentary evidence the classical instance of the historical analysis of science as a social phenomenon. Merton conceived of science as a cultural artefact, a manifestation of intellectual energy that is stimulated, checked or modified by the structure, beliefs and aspirations of the society with which this scientific activity is associated. Put thus crudely the idea seems almost a truism; of course no one in writing the history of science would ever divorce it completely from society's beliefs and structure. Merton's monograph was far from being an exercise in the obvious, however, nor were the historiographical themes with which it was concerned trivial. It was Merton's contention that the historical study of a past society can provide principles of historical explanation which are complementary to, if they do not replace, those offered by the historian of science. Particularly, sociological history provides (if I follow Merton's view of 1938 correctly) principles sufficing to explain that crucial event, the scientific revolution of the seventeenth century, even though the provision of such an explanation was not Merton's chief or explicit concern. In fact Merton may be said to have insisted that the major displacements in science do require sociological explanations.

    Merton's challenge was not at once accepted and his study was greeted rather with the admiration it deserved than with

*A. Rupert Hall, 'Merton Revisited, *or* Science and Society in the Seventeenth Century', *History of Science*, 1963, 2, 1–16.

[1] *Osiris*, iv (1938), 360–632. It is much to be desired that this important issue – containing in addition A. C. Klebs's *Incunabula scientifica et medica* – might be speedily reprinted. In what follows I use the term 'social' (etc.) where 'socio-cultural', 'socio-economic' or the like might be more exact, for the sake of simplicity. Definition of the exact nature of the external influence is not material to this consideration.

argument or criticism. Looking back one can see why: Merton's work was the culmination of an established tradition, not the beginning of a new one. To say that it aroused no great astonishment does not detract from its importance, which lay in making a strong case for the sociological explanation in one country at one time. As Merton himself generously acknowledged, his thesis was not (in broad terms) singular to himself. But Merton could justly regard himself as offering clear ideas backed by massive evidence, where his predecessors had brought forward little more than intuitions.

A current of historiography that favoured 'externalist' explanations – ones deriving from the general cultural, economic and social state of a nation or community of nations – ran strongly in the nineteen twenties and thirties. It derived its ultimate strength from two majestic Victorian conceptions: Marx's observation that the character of a society is largely determined by its economy, together with the compatible though distinct discovery of the anthropologists that 'culture' is a unity. Adding these two ideas together, one is led to conclude that a man's thoughts on any one topic – say, celestial mechanics – are not independent of his thoughts on all other topics, nor of the economic state of the society in which he lives. So far, if we allow that 'not independent of' is by no means equivalent to 'causally determined by', we have a historiographical notion that is, today, hardly open to dispute. Some thirty years ago, however, historians were more apt to regard the case as one of causal determinism and to suppose that any correlation between an intellectual event A and a social event B could be understood as justifying the view that B in some sense 'caused' A, or at least was a necessary condition for the occurrence of A. Such interpretations of historical occurrences in the less fundamental realms of politics, religion and so on by reference to other phenomena in the more fundamental realms of economics seemed to promise escape from the general mistiness and subjectivism of historical explanation.

Social explanations in history appeared objective and certain because they avoid emphasis on individuality and the hazardous significance of the individual. Authoritative models were provided by (for example) Max Weber and R. H. Tawney, whose *Religion and the rise of Capitalism* was published in 1926. Merton refers to the latter five times; remarking that 'It is misleading to assume that [the] foci of scientific interest are exclusively due to the intrinsic developments within the various sciences', he credits to Max Weber the observation that scientists commonly select for treatment problems which are vitally linked with the dominant values and interests of the day.[2]

[2] Merton, *loc. cit.*, 413.

Quotations from the philosopher-historian A. N. Whitehead, the literary historian R. F. Jones, the economic historian G. N. Clark and such historians of science as Dorothy Stimson and Martha Ornstein add further support to Merton's point of view; even E. A. Burtt, who really belongs to a very different school of intellectual history, yields passages to the same effect.[3] For his most uncompromising example of the 'externalist' historiography of science, however, Merton turned to an essay 'On the social and economic roots of Newton's *Principia*' by a Russian historian, B. Hessen, which is indeed a collector's piece.[4]

There is no need now to go back beyond Merton's monograph. 'Science, technology and society in seventeenth-century England' is both more complete and more sophisticated than any of its precursors. Merton saw the problem he proposed to himself as consisting of two parts: 1. why did 'scientific development in England become especially marked about the middle of the seventeenth century?'[5] and 2. 'why was there a strong preponderance of interest, among those concerned, in the physical sciences?' That each part of the problem was real – that is, that the characteristic to be investigated was genuine – Merton established by quite elaborate statistical analyses, as well as by the independent testimony of historians of science.

To each part of the problem Merton devoted a distinct social explanation. In order to account for the increase of interest in science that took place in England, he argued that a distinct change in values associated with Puritanism favoured science; to account for the partiality of this interest towards physical science he instanced the problems of engineering, navigation, warfare and so forth that could be solved by means of physical science. I shall consider each of these explanations in turn, and then the

---

[3] E. A. Burtt, *Metaphysical foundations of modern physical science* (1924, repr. London, 1949); G. N. Clark, *The seventeenth century* (Oxford, 1929, 1947), *The later Stuarts* (Oxford, 1934); R. F. Jones, *Ancients and Moderns* (St Louis, 1936); Martha Ornstein, *The role of scientific societies in the seventeenth century* (pr. pr. 1913, Chicago 1928 etc.); Dorothy Stimson, 'Puritanism and the "new philosophy" in seventeenth-century England', *Bulletin of the Institute for the History of Medicine*, iii (1935), 321–34; A. N. Whitehead, *Science and the modern world* (New York, 1931). Burtt (p. 211) asserts that Newton was 'practical'; this is associated with his over-emphasis of Newton's positivism. Miss Stimson briefly links Puritanism and the Royal Society once more in *Scientists and amateurs* (New York, 1948), 34–5.

[4] *Science at the cross-roads* (London, 1932), 147–212. Merton, 565, draws attention to G. N. Clark's criticism of this essay in *Science and social welfare in the Age of Newton* (Oxford, 1937) but it is not wholly clear to me that Merton's monograph is not, in less measure, liable to some of the same criticisms. In particular, Merton hardly stresses the significance of the intrinsic interest of science upon which Clark (86–91) properly insists.

[5] Merton, 402.

general issue of the balance between social and other forms of explanation in the history of science.

SCIENCE AND THE PURITAN ETHIC

The argument here closely parallels Tawney's in *Religion and the rise of Capitalism*. Not only (according to Merton and others) did Puritanism – or rather not the Puritan theology but the Puritan spirit – encourage scentific investigation, but it stimulated precisely that kind of scientific inquiry that flourished most in England:

> Experiment was the scientific expression of the practical, active and methodical bents of the Puritan. This is not to say, of course, that experiment was derived in any sense from Puritanism. But it serves to account for the ardent support of the new experimental science by those who had their eyes turned towards the other world and their feet firmly planted on this.[6]

That Boyle and many others had justified their work in science as a kind of practical divine service – it glorified God's creation in men's eyes, and so forth – seemed at least to indicate a strong link between science and religion, even though (as Merton of course was aware) neither Bacon the father of empiricism, nor Boyle the Christian virtuoso, was himself a Puritan in any meaningful sense of that term. Somewhat more cogently, Merton pointed to a strong Puritan bias among the early Fellows of the Royal Society and to the explicit association of the Society with Puritanism urged by the Society's detractors. He also quoted, as further direct evidence of the Puritan spur to science, a passage from Richard Baxter's *Christian directory* written in 1664–5:

> the very exercise of love to God and man, and of a heavenly mind and holy life, hath a sensible pleasure in itself, and delighteth the man who is so employed.... What delight had the inventors of the sea-chart and magnetic attraction, and of printing, and of guns, in their inventions! What pleasure had Galileo in his telescopes, in finding out the inequalities and shady parts of the moon, the Medicean planets [etc.]....[7]

On the other hand, Merton cited some evidence that the compatibility of science with those ideas of religion and virtue that he associated with Puritanism was not universal. Not to stress the

[6] *Ibid.*, 452.
[7] *Ibid.*, 435.

Middle Ages, which he regarded as essentially antipathetic to science, he instanced the passivity or quietism associated with the teachings of the Jansenists.[8] However, Merton was careful not to make the causal inference between science and religion too strong: particular discoveries are not, he declared, to be 'directly attributed to the sanction of science by religion', while the peculiar distinction of Puritanism was that it made science 'socially acceptable ... a laudable rather than an unsavoury occupation' so that more men were enticed into it.[9]

This summary does not do justice to Merton's qualifications and reservations any more than it does to the impressive amount of evidence he collected; nevertheless, a reader today will be bound to urge certain questions. Seeking to test the significance of the Puritan ethic, it will strike him that this is notably irrelevant to the efflorescence of medical science in sixteenth-century Italy, and no less to the successes of that brilliant group in France which preceded the Royal Society by a few years. Not only were Gassendi, Mersenne, Descartes, Pascal, Roberval, Bouillaud and so on pious Catholics; several of them were priests. Even in England, it is trivially obvious that whatever the importance of events in the Puritan 1640s and 1650s, science actually flourished and achieved something under the royalist, Anglican re-action from 1660 onwards. Clearly, the most that can be said is that in England (and some other Protestant countries) the ascendancy of a markedly radical wing of the faith seems to be linked with scientific vigour; the link is obviously not *essential* to science as such, for counter-instances are too numerous; it is therefore doubtful whether the statements about the deep, intrinsic bonds between the spirit of Puritanism and the spirit of science can be considered reliable. At least, one cannot give credit to them upon a simple inductive basis, for when one is contemplating the issue of principle the effect of Urban VIII's views upon (say) Galileo and Descartes is of no greater weight than the equally hostile opinions of Luther and Melancthon.

Iteration and exemplification cannot, in any case, make the proposition 'many scientists are Protestants' equivalent to the statement 'men are scientists because they are Protestants'. If induction by enumeration fails, as it must in this instance, what permits the inference that the association of science and Protestantism is more than a temporal correlation? Not the argument that science is justified by religion in Puritan eyes: for Catholics and Anglicans use this justification also. In the presentation of *laborare est orare* Puritanism had some polemical ad-

<hr>

[8] *Ibid.*, 479–80. Merton mentioned Pascal's renunciation of science but not Barrow's.

[9] *Ibid.*, 434.

vantages, certainly, but as Merton admitted the basic ideas were taken by Puritans from the Catholic tradition and they were, indeed, employed by such Catholic apologists of science as Gassendi and Malebranche. Conversely, there were extreme Protestant sects such as the Quakers who were as quietist as the Jansenists:[9a] in seventeenth-century religion it is difficult to find any characteristic of one party that does not have a mirror-image in the other. In place of any solid grounds for the inference one is apt to find something like the following:

> Moreover, as Troeltsch has suggested, Calvinism which abolished the absolute goodness of the Godhead tended to an emphasis on the individual and the empirical, the practically untramelled and utilitarian judgment of things. He finds in the influence of this spirit a most important factor of the empirical and positivist tendencies of Anglo-Saxon thought.[10]

How this statement could be proved is not very obvious; what would count as a refutation of it is still less clear. To that extent it must be judged nebulous and certainly incapable of serving as the fulcrum of an inference.

For reasons that will be considered later there has been during recent years little discussion of the role of religion in the scientific revolution. In 1958 one historian, R. S. Westfall, expressed himself cautiously:

> The influence of Protestantism on natural science is nebulous and difficult to determine. It can be suggested, however, that Protestantism provided an atmosphere more conducive to scientific investigation as such than was Catholicism; perhaps also Protestantism was more conducive to the acceptance of the peculiar mechanical conception of nature which accompanied early modern science and to its reconciliation with religious beliefs.[11]

Since development of this point lay outside the scope of Westfall's book he did not pursue the question of the causal

---

[9a] Miss Rosalie L. Colie (*Light and enlightenment, a study of the Cambridge Platonists and the Dutch Arminians*, Cambridge, 1957, 4) remarks: 'fundamentalist sects tended to fear research into the natural sciences ... to fear that the study of the phenomena of natural science might prove, as it traditionally was viewed, as the easy sliding pathway to atheism, or at least to scepticism'.

[10] *Ibid.*, 452.

[11] Richard S. Westfall, *Science and religion in seventeenth century England* (New Haven, 1958), 7. In a footnote the author adds, 'Although I believe that some connection between Puritanism and early modern science (in England, presumably) has been established, the definitive treatment of it remains to be written.'

relation further, and perhaps would be understood as indicating no more than a correlation between science and Puritanism in seventeenth-century England. His comment is of interest, however, in suggesting that extension of the question to a general debate between Catholic and Protestant that had been discussed some ten years earlier, and indeed, by Merton. For it is not a great step from the idea of the 'Puritan spur' to science in England to the view that Protestantism (whose scientific martyrs are somewhat less notorious than Bruno and Galileo) has invariably encouraged science in greater measure than Catholicism. Thus Merton:

> Uniformly, then available statistics indicate the undue [i.e. greater than random] tendency, on the basis of proportion in the total population, of Protestants to turn to scientific and technologic studies.... What are the relevant frequencies of Protestants and Catholics among scientists? [With reservations], proportionately speaking, Protestants constitute an overwhelming majority of the leading scientists.[12]

The causal inference which Merton does not draw here is firmly made by Jean Pelseneer: 'nous croyons avoir établi le rôle primordial de la Réforme dans la génèse de la science moderne'.[13] Again, in a general discussion of the history of the social relations of science S. Lilley warmly endorsed Merton's conclusions, describing the latter's monograph as 'a direct and scientific discussion of cause and effect', from which it followed that 'Puritanism in England in the latter part of the seventeenth century provided an ethic which encouraged the pursuit of science'. Somewhat weakening his position Lilley then endorsed Merton's refusal to describe Puritanism as the 'ultimate cause' of the scientific movement in England, and introduced a curious escape-clause: 'Whatever the cause it could have been effective in that period only if it had found a religious means of expression.'[14] Now, if this means anything serious, it is that religion was but a 'means of expression' for some effective cause (which was not Merton's view); that is to say – since any effective cause has *ex hypothesi* a religious expression – the analysis of religious expressions can tell us nothing about the nature of the true cause. For Merton and other Protestant exponents, however, Puritanism was if not a cause of the scientific revolution in England a necessary concomitant of

---

[12] Merton, *loc. cit.*, 12.
[13] Jean Pelseneer, 'Les Influences dans l'Histoire des Sciences', *Archives internationales d'histoire des sciences*, Année I (1948), 349. Cf. *idem*. 'L'Origine Protestante de la science moderne', *Lychnos*, 1946–7.
[14] S. Lilley, 'Social Aspects of the History of Science', *Archives internationales d'histoire des sciences*, 2e Année (1949), 376–443. My quotations are from pp. 435–7.

it, and this was determined by considering the religious expression.

If Lilley had stated more plainly that certain forms of religious expression and some of the language used about science
in the seventeenth century were related products having a
common intellectual parentage he would have made an important point, and one whose recognition has contributed to the
failure of interest in the Puritan or Protestant explanation of
science. The weakness was there from the first in (for example)
the reluctance of Merton to declare precisely what the relation
between religion and science was. If Puritanism was not the
'ultimate cause' of (say) the *Principia*, was it *a* cause? Was the
religious encouragement of science the decisive factor or not?
If it was not, then the fact that men are Catholic or Protestant
is about as significant in the history of science as whether they
wear breeches or trousers. But if Puritanism or Protestantism
made the decisive difference – as Pelseneer maintains – then massive proof and argument is required in demonstration. That, as
Westfall pointed out, has still not been provided.

SCIENCE AND TECHNOLOGY

Merton linked the two parts of his sociological study with these
words:

> if this congeniality of the Puritan and the scientific temper
> partly explains the increased tempo of scientific activity dur-
> ing the later seventeenth century, by no means does it account
> for the particular foci of scientific and technologic investiga-
> tion. ... Was the choice of problems a wholly personal con-
> cern, completely unrelated to the socio-cultural background?
> Or was this selection significantly limited and guided by social
> forces?

Once more, Merton made a statistical analysis – this time of
Birch's *History of the Royal Society* – in order to display the
character of scientific work; he assigned about 40 per cent of it
to the category of 'pure science' and the greater part of the rest
to the fields of sea-transport, mining and military technology.[14a]
After further strengthening his case by a review of the activities
and attitudes of individual scientists, Merton concluded that the
seventeenth-century English scientists' choice of problem was
much influenced by socio-economic considerations. Yet he was

[14a] Other estimates make the relative proportion of pure scientific activity
much higher; the subjective element in such classification is inevitably
quite large. If one weighed *books* on pure science against those on technology the preponderance of the former would be enormous.

clearly far from supposing that science was *determined* by outside pressures,[15] as Hessen had suggested, and lately he has made
this point clearer still; for Merton technological considerations
are not *all*, but neither are they *nothing*.[16]

This opinion is unexceptionable. No one can deny that conceptual science, let alone experimental science, is shaped by the
technological equipment of the time in some measure; but the
interesting question is: how much and in what way? Is science
(as it were) an unconscious as well as a conscious instrument of
society, or is it not? To say merely, for example, that X was a
scientist and X was also interested in practical problems of technology, is not really to tell us very much; the bare information
certainly permits no inference about the relation between X's
scientific and technological interests. If X is the Royal Society as
depicted in Birch's *History*, Merton's analysis will tell us that
many Fellows were more interested in craft problems than in
scientific ones; that a Baconian view of the utility of science was
commonplace; and that men had a naive view of the relationship
between pure science and the mastery of nature. Equally, the
observation of Walter Houghton:

> it was primarily the acquisitive temper of the middle class,
> building on the heritage of Bacon and the social reformers,
> that directed the virtuosi to the History of Trades[17]

is readily justifiable: Houghton has not made the mistake of
identifying science with either the concerns of the virtuosi or
social reform. But from such information, valuable and interesting as it is, we do not learn what seventeenth-century *science*
was, nor does it serve to answer Merton's question: why were
people more interested in physics than in biology? Nor does it
answer Hessen's. Such inquiries tell us nothing about Boyle, or
Hooke, or Newton, that is significant to consideration of their
work as scientists. It is really of little benefit to an understanding
of the scientific revolution from Galileo to Newton that quite a
lot of men were interested in ships, cabbages, and sealing-wax.

As with the religious issue, the matter must be clearly and
definitely put if it is to have significance. When and in what circumstances is one entitled to infer that a particular piece of

[15] Merton, 563–5.
[16] *Critical problems in the history of science* (Madison, 1959), 27–8.
[17] Walter E. Houghton Jr, 'The History of Trades', *Journal of the history of
ideas*, ii (1941), 50. The distinction between 'virtuoso' and 'scientist' is
clearly drawn by the same writer in 'The English Virtuoso in the Seventeenth Century' (*ibid.*, iii (1942), 51–73 and 190–219), e.g. p. 194: 'In a world,
the virtuoso stops at the very point where the genuine scientist really
begins....' Now many Fellows of the Royal Society would properly be
described as virtuosi, which did not mean that they were scientists, natural
philosophers, 'physiologists' or 'naturalists'.

scientific work was done for some extra-scientific reason? Those who maintain that often or in some telling way this is the case should lay down their principles of inference. To consider a recent example: by 1940 many physicists knew that the release of nuclear energy was possible, and many worked on the problem during subsequent years. Does this mean – by inference – that all physicists working in atomic physics before 1940 did so because they believed that their work would lead to the technological use of nuclear energy? Of course not. What is the difference when Newton wrote in the scholium to Proposition XXXIV of Book II of the *Principia*: 'This proposition I conceive may be of use in the building of ships'? Was Newton's interest in physics conditioned by the needs (in applied hydrodynamics) of the society in which he lived? It is trivially obvious that Newton could not have written these words if he had been unaware of things called ships, and indeed could not have written the *Principia* at all if he had not been aware of moving bodies, pendulums and so forth. It is perhaps a little more interesting that a mathematician should think such a remark worth making at a time when no master-shipwright employed mathematical theory or would have admitted the competence of a mathematical physicist to instruct him. Yet this statement of Newton's is quoted in a portion of Merton's monograph from which the conclusion is drawn:

> In general, then, it may be said that the contemporary scientists, ranging from the indefatigable virtuoso Petty to the nonpareil Newton, definitely focused their attention upon technical tasks made prominent by problems of navigation and upon derivative scientific research.[18]

To me, this makes Newton sound like a superior carpenter, cartographer, or compass-maker; it puts him in the class of such excellent and learned practitioners as Captain Samuel Sturmy or Joseph Moxon. An analysis that confuses mathematical physics with mathematical technology in this way bewilders rather than assists the historian of science.

The question of economic influence has proved to be of far less interest in the last few years than it was in the nineteen thirties. Another major investigator of the sociology of science, Edgar Zilsel, was prevented by death from completing his work, which has never been further extended.[19] Zilsel, whose main

[18] Merton, *loc. cit.*, 540–1.
[19] Three of Zilsel's articles appeared in early volumes of the *Journal of the history of ideas*. For a bibliography and comment, see that Journal, reprinted in *Roots of scientific thought* (ed. Philip P. Wiener and Aaron Noland, New York, 1957), 281.

thesis it was that modern science originated in the injection of new ideas and ambitions from craft sources into the aridity of traditional scholarship, took a far more economically-determinist line than did Merton. This may be illustrated by one brief judgment upon Francis Bacon:

> Manifestly, the idea of science we usually regard as 'Baconian' is rooted in the requirements of early capitalistic economy and technology; its rudiments first appear in treatises of fifteenth-century craftsmen.[20]

That is to say, Baconian science is the blind servant of economic purpose, of the capitalism whose requirements must be satisfied by appropriate intellectual manoeuvres. If this is so, then the scientist's sense of freedom, that he may choose to be either a Copernican or an Aristotelian for instance, is a mere illusion; society compels him to be progressive and to take the former alternative (which Bacon himself rejected!). So far as this view was related by Zilsel to Bacon specifically he was exaggerating a familiar emphasis on Bacon as the 'philosopher of industrial science'.[21] That Bacon believed in the pursuit of science for its benefits to society there can be no doubt, just as there is also no doubt that he preferred luciferous to lucriferous experiments and regarded a reform of logic as the essential step towards sound science. Benjamin Farrington has expressed this utilitarian aspect of Bacon insistently but not unfairly; for example:

> Bacon is not, like other scientists, working in a chosen field in the light of a long tradition. Rather he makes himself the herald of a revolution in the life of humanity, which he calls a birth of time.[22]

What has been all too often forgotten (by the would-be friends as well as the enemies of Bacon) is that he was not so stupid as to suppose that a sound, verifiable science could be created merely by believing it to be desirable; one had to determine the intellectual structure upon which such a science could be framed.

In its crudest forms at any rate the socio-economic interpretation of the scientific revolution as an offshoot of rising capitalism and mercantile militarism has perished without comment. Its unilluminating conclusions rested on defective logic and improbable psychology; very often, as I myself have tried to reveal,

---

[20] 'The Genesis of the Idea of Scientific Progress', *Journal of the history of ideas*, vi (1945), 346; *Roots of scientific thought*, 273.
[21] Benjamin Farrington, *Francis Bacon, philosopher of industrial science* (New York, 1949).
[22] *Ibid.*, 141.

the true situation is far too complicated to yield such simple generalisations as 'mathematicians were inspired to seek solutions to gunners' problems'.[23] In fact the influence of the art of war on seventeenth-century physics was negligible though (remembering Merton's words) we must not say there was *no* such influence.[24] Hence some of the strongest reasons for the decline of the economic hypothesis are well expressed in the words of one of the most distinguished of modern economic historians, John W. Nef:

> If we examine the background of the intellectual revolution that is responsible for the industrial world in which we live today, we find little to support the view that modern science resulted from industrial progress in the north of Europe between the Reformation and the (English) Civil War. During these times of decisive change in rational procedures it was the mind itself, not economic institutions nor economic development, which called the new tunes and composed most of the variations which the greatest scientists were playing on them. The revolutionary scientific discoveries by Gilbert, Harvey, Galileo and Kepler, like the new mathematics of Descartes, Desargues, Fermat and Pascal, were of no immediate practical use. Freedom, rather than necessity, was the principal power behind the scientific revolution.[25]

Thus recent historians reverse the arrow of economic inference: social forms do not dominate mind; rather, in the long run, mind determines social forms.

THE ASCENDANCY OF THE INTELLECT

In 1939, one year after Merton's monograph, there appeared the *Études galiléennes* of Alexandre Koyré. No contributions to the history of science could be less alike. It is beside my purpose to develop the contrast, save by the obvious remark that as Merton summed up one epoch, that of the socio-economic historian,

---

[23] Cf. A. R. Hall, *Ballistics in the seventeenth century* (Cambridge, 1952); here the strength of the genetic, intellectual current as compared with external pressure is quite obvious.

[24] For Merton's own discussion of ballistics, see *loc cit.* 544–57. E. J. Walter ('Warum gab es im Alterum Keine Dynamik', *Archives internationales d'histoire des sciences*, Année I (1948) 363–82) argued that the invention of artillery was the cause of the early modern interest in dynamics. He made no reference to the medieval (pre-gunpowder) tradition of dynamical and kinematical inquiry.

[25] John W. Nef, *Cultural foundations of industrial civilization* (Cambridge, 1958), 63–4.

Koyré opened another, that of the intellectual historian. Of course Koyré was no more first in the field than Merton was; in their different ways Tannery, Duhem, Cassirer, Mach, Meyerson and Lovejoy had initiated the history of ideas long before. None of Koyré's predecessors, however, had begun that analysis of the scientific revolution as a phenomenon of intellectual history which Koyré has made peculiarly his own. Among the younger historians of science especially his has been the dominant influence through the last ten or fifteen years, and this influence has had a marked effect in withdrawing interest from externalist explanations; other factors have of course worked in the same direction.

Such externalist forms of historical explanation as the sociological tend to confine the intellectual development of science within rather narrow bounds; it is a fundamental hypothesis of this historiography that the gross character of the science of any epoch is shaped externally, the intellectual or internal structure of science effecting only the minutiae and technicalities. To summarise Merton's view, for instance:

> short-time fluctuations of interest in mathematics are largely explicable in terms of the appearance of important contributions by individual mathematicians ... the foci of interest within the general field are partially determined by the nature of the problems which have been explained or brought to light. [Further, the] conclusion that the minor, short-time fluctuations in scientific interest are primarily determined by the internal history of the science in question is borne out by other facts. [The influence of Gilbert and Harvey is discussed.] In a sense, then, the study of these short-time fluctuations would seem the province of the historian of science rather than that of the sociologist or student of culture.[26]

Here, it is clear the 'long-time' fluctuations are not assigned to the province of the historian of science. Such a view is consistent with a 'ripeness of time' concept of discovery or originality: we cannot (according to this concept) attach any special significance to the work of Newton in 1687, Darwin in 1859, or Einstein in 1905 because the time was ripe on each occasion for the work[27] and if Newton, Darwin or Einstein had not written as they did some one else (Hooke, Wallace) would have served the same function. Only in a shorthand way therefore did Newton and the others have a permanent influence on science. Merton did not teach this view, but he did write that

[26] Merton, *loc. cit.*, 407–9.
[27] It is of course a necessary corollary that unappreciated work such as Mendel's fall under the 'unripeness of time' provision.

specific discoveries and inventions belong to the internal history of science and are largely independent of factors other than the purely scientific.[28]

A true, but a curiously negative statement. Why should not the general development of (say) astronomy in the seventeenth century be 'largely independent of factors other than the purely scientific' and not merely the discovery of a fifth satellite of Saturn? This latter opinion has indeed been adopted by those who have followed Koyré in opposing the endeavour to credit the strategy of the scientific revolution to non-scientific influences. In the *Études* Koyré himself renounced just that liaison between modern physical science and empiricism which was regarded as crucial in the early nineteen-thirties; he has rejected also the thesis that classical science is 'active' in the way postulated by the Protestant historians.[29] For Koyré and many others since – as earlier for Burtt – the scientific revolution is to be understood as a transformation of intellectual attitudes:

> Aussi croyons-nous, que l'attitude intellectuelle de la science classique pourrait être charactéerisée par ces deux moments, étroitement liés d'ailleurs : géométrisation de l'espace, et dissolution du Cosmos ... cette attitude intellectuelle nous paraît avoir été le fruit d'une mutation décisive.... C'est qu'il s'agissait non pas de combattre des théories erronées, ou insuffisantes, mais de *transformer les cadres de l'intelligence elle-même....*[30]

There is no suggestion here that the new intellectual attitude was generated by or dependent upon anything external to science, nor does Koyré ever contemplate such a thing. The intellectual change is one whose explanation must be sought in the history of the intellect; to this extent (and we need not pause now to expound all the obvious provisos about microscopes, X-rays, cyclotrons and so forth) the history of science is strictly analogous to the history of philosophy. It is no accident that Koyré himself is a philosopher, nor that an English philosopher-historian should have expressed in *The idea of Nature* a vision of the scientific revolution similar to his. When Collingwood wrote

> the Renassance philosophers enrolled themselves under the banner of Plato against the Aristotelians, until Galileo, the true father of modern science, restated the Pythagorean-

[28] Merton, *loc. cit.*, 434.
[29] Alexandre Koyré, *Études galiléennes* (*Actualites scientifiques et industrielles*, 852–4, Paris, 1939), 6–7. This thought leads Koyré to an excessively stringent critique of Bacon (6, n. 4), indeed his Platonist, anti-empiricist thesis is here expressed in an extreme and vulnerable form.
[30] *Ibid.*, 9, italics added.

Platonic standpoint in his own words by proclaiming that the book of nature is a book written by God in the language of mathematics.[31]

he asserted, as Koyré has asserted, that modern science is of its own intellectual right fundamental and absolute; it is not derivative from some other displacement in civilisation as the reformation or the rise of capitalism. The historians of religion have never claimed that the reformation 'transformed the very structure of the intellect' and it would be indeed odd if someone holding this view of the transcendent signficance of the scientific revolution should also consider it as a mere epiphenomenon. One who has written on the history of religion, Herbert Butterfield, put it no less strongly ten years later, declaring that the scientific revolution 'outshines everything since the rise of Christianity and reduces the Renaissance and Reformation to the rank of mere episodes, mere internal displacements, within the system of medieval Christendom'.[32]

if modern science is the fruit of an intellectual mutation its genesis must be considered in relation to an intellectual tradition; to quote Butterfield once more, its sources stretch far 'back in an unmistakably continuous line to a period much earlier' than the sixteenth century.[32] Those who find the origins of science in the Puritan–capitalist complex, however, have no need for and see little value in the evidence for continuity in scientific thought. On the whole they have been empiricists rather than rationalists. Despite the scholarly researches of Duhem, Sudhoff, Little and many others, the Middle Ages did not get a good press from historians of science during the first two decades of this century; only after Sarton, Haskins, Thorndike and their generation had filled in many more details and suggested new interpretations did Duhem's thesis command widespread attention. Even in 1948 Jean Pelseneer wrote of Duhem:

Nul plus que lui n'a donné, quand on le lit, l'impression d'une continuité si complète dans l'histoire de la science, que l'on finit par douter d'un progrès véritable; chaque auteur paraît n'avoir fait que soubir les connaissances de ses prédécesseurs.... L'influence reçue étant en raison inverse du mérite, de l'originalité, il en résulte l'impossibilité de planifier avec succès la recherche scientifique.[33]

[31] R. G. Collingwood, *The idea of Nature* (Oxford, 1945); Galaxy Books, 1961, 94. This book was largely written in 1933-4 and revised in 1939; it would probably have had a greater impact upon historians of science if its publication had been less long delayed.

[32] Herbert Butterfield, *The origins of modern science* (London, 1949), viii.

[33] Jean Pelseneer, 'Les Influences dans l'Histoire des Sciences', *Archives internationales d'histoire des sciences*, Année I (1948), 348-53. For a far

That is, the very measure of the genius which could give birth to modern science is the fact that its departure from past traditions was so great, and effected so complete a breach of continuity. Merton, who made no reference to either Duhem or Wohlwill, saw a parallel lack of continuity in the attitudes of society to science. He contrasted Richard Baxter's view of science with that of the Middle Ages as he saw it:

> To regard with high esteem scientific discoveries attained empirically and without reference to Scriptural or other sacred authority would have been almost as heretical as making the discoveries themselves. As Professor Haskins has observed, the scientific spirit of Christian Europe in the Middle Ages was not liberated from the respect for authority which was characteristic of that epoch, whereas Puritan authority was enunciating the very doctrines which furthered interest in science and, ultimately, lack of concern with religion itself.[34]

Neither Pelseneer's criticism nor Merton's comparison is wholly unjust. Nevertheless most historians would nowadays emphasise the discontinuity between medieval and modern science much less strongly and in very different terms. Certainly dissent from Duhem's thesis does exist – that thesis has been firmly criticised by Anneliese Maier for instance – and some of the most effective of the intellectual historians, Koyré among them, are far from regarding the scientific revolution as fully prepared in the Middle Ages. Meanwhile, different forms of the case for continuity in dynamics, kinematics, optics, epistemology and so on have been prepared by Marshall Clagett,[35] A. C. Crombie, E. A. Moody and J. H. Randall; even if their work is not considered conclusive in every respect it is far from being negligible. In fact the intellectual historians are by no means divided among themselves on the issue of continuity in the way that they, as a group, are divided from the socio-economic historians. All are agreed, for example, that early modern science was in some measure indebted to medieval science; and that if seventeenth-century concepts are not identical with those of the fourteenth there is an intellectual connection between them.

---

stronger attack on Duhem's historiography of Galileo and its exponents, see Aldo Mieli 'Il Tricentario dei "Discorsi e Dimostrazioni Matematiche" di Galileo Galilei', *Archeion*, xxi (1938).

[34] Merton, *loc. cit.*, 436. It is fitting to draw attention to the distinction that Merton here made between the genetic element in scientific discovery and the 'cultural animus' which was so favourable to science in the seventeenth century.

[35] Especially *The Science of mechanics in the middle ages* (Madison, 1959) in which all the other bibliographical allusions of this paragraph may be explored, if necessary.

Even without making a detailed review of the work of other historians of science active at the present time it is clear that the trend towards intellectual history is strong and universal. Since the journal *Centaurus* published in 1953 a special group of articles on the social relations of science no single article that can be judged to represent the sociological interpretation of history has appeared in that periodical, or *Isis*, *Annals of science*, *Revue d'histoire des sciences*, or the *Archives internationales*. There has been little discussion of the historiographical issue:[36] indeed, it sometimes seems that the case for setting the development of scientific thought in its broader historical context is condemned before it is heard, though one knows from personal conversations that this is not neglected in pedagogic practice. Clearly, externalist explanations of the history of science have lost their interest as well as their interpretative capacity. One reason for this may be that such explanations tell us very little about science itself; about the reception of Newton's optical discoveries, or the significance of Galileo's ideas in mechanics, or about concepts of combustion and animal heat. Social and economic relations are rather concerned with the scientific movement than with science as a system of knowledge of nature (theoretical and practical); they help us to understand the public face of science and the public reaction to scientists; to evaluate the propaganda that scientists distribute about themselves, and occasionally – but only occasionally – to see why the subject of scientific discussion takes a new turn. But to understand the true contemporary significance of some piece of work in science, to explore its antecedents and effects, in other words to recreate critically the true historical situation, for this we must treat science as intellectual history, even experimental science. A sociologist like Merton understood this, of course; what he doubted was the significance of such intellectual history divorced from the social context which was, naturally, his main focus of interest.

Profoundly different historical points of view are involved. It is not enough to suggest, as Lilley modestly did, that there is a bit of truth in both of them so that

the development of science can be fully understood only if the internal and external types of influence are considered together and in their mutual interaction.[37]

(The suggestion that the very stuff of science, that which it *is* at any moment, should ever be considered as an internal *influence*,

[36] An article of my own has touched on this matter; cf. *Critical problems in the history of science*, ed. Marshall Clagett (Madison, 1959), 3–23.
[37] S. Lilley, 'Cause and Effect in the History of Science', *Centaurus*, iii (1953), 59.

is rather curious.) To suppose that it is not worth while to take sides or that the determination of the historian's own attitude to the issue is not significant is to jeopardise the existence of the historiography of science as more than narration and chronicle. For example: how is the historian to conceive of science, before he undertakes to trace its development; is he to conceive it as above all a deep intellectual enterprise whose object is it to gain some comprehension of the cosmos in terms which are, in the last resort, philosophical? Or as an instruction-book for a bag of tricks by which men master natural resources and each other? Is a scientific theory a partial, temporally-limited vision of nature or a useful message printed on a little white card that pops out of a machine when the social animal presses the button – different cards for different buttons, of course? I have deliberately given an exaggerated emphasis to these rhetorical questions in order to indicate the violent imbalance between two points of view that one simply cannot ignore nor amalgamate. In the same way the historian's concept of the scientific revolution of the seventeenth century is historiographically dependent. One issue between the externalist and the internalist interpretation is this: was the beginning of modern science the outstanding feature of early modern civilisation, or must it yield in importance to others, such as the Reformation or the development of capitalism? Before 1940 most general historians and many historians of science would have adopted the latter position; since 1940 nearly all historians have adopted the former one. Why this change should have come about it is not hard to imagine.

By this I do not mean to suggest that the problems raised by the sociologists of science are obsolete; on the contrary, as some scientists like J. D. Bernal have been saying for a long time and many more are saying now, they are immensely real and direct at this moment. Consequently the historical evolution of this situation is of historical significance too, and I believe we shall return to its consideration when a certain revulsion from the treatment of scientists as puppets has been overcome, when (if ever) we are less guiltily involved in the situation ourselves so that we can review it without passion, and when a fresh approach has been worked out. This will not, I imagine, take the form so much of a fusion between two opposite positions in the manner of the Hegelian dialectic, as the demarcation of their respective fields of application with some degree of accuracy. There may also develop a socio-techno-economic historiography whose study will be the gradual transformation of society by science and not (as too often in the past) the rapid transformation of science by society. All this will require a fine analysis, a scrupulous drawing of distinctions and a careful avoidance (except under strict controls) of evidence drawn from subjective, propagandist and programmatic sources. A true sociology of science will deal with what actually happened and could happen, not with what men thought might happen or should happen.

4   Religious Influences in the Rise of Modern Science*

Douglas S. Kemsley

Despite the concentrated attention which the subject has received, the concept of 'the rise of modern science' continues to be surrounded by a variety of somewhat conflicting opinions concerning not only the period and geographical locality on which to focus it, but also its nature and causes.[1]

One particular approach to this historiographical problem has involved a search for contemporary sociological factors which may have provided the necessary stimulus to investigation or produced the spark for the reformation represented by the eruption of science as we know it. Over recent decades, research in this field has been concentrated on the possible influence of the powerful theological currents of the Reformation, particularly with regard to mid-seventeenth-century England, where the scientific movement suddenly attained a new level of significance overshadowing all previous endeavour in scope of interest and numbers involved.

One series of investigations has been concerned with the possible influence of religion on the foundation of the Royal Society of London. Under the date of Wednesday 28 November 1660, the first entry in the earliest Journal Book possessed by the Royal Society records the proposition of a group of men meeting at a weekly scientific gathering 'that some course might be thought of to improve this meeting to a more regular way of debating things, and according to the Manner in other Countreys, where there were voluntary associations of men into Academies for the advancement of various parts of learning'.[2] At the time,

* Douglas S. Kemsley, 'Religious Influences in the Rise of Modern Science: A Review and Criticism, particularly of the "Protestant–Puritan Ethic" Theory', *Annals of Science*, 24, number 3 (September 1968).
[1] H. F. Kearney displays something of the variety of present-day interpretations of the nature of the rise of science in *Origins of the Scientific Revolution*, London, 1964.
[2] Reproduced in full in D. McKie, 'The Origins and Foundations of the Royal Society of London', *Notes and Records of the Royal Society*, 1960, 15, 1: see in particular p. 31; an extract also appears in *Record of the Royal Society*, 1st edn, London, 1897.

this could have referred only to France and Italy, and more especially France,[3] and it would appear at first sight that the foundation of the Royal Society was closely associated with contemporary Continental scientific societies. However, strong evidence exists for a direct continuity between the aims and philosophical temper of those meetings which that of November 1660 was to transform into the Royal Society and those of the Society itself. In his *History of the Royal Society* published in 1667, Sprat mentioned regular meetings for the purpose of reasoning freely upon the works of Nature which had been held in Oxford and London beginning 'some space after the end of the Civil Wars' and continuing during the two decades preceding the giving of the first Charter to the Royal Society in 1662, and regarded them as having 'laid the foundation of all this that follow'd'.[4] Wallis independently gave two separate accounts of those occasions,[5] and elsewhere stressed their continuity with the Royal Society;[6] and as early as 6 January 1660/1, John Evelyn recorded in his Diary his election as 'a Fellow of the Philosophic Society now meeting at Gressham Coll: where was an assembly of divers learned Gent: It being the first meeting since the returne of his Majestie in Lond: but begun some years before at Oxford, and interruptedly here in Lond: during the Rebellion'.[7] The influence of European scientific groups on the foundation of the Royal Society is generally regarded as having provided a stimulus to a more organized form of communal activity rather

[3] M. Ornstein, *The Role of Scientific Societies in the Seventeenth Century*, New York, 1913; H. Brown, *Scientific Organizations in Seventeenth-Century France*, Baltimore, 1934.
[4] Thomas Sprat, *History of the Royal Society*, London, 1667; facsimile reproduction edited by J. I. Cope and H. W. Jones, London, 1959, p. 53.
[5] John Wallis: (a) letter to Dr Smith of Magdalen College, Oxford, dated 29 January 1696/7, printed as No. XI of the Appendices to the Publisher's Preface to *Peter Langtofts' Chronicle* in the *Works* of Thomas Hearne; reproduced in *Record of the Royal Society*, 1st edn, 1897, and in part in R. H. Syfret, 'The Origins of the Royal Society', *Notes and Records of the Royal Society*, 1948, 5, 75; and (b) *A Defence of the Royal Society and the Philosophical Transactions, Particularly those of 1670, in Answer to the Cavils of Dr William Holder*, London, 1678; reproduced in C. R. Weld, *History of the Royal Society*, 1848, and in part in R. H. Syfret, *loc cit.* (a).
[6] John Wallis, letter to Henry Oldenburg, reproduced by the latter in *Phil. Trans.*, 1673, 8, 6146–50. The relevant part of the letter reads: '... circiter menses Junii, Juliique, Anni 1657, atque rem jam tum apud nostros notissimam fuisse; utpote inter eos (Geometras aliosque), qui (*Societatis Regiae* appellationem nondem adepti) tum solebant in Greshamensi Collegio (post habitas ibidem praelectiones Mathematicas) statisdiebus convenire, publicatam et cum plausu acceptam ...'
[7] John Evelyn, *Diary*, London, 1959; the editor (E. S. de Beer), observes in a footnote to this entry that Evelyn's opinion that this was the 'first meeting' since the King's return is inaccurate. Evelyn had been suggested as a possible member at the earlier meeting on 28 November 1660 and was proposed for election at the meeting of 26 December 1660.

than as a source of inspiration to a scientific temper, since clearly this had existed in England independently of the Continental academies. The 'foundation' of the Royal Society has therefore usually been studied in terms of the origins of those early meetings.

Research on the possible influence of religious factors on the foundation of the Royal Society has been directed primarily to the religious affiliations and associations of those individuals whom both Sprat and Wallis recorded as participants in the pre-Royal Society group, with the basic historical fact in mind that their meetings began and continued for nearly two decades when that amorphous brand of Protestantism known as Puritanism held sway in the religious field, corresponding fairly closely with the political era of 'the Commonwealth' (1649–60). Some thirty years ago, Stimson[8] advanced her thesis that Puritanism had been an important factor in making conditions in England favourable to the growth of science, through its emphasis on the right of private judgment, its critical spirit, its insistence upon knowledge and reason, independence, and uprightness of character, and its demand that men spend their time profitably. She investigated the religious affiliations of the nine men named in Wallis's accounts, together with Wallis himself, and concluded that only one was 'definitely Royalist' (and therefore presumably Anglican rather than Puritan), two could not be categorized, while the remaining seven were all 'Puritan in training and Parliamentary in their affiliation'. Stimson then extended her study to the one hundred and nineteen men who constituted the Royal Society at its legal incorporation in 1662, and concluded that nearly half of the eighty-seven for whom relevant information was available 'had had Puritan experience in greater or less degree'. McKie took up this point, and, while agreeing with Stimson that the politics of those named by Wallis tended decidedly towards the Parliamentary cause, pointed out that the twelve men who on 28 November 1660 decided to found 'a College for the Promoting of Physico–Mathematicall Experimentall Learning' were decidedly more Royalist than the earlier company had been Parliamentary.[9]

Now, on the one hand, this observation does not involve any necessary refutation of Stimson's thesis, for although those of Parliamentary or Royalist politics were generally associated with Puritanism and Anglicanism respectively during the Common-

[8] H. D. Stimson, 'Puritanism and the New Philosophy in Seventeeth-Century England', *Bull. Inst. Hist. Med.*, 1935, 3, 321; the same argument reappears as part of her study, 'Amateurs of Science in Seventeenth Century England', *Isis*, 1939, 31, 32, and in her book *Scientists and Amateurs*, New York, 1948.

[9] McKie, *op. cit.*, p. 31.

wealth, the close link between religion and politics cannot be carried over into the early period of the Restoration, in which for two years complete religious freedom was enjoyed under the Declaration of Breda, dated by King Charles II at Breda 4/14 April 1660.[10] In November of that year, one could have been strongly Royalist politically and yet devoutly Puritanical, a state which obtained until May 1662, when the 'liberty to tender conscience' in matters of religion was annulled by the Caroline Act of Uniformity,[11] only two months before the Royal Society was granted its first charter of incorporation. On the other hand, McKie's point underlines the fact that Stimson's statistics for those who formed the first Fellows under the 1662 charter cannot be regarded as significant evidence for the centrality of Puritanism as a motivating force of the Society's incorporation. Even though the Royal Society was a greatly expanded and organized form of a pre-existing group of men who had shared a common interest in the study of nature and who had indeed 'had Puritan experience', and although the scientific temper exhibited continuity from the Commonwealth to the Restoration, the rapid expansion of scientific endeavour in the first years of the Restoration from the twelve who in November 1660 decided to found a 'Colledge' to well over a hundred in 1662, rising to an annual average of just over two hundred for the period 1666–70, appears to bear no specific relationship to Puritanism.[12] Indeed, one might argue from this evidence, as indeed was done by Sprat and Wallis, that the first meetings in the 1640s were held specifically to *escape from* that inflexible over-confident intellectual temper associated with Puritanism evidenced by internecine conflicts over differing interpretations of the same biblical texts, and that not until Puritan excesses of dogmatism and enthusiasm were replaced by a freer and more critical atmosphere in religion could the scientific spirit flourish. We shall return to this point subsequently.

[10] Reproduced in H. Gee and W. J. Hardy, *Documents Illustrative of English Church History*, London, 1896, p. 585.

[11] The text is given in full in Gee and Hardy, *op. cit.*, p. 600.

[12] Detailed information on the early membership of the society is available in E. S. de Beer, 'The Earliest Fellows of the Royal Society', *Notes and Records of the Royal Society*, 1950, 7, 172; compare also the list of the Fellows of 1667 presented by Sprat, *op. cit.*, p. 431; the *Chronological Register of Fellows of the Royal Society*, 1663–1700, Appendix V, *Record of the Royal Society*, London, 1940 edition; H. G. Lyons, 'The Composition of the Fellowship and the Council of the Society', *Notes and Records of the Royal Society*, 1939, 2, 108; R. P. Stearns, 'Colonial Fellows of the Royal Society of London, 1661–1788', *ibid.*, 1951, 8, 178; R. P. Stearns, 'Fellows of the Royal Society in North Africa and the Levant, 1662–1800', *ibid.*, 1954, 11, 75; and 'Average Number of Ordinary Fellows and of Foreign Members for Each 5-Year Period 1663–1935', Appendix VII, *Record of the Royal Society*, 4th edn, London, 1940.

Stimson's study inspired a group of papers on the relation between the pre-Royal Society meetings and another aspect of seventeenth-century European protestantism, the so-called 'pansophic' movement. Syfret[13] observed that although no specific correlation could be discovered which would identify the early scientific meetings with those of the pansophists Dury, Hartlib and their English circle which had been inspired by the spiritually-oriented Christianity of the Moravian, Comenius, through his books and his visit to England in 1641-2,[14] connexions nevertheless did exist between these two apparently separate groups through the common membership of Theodore Haak. Born of Calvinist parents at Neuhausen, near Worms, Haak had immigrated to England in 1625. He was ordained deacon by the Anglican Bishop of Exeter, Joseph Hall, about 1629, but never became a priest. During the interregnum, he sided with the Parliament, and was appointed by the Puritan Westminster Assembly of Divines (of which incidentally Wallis was an assistant clerk), to translate the so-called Calvinistic 'Dutch Annotations' on the bible into English.[15] The significance of Haak springs from Wallis's reference to him as the one 'who, I think, gave the first occasion, and first suggested those meetings' of the London scientific group in 1645. Although he was apparently not present at the November 1660 meeting at which the decision to constitute the organization was reached, Haak's name appears subsequently in the list of Fellows elected to the embryo Royal Society on 4 December 1661.[16] Syfret suggested that Haak had initiated the London meetings as one part of the Comenian pansophic plan conceived in 1641-2 to reform and re-unify all education, philosophy and social activity in England as specific aspects of a reformed spiritual Christianity, and that Haak's scientific correspondence with Mersenne, the Minorite friar, in the late 1630s, largely reflected matters of pansophic interest. Her argument was virtually a development of Young's earlier thesis.[14]

Turnbull[17] considered that although Haak was indeed one of

[13] R. H. Syfret, 'The Origins of the Royal Society', in Notes and Records of the Royal Society, 1948, 5, 75.

[14] R. F. Young, 'The Visit of Comenius to London in 1641-2 and its Bearing on the Origins of the Royal Society', ibid., 1940-1, 3, 159; this was itself stimulated by the paper by D. Stimson, 'Comenius and the Invisible College', Isis, 1935, 23, 373. Further information on Comenius and the English pansophists is available in the introductory essays of M. W. Keatinge, The Great Didactic of John Amos Comenius, London, 2nd edn, 1910, and in G. H. Turnbull, Hartlib, Dury and Comenius – Gleanings from Hartlib's Papers, London and Liverpool, 1947.

[15] Entry under HAAK, The Dictionary of National Biography; see also P. R. Barnett, Theodore Haak F.R.S., 1605-90, The Hague, 1962.

[16] E. S. de Beer, op. cit. (footnote 12).

[17] G. H. Turnbull, 'Samuel Hartlib's Influence on the Early History of the Royal Society', Notes and Records of the Royal Society, 1953, 10, 101.

those who welcomed Comenius on his visit to England, there was
no evidence for Haak's collaboration in Comenius's scheme of
Pansophia. He accorded Haak a place in the scientific group, but
contended that the Haak–Mersenne correspondence was purely
scientific, with no specific relation to Pansophism. Turnbull then
turned his attention to the possible influence on the English
scientific movement of Samuel Hartlib, a central figure in English
pansophism and an enthusiastic and prolific collector, seeker and
disseminator of scientific information to and for the London
group, but concluded that Hartlib was not a member of that
group, and had no hand in the foundation of the Royal Society,
and no direct influence on its early history.[18]

Barnett[19] took up the case for the significance of Haak, and
introduced new evidence not only for his intimate involvement
with the Comenian pansophists, but also for his deep personal
interest in natural philosophy. Although she was careful to note
that the Royal Society was not necessarily a direct result of the
earlier idealistic plans, Barnett showed unequivocally that Haak
saw the Society not merely as an organization for scientific
studies, but as a means to deepen man's understanding both of
his fellows and of the Creator by investigating the created world.[20]
Cope[21] also accorded Haak the dual role of a Comenian pansoph-
ist and the initial inspirer of the London scientific meetings.
Recently, Purver[22] has differentiated between the scientific group
referred to by Sprat and that which Wallis associated with the
London Haakian meetings in one of his accounts, as representing
two interpretations of Bacon's vision, the one a true reflection in

---

[18] Previously, Stimson had also described Hartlib, together with Haak, and
Henry Oldenburg, first secretary of the Royal Society, as 'intelligencers'
rather than scientific creators or initiators: D. Stimson, 'Haak, Hartlib and
Oldenburg: Intelligencers', *Isis*, 1939, *31*, 309.
[19] P. R. Barnett, 'Theodore Haak and the Early Years of the Royal Society',
Ann. Sci., 1957, *13*, 205.
[20] Similar evidence is also available in a letter from Haak to John Winthrop,
Governor of Connecticut, dated 29 October 1667 from Westminster,
advising the latter that Haak was sending a copy of Sprat's *History*; he
speaks of the 'generous and noble undertakings' of the Royal Society, and
refers to 'those noble grounds for Mankinds improving the Treasures
God hath communicated to them so abundantly throughout all the world,
and that we may yet more enjoy and prayse his goodnesse, serving Him &
one another with all chearfullnesse & industry, and ever thereby more
and more reconciling ye estrangednesse of ye minds of mankinde amongst
themselves, that they may be willing to listen to more and more & still
better Truths & Union'; reproduced in 'President's Description of Correspondence of Several of the Founders of the Royal Society in England with
Governor John Winthrop of Connecticut between 1661 and 1672', *Proc.
Massachusetts Hist. Soc.*, 1878, p. 206.
[21] J. I. Cope, 'Origins of the Royal Society', Appendix A to Sprat's *History*
(1959). See footnote 4.
[22] M. Purver, *The Royal Society; Concept and Creation*, London, 1967.

which nature revealed the power but not the will of God, and the other a utopian pansophism in which theology continued to be interwoven with philosophy, and she has argued that as a consequence only the former may be taken as the true precursor of the Royal Society. Now this distinction is important as a matter of factual history, but for present purposes, although it would eliminate the direct relevance of Haak and Protestant pansophism to the rise of modern science, it does not affect Stimson's case for the influence of Puritanism on the foundation of the Royal Society.

Investigations of the nature of the relation between Puritanism or Protestantism and the rise of modern science in England have not been confined to discussions specifically concerned with the foundation of the Royal Society or with Haak's place in that history. Jones devoted three chapters of his classic study *Ancients and Moderns* to a survey of the several schemes for the general advancement of learning and piety, the revolt against the authority of Aristotle and the ancients, and the general progress of science which marked the two decades of the so-called 'Puritan era' in England, and subsequently produced further evidence for his assertion that the chief supporters of science before the Restoration had been a group of 'scientifically minded Puritans'.[23] Almost concurrently with Jones's book, Merton published the first of his two sociological studies on the inter-relation of Puritanism and science,[24] in which he argued that 'the Puritan ethic, as an ideal-typical expression of the value-attitudes basic to ascetic Protestantism generally, so canalized the interests of seventeenth-century Englishmen as to constitute an important *element* in the enhanced cultivation of science'. Turner,[25] having described Puritanism as 'the essence of Protestantism' on the ground that its only authority was the bible, extended Stimson's biographical approach to cover the whole century. Because of their interest in the bible, Boyle and Ray, Wallis and Wilkins took their place as 'Puritans' along with some sixteen other contemporary English scientists; and even Isaac Newton, whom Turner acknowledged was no 'true Puritan', was fitted into the argument as belonging 'to the Puritan type' on the same basis.

All these studies have focused their attention on the English

[23] R. F. Jones, *Ancients and Moderns, A Study of the Rise of the Scientific Movement in Seventeenth-Century England*, St Louis, 1936; second edn, 1961; reprinted Berkeley and Los Angeles, 1965 (see p. 227 for 'scientifically-minded Puritans'); and R. F. Jones, 'Puritanism, Science and Christ Church', *Isis*, 1939, *31*, 65.
[24] R. K. Merton, 'Puritanism, Pietism and Science', *Sociological Rev.*, 1936, *28*, 1.
[25] C. E. A. Turner, 'Puritan Origins in Science', *Faith and Thought* (the journal of The Philosophical Society of Great Britain, also known as The Victoria Institute), 1949, *81*, 85.

scene. However, a second line of research has been concerned with the broader field of the religious affiliations of European scientists in general. Investigations on this point date back to 1873, when Alphonse de Candolle published his statistical analyses of the historical development of the various sciences.[26] A substantial portion of his detailed study was concerned with classifications of the leading European scientists of international repute over the previous two centuries with regard to such factors as education, race, language and religious belief. Under the heading 'Influence of Religion', de Candolle showed that in the period 1666 to 1869, seventy-one of the ninety-two foreign members of the French Academy of Sciences had been non-Roman Catholics – a group he labelled 'Protestant', while recognizing the variety which this designation covered – and sixteen had been Roman Catholic, the remaining five being either of indeterminate religious affiliation, or members of the Jewish faith. At the same time, the respective religious populations of Europe in 1873 outside France from whom these foreign members could have been drawn were one hundred and seven million Roman Catholics and sixty-eight million Protestants. The conclusion is clear. Assuming that the proportion of Roman Catholics to Protestants had been constant from 1666 at the 1873 ratio, one might have expected nearly twice as many Roman Catholics as Protestants among scientists sufficiently eminent to have been elected to foreign membership of the French Academy, but in fact the actual ratio had been over four to one in the reverse direction. De Candolle also observed in passing that, of the twenty-two foreign members of the Academy who had been of English nationality, not one had been a Roman Catholic.

Since these observations had been concerned with foreign members of the French Academy, they took on account of the 'very numerous' French scientists over the two centuries. De Candolle therefore extended his study to this group by noting the religious affiliations of the foreign members of the Royal Society of London in 1829 and 1869, at which times the numbers of French foreign members had been highest. He found that in both years foreign members of the English Society were divided roughly equally between Roman and non-Roman affiliations, and yet, outside England, there were four times as many Roman Catholics as Protestants. These figures thus substantiated his former findings, and lead to the generalization that Protestants had formed a disproportionately large section of the international scientific community of Europe in the preceding two centuries.

[26] Alphonse de Candolle, *Histoire des Sciences et des Savants depuis Deux Siècles, suivie d'autres Etudes sur des Sujets Scientifiques, en particulier sur la Sélection dans L'Espèce Humaine* Genève–Bale–Lyon, 1873.

De Candolle interpreted his findings as an indication of the effect of two different modes of religious upbringing on the general ability or otherwise of an individual to render knowledge progressive. He specifically discounted any effect of actual dogmas, particularly those concerned with life after death, in retarding scientific achievement by possible diversion of attention from the present, since such doctrines were not confined to Roman Catholicism, and moreover, the degree to which any individual had been actually committed to them was indefinable despite verbal profession. He suggested rather that the observed variation between numbers of Protestant and Roman Catholic scientists was attributable to differences in general education and mental habit, the former having grown up in the spirit of individual free choice and under a less intense authoritarianism than the latter, so that their 'faculty of curiosity', 'the mother of the sciences', had been less affected.

De Candolle's research is not directly concerned with the origins but rather with the subsequent development of modern science. However Pelseneer extended the study of religious affiliations of European scientists back into the sixteenth century,[27] and pointed out that of the two hundred and fifty individuals responsible for over three hundred scientific publications during the period 1521–1600 – the era in which he considered modern science could be said to have been born – the majority had been either Protestant or were regarded at the time as sympathetic to the Reformation; for the particular decades 1581–1600, the ratio of Protestant to Roman Catholic authors of scientific works was as high as six to one. Pelseneer concluded from this that 'modern science was born of the Reformation'.

In the light of the evidence presented so far, whether relating only to England or concerned with the wider horizons of Europe, there can be little doubt that non-Roman Catholics exhibited a significantly greater predilection for the study of nature over the whole period from the early sixteenth to the mid-nineteenth centuries than did Roman Catholics. It has been an easy step for scholars to assume that the two lines of evidence we have considered so far are closely linked, and that the sudden rapid rise of modern science in mid-seventeenth-century England was a direct outcome of the Puritan ascendancy from 1640 to 1660. Attempts have therefore been made to determine the nature of the supposed influence on science of those movements for ecclesiastical and doctrinal reforms in sixteenth-century Europe which continued in England into the seventeenth century, and to discover reasons for the particular power it is thought to have

[27] J. Pelseneer, 'L'Origine Protestante de la Science Moderne', *Lychnos*, 1946–7, 246; see also his study 'La Réforme et l'Origine de la Science Moderne', *Revue de l'Université de Bruxelles*, 1954, 5, 406.

exerted on science. Two lines of thought on these matters may be traced.

On the one hand, Mason has argued for a direct influence of Reformation theology as a significant factor in the rise of modern science and to explain Protestant dominance in scientific interests.[28a] Despite its congruity with science, Mason rejected the possibility of any vital influence of Lutheranism, both because its geographical coverage was not coextensive with areas exhibiting scientific activity, and also because he considered that its emphasis on justification by an inner faith reduced 'works', of which the acquisition and use of knowledge was one, to a minor role. However, he considered that the main European centres of early scientific activity were also consistently centres of a Calvinist type of ecclesiastical reform – England, the Puritans and the reformed Church of England; France with its Huguenots and those 'Puritans within the creed', the Jansenists; and Holland with its Calvinist sects – and that the peculiar emphasis on the continuous performance of good works as an indication that a man was indeed 'saved' which characterized the English as distinct from the Dutch, Scottish or French variants of Calvinism provided the motive power for the rise of science in Puritan England.[28b] Mason attributed the general Protestant interest in science to what he described as 'a certain congruity between the more abstract elements of the Protestant theologies and the theories of modern science', to be seen in the rejection of the concept of hierarchy by reformers and then by early modern scientists. As the early Calvinists disavowed the concept of a hierarchical government of the universe in theology, so also did Copernicus in the physical structure of the macrocosm in the field of astronomy; both substituted an absolutist centre. Again, Mason held that a similar transition, this time actually influenced by the theological change, occurred in the conception of the microcosm, the little world of the human body. Mason pointed to the speculations of Servetus, who, basing his argument on the Reformation reinstatement of the equality of each individual soul in the eyes of God, as opposed to a hierarchical scale of souls of differing religious merit, rejected the hierarchical liver-heart-brain model of the human body derived from Galen

[28a] S. F. Mason, 'The Scientific Revolution and the Protestant Reformation': Pt 1, 'Calvin and Servetus in Relation to the New Astronomy and the Theory of the Circulation of the Blood', *Ann. Sci.*, 1953, 9, 64; Pt 2, 'Lutheranism in Relation to Iatrochemistry and the German Nature Philosophy', *Ann. Sci.*, 1953, 9, 154.
[28b] The argument is clarified in Mason's book, *Main Currents of Scientific Thought*, London, 1956, chap. 16. Reformation theology, regarded as monolithically Calvinist, is likewise conceived to be the prime mover in the development of modern science by E. L. Hebden Taylor, 'The Reformation and the Development of Modern Science', *The Churchman*, 1968, 82, 87.

and substituted his theory of a single system centred on the heart.

On the other hand, several scholars, notably Merton,[29] Hooykaas,[30] Kocher[31] and Dillenberger,[32] have pointed out that not only was there nothing in the dogmas of Catholicism, Protestantism or Puritanism which made any one of them either more or less favourable to science in general than the others, but also that Puritanism itself was not homogeneous. This needs little substantiation; Thomas Edwards, staunch Presbyterian opponent of Independency and tolerationism, listed seventeen major religious groups in the Puritan England of 1646.[33] Nevertheless, these scholars have all maintained that the close association between the scientific endeavour and English Puritanism generally could be taken to mean that the latter encouraged science far more than other forms of Christianity, and that since Calvinism represents the ideal form of Puritanism, the impetus to modern science must be associated with the developed English form of Calvinism. The general argument which has emerged is that even though the influence of Protestantism on the rise of science cannot be attributed directly to a specific theology, science received its impetus from a Protestant – Merton[24] also calls it more specifically a Puritan – 'ethic' or 'ethos' found primarily in Calvinism.[34] This thesis takes account of three particular points: the preponderance of Protestants in science in the sixteenth century; the theological differences between Lutheranism and other forms of Protestantism, particularly its precepts of justification by faith only and its tendency to elevate penitent grief above constructive action; and the upsurge of English science during the Puritan era. Its protagonists describe the so-called Protestant 'ethic' as a drive to

[29] R. K. Merton, 'Science, Technology and Society in Seventeeth-Century England', *Osiris*, 1938, 4, 360.

[30] R. Hooykaas, 'Science and Reformation', *J. World Hist.*, 1956, 3, 109, 781.

[31] P. H. Kocher, *Science and Religion in Elizabethan England*, San Marino (Calif.), 1953.

[32] J. Dillenberger, *Protestant Thought and Natural Science, an Historical Interpretation*, London, 1961.

[33] Thomas Edwards, *Gangraena; or, a Catalogue and Discovery of many of the Errors, Heresies, Blasphemies, and Pernicious Practices of the Sectaries of this Time*, London, 1646; a convenient description of English sects and sectaries in the mid-1640s, including material from Edwards, is available in D. Masson, *The Life of John Milton; Narrated in Connexion with the Political, Ecclesiastical and Literary History of his Time*, vol. iii, pp. 136–59; new edn, Gloucester (Mass.), 1965.

[34] In introducing this concept, Merton was consciously extending the earlier thesis that a Protestant 'ethos' had stimulated the growth of capitalism: see M. Weber, *The Protestant Ethic and the Rise of Capitalism*, tr. T. Parsons, New York, 1930, and the extensive literature that has grown up around that theory, especially R. W. Green, *Protestantism and Capitalism – The Weber Thesis and its Critics*, Boston, 1959.

illuminate ever more intensely the glory of God, and to provide increasingly for the relief of man's estate and the advantage of individual and nation alike, concepts which certainly found frequent expression during the whole period in question, particularly in mid-seventeenth-century England, and which are commonly regarded in the theory (as for example by Merton)[24, 29] as the hallmarks of this sterling spirit. If they formed no specific part of Protestant theology generally, or of Calvinism in particular, it is argued that these emphases were derived directly from and were characteristic and concrete expressions of the Protestant doctrines of the otherness of God and the significance of each Christian individual and community in His eyes, features which found their strongest expression among the English Puritans. Kocher, writing specifically of sixteenth-century England, believed that he had located the source of this Calvinistic scientific ethic in what he described as Calvin's 'crucial distinction between the total ruin wrought by original sin on man's moral and religious faculties, and the only partial corruption of his practical intellect', and suggested that this feature 'saved Calvinism from scepticism about natural science' and was 'so incalculably important for the future of science in England'. In his opinion, 'it was lucky for Elizabethan scientists that the prevailing climate of theology in which they worked had been set by Calvin and transmitted to England'.[35] Rosen was equally definitive in declaring that 'it may be asserted without contradiction that Puritanism was one of the major motive forces of the new experimental science'.[36] According to this theory, the rise of modern science was dependent, albeit indirectly, on Calvin's theology.

Other writers have rejected any relation between Puritanism and science,[37] and yet others have replaced the theory of an influence of Reformed religion on science by a consideration of the developing harmony between the two areas of knowledge.

[35] Kocher, op. cit. [footnote 31], p. 10; in support of his argument, Kocher quoted Calvin's eulogy of 'the writings of the olde men' and his 'great admiration of their witte' in 'Phisicke' and 'the Mathematicall sciences', and of 'that marvellous light of trueth that shineth in them' (Institutes, 1587 edn, tr. Th. Norton, fol. 81 r and v). However, this may be regarded as Calvin's narrowing down to the knowledge of nature of an early Christian argument for the existence of truth, including that in moral and religious fields, beyond the bounds of Judaeo-Christianity (see, e.g., Justin Martyr, 1 Apol. 46; 2 Apol. 13). The problem had come to the fore again in Calvin's time with the discovery of new lands and gave rise to the many contemporary arguments for and against the 'invisible church': see, e.g., H. F. Woodhouse, The Doctrine of the Church in Anglican Theology, 1547–1603, S.P.C.K., London, 1954.
[36] E. Rosen, 'Left-Wing Puritanism and Science', Bull. Hist. Med., 1944, 15.
[37] M. M. Knappen, Tudor Puritanism, Chicago, 1939, pp. 478–80; and M. H. Curti, Oxford and Cambridge in Tension, 1558–1642, Oxford, 1959, pp. 247–9 and Note M, pp. 287–8.

Thus, Westfall[38] maintains that a state of co-existent separation between science and religion existed in seventeenth-century England; although he admits that some connexion between Puritanism and early modern science has been established, he insists that the influence of Protestantism on natural science is nebulous and difficult to isolate, and concludes that a definitive treatment has not yet been offered. Rabb[39] has pointed to the difficulty of joining the obvious influence of Francis Bacon to Puritanism in the development of English science, despite the description of Bacon as the son of a 'learned, eloquent and religious woman, full of puritanical fervour'[40] invoked by Merton:[29] and having drawn attention again to the point that the Puritans' theoretical approval of science was no more pronounced than that of non-Puritans, he concludes that Puritanism itself did not stimulate scientific activity, nor can it be regarded as a main factor or a tangible cause in the rise of modern science, and offers the alternative opinion that it was the seventeenth-century 'spirit of revolution', expressed first in the theological and then in the philosophical field, which provided the impetus required to reject the old and adopt the convenient ready-made Baconian philosophy. Rabb would explain the contemporaneity of Puritanism and science not in terms of the effect of the one in giving rise to the other, but as twin effects, one following hard on the heels of the other, arising from a common cause. In similar vein, Hill, having intentionally disregarded Puritanism in his study of the intellectual origins of the so-called 'revolution' in seventeenth-century England, suggested that the concurrent reconstructions in science, history and law were, together with Puritanism, different aspects of a single revolution.[41]

Mason[28] related his understanding of the significance of Calvinist theology discussed above to the developing harmony between science and religion by regarding the influence of Calvinism as merely latent until the 1640s. Prior to that time, according to Mason, the scientific endeavour was retarded by tensions between particular biblical statements and the observed world which had been created by the literalistic mode of scriptural interpretation

---

[38] R. S. Westfall, 'Science and Religion in Seventeenth-Century England', *Yale Historical Publications, Miscellany 67*, New Haven and London, 1958.
[39] T. K. Rabb, 'Puritanism and the Rise of Experimental Science in England', *J. World Hist.*, 1962, 7, 1; reprinted in *The Rise of Science in Relation to Society* (ed. L. M. Marsak), London, 1964.
[40] Mary Stuart, *Francis Bacon*, London 1932, p. 6. Even Bacon himself becomes not merely 'one of Calvin's successors' but the epitome of 'Calvinist thinkers', according to E. L. Hebden Taylor, *The Churchman*, 1968, 82, 87.
[41] C. Hill, *Intellectual Origins of the English Revolution*, Oxford, 1965; see p. 300.

employed in early Protestantism, but then, with the advent of such scientifically-minded Puritans as Wilkins, Boyle and Sprat, who rejected biblical literalism, 'modern science and Calvinist theology reached a *modus vivendi* and some degree of integration'.

CRITICISMS OF CURRENT THEORIES

Now let us reconsider the present state of these studies. Two main lines of evidence are well marked. Meetings devoted to the study of nature, begun in England at a time of Puritan dominance in politics and religion, subsequently developed into the Royal Society through legal incorporation and an increased degree of internal organization, but without change in the aims and scientific temper of the members. Again, a general Protestant predilection for the study of science in the sixteenth and seventeenth centuries seems incontrovertible. However, current understanding of the relationship between these points and also of each of them to the rise of science may be criticized on several grounds.

Firstly, Mason's view that modern science, previously retarded by a literalistic interpretation of the bible, developed only when 'scientifically-minded Puritans' influenced Protestantism and removed this supposed barrier to progress, not only fails to relate the possession of a 'scientific mind' by some isolated individuals whom he would regard as ideal Calvinists to Calvinist theology, but confuses non-literalism with the use of the idea of 'accommodation', and, in supposing that this technique was first employed in mid-seventeenth-century England, overlooks its frequent and common earlier use by Christians of Calvinist and other persuasions. Certainly there were 'tensions' or discrepancies between particular biblical statements and other knowledge. Those which particularly exercised the minds of sixteenth- and seventeenth-century thinkers were the contrasts between current astronomical understanding of the relative sizes of the sun (one hundred and sixty-six times the diameter of the earth) and the moon (one thirty-ninth of the earth)[42] and the biblical description of the moon as a 'great light' comparable in size to the sun (Gen. I. 16), and between the Copernican theory of the sun's immovability and the earth's motion, and texts such as Eccles. i, 4–5, 'the earth abideth for ever; the sun also ariseth, and the sun goeth down, and hasteth to his place where he arose'. To those not prepared to dismiss either the biblical books or nature *in toto* because of these contrasts, the commonly accepted solution lay in pointing out that such biblical statements reflected ordinary

[42] See, e.g., F. R. Johnson, *Astronomical Thought in Renaissance England.* Baltimore, 1937, pp. 57 f.

visual observation and human understanding, and were perfectly 'sensible', while the more sophisticated 'reasonable' understanding newly available to men had been known all along by God, the common 'author' of the bible and the book of nature, but that He had purposely refrained from revealing the true description of the universe to the people of old testament times in order not to divert their attention by 'non-sensical' statements from the religious behavioural philosophy He wished to impart. As Wilkins put it, the Holy Ghost inspired the writers of Scripture 'only with the Knowledge of those things whereof they were to be Penmen, and that they were not better skilled in Points of Philosophy than others', even though their religious apprehension was perhaps greater.[43] This theory of God's 'accommodation' of His knowledge to common sensual appearances was not a device by which the plain meaning of the texts in question was exchanged for a figurative sense, but rather an explanation – and to the men of the time a meaningful and sensible one – of differences between the understanding of particular natural phenomena at different periods in history. Nor was Wilkins by any means the first to use this argument. He himself cited several earlier biblical commentators to support his 'scientific' solution of the tension, including Calvin, who in his *Commentary on Genesis* had concluded that 'Moses rather frameth himself to common use', since 'he had rather respect to us, then to the starres, even as it became a Devine'.[44] Although here it was Moses, privy to God's mind, rather than God Himself who had 'accommodated' his understanding to that of the general populace, the basic concept was fundamentally the same. Some fifty years prior to Calvin, John Colet had employed the idea of Mosaic accommodation, drawn from the great annotated bible of the day,[45] when discussing the biblical account of creation:

[43] John Wilkins, *A Discourse Concerning a New Planet*, 1640; Proposition I.
[44] John Calvin, *In primum Moses librum, qui Genesis vocatur, Commentarius*, Geneva, 1554; English transln, *A Commentarie of John Calvine upon the first booke of Moses, called Genesis*, London, 1578; on Gen. 1. 16: Calvin's supposed anti-Copernican attitude, which for nearly a century had been attributed to him, has been shown recently to be without foundation, see E. Rosen, 'Calvin's Attitude Toward Copernicus', *J. Hist. Ideas*, 1960, 21, 431; cf. also the acceptance of Copernicanism among other Puritans, D. Fleming, *The Judgment upon Copernicus in Puritan New England*, pp. 160–75 of *L'Aventure de l'Esprit*, vol. ii, Mélanges A. Koyré, Paris, 1964; and for Calvin's high estimate of the revelatory value of nature in general and astronomy in particular, T. H. L. Parker, *The Doctrine of the Knowledge of God; A Study in the Theology of John Calvin*, Edinburgh and London, 1952, chapter 1.
[45] De Lyra, *Glossa ordinaria*, in *Biblia Latina cum glossa*, vol. i, p. 23: 'Moses was speaking to an uneducated people, who could not take in spiritual ideas, but only gross and bodily ones: and on that account he made no mention of the creation of angels' (quoted in J. H. Lupton, *A Life of Dean Colet*, 1887, p. 248).

'Moses proceeds in due order to deal with particular objects and set before us the arrangement of the universe in detail. And this he does in such a way, in my opinion, that we may perceive him to have regard to popular conceptions, and to the uneducated multitude whom he taught'.[46] Indeed, the theory was employed about A.D. 400 by John Chrysostom in his second homily on the first chapter of Genesis,[47] and, applied either to God or to a biblical writer, it was made use of continually, and not only in questions of astronomy, by Anglican and Calvinist theologian-scientists of sixteenth-century England[48] and others.[49] Moreover, although it predominated among Protestants, its use was not confined to them. Galileo, a devout Roman Catholic, related the Copernican understanding of the earth's motion to the biblical concept of its immovability in precisely the same way : 'since it was very obvious that it was necessary to attribute motion to the sun and rest to the earth, in order not to confound the shallow understanding of the common people and make them obstinate and perverse about believing in the principal articles of the faith, it is no wonder that this was very wisely done in the divine scriptures'; but although he was supported in this attitude by Friar Thomas Campanella's *Defence of Galileo*, the Roman Catholic superiors of the day were not prepared to accept the idea of accommodation.[50] In general, it cannot be said that new scientific theories or discoveries were either retarded by one understanding of particular biblical texts referring to nature, or, conversely, enabled to develop through a supposed enlightenment and eman-

[46] John Colet, *Letters to Radalphus on the Mosaic Account of the Creation, ca.* 1500; first printed in J. H. Lupton, *A Life of Dean Colet*, 1887, Appendix, pp. 246 ff.; see p. 251.
[47] John Chrysostom, *Second Homily on Genesis, Chapter one, ca.* A.D. 400; in *Patrologica Græca* (ed. P. G. Migne), vol. iv, col. 29, para 2.
[48] Kocher, *op. cit.* [footnote 31], pp. 38–40; also Ed. Wright's preface to Gilbert's *De Magnete*, 1600, in defence of the earth's motion : 'it was not the purpose of Moses or the Prophets to set forth any mathematical or physical subtleties, but rather to accommodate themselves to the understanding of the vulgar and to ordinary methods of speech, much as nurses are accustomed to accommodate themselves to their infants'. Kocher has explored this distinction between literalism and 'accommodation' by early English astronomers, in 'Use of the Bible in English Astronomical Treatises during the Renaissance' (*Huntington Library Quarterly*, 1945–6, 9, 109–20).
[49] A. Williams, *The Common Expositor; An Account of the Commentaries on Genesis*, 1527–1633, North Carolina, 1948, especially pp. 176–8; and Thomas Aquinas, *Summa Theologiæ*, Pt 1, Q. 68, Art. 3.
[50] Galileo, *Letter to Madame Christina of Lorraine, Grand Duchess of Tuscany, Concerning The Use of Biblical Quotations in Matters of Science*, 1615; reprinted in *Discoveries and Opinions of Galileo* (ed. S. Drake), New York, 1957; and Thomas Campanella, *The Defence of Galileo* [*whether his philosophy*] *is in Harmony with or Opposed to the Holy Scriptures*, 1622, transl. G. McColley, Smith College Studies in History, vol. xxii, Nos. 3–4, Northampton, Mass., 1937.

cipation from the bible of 'scientifically-minded' men, Puritans or otherwise, for indeed tensions only existed at all because particular discoveries or theories in natural philosophy *had already been made or advanced*. Certainly, the possibility of solving those tensions and of accepting new theories and discoveries presented no difficulty to those willing and able to accept the explanation of God's 'accommodation', and with it the unspoken corollary of a present revelatory process, while those who attempted to confine God's revelatory activity to the biblical period found either the biblical or the scientific knowledge untenable, and became in consequence either atheistic scientists or anti-scientific churchmen; but that distinction, and the differentiation of the boundaries between the two points of view, would take us deep into fifteenth-, sixteenth- and seventeenth-century theologies, and is not the issue here.

Secondly, the terms 'Protestant', 'Puritan' and Calvinist' have come to be used interchangeably, although 'Protestant' in de Candolle's and Pelseneer's sense applied to all non-Roman Catholics generally. This is of particular importance for a historically accurate interpretation of the situation in mid-seventeenth century England, where from 1640 or so onwards, Puritans and Anglicans were, despite internal differences within both groups, identifiably separate species, making it scarcely meaningful to label all who lived and wrote during the Puritan era as 'Puritans'. Indeed, there is clear evidence that at least part of the scientifically minded group scarcely represented an ideal Calvinism during the interregnum. 'S.P.', writing in 1662 of the 'latitude-men' who in the Church of England of the day were known to be 'followers for the most part of the new Philosophy', observed that during the preceding two decades they had been regarded with a jaundiced eye by each of the mutually antagonistic Presbyterian and Independent parties: they 'are such, whose fortune it was to be born so late, as to have their education in the University, since the beginning of the unhappy troubles of this Kingdom ... they were so far from being sowred with the leaven of the times they lived in, that they were always looked upon with an evil eye by the successive usurping powers, and the general outcry was, that the whole University was ... full of men of a Prelatical Spirit ... because they were generally ordained by Bishops; and in opposition to that hide-bound, strait-lac'd spirit that did then prevail, they were called Latitude-men'.[51] This attitude, standing in marked contrast to that of the Calvinistic 'Narrow-men', had its direct antecedent in the outlook of 'the ever-memorable John Hales'.

[51] 'S.P.', *A Brief Account of the New Sect of Latitude-Men, Together with some reflections upon the New Philosophy*, Cambridge, 1662, p. 5; facsimile reprint by The Augustan Reprint Society, Clark Memorial Library, University of California, Los Angeles, 1963.

As an official Anglican observer at the Synod of Dort (Dortrecht) in 1618–19, Hales, together with several of his colleagues, had been unable to reconcile his understanding that the 'grace of redemption' was, without exception, general to all men, with the boundaries the Calvinists believed existed to that grace, and so had 'bid John Calvin goodnight'.[52] Sprat similarly distinguishes between the intellectual temper of the pre-Royal Society group and that which characterized the 'Twenty Years Melancholy' during which they had met: 'the University had, at that time, many Members of its own, who had begun a free way of reasoning, ... their first purpose was no more, then onely the satisfaction of breathing a freer air, and of conversing in quiet with one another, without being ingag'd in the passions, and madness of that dismal Age ... such spiritual Frensies, which did then bear Rule, can never stand long, before a cleer, and a deep skill, in Nature. It is almost impossible that they, who converse much with the subtilty, of things, should be deluded by such thick deceits.... For such a candid, and unpassionate company, as that was, and for such a gloomy season, what could have been a fitter Subject to pitch upon, than Natural Philosophy? To have been always tossing about some Theological question, would have been, to have made that their private diversion, the excess of which they themselves dislik'd in publick'. The subject to which these men had devoted themselves, Philosophy, had 'been always Loyal in the worst of times: For although the King's enemies had gain'd all other advantages ... yet they could never, by all their Victories, bring over the Reason of men to their Party'.[53]

The same two authors provide mutually substantiating evidence for a continuity in the decidedly non-Puritan outlook of these new philosophers at the Restoration. 'S.P.''s pamphlet was penned only four days before Royal assent was given to the Caroline Act of Uniformity, one purpose of which was to reinstate the Book of Common Prayer as the only form to be followed by all Englishmen in the public worship of God. For a

[52] *Golden Remains of the Ever-Memorable Mr John Hales, of Eaton-Colledge*, Third Impression, *With Additions* ... [including] *Letters and Expresses Concerning the Synod of Dort*, London, 1688 (3rd impression, 1657). The centrality of the question concerning grace may be seen in the letter on p. 580 from George Carleton, Lord Bishop of Llandaff, head of the English delegation to the Synod, to the Archbishop of Canterbury, 18 February 1618. Hales's comment on bidding Calvin 'goodnight' appears in the letter of Anthony Farindon to the Editor of the *Golden Remains*, dated 17 September 1657, and printed as a preface to it. The influence of Hales and the anti-Calvinist attitude of the Latitudinarians during the Puritan era is discussed by M. Nicolson, 'Christ's College and the Latitude-Men', *Modern Philology*, 1929, 27, 35.

[53] Sprat, *op cit.* [footnote 4], pp. 53–9; see also p. 152. Their distinctive rejection of theological topics is endorsed by Wallis's comments, refs 5a and 5b.

century, certain features in that book had formed the main bones of contention between the Puritan and non-Puritan factions, and in 1662 Puritan antagonism to them was still as immovable as ever, as the events of the Savoy Conference called in the previous year by Charles II to 'advise upon and review' them clearly show.[54] Writing of the attitude of the Latitude-men to the impending reinstatement of this hallmark of non-Puritanism, 'S.P.' observed that 'as for the Rites and Ceremonies of Divine Worship, they do highly approve that vertuous mediocrity [powerful mean] which our Church observes between the meretricious gaudiness of the Church of Rome, and the squalid sluttery of Fanatick conventicles'.[55] Again, Sprat decried the iconoclastic spirit of 'some forward assertors of new Philosophy' of his own day, who, contrary to the outlook of its true disciples, 'have come as furiously to the purging of Philosophy, as our Modern Zealots did to the Reformation of Religion'; in attempting to purify philosophy they were in danger of throwing out the baby with the bathwater, as he believed those who had set out to purify religion had done. Sprat's judgment that 'the one Party is as justly to be condemn'd, as the other'[56] is an unequivocal denial of the validity of the zealously purifying ethos of Puritanism in the reformation not only of religion but also of philosophy.

Modern interpreters, faced with Sprat's quite definite anti-Puritan statements, have maintained their theory either by ignoring these comments or by attributing to him 'a pliable nature',[57] categorizing him as having 'belonged to the Calvinist tradition',[58]

[54] Primary evidence for earlier differences is available in Richard Hooker, *Of the Laws of Ecclesiastical Policy*, 1595 and 1597. The continuing antagonism of the Puritan faction to the Book of Common Prayer, at least in certain points, during the century to 1662 is discussed at length in F. E. Brightman and K. D. Mackenzie, *The History of the Book of Common Prayer Down to 1662*, pp. 130–97, in ed. W. K. Lowther Clarke, *Liturgy and Worship*, S.P.C.K., London, 1932, and in greater detail in E. Daniel, *The Prayer-Book, its History, Language and Contents*, 26th edn, Redhill, Surrey, 1948; F. Procter and W. H. Frere, *A New History of the Book of Common Prayer*, 3rd impression, 1908; C. Neil and J. M. Willoughby, *The Tutorial Prayer Book*, 3rd impression, London, 1959. General discussions of the relations between the Puritan and non-Puritan factions over the same period are available in: J. F. N. New, *Anglican and Puritan – The Basis of Opposition, 1558–1640*; I. Calder, *Activities of the Puritan Faction in the Church of England, 1625–33*, 1957; H. O. Wakeman, *The Church and the Puritans, 1570–1660*, 1911; D. Neal, *History of the Puritans from 1517 to 1688* (new edn, ed. J. Toulmin), 5 vols, 1793–7; C. Hill, *Society and Puritanism in Pre-Revolutionary England*, New York, 1964; J. B. Marsden, *The History of the Early Puritans from the Reformation to the Opening of the Civil War in 1642*, London, 1850; and G. H. Curteis, *Dissent in its Relation to the Church of England*, London, 1872 (frequently reprinted).
[55] 'S.P.', *op. cit.* [footnote 51], pp. 7–8.
[56] Sprat, *op. cit.* [footnote 4], pp. 328–9.
[57] Rabb, *op. cit.* [footnote 39], p. 18.
[58] Mason, *op. cit.* [footnote 28a], p. 66.

or, in open contradiction to his own words, arguing that he 'really reveals here the underlying affinity between Puritanism and science'.[59] But this is to mistake an association of contemporaneity for a necessary relationship, to misunderstand that association just as the vituperative Stubbe had in calling Joseph Glanville, a clerical Fellow of the Royal Society, 'a Renegado-presbyter turned Latitudinarian';[60] for Glanville himself, writing of the attitude of the Latitude-men to the enthusiasms of the inter-regnum, observed that they 'knew, that Truth would have the advantage, could it but procure an impartial Tryal: That the False Doctrines, and Fanatical Practices of the Times would be detected and sham'd ... and that those Old Truths that were exploded with so much abhorrence, would, in all likelyhood, gain upon the Judgments and Affections of all that were free, and durst to be inquisitive'.[61] Protestants perhaps; but Puritans – in the sense of being aligned with an ideal Calvinism opposed to Anglicanism – or even 'scientifically minded' Puritans, many English new philosophers were not.

Thirdly, despite the very frequent use of the twin formulae 'the glory of God' and 'the benefit of mankind' by Puritans, the concepts do not characterize either Puritanism in particular or Protestantism in general. Although not yet associated with natural science, they may be found more than a century earlier in as public a place as the preamble to the annual printings of the Statutes and Acts of England. From at least as early as 1510 and until 1533, the texts of the laws of England were promulgated 'to the honour of almyghty god and of holy churche and for the weale and profyte of this his realme'; from 1534 the heading took an amended form, 'to the glory of God and for the common-weal and profite of this Kingdom'.[62] Although the changes no doubt reflect Henry's protesting abrogation of Papal authority in England – the first Act of 1534 (26 Hen. VIII cap. 1) was the so-called Supremacy Act, 'The King's Grace to be Authorized Supreme Head of the Church of England, and to have Authority

[59] Jones, *op. cit.* [footnote 23], 2nd edn, p. 334, Notes to chap. 8, no. 102.

[60] Henry Stubbe, *A Preface against Ecebolius Glanvil*, 1671, p. 34; for accounts of Stubbe's criticisms of the Royal Society, see R. H. Syfret, 'Some Early Critics of the Royal Society', *Notes and Records of the Royal Society*, 1951, 8, 20; J. I. Cope and H. W. Jones, *Aftermath; Stubbe's Attack on The Royal Society*, Appendix B to Sprat's History (footnote 4); and H. W. Jones, 'Mid-Seventeenth-Century Science: Some Polemics', *Osiris*, 1950, 9, 254–74.

[61] Joseph Glanville, *Anti-Fanatical Religion and Free Philosophy*, p. 13, in *Essays upon Several Important Subjects*, 1676; see also W. A. Shaw, *A History of the English Church during the Civil Wars and under the Commonwealth, 1640–60*, 2 vols, 1900.

[62] See, e.g., *The Statutes at Large from Magna Charta to the end of the last Parliament*, 1761, ed. O. Ruffhead, 8 vols, London, 1763.

to Redress all Errors, Heresies and Abuses in the Same'[63] – it is clear that the concepts of God's glory and community benefit had been employed as the earnest of the 'proper' direction of an ethic well before either Calvin or his predecessor, Luther, protested.

Again, the Society of Jesus, approved by Pope Paul III in 1540, centred its *raison d'être* on Ignatius of Loyola's *Spiritual Exercises* and his *Constitutions of the Society of Jesus*, the pages of each of which are so liberally seasoned with the idealisms of 'the greater glory of God' and the salvation of souls of men that the former, in its Latin form 'ad majorem Dei gloriam', rapidly became the motto of that Society.[64] The *Exercises* frequently refer to God as 'Creator and Lord', and Point 2 of the 'Contemplation for Obtaining Love' in the Fourth Week of the *Exercises* relates directly to nature: 'consider how God dwells in the creatures: in the elements, giving them being: in the plants, giving them growth: in the animals giving them sensation: in men, giving them understanding'; the theme is continued in Point 3: 'consider how God works and labours on my behalf in all created things ... as in the heavens, elements, plants, fruits, flocks'. If the rise of modern science is to be ascribed to the influence of a Protestant ethic, that ethic cannot be characterized by its appeal to or emphasis on the glory of God or the good of mankind, either in general terms or specifically in relation to nature, for these were mediaeval Christian commonplaces. Nor again, be it noted, can these concepts be taken as the source or the impetus which led to modern science. Some confirmation of this point of criticism occurs in the two charters of the Royal Society. The First Charter granted by Charles II in 1662 referred to the application of the Society's studies 'to further promoting by the authority of experiments the sciences of natural things and of useful arts', and not till the Second Charter of 1663 – some three years after the Restoration and one year after the Act of Uniformity, scarcely at a time of significant public Puritan influence – were the words 'to the glory of God the Creator and the advantage of the human race' added.[65]

[63] The text is available in Gee and Hardy [footnote 10], p. 243.
[64] See, e.g., the edition of St Ignatius of Loyola, *The Spiritual Exercise*, tr. from the Spanish by W. H. Longridge, London, 1919; and *Constitutiones Societatis Jesu, Apud Curiam Praepositi Generalis*, ed. W. H. Longridge, Rome 1943. F. X. Lawlor ('The Doctrine of Grace in the Spiritual Exercises', *Theological Studies*, 1942, 3, 513) counted some 135 uses of the formula, and another 150 locutions such as 'ad majus servitium Dei' and 'ad majus Dei obsequium' in the Spiritual Exercises; and a photograph of a statue of Ignatius erected in 1741 which strikingly illustrates the centrality of the formula in the writings of Ignatius appears in the entry *Jesuits* in the *New Catholic Encyclopaedia*, New York, 1967.
[65] *Record of the Royal Society of London*, 1st edn, 1877, pp. 31, 58, where Latin texts and contemporary English translations of both Charters are

Fourthly, the association of the rise of modern science with the Puritan era is generally considered to be reflected in a sudden expansion in volume of literature devoted to scientific subjects. For example, Merton[29] has drawn a series of graphs showing 'shifts of initial interests' in England from 1601 to 1700, in which the literature devoted to science is shown to have risen from some 2 per cent of the total at the beginning of the seventeenth century to about 5 per cent in 1640, followed immediately by a steeper rise to 7–8 per cent of the total for the ensuing decades (apart from a short-period drop to 4 per cent during the Civil Wars). However, the figures given by Klotz[66] for 'science' in her 'Subject Analysis of English Imprints for Every Tenth Year from 1480 to 1640', when expressed as percentages of total imprints, are: 1600, 8 per cent; 1610, 6 per cent; 1620, 4 per cent; 1630, 13 per cent; and 1640, 5 per cent. Certainly, no two scholars would necessarily accord precisely the same boundaries to the 'scientific' area, nor would they necessarily place any particular book or pamphlet in the same category, but the differences between these percentages in corresponding years are sufficiently large to preclude the use of the former as evidence for a significant expansion of English scientific literature from 1640 onwards. 'The rise of modern science' in seventeenth-century England cannot be illustrated by any significant increase in the output of scientific literature, and requires some other criterion for its definition.[67]

In the fifth place, the supposed relation between the origins of modern science and one particular aspect of Christianity does not allow due weight to be given to evidence relating to other expressions of Christian faith and to the non-sectarian nature of science. On the religious side, despite the difficulties faced by a Galileo and the cautious hesitancy of a Copernicus, the fact remains that prior to the Reformation the Roman Catholic church had done much to support and advance the science of the day, and virtually all mediaeval European scientists were of that faith.[68] Writing of his own times, Sprat observed that

given; an English version of the 1663 Charter is also quoted by Sprat, op. cit., p. 134.
[66] E. L. Klotz, 'A Subject Analysis of English Imprints for Every Tenth Year from 1480 to 1640', Huntingdon Library Quarterly, 1937–8, 1, 417.
[67] The earlier percentages for scientific works as a proportion of the total English literature which may be derived from Klotz's table (op. cit., footnote 66) are of no small interest: 1490, 20%; 1500, 4%; 1510, 3%; 1520, 4%; 1530, 11%; 1540, 14%; 1550, 6%; 1560, 11%; 1570, 4%; 1580, 9%; 1590, 10%. Apart from the 1490 figure, which cannot be considered significant because of the small total of only ten imprints, these figures suggest a fluctuating ratio but no significant increase in the proportion of English literature devoted to science over the whole period 1500–1640.
[68] See, e.g., the professedly apologetic work by J. J. Walsh, The Popes and Science, The History of the Papal Relations to Science during the Middle Ages and down to our own Time, London, 1912; and R. Hooykaas, 'Science

the Church of Rome has indeed of late look'd more favourably upon it [experimental knowledge]. They will now condemn no man for asserting the Antipodes: The severity with which they handled Galileo, seems now very much abated: they now permit their Jesuits to bestow some labours upon Natural Observations, for which they have great advantages by their Travails; and their Clergy may justly claim some share in the honor, as long as the Immortal Names of Mersennus and Gassendus shall live.[69]

On the secular side, the possible significance of Gresham College,[70] and the powerful influence of Francis Bacon on both the foundation of the Royal Society and the theme of Sprat's *History*[71] seem to bear little or no relation to the theory of a Protestant 'ethic', particularly when one recalls Bacon's absolute distinction between the contents of the bible and the book of nature,[72] the absence of a specifically Protestant or Puritan theological argument for science in Sprat's discussion of the relations between new philosophy and religion,[73] the overt recognition by both Bacon and Sprat of the earlier attainments – and shortcomings – in natural knowledge by non-Christians, especially the Islambic Arabs and pre-Christian Greeks,[74] and the tolerant attitude of the Royal Society to Roman Catholicism which aroused Stubbe's Anglican ire.[75] Above all, the Society was itself avowedly non-sectarian: in Sprat's words, 'it is to be noted, that they have freely admitted Men of different Religions, Countries, and Professions of Life ... they openly profess, not to lay the Foundation of an English, Scottish, Irish, Popish or Protestant Philosophy; but a Philosophy of Mankind';[76] and again, through the design of uniting men's 'Hands and Reasons', 'men of disagreeing parties,

---

and Theology in the Middle Ages', *Free University Quarterly*, vol. 3, pp. 74–142.

[69] Sprat, *op. cit.*, p. 373; on Gassendi, see J. T. Clark, 'Pierre Gassendi, and the Physics of Galileo', *Isis*, 1963, 5, 54; and G. S. Brett, *The Philosophy of Gassendi*, London, 1908.

[70] McKie, *op. cit.* [footnote 2]; and H. Hartley, 'Gresham College and the Royal Society', *Notes and Records of the Royal Society*, 1961, 5, 16, 125; Purver, *op. cit.*, pp. 183 ff., has suggested that the supposed influence of Gresham College on the foundation of the Royal Society is 'a mare's nest'.

[71] H. Fisch and H. W. Jones, 'Bacon's Influence on Sprat's "History of the Royal Society" ', *Modern Language Quarterly*, 1951, 12, 399–406; and for the reinstatement of Bacon as the originator of that new philosophy of which the Royal Society was a communal incarnation, see Purver, *op. cit.*

[72] F. Bacon, *The Advancement of Learning*, Bk 9, 1623; *Works*, ed. Spedding *et al.*, vol. v, pp. 111 ff.

[73] Sprat, *op. cit.*, pp. 345–78.

[74] See, e.g., F. Bacon, *The Advancement of Learning*, Bk 1, *passim*; and Sprat, *op. cit.*, pp. 5–15 and 45–6.

[75] See works cited in footnote 60.

[76] Sprat, *op. cit.*, p. 63.

and ways of life, have forgotten to hate, and have met in the unanimous advancement of the same Works. There the Soldier, the Tradesman, the Merchant, the Scholar, the Gentleman, the Courtier, the Divine, the Presbyterian, the Papist, the Independent, and those of Orthodox Judgment, have laid aside their names of distinction, and calmly conspir'd in a mutual agreement of labors and desires'.[77] The Royal Society and English science were not regarded by these leading spokesmen as in any way representing a particular religious outlook, whether Puritan, Anglican or some other, but indeed as the converse, a philosophy unbounded by the tenets of any philosophical sect or particular religious system, in which all men might engage freely in one community and with mutual profit.

Sixthly, despite the supreme importance for the rise of science which Kocher attributed to Calvin's distinction between the total depravity of man's moral and religious faculties and the only partial corruption of his practical intellect, both Bacon and the Royal Society made another and, for them, vital distinction in the field of human knowledge between the use of rational and logical thought in natural theology and philosophy on the one hand, for which they readily praised both the ancients and the schoolmen, and on the other, the repeated failure of earlier philosophers to have begun their logical constructions from a true and circumspect assessment of the primary evidence.[78] They believed that the previous failure of natural knowledge to advance significantly beyond Aristotle lay primarily in this fatal weakness preceding logic, which the philosophy described in *The Advancement of Learning*, the *Novum Organum*, and the 'new philosophy' of the Royal Society was designed specifically to overcome. In contrast to Kocher's theory, Bacon explicitly believed that man 'fell at the same time from his state of innocency and from his dominion over creation. Both of these losses, can even in this life be in some part repaired; the former by religion and faith, the latter by arts and sciences';[79] and, recognizing that 'the errors which have hitherto prevailed, and which will prevail for ever, should (if the mind be left to go its own way) either by the natural force of the understanding or by help of the aids and instruments of Logic, one by one correct themselves, was not a thing to be hoped for; because the primary notions of things which the mind readily and passively imbibes, stores up and accumulates (and it is from them that all the rest flow) are false, confused, and over-hastily abstracted from the facts', he set him-

---

[77] *Ibid.*, p. 427; the religious policy of the Royal Society is discussed at greater length by Purver, *op. cit.* [footnote 22].
[78] See, e.g., Sprat, *op. cit.*, pp. 15, 18, 30.
[79] F. Bacon, *Novum Organum*, Bk 2, in *Works*, ed. Spedding *et al.*, vol. iv, pp. 247–8; cf. also *Valerius Terminus*, in *Works*, vol. iii, p. 217.

self the task of restoring 'to its perfect and original condition', or at least improving, the ability of the mind of man to apprehend the nature of things.[80] Belief in the total corruption of man's practical intellect and a recognition of his recurring though often unconscious desire to worship the idols of the human mind were necessary preliminaries to their great instauration.

Seventhly, neither Sprat nor his contemporaries regarded a Christian, or more specifically a Protestant, outlook as either a necessary prerequisite or a consequence of the study of nature. The Royal Society's disavowal of loyalty to any one particular aspect of Christianity[81] is borne out in two further ways. First, although Sprat recognized the fundamental necessity for the natural philosopher to possess certain qualities in close accord with those ideally present in Christians[82] – he should be modest and humble, willing to be taught, with a receptive and pliable mind, not prone to condemning the efforts of others,[83] candid and 'unpassionate',[84] 'embracing all assistance',[85] with a searching spirit[86] guided by a critical and reiterated scrutiny of evidence[87] – he wished it to be understood that 'it might not be thought that I have defended every particular Sercher into Nature', as far as their religious views, for some were 'disaffected towards hevenly things' and 'negligent in the Worship of God', and 'by their carelessness of a Future Estate, have brought a discredit on Knowledge itself'.[88] Again, although Sprat was quick to point out that 'the Greatest and most Reverend of our churchmen, by their care, and passion, and indeavours, in advancing this Institution, have taken off the unjust scandal from Natural knowledge, that it is an Enemy to Divinity'[89] – his list of Fellows included the Lord Archbishop of Canterbury (Gilbert Sheldon), the Lord Archbishop of York (Richard Sterne), and the Lord Bishops of London (Humfrey Henchman), Rochester (John Dolben), Winchester (George Morley), and Exeter (Seth Ward)[90] – he also pointed out that the differing opinions of the Christian faith which had flourished since the Reformation had much retarded the knowledge of nature,[91] and that the Royal Society, by admitting men

---

[80] F. Bacon, The Great Instauration, Proemium, in Works, ed. Spedding et al., vol. iv, p. 7.
[81] Sprat, op. cit., p. 63.
[82] Sprat, op. cit., pp. 348–69; see also M. E. Prior, 'Bacon's Man of Science', J. Hist. Ideas, 1954, 15, 348.
[83] Sprat, op. cit., pp. 33–4.
[84] Ibid., p. 55.
[85] Ibid., p. 67.
[86] Ibid., p. 125.
[87] Ibid., p. 99.
[88] Ibid., p. 375.
[89] Ibid., p. 132.
[90] Ibid., pp. 431–3.
[91] Ibid., p. 25.

of all professions, including Divinity, intended to prevent one discipline from outweighing the others.[92] 'The whole care is not to be trusted to single men,' he observed; 'not to a Company all of one mind; not to Philosophers; not to devout and religious men alone'; for 'by all these we have been already deluded; even by those whom I last nam'd, who ought most of all to abhor falsehood; of whom yet many have multiply'd upon us, infinite Stories, and false Miracles, without any regard to Conscience, or Truth'.[93] He later discussed at length Puritan excesses with regard to supposed prophecies and pretended miracles, and their lack of affinity with the temper of the experimental philosopher.[94]

The *History* also makes it clear that in Sprat's eyes, the study of nature involved no necessary religious *consequence* for the scientist. Negatively, he took great pains, in the face of objections 'of some devout men against Knowledge, and chiefly that of Experiments',[95] to make out the case that 'Experiments of Natural things, do neither darken our eies, nor deceive our minds, nor deprave our hearts'.[96] Natural philosophy did not lead its followers away from Christianity into an inevitable atheism. Positively, Sprat insisted that natural philosophy ought not to be condemned merely because it disregarded theology, but that on the contrary it deserved 'so little to be esteem'd impious, that it ought rather to be reckon'd as Divine';[97] at the very least, 'it lies in the Natural Philosophers hands, best to advance that part of Divinity, which, though it fills not the mind, with such tender, and powerful contemplations, as that which shews us Man's Redemption by a Mediator; yet it is by no means to be passed by unregarded: but is an excellent ground to establish the other'.[98] New philosophy could lead men 'to admit a Deity', but Sprat did not go beyond concluding 'that the doubtful, the scrupulous, the diligent Observer of Nature, is neerer to make a modest, a severe, a meek, an humble Christian, than the man of Speculative Science'.[99]

[92] *Ibid.*, p. 66.
[93] *Ibid.*, pp. 73–4.
[94] *Ibid.*, pp. 357–65.
[95] H. Schulz discusses these objections in detail in his *Milton and Forbidden Knowledge*, 1955.
[96] Sprat, *op. cit.*, p. 347; cf. also p. 26; Sprat's total argument on this point occupies pp. 348–69.
[97] *Ibid.*, p. 351.
[98] *Ibid.*, p. 82.
[99] *Ibid.*, pp. 349 and 367.

SEVENTEENTH-CENTURY EVIDENCE FOR A
REVISED THEORY

Finally, we must consider the existence of a specific appreciation by Sprat of the influence which the religious reformation of the previous century had exerted on the rise of new philosophy. Most scholars who have been concerned with associations between the reformation and modern science, and particularly with the foundation of the Royal Society, – including McKie,[2] Stimson,[8] Syfret,[13] Barnett,[19] Cope,[21] Purver,[22] Jones,[23] Merton,[24] Turner,[25] Merton,[29] Hooykaas,[30] Kocher,[31] Westfall[38] and Rabb[39] – neither refer to nor discuss Sprat's remarks, which nevertheless are a source of primary evidence and presumably reflect the opinion of Fellows of the Royal Society on whose behalf he had written his the semi-official apologia.[100] The particular section reads as follows:

> The Church of England will not only be safe amidst the consequences of a Rational Age, but amidst all the improvements of Knowledge, and the subversion of old Opinions about Nature, and introduction of new ways of Reasoning thereon. This will be evident, when we behold the agreement that is between the present Design of the Royal Society, and that of our Church in its beginning. They both may lay equal claim to the word Reformation; the one having compass'd it in Religion, the other purposing it in Philosophy. They both have taken a like cours to bring this about; each of them passing by the corrupt Copies, and referring themselves to the perfect Originals for their instruction; the one to the Scripture, the other to the large Volume of the Creatures. They are both unjustly accus'd by their enemies of the same crimes, of having forsaken the Ancient Traditions, and ventur'd on Novelties. They both suppose alike, that their Ancestors might err; and yet retain a sufficient reverence for them. They both follow the great Praecept of the Apostle, of Trying all things. Such is the Harmony between their Interests and Tempers ... the Church of England ... arose on the same Method, though in different works ... [and] Heroically passed through the same difficulties....[101]

Having drawn these parallels between the first step in the two reformations, that is the 'subversion of old opinions' about the

---

[100] The circumstances under which Sprat wrote the *History* are outlined in the *Introduction* by J. I. Cope to the edition of 1959 [footnote 4]; the guidance and concurrence of the Society throughout the writing and publication of the *History* are fully attested by Purver, *op. cit.* [footnote 22].

[101] Sprat, *op. cit.*, pp. 370–1.

written book of God, the Scriptures, and the same process with regard to the other book of God, 'the large volume of the Creatures', Sprat goes on to allude, albeit very concisely, to the constructive aspect of both reformations, the 'introduction of new ways of Reasoning' developed first in the religious reformation by the Church of England for re-interpretation of the bible, and now being employed by the Royal Society in the re-interpretation of the book of nature. He writes:

> The present Inquiring Temper of this Age was at first pro-duc'd by the liberty of judging, and searching, and reasoning, which was us'd in the first Reformation. Though I cannot carry the Institution of the Royal Society many years back, yet the seeds of it were sown in King Edward the Sixth's, and Queen Elizabeth's Reign; and ever since that time Experimental Learning has still retained some vital heat, though it wanted the opportunities of ripening itself, which now it injoys. The Church of England therefore may justly be styl'd the Mother of this sort of Knowledge; and so the care of its nourishment and prosperity peculiarly lyes upon it.[102]

Scholars who have mentioned these remarks have found in them the expression of 'a consonance of aim between early modern science and Protestantism',[103] or simply a comparison – Hill describes it as 'obvious' – between the scientific revolution and the Protestant reformation,[104] but they appear to have overlooked not only the contradictions and difficulties these pose for the 'Puritan ethic' theory, but also the implications they contain for a more complete understanding of the rise of modern science.

Clearly, Sprat is not making any claim for the theological content of mid-sixteenth-century Anglicanism as the source of the rise of modern science. Neither at this point nor elsewhere in the *History* does he employ or refer to the influence of any theological tenet, whether specifically Anglican, Calvinist, Puritan or Protestant, or of any 'ethos' arising from theology, as the source of the total reformation of philosophy on which he and the Royal Society were then engaged, and which he clearly distinguished from that general restoration of learning which had accompanied the religious reformation.[105] Indeed, in the light of

---

[102] *Ibid.*, p. 372.
[103] Mason, *op. cit.* [footnote 28a], p. 66.
[104] Dillenberger, *op. cit.* [footnote 32], p. 130; Hill, *op. cit.* [footnote 41], p. 25.
[105] Sprat, *op. cit.*, p. 22; the general nature of this observation on the restoration of learning is akin to Bacon's comment that at the time of the reformation, 'a renovation and new spring of all other knowledges' took place (*Works*, vol. iii, p. 300); both Bacon and Sprat distinguish between that sixteenth century *restoration* of learning common to Europe and the 'great instauration' of philosophy which one planned and the other found incorporated in the activities of the Royal Society.

known reactions against the Royal Society by an influential section of Anglicans, and the apologetic tenor of Sprat's *History*, it
would be as misleading to ascribe the scientific 'liberty of judging
and searching and reasoning' to all Anglicans, as to deny that
some Calvinists and members of other religious persuasions exhibited this scientific spirit. *Religious denominational labels are
simply not sufficient to explain all known aspects of the phenomenon.* Nevertheless, Sprat was drawing attention to the facts
that each movement was a reformation in the use of evidence
and the method of interpretation of its relevant 'book', and that
the 'cours' which the Royal Society was following in philosophy
was derived from and identical with that employed by the
Church of England in biblical evidence a century earlier, on
which the English reformation was based. In both reformations
this involved the critical and not merely iconoclastic 'subversion
of old opinions' in the interpretations of particular features in
each 'book', and the 'introduction of new ways of Reasoning
thereon'. Now if Sprat's parallel can be sustained and supported
in detail on both these points, there would be sound reason to
regard the use of those approaches to evidence and interpretation employed in the English reformation as the source of the
scientific methodology of the Royal Society. Certainly the Anglican 'via media', clearly outlined in several reformation documents dealing specifically with the 'official' Anglican philosophy
of biblical interpretation, differed significantly from the philosophies of Puritan Anglicans and other Protestants on the one
side and of Roman Catholics on the other in a closely similar
way to that in which the 'cours' of new philosophy employed by
the Royal Society can be clearly distinguished from those of such
new systems as Cartesian philosophy on the one hand, and that
of contemporary old philosophers on the other. Further clarification of such parallels is clearly desirable, and would also presumably enable an acceptable interpretation of the sociological evidences reviewed earlier to emerge.

5 The Grand Design – A New Physics*

I. B. Cohen

The publication of Isaac Newton's *Principia* in 1687 was one of the most notable events in the whole history of physical science. In it one may find the culmination of thousands of years of striving to comprehend the system of the world, the principles of force and of motion, and the physics of bodies moving in different media. It is no small testimony to the vitality of Newton's scientific genius that although the physics of the *Principia* has been altered, improved, and challenged ever since, we still set about solving most problems of celestial mechanics and the physics of gross bodies proceeding essentially as Newton did some three hundred years ago. And if this is not enough to satisfy the canons of greatness, Newton was equally great as a pure mathematician. He invented the differential and integral calculus (produced simultaneously and independently by the German philosopher Gottfried Wilhelm Leibniz), which is the language of physics; he developed the binomial theorem and various properties of infinite series; and he laid the foundations for the calculus of variations. In optics Newton began the experimental study of the analysis and composition of light, showing that white light is a mixture of light of many colors, each having a characteristic index of refraction. Upon these researches have risen the science of spectroscopy and the methods of color analysis. Newton invented a reflecting telescope and so showed astronomers how to transcend the limitations of telescopes built of lenses. All in all, it was a fantastic scientific achievement – of a kind that has never been equalled.

In this book[1] we shall deal exclusively with Newton's system of dynamics and gravitation, the central problems for which the preceding chapters have been a preparation. If you have read them carefully, you have in mind all but one of the major ingredients requisite to an understanding of the Newtonian system of the world. But even if that one were to be given – the analysis

---

*I. B. Cohen, 'The Grand Design – A New Physics', Chapter 7 of *The Birth of a New Physics*, Heinemann Educational Books, 1961.
[1] *The Birth of a New Physics*.

of uniform circular motion – the guiding hand of Newton would still be required to put the ingredients together. It took genius to supply the new concept of universal gravitation. Let us see what Newton actually did.

First of all, it must be understood that Galileo himself never attempted to display any scheme of mechanics that would account for the movement of the planets, or of their satellites. As for Copernicus, the *De revolutionibus* contains no important insight into a celestial mechanics. Kepler had tried to supply a celestial mechanism, but the result was never a very happy one. He held that the *anima motrix* emanating from the sun would cause planets to revolve about the sun in circles. He further supposed that magnetic interaction of sun and planet would shift the planet during an otherwise circular revolution into an elliptical orbit. Others who contemplated the problems of planetary motion proposed systems of mechanics containing certain features that were later to appear in Newtonian dynamics. One of these was Robert Hooke, who quite understandably thought that Newton should have given him more credit than a mere passing reference for having anticipated parts of the laws of dynamics and gravitation.

NEWTONIAN ANTICIPATIONS

The climactic chapter in the discovery of the mechanics of the universe starts with a pretty story. By the third quarter of the seventeenth century a group of men had become so eager to advance the new mathematical experimental sciences that they banded together to perform experiments in concert, to present problems for solution to one another, to report on their own researches and on those of others as revealed by correspondence, books, and pamphlets. Thus it came about that Robert Hooke, Edmund Halley, and Sir Christopher Wren, England's foremost architect, met to discuss the question, Under what law of force would a planet follow an elliptical orbit? From Kepler's laws – especially the third or harmonic law, but also the second or law of areas – it was clear that the sun somehow or other must control or at least affect the motion of a planet in accordance with the relative proximity of the planet to the sun. Even if the particular mechanisms proposed by Kepler (an *anima motrix* and a magnetic force) had to be rejected, there could be no doubt that some kind of planet–sun interaction keeps the planets in their courses. Furthermore, a more acute intuition than Kepler's would sense that any force emanating from the sun must spread out in all directions from that body, presumably diminishing according to the inverse of the square of the distance from the sun – as light diminishes in intensity in relation to distance. But to say this much is a very different thing from *proving* it mathematically. For to prove it would require a complete physics with mathematical methods for solving all the attendant and consequent problems. When he declined to credit authors who tossed off general statements without being able to prove them mathematically or fit them into a valid framework of dynamics, Newton was quite justified in saying, as he did of Hooke's claims: 'Now is not this very fine! Mathematicians that find out, settle, and do all the business, must content themselves with being nothing but dry calculators and drudges; and another, that does nothing but pretend and grasp at all things, must carry away all the invention, as well as those that were to follow him as of those that went before.'

In any event, by January 1684, Halley had concluded that the force acting on planets to keep them in their orbits 'decreased in the proportion of the squares of the distances reciprocally',

$$F \propto \frac{1}{D^2}$$

but he was not able to deduce from that hypothesis the observed motions of the celestial bodies. When Wren and Hooke met later in the month, they agreed with Halley's supposition of a solar force. Hooke boasted 'that upon that principle all the laws of the celestial motions were to be [i.e. could be] demonstrated, and that he himself had done it'. But despite repeated urgings and Wren's offer of a considerable monetary prize, Hooke did not – and presumably could not – produce a solution. Six months later, in August 1684, Halley decided to go to Cambridge to consult Isaac Newton. On his arrival he learned the 'good news' that Newton 'had brought this demonstration to perfection'. Here is an almost contemporaneous account of that visit:

Without mentioning either his own speculations, or those of Hooke and Wren, he at once indicated the object of his visit by asking Newton what would be the curve described by the planets on the supposition that gravity diminished as the square of the distance. Newton immediately answered, *an Ellipse*. Struck with joy and amazement, Halley asked him how he knew it? 'Why,' replied he, 'I have calculated it'; and being asked for the calculation, he could not find it, but promised to send it to him. After Halley left Cambridge, Newton endeavoured to reproduce the calculation, but did not succeed in obtaining the same result. Upon examining carefully his diagram and calculations, he found that in describing an ellipse coarsely with his own hand, he had drawn the two axes of the curve instead of two conjugate diameters somewhat inclined to one another. When this mistake was corrected he obtained the result which he had announced to Halley.

Spurred on by Halley's visit, Newton resumed work on a subject that had commanded his attention in his twenties when he had laid the foundations of his other great scientific discoveries: the nature of white light and color and the differential and integral calculus. He now put his investigations in order, made great progress, and in the fall term of the year, discussed his research in a series of lectures on dynamics which he gave at Cambridge University, as required by his professorship. Eventually, with Halley's encouragement, the draft of these lectures, *De motu corporum*, grew into one of the greatest and most influential books any man has yet conceived. Many a scientist has echoed the sentiment which Halley expressed in the ode he wrote as a preface to Newton's *Principia* (or, to give Newton's masterpiece its full title, *Philosophiae naturalis principia mathematica, The Mathematical Principles of Natural Philosophy*, London, 1687):

> Then ye who now on heavenly far,
> Come celebrate with me in song the name
> Of Newton, to the Muses dear; for he
> Unlocked the hidden treasuries of Truth:
> So richly through his mind had Phoebus cast
> The radiance of his own divinity.
> Nearer the gods no mortal may approach.

THE 'PRINCIPIA'

The *Principia* is divided into three parts or 'books'; we shall concentrate on the first and third. In Book One Newton develops the general principles of the dynamics of moving bodies, and in Book Three he applies the principles to the mechanism of the universe. Book Two, which we shall not discuss, deals with fluid mechanics and the motion of bodies in various types of resisting media, the theory of waves and other aspects of general physics.

In Book One, immediately following the Preface, a set of Definitions, and a discussion of the nature of time and space, Newton presented the 'Axioms, or Laws of Motion':

Law I
Every body continues in its state of rest, or of uniform motion in a right [straight] line, unless it is compelled to change that state by forces impressed upon it.

Law II

The change of motion is proportional to the motive force impressed; and is made in the direction of the right line in which that force is impressed.

We should observe that the forces needed to change the 'state of rest or of uniform motion in a right line' of a body can never be at right angles to the direction of motion of the body. [...] This law of motion is sometimes called the 'Principle of Inertia', and the property that material bodies have of continuing in a state of rest or of uniform motion in a right line is sometimes known as the body's inertia.[2]

Newton illustrated Law I by reference to projectiles which continue in their forward motions 'so far as they are not retarded by the resistance of the air, or impelled downward by the force of gravity', and he referred also to 'the greater bodies of planets and comets'. At this one stroke Newton postulated the opposite view of Aristotelian physics. In the latter no celestial body could move uniformly in a straight line in the absence of a force, because this would be a 'violent' motion and so contrary to its nature. Nor could a terrestrial object, as we have seen, move along its 'natural' straight line without an external mover or an internal motive force. Newton, presenting a physics that applies simultaneously to both terrestrial and celestial objects, stated that in the absence of a force bodies do not necessarily stand still as Aristotle supposed, but they may move at constant rectilinear speed. This 'indifference' of all sorts of bodies to rest or uniform straight line motion in the absence of a force clearly is an advanced form of Galileo's statement in his *Letters on the Solar Spots* (page 125), the difference being that in that work Galileo was writing about uniform motion along a great spherical surface concentric with the earth.

Newton said of the Laws of Motion that they were 'such principles as have been received by mathematicians, and ... confirmed by [an] abundance of experiments. By the first two Laws and the first two Corollaries, Galileo discovered that the descent of bodies varies as the square of the time and that the motion of projectiles is in the curve of a parabola: experience agreeing with both, unless so far as these motions are a little retarded by the resis-

[2] The earliest known statement of this law was made by René Descartes in a work that he did not publish. It appeared in print for the first time in a work by Pierre Gassendi. But prior to Newton's *Principia* there was no completely developed inertial physics. It is not without significance that this book of Descartes was based on the Copernican point of view; Descartes suppressed it on learning of the condemnation of Galileo. Gassendi likewise was a Copernican. He actually made experiments with objects let fall from moving ships and moving carriages to test Galileo's conclusions.

tance of the air.' The 'two Corollaries' deal with methods used by Galileo and many of his predecessors to combine two different forces or two independent motions. Fifty years after the publication of Galileo's *Two New Sciences* it was difficult for Newton, who had already established an inertial physics to conceive that Galileo could have come as close as he had to the concept of inertia without having taken full leave of circularity and having stated a true principle of linear inertia.

Newton was being very generous to Galileo because, however it may be argued that Galileo 'really did' have the law of inertia or Newton's Law I, a great stretch of the imagination is required to assign any credit to Galileo for Law II. This law has two parts. In the second half of Newton's statement of Law II the 'change in motion' produced by an 'impressed' or 'motive' force – whether that be a change in the speed with which a body moves or a change in the direction in which it is moving – is said to be 'in the direction of the right line in which that force is impressed'. This much is certainly implied in Galileo's analysis of projectile motion because Galileo assumed that in the forward direction there was no acceleration because there was no horizontal force, except the negligible action of air friction; but in the vertical direction there was an acceleration or continual increase of downward speed, because of the downward-acting weight force. But the first part of Law I – that the change in the magnitude of the motion is proportional to the motive force – is something else again; only a Newton could have seen it in Galileo's studies of falling bodies. This part of the law says that if an object were to be acted on first by one force F_1 and then by some other force F_2, the accelerations or changes in speed produced, A_1 and A_2, would be proportional to the forces, or that

$$\frac{F_1}{F_2} = \frac{A_1}{A_2} \text{ or}$$

$$\frac{F_1}{A_1} = \frac{F_2}{A_2}$$

But in analysing falling, Galileo was dealing with a situation in which only one force acted on each body, its weight W, and the acceleration it produced was g the acceleration of a freely falling body.

While Aristotle had said that a given force gives an object a certain characteristic speed, Newton now said that a given force always produces in that body a definite acceleration A. To find the speed V, we must know how long a time T the force acted, or how long the object had been accelerated, so that Galileo's law

$$V = AT$$

may be applied.

At this point let us try a thought-experiment, in which we assume we have two cubes of aluminium, one just twice the volume of the other. (Incidentally, to 'duplicate' a cube – or make a cube having exactly twice the volume as some given cube – is as impossible within the framework of Euclidean geometry as to trisect an angle or to square a circle.) We now subject the smaller cube to a series of forces F_1, F_2, F_3 ... and determine the corresponding accelerations A_1, A_2, A_3 ... In accordance with Law II we would find that there is a certain constant value of the ratio of force to acceleration

$$\frac{F_1}{A_1} = \frac{F_2}{A_2} = \frac{F_3}{A_3} = \ldots = m_s$$

which for this object we may call m_ss. We now repeat the operations with the larger cube and find that the same set of forces F_1, F_2, F_3 ... respectively produces *another* set of accelerations a_1, a_2, a_3 ... In accordance with Newton's second law, the force-acceleration ratio is again a constant which for this object we may call m_l

$$\frac{F_1}{a_1} = \frac{F_2}{a_2} = \frac{F_3}{a_3} = \ldots = m_l$$

For the larger object the constant proves to be just twice as large as the constant obtained for the smaller one and, in general, so long as we deal with a single variety of matter like pure aluminium, *this constant* is proportional to the volume and so *is a measure of the amount of aluminium in any sample*. This particular constant is a measure of an object's resistance to acceleration, or a measure of the tendency of that object to stay as it is – either at rest, or in motion in a straight line. For observe that m_l was twice m_s; to give both objects the same acceleration or change in motion the force required for the larger object is just twice what it must be for the smaller. The tendency of any object to continue in its state of motion (at constant speed in a straight line) or its state of rest is called its *inertia*; hence, Newton's Law I is also called the principle of inertia. The constant determined by finding the constant force-acceleration ratio for any given body may thus be called *the body's inertia*. But for our aluminium blocks this same constant is also a measure of the 'quantity of matter' in the object, which is called its *mass*. We now make precise the condition that two objects of different material – say one of brass and the other of wood – shall have the same 'qauntity of matter': it is that they have the *same mass* as determined by the force-acceleration ratio, or the *same inertia*.

In ordinary life, we do not compare the 'quantity of matter' in objects in terms of their inertias, but in terms of their weight.

Newtonian physics makes it clear why we can, and through its clarification we are able to understand why at any place on the earth two unequal weights in a vacuum fall at the same rate. But we may observe that in at least one common situation we always compare the inertias of objects rather than their weights. This happens when a person hefts two objects to find which is heavier, or has the greater mass. He does not hold them out to see which pulls down more on his arm; instead, he moves them up and down to find which is easier to move. In this way he determines which has the greater resistance to a change in its state of motion in a straight line or of rest – that is, which has the greater inertia.

FINAL FORMULATION OF THE LAW OF INERTIA

At one point in his *Discourses and Demonstrations Concerning Two New Sciences* Galileo imagined the motion of a ball rolling along a plane 'with a motion which is uniform and perpetual, provided the plane has no limits'. A plane without limit is all right for a pure mathematician, who is a Platonist in any case. But Galileo was a man who combined just such a Platonism with a concern for applications to the real world of sensory experience. In the *Two New Sciences* Galileo was not interested in abstractions as such, but in the analysis of real motions on or near the earth. So we understand that having talked about a plane without limit, he does not continue with such a fancy, but asks what would happen on such a plane if it were a real earthly plane, which for him means that it is 'limited and elevated'. The ball, in the real world of physics, falls off the plane and begins to fall to the ground. In this case,

> ... the moving particle, which we imagine to be a heavy one, will on passing over the edge of the plane acquire, in addition to its previous uniform and perpetual motion, a downward propensity due to its own weight; so that the resulting motion which I call projection is compounded of one which is uniform and horizontal and of another with is vertical and naturally accelerated.

Unlike Galileo, Newton made a clear separation between the world of abstract mathematics and the world of physics, which he still called philosophy. Thus the *Principia* included both 'mathematical principles' as such and those that could be applied in 'natural philosophy', but Galileo's *Two New Sciences* included only those mathematical conditions exemplified in nature. For instance, Newton plainly knew that the attractive force exerted by the sun on a planet varies as the inverse-square of the distance,

$$F \propto \frac{1}{D^2}$$

but in Book One of the *Principia* he explored the consequences not only of this particular force but of others with quite different dependence on the distance, including

$$F \propto D$$

$$F \propto \frac{1}{D^3}$$

'THE SYSTEM OF THE WORLD'

At the beginning of Book Three, which was devoted to 'The System of the World', Newton explained how it differed from the preceding two, which had been dealing with 'The Motion of Bodies'.

> In the preceding Books I have laid down ... principles not philosophical [pertaining to physics] but mathematical: such, namely, as we may build our reasonings upon in philosophical inquiries. These principles are laws and conditions of certain motions, and powers or forces, which chiefly have respect to philosophy; but, lest they should have appeared of themselves dry and barren, I have illustrated them here and there with some philosophical scholiums, giving an account of such things as are of a more general nature, and which philosophy seems chiefly to be founded on: such as the density and the resistance of bodies, spaces void of all bodies, and the motion of light and sounds. It remains that, from the same principles, I now demonstrate the System of the World.

I believe it fair to say that it was the freedom to consider problems either in a purely mathematical way or in a 'philosophical' (or physical) way that enabled Newton to express the first law and to develop a complete inertial physics. After all, physics as a science may be developed in a mathematical way but it always must rest on experience – and experience never shows us pure inertial motion. Even in the limited examples of linear inertia discussed by Galileo, there was always some air friction and the motion ceased almost at once, as when a projectile strikes the ground. In the whole range of physics explored by Galileo there is no example of a physical object that has even a component of pure inertial motion for more than a very short time.

It was perhaps for this reason that Galileo never framed a general law of inertia. He was too much a physicist.

But as a mathematician Newton could easily conceive of a body's moving along a straight line at constant speed forever. The concept 'forever', which implies an infinite universe, held no terror for him. Observe that his statement of the law of inertia, that it is the natural condition for bodies to move in straight lines at constant speed forever, occurs in Book One of the *Principia*, the portion said by him to be mathematical rather than physical. Now, if it is the natural condition of motion for bodies to move uniformly in straight lines, then this kind of inertial motion must characterize the planets. But the planets do not move in straight lines, but rather along ellipses. Using a kind of Galilean approach to this single problem, Newton could say that the planets must therefore be subject to two motions: one inertial (along a straight line at constant speed) and one always at right angles to that straight line drawing each planet toward its orbit.

Though moving in a straight line, each planet nevertheless represents the best example of inertial motion observable in the universe. But for that component of inertial motion, the force that continually draws the planet away from the straight line would draw the planet in toward the sun until the two bodies collided. Newton once used this argument to prove the existence of God. If the planets had not received a push to give them an inertial (or tangential) component of motion, he said, the solar attractive force would not draw them into an orbit but instead would move each planet in a straight line toward the sun itself. Hence the universe could not be explained in terms of matter alone.

For Galileo pure circular motion could still be inertial, as in the example of an object on or near the surface of the earth. But for Newton pure circular motion was not inertial; it was accelerated and required a force for its continuance. Thus it was Newton who finally shattered the bonds of 'circularity' which still had held Galileo in thrall. And so we may understand that it was Newton who showed how to build a celestial mechanics based on the laws of motion: since their elliptical (or almost circular) orbital motion is not purely inertial, it requires the constant action of a force, which turns out to be the force of universal gravitation.

Thus Newton, again unlike Galileo, set out to 'demonstrate the System of the World', or – as we would say today – to show how the general laws of terrestrial motion may be applied to the planets and to their satellites.

In the first theorem of the *Principia* Newton showed that if a body were to move with a purely inertial motion, then with respect to any point not on the line of motion, the law of equal areas must apply. In other words, a line drawn from any such body to such a point will sweep out equal areas in equal times. Conceive a body moving with purely inertial motion along the straight line of which *PQ* is a segment. Then in a set of equal time intervals (fig. 1) the body will move through equal distances

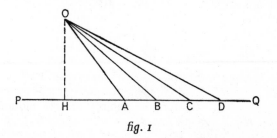

fig. 1

AB, *BC*, *DC*, ... because, as Galileo showed, in uniform motion a body moves through equal distances in equal times. But observe that a line from the point *O* sweeps out equal areas in these equal times, or that the areas of triangles *OAB*, *OBC*, *OCD*, ... are equal. The reason is that the area of a triangle is one-half the product of its altitude and its base; and all these triangles have the same altitude *OH* and equal bases. Since

$$AB = BC = CD = \ldots$$

it is true that

$$\tfrac{1}{2}AB \times OH = \tfrac{1}{2}BC \times OH = \tfrac{1}{2}CD \times OH = \ldots$$

or

area of $\triangle OAB$ = area of $\triangle OBC$ = area of $\triangle OCD = \ldots$

Thus the very first theorem proved in the *Principia* showed that purely inertial motion leads to a law of equal areas, and so is related to Kepler's second law. Newton then proved that if at regular intervals of time, a body moving with purely inertial motion were to receive a momentary impulse (a force acting for an instant only), all these impulses being directed toward the same point *S*, then the body would move in each of the equal time-intervals between impulses so that a line from it to *S* would sweep out equal areas. This situation is shown in figure 2. When the body reaches the point *B* it receives an impulse toward *S*. The new motion is a combination of the original motion along *AB* and a motion toward *S*, which produces a uniform rectilinear motion toward *C*, etc.: The triangles *SAB*, *SBC*, and *SCD* ... have the same area. The next step, according to Newton, is as follows:

... Now let the number of those triangles be augmented, and their breadth diminished *in infinitum*; and (by Cor. iv, Lem. iii) their ultimate perimeter *ADF* will be a curved line: and therefore the centripetal force, by which the body is con-

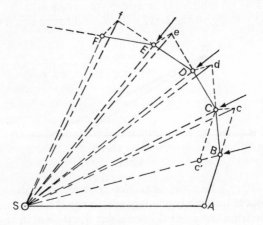

fig. 2. *If at* B *the body had received no impulse, it would, during time* T, *have moved along the continuation of* AB *to* c. *The impulse at* B, *however, gives the body a component of motion toward* S. *During* T *if the body's only motion came from that impulse, it would have moved from* B *to* c′. *The combination of these two movements,* Bc *and* Bc′, *results during time* T *in a movement from* B *To* C. *Newton proved that the area of the triangle* SBC *is equal to the area of the triangle* SBc. *Hence, even when there is an impulsive force directed toward* S, *the law of equal areas holds.*

tinually drawn back from the tangent of this curve, will act continually; and any described areas *SADS, SAFS,* which are always proportional to the times of description, will, in this case also, be proportional to those times. Q.E.D.

In this way Newton proceeded to prove:

PROPOSITION I. THEOREM I
The areas which revolving bodies describe by radii drawn to an immovable centre of force do lie in the same immovable planes, and are proportional to the times in which they are described.

In simple language, Newton proved in the first theorem of Book One of the *Principia* that if a body is continually drawn toward some center of force, its otherwise inertial motion will be transformed into motion along a curve, and that a line from the center of force to the body will sweep out equal areas in equal times. In Proposition II (Theorem II) he proved that if a body moves along a curve so that the areas described by a line from the body to any point are proportional to the times, there must be a 'central' (centripetal) force continuously urging the body toward that point. The significance of Kepler's Law II does not appear until Proposition XI when Newton sets out to find 'the law of the centripetal force tending to the focus of the ellipse'. This force varies 'inversely as the square of the distance'. Then Newton proves that if a body moving in an hyperbola or in a parabola is acted on by a centripetal force tending to the focus, the force still varies inversely as the distance. Several theorems later, in Proposition XVII, Newton proves the converse, that if a body moves subject to a centripetal force varying inversely as the square of the distance, the path of the body must be a conic section: an ellipse, a parabola, or hyperbola.

We may note that Newton has treated Kepler's laws exactly in the same order as Kepler himself: first the law of areas as a general theorem, and only later the particular shape of planetary orbits as ellipses. What seemed at first to be a rather odd way of proceeding has been shown to represent a fundamental logical progression of a kind that is the opposite of the sequence that would have been followed in an empirical or observational approach.

In Newton's reasoning about the action of a centripetal force on a body moving with purely inertial motion, mathematical analysis, for the first time, disclosed the true meaning of Kepler's 'second law' of equal areas! Newton's reasoning showed that this law implied a center of force for the motion of each planet. Since the equal areas in planetary motion are reckoned with respect to the sun, Kepler's second law becomes in Newton's treatment the basis for proving rigorously that a central force emanating from the sun attracts all the planets.

So much for the problem raised by Halley. Had Newton stopped his work at this point, we would still admire his achievement enormously. But Newton went on and the results were even more outstanding.

THE MASTER-STROKE: UNIVERSAL GRAVITATION

In Book Three of the *Principia*, Newton showed that as Jupiter's satellites move in orbits around their planet, a line from Jupiter to each satellite will 'describe areas proportional to the times of description' and that the ratio of the squares of their times to the cubes of their mean distances from the center of Jupiter is a constant, although a constant having a different value from the constant for the motion of the planets. Thus if T_1, T_2, T_3, T_4 be the periodic times of the satellites, and a_1, a_2, a_3, a_4 be their respective mean distances from Jupiter,

$$\frac{(a_1)^3}{(T_1)^2} = \frac{(a_2)^3}{(T_2)^2} = \frac{(a_3)^3}{(T_3)^2} = \frac{(a_4)^3}{(T_4)^2}$$

Not only do these laws of Kepler's apply to the Jovian system, but they also apply to the five satellites of Saturn known to Newton – a result wholly unknown to Kepler. The third law of Kepler could not be applied to the earth's moon because there is only one moon, but Newton did state that its motion accorded to the law of equal areas. Hence, one may see that there is a central force, varying as the inverse-square of the distance, that holds each planet to an orbit around the sun and each planetary satellite to an orbit around its planet.

Now Newton makes the master-stroke. He shows that a single universal force (a) keeps the planets in their orbits around the sun, (b) holds the satellites in their orbits, (c) causes falling objects to descend as observed, (d) holds objects on the earth, and (e) causes the tides. It is the force called *universal gravitation*, and its fundamental law may be written

$$F = G\,\frac{mm'}{D^2}$$

This law says that between any two bodies whatsoever, of masses m and m', wherever they may be in the universe, separated by a distance D, there is a force of attraction which is *mutual*, and each body attracts the other with a force of identical magnitude, which is *directly proportional to the product of the two masses and inversely proportional to the square of the distance between them*. G is a constant of proportionality, and it has the same value in all circumstances – whether in the mutual attraction of a stone and the earth, of the earth and the moon, of the sun and Jupiter, of one star and another, or of two pebbles on a beach. This constant G is called the *constant of universal gravitation* and may be compared to other 'universal' constants – of which there are not very many in the whole of science – such as c, the speed of light, which figures so prominently in Relativity, or h, Planck's constant, which is so basic in Quantum Theory.

How did Newton find his law? It is difficult to tell in detail, but we can reconstruct some of the basic aspects of the discovery. From a later memorandum (about 1714), we learn that

Newton as a young man 'began to think of gravity extending to the orb of the moon, and having found out how to estimate the force with which a globe revolving within a sphere presses the surface of the sphere, from Kepler's Rule of the periodical times of the planets being in a sesquialterate proportion [i.e., as the $\frac{3}{2}$ power] of their distances from the centres of their orbs, I deduced that the forces which keep the planets in their orbs must [be] reciprocally as the squares of their distances from the centres about which they revolve: and thereby compared the force requisite to keep the moon in her orb with the force of gravity at the surface of the earth, and found them answer [i.e., agree] pretty nearly.'

With this statement as guide, let us consider first a globe of mass m and speed v moving along a circle of radius r. Then, as Newton found out, and as the great Dutch physicist Christian Huygens (1629–95) also discovered (and to Newton's chagrin, published first), there must be a central acceleration, of magnitude v^2/r. That is, an acceleration follows from the fact that the globe is not at rest nor moving at constant speed in a straight line; from Law I and Law II, there must be a force and hence an acceleration. We shall not prove that this acceleration has a magnitude v^2/r, but that it is directed toward the center you can see if you whirl a ball in a circle at the end of a string. A force is needed to pull the ball constantly toward the center, and from Law II the acceleration must always have the same direction as the accelerating force. Thus for a planet of mass m, moving approximately in a circle of radius r at speed v, there must be a central force F of magnitude

$$F = mA = m\frac{v^2}{r}$$

If T is the period, or time for the planet to move through 360°, then in time T the planet moves once around a circle of radius r, or through a circumference of $2\pi r$. Hence the speed v is $2\pi r/T$, and

$$F = mA = mv^2 \times \frac{1}{r} = m\left[\frac{2\pi r}{T}\right]^2 \times \frac{1}{r}$$

$$= m \times \frac{4\pi^2 r^2}{T^2} \times \frac{1}{r}$$

$$= m \times \frac{4\pi^2 r^3}{T^2} \times \frac{1}{r} \times \frac{1}{r}$$

$$= \frac{4\pi^2 m \times r^3}{T^2 \times r^2} = \frac{4\pi^2 m}{r^2} \times \frac{r^3}{T^2}$$

Since for every planet in the solar system, r^3/T^2 has the same value K (by Kepler's rule or third law),

$$F = \frac{4\pi^2 m}{r^2} \times K = 4\pi^2 K \frac{m}{r^2}$$

The radius r of the circular orbit corresponds in reality to D the average distance of a planet from the sun. Hence, for any planet the law of force keeping it in its orbit must be

$$F = 4\pi^2 K \frac{m}{D^2}$$

where m is the mass of the planet, D is the average distance of the planet from the sun, K is 'Kepler's constant' for the solar system (equal to the cube of the mean distance of any planet from the sun divided by the square of its period of revolution), and F is the force with which the sun attracts the planet and draws it continually off its purely inertial path into an ellipse. Thus far mathematics and logic may lead a man of superior wit who knows the Newtonian laws of motion and the principles of circular motion.

But now we rewrite the equation as

$$F = \left[\frac{4\pi^2 K}{M_s} \right] \frac{M_s m}{D^2}$$

where M_s is the mass of the sun and say that the quantity

$$\frac{4\pi^2 K}{M_s} = G$$

is a *universal constant*, that the law

$$F = G \frac{M_s m}{D^2}$$

is not limited to the force between the sun and a planet. It applies also to every pair of objects in the universe, M_s and m becoming the masses m and m' of those two objects and D becoming the distance between them:

$$F = G \frac{mm'}{D^2}$$

There is no mathematics – whether algebra, geometry, or the calculus – to justify this bold step. One can say of it only that it is one of those triumphs that humble ordinary men in the presence of genius. And just think what this law implies. For instance, this book that you hold in your hands attracts the sun in a calculable degree; it is the same force that makes the moon follow its orbit and an apple fall from the tree. Late in life

Newton said it was this last comparison that inspired his great discovery.

The moon (see fig 3) if not attracted by the earth would have a purely inertial motion and in a small time t would move uniformly along a straight line (a tangent) from A to B. It does not, said Newton, because while its inertial motion would have carried it from A to B, the gravitational attraction of the earth

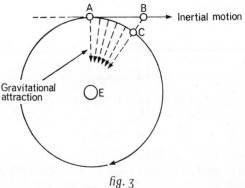

fig. 3

will have made it fall toward the earth from the line AB to C. Thus the moon's departure from a purely inertial rectilinear path is caused by its continual 'falling' toward the earth – and its falling is just like the falling of an apple. Is this true? Well, Newton put the proposition to a test, as follows:

Why does an apple of mass m fall to the earth? It does so, we may now say, because there is a force of universal gravitation between it and the earth, whose mass is M_e. But what is the distance between the earth and the apple? Is it the few feet from the apple to the ground? Newton eventually was able to prove that the attraction between a small object and a more or less homogeneous and more or less spherical body is exactly the same as if all the large mass of the body were concentrated at its geometric center. This theorem means that in considering the mutual attraction of earth and apple, the distance D in the law of universal gravitation may be taken to be the earth's radius, R_e. Hence the law states that the attraction between the earth and an apple is:

$$F = G \frac{mM_e}{R_e^2}$$

where m is the mass of the apple, M_e the mass of the earth and R_e the earth's radius. But this is an expression for the *weight* W of the apple, because the weight of any terrestrial object is merely the magnitude of the force with which it is gravitationally attracted by the earth. Thus,

$$W = G\frac{mM_e}{R_e^2}$$

There is a second way of writing an equation for the weight of an apple or of any other terrestrial object of mass m. We use Newton's Law II, which says that the mass m of any object is the ratio of the force acting on the object to the acceleration produced by that force,

$$m = \frac{F}{A}$$

or

$$F = mA$$

Note that when an apple falls from the tree, the force pulling it down is its weight W, so that

$$W = mA$$

Since we now have two different mathematical statements of the same force or weight W, they must be equal to each other, or

$$mA = G\frac{mM_e}{R_e^2}$$

and we can divide both sides by m to get

$$A = G\frac{M_e}{R_e^2}$$

So, by Newtonian principles, we have at once explained why at any spot on this earth all objects – whatever their mass m or weight W may be – will have the same acceleration A when they fall freely, as in a vacuum. The last equation shows that this acceleration of free fall is determined by the mass M_e and radius R_e of the earth and a universal constant G, none of which *depends in any way* on the particular mass m or weight W of the falling body.

Now let us write the last equation in a slightly different way,

$$A = G\frac{M_e}{D_e^2}$$

where D_e stands for the distance from the center of the earth. At or near the earth's surface D_e is merely the earth's radius R_e. Now consider a body placed at a distance D_e of 60 earth-radii from the earth's center. With what acceleration A' will it fall toward the center of the earth? The acceleration A' will be

$$A' = G\frac{M_e}{(60\,R_e)^2} = G\frac{M_e}{3600\,R_e^2} = \frac{1}{3600}\,G\frac{M_e}{R_e^2}$$

We just saw that at the surface of the earth an apple or any other object will have a downward acceleration equal to

$$G \frac{M_e}{R_e^2},$$

and now we have proved that an object at 60 earth-radii will have an acceleration just $\frac{1}{3600}$ of that value. On the average, a body at the earth's surface falls in one second toward the earth through a distance of 16·08 feet, so that out at a distance of 60 earth-radii from the earth's center a body should fall

$$\tfrac{1}{3600} \times 16\cdot08 \text{ feet} = \tfrac{1}{3600} \times 16\cdot08 \times 12 \text{ inches} = 0\cdot0536 \text{ inches}$$

It happens that there is a body out in space at a distance of 60 earth-radii and so Newton had a subject for testing his theory of universal gravitation. If the same gravitational force makes both the apple and the moon fall, then in one second the moon must have fallen through 0·0536 inches from its inertial path to stay on its orbit. A rough computation, based on the simplifying assumptions that the moon's orbit is a perfect circle and that the moon moves uniformly without being affected by the gravitational attraction of the sun, yields a distance fallen in one second of 0·0539 inches – or a remarkable agreement to within 0·0003 inches! Another way of seeing how closely observation agrees with theory is to observe that the two values differ by 3 parts in about 500, which is the same as 6 parts in 1000 or 0·6 parts per hundred (0·6 per cent). Another way of seeing how this calculation can be made (perhaps following the lead Newton himself gave in the quotation on page 117) is as follows:

1. For a body on earth (the apple)

$$g = \frac{GM_e}{R_e^2}$$

2. For the moon (Kepler's Third Law)

$$K = \frac{R_m^3}{T_m^2} = \frac{GM_e}{4\pi^2}$$

Then

$$G = \frac{4\pi^2 R_m^3}{R_e^2 T_m^2} = 4\pi^2 \left[\frac{R_m}{R_e}\right]^3 \frac{R_e}{T_m^2}$$

Put

$$\frac{R_m}{R_e} = 60, \quad R_e = 4{,}000 \times 5{,}280 \text{ feet}$$

$$T_m = 28d = 28 \times 24 \times 3600 \text{ sec}$$

Gives

$$G = 31 \text{ ft/sec}^2$$

Newton said, in the autobiographical memorandum I have quoted, that he 'compared the force requisite to keep the moon in her orb with the force of gravity at the surface of the earth'.

In Book III of the *Principia*, Newton shows that the moon, in order to keep along its observed orbit, falls away from its straight line inertial path, through a distance of $15\frac{1}{12}$ Paris feet (an old measure) in every minute. Imagine the moon, he says, 'deprived of all motion to be let go, so as to descend toward the earth with the impulse of all that force by which ... it is retained in its orb'. In one minute of time it will descend through the same distance that it does when this descent occurs together with the normal inertial motion. Next, assume that this motion toward the earth is due to gravity, a force that varies inversely as the square of the distance. Then, at the surface of the earth this force would be greater by a factor 60×60 than at the moon's orbit. Since the acceleration is by Newton's Second Law, proportional to the accelerating force, a body brought from the moon's orbit to the earth's surface would have an increase in its acceleration of 60×60. Thus, Newton argues, if gravity is a force varying inversely as the square of the distance, a body at the earth's surface should fall through a distance of $60 \times 60 \times 15\frac{1}{12}$ Paris feet in one minute, or $15\frac{1}{12}$ Paris feet in one second.

From Huygens's pendulum experiment Newton obtained the result that on earth (at the latitude of Paris) a body falls just about that far. Thus it is proved that it is the force of the earth's gravity that retains the moon in its orbit. In making the computation, Newton predicted from observations of the moon's motion and from gravitation theory that the distance fallen by a body on earth in one second would be 15 Paris feet, 1 inch and $1\frac{4}{9}$ lines (1 line = $\frac{1}{12}$ inch). Huygen's result for free fall at Paris was 15 Paris feet, 1 inch, $1\frac{7}{9}$ lines. The difference was $\frac{3}{9}$ or $\frac{1}{3}$ of a line and hence $\frac{1}{36}$ of an inch – a very small number indeed. By the time he wrote the *Principia*, he had found a far better agreement theory and observation than in that rough test he had made twenty years earlier.

Newton said that in this test observation agreed with prediction 'pretty nearly'. Two factors were involved. First, he chose a poor value of the earth's radius and so obtained bad numerical results, agreeing only roughly or 'pretty nearly'. Second, since he had not then been able to prove rigorously that a homogeneous sphere attracts gravitationally as if all its mass were concentrated at its center, the proof was at best rough and approximate.

But this test proved to Newton that his concept of universal gravitation was valid. You can appreciate how remarkable it was when you consider the nature of the constant G. We saw earlier that

$$G = \frac{4\pi^2 K}{M_s}$$

and we may well ask what either K (the cube of any planet's distance from the sun divided by the square of the periodic time of that planet's revolution about the sun) or M_s (the mass of the sun) has to do with either the earth's pull on a stone or the earth's pull on the moon. If the fact that the earth happens to be within the solar system lessens the wonder that G should apply to the stone and the moon, consider a system of double stars located millions of light-years away from the solar system. Such a pair of stars may form an eclipsing binary, in which one of the stars encircles the other as the moon encircles the earth. Way out there, beyond any possible influence of the sun, the same constant

$$G = \frac{4\pi^2 K}{M_s}$$

applies to the attraction of each of the stars by the other. This is a universal constant *in spite of the fact* that in the form in which Newton discovered it, it was based on elements in *our solar system*. Evidently, the act of dividing the Kepler constant by the mass of the central body about which the others revolve eliminates any special aspects of that particular system – whether of planets revolving about Jupiter or Saturn.

THE DIMENSIONS OF THE ACHIEVEMENT

A few further achievements of Newtonian dynamics, or gravitation theory, will enable us to comprehend its heroic dimensions. Suppose the earth were not quite a perfect sphere, but were oblate – flattened at the poles and bulging at the equator. Consider now the acceleration A of a freely falling body at a pole, at the equator and at two intermediate points a and b. Clearly the 'radius' R of the earth, or distance from the center, would increase from the pole to the equator, so that

$$R_p < R_b < R_a < R_e$$

As a result the acceleration A of free fall at those places would have different values:

$$A_p = G\frac{M_e}{R_p^2}; \; A_b = G\frac{M_e}{R_b^2}; \; A_a = \frac{M_e}{R_a^2}; \; A_e = \frac{M_e}{R_e^2}$$

so that

$$A_p > A_b > A_a > A_e$$

The following data, obtained from actual experiment, show the acceleration varies with latitude:

Latitude	Acceleration of free fall	
0° (equator)	978·039 cm/sec²	32·0878 ft/sec·
20°	978·641	32·1076
40°	980·171	32·1578
90°	981·918	32·2151
60	983·217	32·2577

In Newton's day, the acceleration of free fall was found by determining the length of a seconds pendulum – one that has a period of 2 seconds. The equation for the period T of a common pendulum swinging through a short arc is

$$T = 2\pi\sqrt{\frac{l}{g}}$$

where l is the length of the pendulum (computed from the point of support to the center of the bob) and g is the acceleration of free fall. Halley found that when he went from London to St Helena it was necessary to shorten the length of his pendulum in order to have it continue to beat seconds. Newton's mechanics not only explains this variation, but it leads to a prediction of the shape of the earth, an oblate spheroid, flattened at the poles and bulging at the equator.

The variations in g, the acceleration of free fall, lead to variations in the weight of any physical object transported from one latitude to another. A complete analysis of this variation in weight requires the consideration of a second factor, the force arising from the rotation of the object along with the earth. The factor that enters here is v^2/r where v is the linear speed along a circle and r the circle's radius. At different latitudes, there will be different values of both v and r. Furthermore, to relate the rotational effect to weight, a component must be taken along a line from the center of the earth to the position in question, since the rotational effect occurs in the plane of circular motion, or along a parallel of latitude. It is because of these rotational forces that the earth, according to Newtonian physics, acquired its shape.

A second consequence of the equatorial bulge is the precession of the equinoxes. In actual fact, the difference between the polar and equatorial radii of the earth may not seem very great

equatorial radius = 6378·388 km = 3963·44 miles
polar radius = 6356·909 km = 3949·99 miles

But if we represent the earth with an 18-inch globe, the difference between the smallest and greatest diameters would be about

$\frac{1}{16}$ of an inch. Newton showed that precession occurs because the earth is spinning on an axis inclined to the plane of its orbit, the plane of the ecliptic. In addition to the gravitational attraction that keeps the earth in its orbit, the sun exerts a pull on the bulge, thus tending to straighten the axis. The sun tends to make the earth's axis perpendicular to the plane of the ecliptic (fig. 4A)

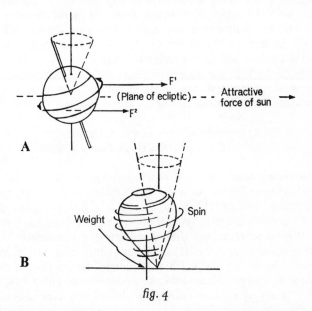

fig. 4

or make the plane of the bulge coincide with the plane of the ecliptic. At the same time the moon's pull tends to make the plane of the bulge coincide with the plane of its orbit (inclined at about 5° to the plane of the ecliptic). If the earth were a perfect sphere the pull on it of sun or moon would be symmetrical and there would be no tendency for the axis of rotation to 'straighten out'; the lines of action of the gravitational pulls of sun and moon would pass through the earth's center.

Now it is a result in Newtonian physics that if a force is exerted so as to change the orientation of the axis of a spinning body, the effect will be that the axis itself, rather than changing its orientation, will undergo a conical motion. This effect may be seen in a spinning top. The axis of rotation is usually not absolutely vertical. The weight of the top tends therefore to turn the axis about the spinning point so as to make the axis horizontal. The weight tends to produce a rotation whose axis is at right angles to that of the top's spin, and the result is the conical motion of the axis shown in figure 4B. The phenomenon of precession had been known since its discovery in the second century

B.C. by Hipparchus, but its cause had been wholly unknown before Newton. Newton's explanation not only resolved an ancient
mystery, but was an example of how one could predict the
precise shape of the earth by applying theory to astronomical
observations. Newton's predictions were verified when the French
mathematician Pierre L. M. de Maupertuis measured the length of
a degree of arc along a meridian in Lapland and compared the
result with the length of a degree along the meridian nearer the
equator. The result was an impressive victory for the new science.

Yet another achievement of the Newtonian theory was a
general explanation of the tides relating them to gravitational
action of the sun and moon on the waters of the oceans. We
may well understand the spirit of admiration that inspired
Alexander Pope's famous couplet

> Nature and Nature's Laws lay hid in night
> God said, Let Newton be, and all was light.

In seeing how the Newtonian mechanics enabled man to
explain the motions of planets, moons, falling stones, tides, trains,
automobiles, and anything else that is accelerated – speeded up,
slowed down, started in its motion or stopped – we have solved
our original problem. But there remain one or two items that require a word or so more. It is true, as Galileo observed, that for
ordinary bodies on the earth (which may be considered as revolving in a large elliptic orbit at an average distance from the
sun of about 93 million miles), the situation is very much like
being on something that is moving in a straight line, and there
is an indifference to uniform rectilinear motion and to rest so
far as all the dynamical problems are concerned. On the rotating
earth, where the arc during any time interval such as the flight
of a bullet is a part of a 'circle' smaller than the annual orbit,
another Newtonian kind of principle can be invoked, the principle of the conservation of angular momentum.

The angular momentum of a small object rotating in a circle
(as a stone held on the top of a tower on a rotating earth) is given
by the expression mvr where r is the radius of rotation, m the
mass, and v the speed along the circle. The principle says that
under a large variety of conditions (specifically, in all circumstances in which there is no external force of a special kind), the
angular momentum remains constant.

An example may be given. A man stands on a whirling plat-
form, with his arms outstretched and clutching a 10-pound
weight in each hand. He is set whirling slowly on the turntable
and then is told to bring his hands in toward his body along a
horizontal plane so that he looks like figure 5. He finds that he
spins faster and faster. Stretching his arms out once again will

fig. 5

slow him down. For anyone who has never seen such a demon-stration before (it is a standard figure in ice skating) the first encounter can be quite startling. Now let us see why these changes occurred. The speed v with which the masses m held in his hands move around is

$$v = \frac{2\pi r}{t}$$

where t is the time for a complete rotation, during which each mass m moves through a circumference of a circle of radius r. At first the angular momentum is

$$mvr = m \times \frac{2\pi r}{t} \times r = \frac{2\pi m r^2}{t}$$

But as the man brings his arms in to his chest he makes r very much smaller. If

$$\frac{2\pi m r^2}{t}$$

is to keep the same value, as the law of conservation demands, then t must get smaller too, which means that the time for a revolution becomes smaller as r diminishes.

What has this to do with a stone falling from a tower? At the top of the tower the radius of rotation is $R + r$ where R is the radius of the earth and r the height of the tower. When the stone strikes the ground, the radius of rotation is R. Therefore, like the masses drawn inward by the whirling mass, the stone must be moving around in a smaller circle when at the base of the tower than at the top, and so will whirl more quickly. Far from being left behind, the stone, according to our theory, should get a little ahead of the tower. How great an effect is this? Since the problem depends on t, the time for a rotation through 360°, we can get a much better idea of the magnitude of the problem if we study the angular speed than if we consider some linear speed. Look at the hands of a moving clock, paying particular attention to the hour hand. By how much does it appear to shift in, say, five minutes, which corresponds to dropping a ball from a much greater height than the Empire State Building? Not by any discernible degree. Now the rotation of the earth through 360° takes just twice as much time as a complete rotation of the hour hand (12 hours). Since in five minutes the angular motion or rotation of the hour hand is not discernible to the un-aided eye, a motion that is twice as slow produces practically no effect. Except in problems of long-range artillery firing, analy-sis of the movements of the trade winds and other phenomena on a vastly larger scale than the fall of a stone, we may neglect the earth's rotation.

Such was the great Newtonian revolution, which altered the whole structure of science and, indeed, turned the course of Western civilization. How has it fared in the last hundred years? Is the Newtonian mechanics still true?

All too often the misleading statement is made that Relativity theory has shown classical dynamics to be false. Nothing could be further from the truth! Relativistic corrections apply to objects moving at speeds v for which the ratio v/c is a significant quantity, c being the speed of light, or 186,000 miles per second. At the speeds attained in linear accelerators, cyclotrons, and other devices for studying atomic and sub-atomic particles, it is no longer true that the mass m of a physical object remains con-stant. Rather, it is found that the mass in motion is given by the equation

$$m = \frac{m_0}{\sqrt{1 - v^2/c^2}}$$

where m is the mass of an object moving at a speed v relative to the observer and m_0 is the mass of that same object observed at rest. Along with this revision goes Albert Einstein's now familiar equation relating mass and energy, $E = mc^2$, and the denial of the validity of Newton's belief in an 'absolute' space and an 'absolute' time. Well then, might we agree with the new couplet added by J. C. Squire to the one of Pope's we have quoted?

> It did not last; the Devil howling 'Ho,
> Let Einstein be', restored the status quo.

But for the whole range of problems discussed by Newton the motion of stars, planets, moons, airplanes, automobiles, base-v attainable are such that v/c has to all intents and purposes balls, rockets, and every other type of gross body – the speeds the value zero and we can still apply Newtonian dynamics without correction. (There is one example of a failure of Newtonian physics: a very small error in predicting the advance of the perihelion of Mercury – 40" per century! – for which we need to invoke Relativity theory.) Hence for engineering and all physics except a portion of atomic and subatomic physics, it is still the Newtonian physics that explains occurrences in the external world.

While it is true that the Newtonian mechanics is still applicable in the range of phenomena for which it was intended, the student should not make the mistake of thinking that the framework in which the system originally was set is equally valid. Newton believed that there *was* a sense in which space and time were 'absolute' physical entities. Any deep analysis of his writings shows how in his mind his discoveries depended on these 'absolutes'. To be sure, Newton was aware that clocks do not measure absolute time, but only local time, and that we deal in our experiments with local space rather than absolute space. Thus he actually developed not merely a law of gravitational force and a system of rules for computing the answers to problems in mechanics but constructed a complete system based on a world view.

Today, following the Michelson–Morley experiment and Relativity, that world view can no longer be considered a valid basis for physical science, and the Newtonian principles are considered to be only a special, though extremely important, case of a more general system.

Some scientists hold that one of the greatest validations of Newtonian physics has been the set of predictions concerning satellite motions; they have enabled man to launch into orbit a series of artificial moons and to predict what will happen to them out in space. This may be so, but to the historian the greatest achievement of Newtonian science must ever be the first full explanation of the universe on mechanical principles – one set of axioms and a law of universal gravitation that applied to all matter everywhere: on earth as in the heavens. Newton recognized that the one example in nature in which there is pure inertial motion going on and on and on without frictional or other interference to bring it to a halt is the orbital motion of moons and planets. And yet this is not a uniform or unchanging motion along a single straight line, but rather along a constantly changing straight line, because planetary motions are a compounding of inertial motion with a continuing falling away from it. To see that moons and planets exemplify pure inertial motion required the same genius necessary to realize that the planetary law could be generalized into a law of universal attraction for all matter and that the motion of the moon partakes of the motion of the falling apple.

In Newton's genius we see the full significance of both Galilean mechanics and Kepler's laws of planetary motion realized in the development of the inertial principles required for the Copernican–Keplerian universe. A great French mathematician, Joseph Louis Lagrange (1736–1813), best defined Newton's achievement. There is only one law of the universe, he said, and Newton discovered it. Newton did not develop modern dynamics all by himself but depended heavily on certain of his predecessors; the debt in no way lessens the magnitude of his achievement. It only emphasizes the importance of such men as Galileo and Kepler and Huygens, who were great enough to make significant contributions to the Newtonian enterprise. Above all, we may see in Newton's work the degree to which science is a collective and a cumulative activity and we may find in it the measure of the influence of an individual genius on the future of a cooperative scientific effort. In Newton's achievement we see how science advances by heroic exercises of the imagination rather than by patient collecting and sorting of myriads of individual facts. Who, after studying Newton's magnificent contribution to thought, could deny that pure science exemplifies the creative accomplishment of the human spirit at its pinnacle?

6 The Metaphysics of Newton*

E. A. Burtt

Thus far the metaphysical ideas of Newton which we have been investigating exemplify in the main the first and second of the three types distinguished in Section 2 of the present chapter.† They are either appropriated uncritically from the scientific tide of the day or rest upon some feature of his method for their final justification. His treatment of space and time, however, has led us by anticipation into the importance of his ultimately theistic interpretation of the universe, and now as we face the latter more directly it will be helpful first to note that his theological views represent predominantly a metaphysical element of the third type. Religion was a fundamental interest to Newton. It dealt with a realm for the most part different from the object of science; its method was quite disparate, for its conclusions, in the main, were insusceptible of proof or disproof by scientific standards. To be sure, Newton was confident, as we shall see, that certain empirical facts open to anybody's observation, implied unqualifiedly the existence of a God of a certain definite nature and function. God was not detached from the world that science seeks to know; indeed, every true step in natural philosophy brings us nearer to a knowledge of the first cause,[1] and is for this reason to be highly valued – it will enlarge the bounds of moral philosophy also, inasmuch as 'so far as we can know by natural philosophy what is the first cause, what power he has over us, and what benefits we receive from him, so far our duty towards him, as well as that towards one another, will appear to us by the light of nature'.[2] So, although religion and science are fundamentally different interpretations of the universe, each valid in its own way, yet for Newton in the last analysis, the realm of science was dependent on the God of re-

*E. A. Burtt, 'The Metaphysics of Newton', in *The Metaphysical Foundations of Modern Physical Science*, Routledge and Kegan Paul, 2nd revised edn, 1932.
† Omitted – *Ed.*
[1] *Opticks*, p. 345.
[2] *Opticks*, p. 381.

ligion, and led the reverent mind to a fuller assurance of his reality and a readier obedience to his commands. Thus in spite of their incommensurable character and his considerable success in banning religious prejudices from his positive scientific theorems, the fact that God's existence and control was never questioned by the man who wrote almost as many theological dissertations as scientific classics had its strong and significant reactions on positions which he would have called purely scientific.

NEWTON AS THEOLOGIAN

Newton's place in the religious unsettlement of his era would be an interesting topic for studious application. He was accused by the ultra orthodox of being an Arian, apparently on ample grounds. Among other heretical suggestions, he wrote a brief essay on *Two Notable Corruptions of Scripture*,[3] in each case the effect of his thesis being to cast doubt on the traditional assumption that the doctrine of the Trinity was taught in the New Testament. A strongly Arian flavour pervades most of his theological efforts, from which we shall take a quotation or two for another purpose, namely to show that religion was something quite basic to him and in no sense a mere appendage to his science or an accidental addition to his metaphysics. Newton believed that scientific fact involved theism, but he would have been a theist had his scientific powers remained forever dormant. Newton evidently cherished a kind of religious experience, nourished largely, of course, by tradition, that was in the main detachable from the theism postulated as a corollary to science. This fact has its relevant bearings on his clear and continued conviction that the world of science is by no means the whole world.

> We are, therefore, to acknowledge one God, infinite, eternal, omnipresent, omniscient, omnipotent, the creator of all things, most wise, most just, most good, most holy. We must love him, fear him, honour him, trust in him, pray to him, give him thanks, praise him, hallow his name, obey his commandments, and set times apart for his service, as we are directed in the third and fourth Commandments, for this is the love of God, that we keep his commandments, and his commandments are not grievous. I John, v, 3. And these things we must do not to any mediators between him and us, but to him alone, that he may give his angels charge over us, who, being our fellow-servants, are pleased with the worship we give to their God. And this is the first and the principal part of re-

[3] *Opera*, Vol. V.

ligion. This always was, and always will be the religion of God's people, from the beginning to the end of the world.[4]

Newton's longer theological treaties, such as the *Observations on the Prophecies*,[5] but confirm these indications that he was a pious, believing Christian in all that the term then implied, as well as a master scientist.[6] His Arianism was radical for the age,

[4] Brewster, II, 348 ff.
[5] *Opera*, Vol. V.
[6] From a manuscript entitled, *On our Religion to God, to Christ, and the Church*, Brewster, II, 349 ff., the following excerpts are illustrative:

'There is one God, the Father, ever living, omnipresent, omniscient, almighty, the maker of heaven and earth, and one Mediator between God and man, the man Christ Jesus....

'The Father is omniscient, and hath all knowledge originally in his own breast, and communicates knowledge of future things to Jesus Christ; and none in heaven or earth, or under the earth, is worthy to receive knowledge of future things immediately from the Father but the Lamb. And therefore the testimony of Jesus is the spirit of prophecy, and Jesus is the Word or Prophet of God....

'We are to return thanks to the Father alone for creating us, and giving us food and raiment and other blessings of this life, and whatsoever we are to thank him for, or desire that he would do for us, we ask of him immediately in the name of Christ....

'To us there is but one God, the Father, of whom are all things, and one Lord Jesus Christ, by whom are all things, and we by him. That is, we are to worship the Father alone as God Almighty, and Jesus alone as the Lord, the Messiah, the Great King, the Lamb of God who was slain, and hath redeemed us with his blood, and made us kings and priests.'

In a very interesting tract on church union, Brewster, II, 526 ff., Newton adds to his propaganda as a pioneer in that field some propositions on church government:

'It is therefore the duty of bishops and presbyters to govern the people according to the laws of God and the laws of the king, and in their councils to punish offenders according to those laws, and to teach those who do not know the laws of God; but not to make new laws in the name of either God or the king.

'The Church is constituted and her extent and bounds of communion are defined by the laws of God, and these laws are unchangeable.

'The laws of the king extend only to things that are left indifferent and undetermined by the laws of God, and particularly to the revenues and tranquillity of the church, to her courts of justice, and to decency and order in her worship; and all laws about things left indifferent by the laws of God ought to be referred to the civil government....

'To impose any article of communion not imposed from the beginning is a crime of the same nature with that of those Christians of the circumcision who endeavoured to impose circumcision and the observation of the law upon the converted Gentiles. For the law was good if a man could keep it, but we were to be saved not by the works of the law, but by faith in Jesus Christ, and to impose those works as articles of communion, was to make them necessary to salvation, and thereby to make void the faith in Jesus Christ. And there is the same reason against imposing any other article of communion which was not imposed from the beginning. All such impositions are teaching another gospel....

'After baptism we are to live according to the laws of God and the king,

but it did not prevent his approaching the world of science under the necessity of seeing it cloaked by a divine glory and suffused with the religious significance that followed from the conviction that it had been created and ordered by the hands of the God who had been worshipped from his youth as Father of the Christian Saviour and infallible Author of the Christian Scriptures.

Parented in part by this traditional religious indoctrination and experience, in part thrust upon him, as it seemed, by indubitable evidences of intelligent purpose in the cosmic order, the now familiar arguments for the divine origin of the world are spread forth upon the pages of his classic works.

The main business of natural philosophy is to argue from phenomena without feigning hypotheses, and to deduce causes from effects, till we come to the very first cause, which certainly is not mechanical; and not only to unfold the mechanism of the world, but chiefly to resolve these and such like questions. What is there in places almost empty of matter, and whence is it that the sun and planets gravitate towards one another, without dense matter between them? Whence is it that nature doth nothing in vain; and whence arises all that order and beauty which we see in the world? To what end are comets, and whence is it that planets move all one and the same way in orbs concentric, while comets move all manner of ways in orbs very eccentric, and what hinders the fixed stars from falling upon one another? How came the bodies of animals to be contrived with so much art, and for what ends were their several parts?[7] Was the eye contrived without skill in optics, or the ear without knowledge of sounds? How do the motions of the body follow from the will, and whence is the instinct in animals? Is not the sensory of animals that place to which the sensitive substance is present, and into which the sensible species of things are carried through the nerves and brain, that there they may be perceived by their immediate presence to that substance? And these things being rightly dispatched, does it not appear from phenomena that there is a being incorporeal, living, intelligent, omnipresent, who, in infinite space, as it were in his sensory, sees the things themselves intimately, and thoroughly perceives them; and comprehends them wholly by their immediate presence to himself?[8]

---

and to grow in grace and in the knowledge of our Lord Jesus Christ, by practising what we promised before baptism, and studying the Scriptures, and teaching one another in meekness and charity, without imposing their private opinions, or falling out about them.'

[7] Cf. also *Principles*, II, 313; *Opticks*, pp. 378 ff.

[8] *Opticks*, pp. 344 ff.

Here facts whose ultimate causality Newton usually ascribed to the ether seem to be regarded as the direct operation of God, such as gravity and the production of bodily motion by the will. Likewise the theological grounding of the postulate of the simplicity of nature is notable, aligning Newton in this respect with his great scientific forbears. Of these teleological arguments the most cogent to Newton's own mind, and one which he never tired of stressing, reflects his thorough acquaintance with the phenomena of the celestial system – that is, the fact that 'planets move all one and the same way in orbs concentric, while comets move all manner of ways in orbs very eccentric'.[9] In his first letter to Dr Bentley, on the occasion of the latter's tenure of the Boyle lectureship in 1692, this argument is developed in some detail. Bentley had written to Newton, outlining a vast cosmic hypothesis of the creation of the universe from matter evenly dispersed throughout all space, on certain points of which he requested Newton's advice because he had deduced it, as he believed, from Newtonian principles. The latter's reply approved the main features of the scheme, but devoted itself especially to the above argument.

Sir; When I wrote my treatise about our system, I had an eye upon such principles as might work with considering men, for the belief of a Deity; and nothing can rejoice me more than to find it useful for that purpose. But if I have done the public any service this way, it is due to nothing but industry and patient thought. . . .

The same power, whether natural or supernatural, which placed the sun in the centre of the six primary planets, placed *Saturn* in the centre of the orbs of his five secondary planets; and *Jupiter* in the centre of his four secondary planets; and the earth in the centre of the moon's orb; and therefore, had this cause been a blind one without contrivance or design, the sun would have been a body of the same kind with *Saturn*, *Jupiter*, and the earth; that is without light or heat. Why there is one body in our system qualified to give light and heat to all the rest, I know no reason, but because the author of the system thought it convenient: and why there is but one body of this kind, I know no reason, but because one was sufficient to warm and enlighten all the rest. For the Cartesian hypothesis of suns losing their light, and their turning into comets, and comets into planets, can have no place in my system, and is plainly erroneous: because it is certain, that as often as they appear to us, they descended into the system of our planets, lower than the orb of *Jupiter*, and sometimes lower than the orbs of *Venus* and *Mercury*; and yet never

[9] Cf. *Opticks*, p. 378; *Principles*, II, 310.

stay here, but always return from the sun with the same degrees of motion by which they approached him.

To your second query I answer, that the motions, which the planets now have, could not spring from any natural cause alone, but were impressed by an intelligent agent. For since comets descend into the region of our planets, and here move all manner of ways, going sometimes the same way with the planets, sometimes the contrary way, and sometimes in crossways, their planes inclined to the plane of the ecliptic, and at all kinds of angles, it is plain that there is no natural cause which could determine all the planets, both primary and secondary, to move the same way and in the same plane, without any considerable variation: this must have been the effect of counsel. Nor is there any natural cause which could give the planets those just degrees of velocity, in proportion to their distances from the sun, and other central bodies, which were requisite to make them move in such concentric orbs about those bodies. Had the planets been as swift as comets ... or had the distances from the centres, about which they move, been greater or less ... or had the quantity of matter in the sun, or in *Saturn*, *Jupiter*, and the earth, and by consequence their gravitating power, been greater or less than it is; the primary planets could not have revolved about the sun, nor the secondary ones about *Saturn*, *Jupiter*, and the earth, in concentric circles as they do, but would have moved in hyperbolas or parabolas, or in ellipses very eccentric. To make this system, therefore, with all its motions, required a cause which understood, and compared together the quantities of matter in the several bodies of the sun and planets, and the gravitating powers resulting from thence; the several distances of the primary planets from the sun, and of the secondary ones from *Saturn*, *Jupiter*, and the earth; and the velocities, with which these planets could revolve about those quantities of matter in the central bodies; and to compare and adjust all these things together in so great a variety of bodies, argues that cause to be not blind or fortuitous, but very well skilled in mechanics and geometry.[10]

That Newton does not allow his teleology to run riot is evidenced by the concluding paragraphs of this interesting argument for the creation of the solar system by an expert mathematician. Dr Bentley, in his zealous quest for theistic evidences, had suggested the inclination of the earth's axis as an additional proof. Newton thought that this was overdoing the matter, unless the reasoning be cautiously guarded.

[10] *Opera*, IV, 429 ff.

Lastly, I see nothing extraordinary in the inclination of the earth's axis for proving a Deity; unless you will urge it as a contrivance for winter and summer, and for making the earth habitable towards the poles; and that the diurnal rotations of the sun and planets, as they could hardly arise from any cause purely mechanical, so by being determined all the same way with the annual and menstrual motions, they seem to make up that harmony in the system, which, as I explained above, was the effect of choice, rather than chance.

There is yet another argument for a Deity, which I take to be a very strong one; but till the principles on which it is grounded are better received, I think it more advisable to let it sleep.

There is nothing in Newton's later writings to indicate whether any of the arguments there advanced is the one here withheld from Dr Bentley's apologetic zest.

Several times in his Bentley letters Newton took occasion to object to the doctor's assumption that gravity is an essential quality of bodies. This his own experimental principles had led him to refuse to do, as we noted in Section 4.[11] At the same time the prestige of his law of gravitation, and its apparent universality in the world of matter, had encouraged a general impression that gravity was innate in matter according to Newtonian principles, an impression that was further advanced by Cotes's explicit championship of the doctrine in his preface to the second edition of the Principia. 'You sometimes speak of gravity as essential and inherent to matter. Pray do not ascribe that notion to me; for the cause of gravity is what I do not pretend to know, and therefore would take more time to consider it.[12] Nevertheless, Newton held the phenomena to be such, that even with innate gravity the matter of the solar system could not have taken its present form alone; 'gravity may put the planets into motion, but without the divine power it could never put them into such a circulating motion, as they have about the sun';[13] furthermore, if there be innate gravity, it is impossible now for the matter of the earth and all the planets and stars to fly up from them, and become evenly spread throughout all the heavens, without a supernatural power, and certainly that which can never be hereafter without a supernatural power, could never be heretofore without the same power'.[14] Hence, whether with gravity essential to bodies or without, a divine creation is implied.

---

[11] Cf. Principles, II, 161 ff.; 313.
[12] Opera, IV, 437.
[13] Opera, IV, 436 ff.; 439.
[14] Opera, IV, 441.

GOD'S PRESENT DUTIES IN THE COSMIC ECONOMY

Newton thus, because of his powerful religious heritage and with a keen sense for all the facts of order and adaptation in the world, supports with all the vigour of his authoritative pen the view currently accepted by all parties of the ultimately religious genesis of the universe. God originally created masses and set them in motion; likewise the space and time in which they move, as we saw, he constitutes by his presence and continued existence. He is responsible for that intelligent order and regular harmony in the structure of things that makes them the object of exact knowledge and of reverent contemplation. It is when we inquire into the subsequent relations of the Deity to his handiwork that we fall upon those elements in Newton's theology that became of the most profound historical significance. It will be remembered that none of his predecessors among the mechanical interpreters of nature had ventured to be fully consistent in the conception of the world as a mathematical machine. It seemed either impious or dangerous to detach God from continued connexion with the object of his past creative activity. Thus Descartes, for all his mechanical enthusiasm, spoke of God as maintaining the vast machine by his 'general concourse', and even of recreating it constantly because of the supposed discreteness of temporal moments. By More the term 'mechanical' was practically confined to the principle of inertia, God being either directly or indirectly responsible for those further principles in virtue of which things were actively held together in a circulating system. Boyle, in spite of his frequent comparison of the world to the Strassburg clock, piously reiterated the 'general concourse' of Descartes, though without indicating what meaning might be contained in the phrase, and attempted an analysis of the various ways in which God might be said to exert a present providence over the fruit of his labours. It is in Huyghens and Leibniz that we first meet spirits adventurous enough openly to confine the divine activity to the first creation alone, and the latter contemptuously criticized his English contemporaries for insulting the Deity by the insinuation that he had been unable to make a perfect machine at the beginning, but was under the necessity of tinkering with it from time to time in order to keep it in running condition. 'According to their doctrine, God Almighty wants to wind up his watch from time to time, otherwise it would cease to move. He had not, it seems, sufficient foresight to make it a perpetual motion. Nay, the machine of God's making is so imperfect according to these gentlemen, that he is obliged to clean it now and then by an extraordinary concourse, and even to mend it as a clockmaker mends his work; who must consequently be so much the more unskilful a workman, as he is oftener obliged to mend his work and set it right. According to my opinion, the same force and vigour remains always in the world, and only passes from one part of matter to another, agreeably to the laws of nature and the beautiful pre-established order. And I hold that when God works miracles, he does not do it in order to supply the wants of nature, but those of grace. Whoever thinks otherwise, must needs have a very mean notion of the wisdom and power of God.[15]

Now from Newton's writings, as from Boyle's, it is possible to pick passage after passage in which it seems to be assumed that after its first construction the world of nature has been quite independent of God for its continued existence and motion. The world could not have arisen out of a chaos by the mere laws of nature, 'though being once formed, it may continue by those laws for many ages';[16] the frame of nature may be a condensation of various ethereal spirits, 'and after condensation wrought into various forms, at first by the immediate hand of the Creator, and ever since by the power of nature, which, by virtue of the command, increase and multiply, became a complete imitator of the copy set her by the Protoplast';[17] 'in him are all things contained and moved, yet neither affects the other – God suffers nothing from the motion of bodies, bodies find no resistance from the omnipresence of God'.[18] But when we investigate more thoroughly we find that he, no more than Boyle, had any intention of really divorcing God from present control of, and occasional interference with, his vast engine. It is not enough to have the miracles of scripture and the achievements of spiritual grace to appeal to as evidences of continued divine contact with the realm of human affairs. God must also be given a present function in the cosmos at large; we must not allow him to abandon his toils after six days of constructive labour and leave the world of matter to its own devices. Newton's religious prejudices and his aesthetico-scientific assumptions alike arose in rebellion against such an indeterminate vacation for the Deity.

It is noticeable that Newton, in common with the whole voluntaristic British tradition in medieval and modern philosophy, tended to subordinate in God the intellect to the will; above the Creator's wisdom and knowledge is to be stressed his power and dominion. In some passages this emphasis is not present, but usually the proportions are unmistakable. The famous paragraph on the nature of the Deity in the second edition of the *Principia* is the most striking example:

[15] Brewster, II, 285.
[16] *Opticks*, p. 378.
[17] Brewster, I, 392.
[18] *Principles*, II, 311.

This Being governs all things, not as the soul of the world, but as Lord over all; and on account of his dominion he is wont to be called Lord God παντοκράτωρ, or *Universal Ruler* .. The Supreme God is a Being eternal, infinite, absolutely perfect; but a being, however perfect, without dominion, cannot be said to be Lord God. ... It is the dominion of a spiritual being which constitutes a God: a true, supreme, or imaginary dominion makes a true, supreme, or imaginary God. And from his true dominion it follows that the true God is a living, intelligent, and powerful Being; and from his other perfections, that he is supreme, or most perfect ... We know him only by his most wise and excellent contrivances of things, and final causes; we admire him for his perfections; but we reverence and adore him on account of his dominion; for we adore him as his servants; and a god without dominion, providence, and final causes, is nothing else but Fate and Nature.... And thus much concerning God; to discourse of whom from the appearances of things does certainly belong to natural philosophy.[19]

Absurd indeed it would be to deprive a being so portrayed of present control of his creation; accordingly we find Newton assigning to God two very important and specific duties in the daily cosmic economy. For one thing, he actively prevents the fixed stars from collapsing together in the middle of space. This is not taught in the *Principia*; Newton there had confined himself to observing that in order to prevent such a collapse God had set these stars at immense distances from one another.[20] Of course, this expedient would hardly suffice through all the ages of time, hence the reader of Newton is surprised that his author nowhere cites this difficulty as a reason for not imputing gravity to matter beyond the reach of our experimental observations: if the fixed stars do not gravitate, obviously there is no problem. We discover, however, that Newton implicitly thinks of them as possessing gravity, for in the *Opticks* and the third letter to Bentley he assigns it as one of the divine functions constantly to maintain them at their proper intervals.[21] In the former note the question: 'what hinders the fixed stars from falling upon one another?' In the latter, after approving, in the main, Bentley's creation hypothesis, he adds: 'And though the matter were divided at first into several systems, and every system by a divine power constituted like ours; yet would the outside systems descend towards the middlemost; so that this frame of things could not always subsist without a divine power to conserve it....'

In the final query of the *Opticks*, however, we find God made

[19] *Principles*, II, 311 ff. Cf. also *Opticks*, p. 381.
[20] *Principles*, II, 310 ff.
[21] *Opticks*, p. 344; *Opera*, IV, 439 ff.

responsible for a much more intricate task in applied mechanics; he is allotted the duty of providentially reforming the system of the world when the mechanism has so far run out of gear as to demand such a reformation. The active principles of the ether provide for the conservation of motion, but they do not provide sufficiently for overcoming the noted irregularities in the motion of the planets and comets, especially the latter. Due to the gradual disintegration of the comets under the influence of solar heat,[22] and the retardation in their aphelia because of mutual attractions among themselves and between them and the planets; likewise due to the gradual increase in bulk of the planets, owing chiefly to the same causes, the irregularities in nature are on the increase, and the time will come when things must be set right again.

'For while comets move in very eccentric orbs in all manner of positions, blind fate could never make all the planets move in one and the same way in orbs concentric, some inconsiderable irregularities excepted, which may have risen from the mutual actions of comets and planets upon one another, and which will be apt to increase till this system wants a reformation.'[23] God is scientifically required, Newton holds, to fulfil this need, since he is a 'powerful ever-living Agent, who being in all places is more able by his will to move the bodies within his boundless uniform sensorium, and thereby to form and reform the parts of the universe, than we are by our will to move the parts of our own bodies. And yet we are not to consider the world as the body of God, or the several parts thereof, as the parts of God. He is a uniform being, void of organs, members or parts, and they are his creatures subordinate to him, and subservient to his will. . . . And since space is divisible *in infinitum*, and matter is not necessarily in all places, it may be also allowed that God is able to create particles of matter of several sizes and figures, and in several proportions to space, and perhaps of different densities and forces, and thereby to vary the laws of nature, and make worlds of several sorts in several parts of the universe. At least, I see nothing of contradiction in all this.'[24]

Newton thus apparently takes for granted a postulate of extreme importance; he assumes, with so many others who bring an aesthetic interest into science, that the incomparable order, beauty, and harmony which characterize the celestial realm in the large, is to be eternally preserved. It will not be preserved by space, time, mass, and ether alone; its preservation requires the continued exertion of that divine will which freely chose this order and harmony as the ends of his first creative toil. From

[22] *Principles*, II, 293-8.
[23] *Opticks*, p. 378 ff.
[24] *Opticks*, p. 379.

the Protoplast of the whole, God has now descended to become a category among other categories; the facts of continued order, system, and uniformity as observed in the world, are inexplicable apart from him.

THE HISTORICAL RELATIONS OF NEWTON'S THEISM

Contrast this Newtonian teleology with that of the scholastic system. For the latter, God was the final cause of all things just as truly and more significantly than their original former. Ends in nature did not head up in the astronomical harmony; that harmony was itself a means to further ends, such as knowledge, enjoyment, and use on the part of living beings of a higher order, who in turn were made for a still nobler end which completed the divine circuit, to know God and enjoy him forever. God had no purpose; he was the ultimate object of purpose. In the Newtonian world, following Galileo's earlier suggestion, all this further teleology is unceremoniously dropped. The cosmic order of masses in motion according to law, is itself the final good. Man exists to know and applaud it; God exists to tend and preserve it. All the manifold divergent zeals and hopes of men are implicitly denied scope and fulfilment, if they cannot be subjected to the aim of theoretical mechanics, their possessors are left no proper God, for them there is no entrance into the Kingdom of heaven. We are to become devotees of mathematical science; God, now the chief mechanic of the universe, has become the cosmic conservative. His aim is to maintain the *status quo*. The day of novelty is all in the past; there is no further advance in time. Periodic reformation when necessary, by the addition of the indicated masses at the points of space required, but no new creative activity – to this routine of temporal housekeeping is the Deity at present confined.

Historically, the Newtonian attempt thus to keep God on duty was of the very deepest import. It proved a veritable boomerang to his cherished philosophy of religion, that as the result of all his pious ransackings the main providential function he could attribute to the Deity was this cosmic plumbery, this meticulous defence of his arbitrarily imposed mechanical laws against the threatening encroachments of irregularity. Really, the notion of the divine eye as constantly roaming the universe on the search for leaks to mend, or gears to replace in the mighty machinery would have been quite laughable, did not its pitifulness become earlier evident. For to stake the present existence and activity of God on imperfections in the cosmic engine was to court rapid disaster for theology. Not immediately, of course, indeed for many contemporary minds the purging of the world from all secondary qualities and the stress laid on the marvellous regularity of its whirrings only brought into fuller rational relief its divine Creator and governing Will.

> What though in solemn *silence* all
> Move round the *dark* terrestrial ball?
> What though no *real* voice nor sound
> Within their radiant orbs be found?
> In reason's ear they all rejoice,
> And utter forth a glorious voice,
> Forever singing as they shine,
> 'The hand that made us is divine'.[25]

But science moved on, and under the guidance of the less pious but more fruitful hypothesis that it would be possible to extend the mechanical idea over an ever wider realm, Newton's successors accounted one by one for the irregularities that to his mind had appeared essential and increasing if the machine were left to itself. This process of eliminating the providential elements in the world-order reached its climax in the work of the great Laplace, who believed himself to have demonstrated the inherent stability of the universe by showing that all its irregularities are periodical, and subject to an eternal law which prevents them from ever exceeding a stated amount.

While God was thus being deprived of his duties by the further advancement of mechanical science, and men were beginning to wonder whether the self-perpetuating machine thus left stood really in need of any supernatural beginning, Hume's crushing disposal of the ideas of power and causality along another tack were already disturbing the learned world with the suspicion that a First Cause was not as necessary an idea of reason as it had appeared, and Kant was preparing the penetrating analysis which frankly purported to remove God from the realm of knowledge altogether. In short, Newton's cherished theology was rapidly peeled off by all the competent hands that could get at him, and the rest of his metaphysical entities and assumptions, shorn of their religious setting, were left to wander naked and unabashed through the premises of subsequent thought, unchallenged by thorough criticism because supposed as eternally based as the positive scientific conquests of the man who first annexed the boundless firmament to the domain of mathematical mechanics. Space, time, and mass became regarded as permanent and indestructible constituents of the infinite world-order, while the notion of the ether continued to assume unpredictable shapes

[25] *The Spacious Firmament on High*, hymn written by Joseph Addison to the chorus of Haydn's *Creation*, 3rd stanza.

and remains in the scientific thought of today a relic of ancient animism still playing havoc with poor man's attempts to think straight about his world. The only place left for God was in the bare irreducible fact of intelligible order in things, which as regards the cosmos as a whole could not be quite escaped by Hume the sceptic, and as regards the realm of moral relations was all but hypostasized by that ruthless destroyer of age-long theistic proofs, Immanuel Kant. Newton's doctrine is a most interesting and historically important transitional stage between the miraculous providentialism of earlier religious philosophy and the later tendency to identify the Deity with the sheer fact of rational order and harmony. God is still providence, but the main exercise of his miraculous power is just to maintain the exact mathematical regularity in the system of the world without which its intelligibility and beauty would disappear. Furthermore, the subsequent attempt to merge him into that beauty and harmony had itself to battle for a most discouraging and precarious existence. The bulk of thinking men, ever and inevitably anthropomorphic in their theology, could hardly sense religious validity in such theistic substitutes. For them, so far as they were considerably penetrated with science or philosophy, God had been quite eliminated from the scene, and the only thing left to achieve was a single and final step in the mechanization of existence. Here were these residual souls of men, irregularly scattered among the atoms of mass that swam mechanically among the ethereal vapours in time and space, and still retaining vestiges of the Cartesian *res cogitans*. They too must be reduced to mechanical products and parts of the self-regulating cosmic clock. For this the raw materials had already been supplied by Newton's older English contemporaries, Hobbes and Locke, who had applied in this field the method of explanation in terms of simplest parts, merely dropping the mathematical requirement; they likewise simply needed to be purged of a rather alien theological setting to fit appropriately into an ultimate mechanomorphic hypothesis of the whole universe. Such a universalizing of this clockwork naturalism reached its summation in some of the brilliant French minds of the late Enlightenment, notably La Mettrie and the Baron d'Holbach, and in a somewhat different form in nineteenth-century evolutionism.

To follow such developments is obviously quite beyond the scope of an analysis of the metaphysic of early modern science. The rapid elimination of God, however, from the categories, rendered irreversible the projection upon modern philosophy of the notable problem referred to in the introduction and yet racking the brains of thinkers, whose essential relation to the Newtonian metaphysical scheme can hardly therefore be passed over. I refer to the problem of knowledge. As long as the existence of a God to whom the whole realm of matter was intimately present and known, succeeded in maintaining itself as an unquestioned conviction, the problem of how man's soul, shut within the dark room of a ventricle of the brain, could possibly gain trustworthy knowledge of external masses blindly wandering in time and space, naturally became no terrifying puzzle – a spiritual continuity connecting all links in the infinite scene was supplied in God. This is why Boyle's epistemological comments were so weak. But with the farewell of the Deity, the epistemological difficulties of the situation could hardly fail to offer an overwhelming challenge. How could intelligence grasp an inaccessible world in which there was no answering or controlling intelligence? It was by no means an accident that Hume and Kant, the first pair who really banished God from metaphysical philosophy, likewise destroyed by a sceptical critique the current overweening faith in the metaphysical competence of reason. They perceived that the Newtonian world without God must be a world in which the reach and certainty of knowledge is decidedly and closely limited, if indeed the very existence of knowledge at all is possible. This conclusion had already been foreshadowed in the fourth book of Locke's *Essay*, where a pious theism alone saved the inconsistent author from tumbling into the Avernus of scepticism. None of these keen and critical minds, however – and this is the major instructive lesson for students of philosophy in the twentieth century – directed their critical guns on the work of the man who stood in the centre of the whole significant transformation. No one in the learned world could be found to save the brilliant mathematical victories over the realm of physical motion, and at the same time lay bare the big problems involved in the new doctrine of causality, and the inherent ambiguities in the tentative, compromising, and rationally inconstruable form of the Cartesian dualism that had been dragged along like a tribal deity in the course of the campaign. For the claim of absolute and irrefutable demonstration in Newton's name had swept over Europe, and almost everybody had succumbed to its authoritative sway. Wherever was taught as truth the universal formula of gravitation, there was also insinuated as a nimbus of surrounding belief that man is but the puny and local spectator, nay irrelevant produce of an infinitive self-moving engine, which existed eternally before him and will be eternally after him, enshrining the rigour of mathematical relationships while banishing into impotence all ideal imaginations; an engine which consists of raw masses wandering to no purpose in an undiscoverable time and space, and is in general wholly devoid of any qualities that might spell satisfaction for the major interests of human nature save solely the central aim of the mathematical physicist. Indeed, that this aim itself should be rewarded appeared inconsistent and impossible when subjected to the light of clear epistemological analysis.

But if they had directed intelligent criticism in his direction, what radical conclusions would they have been likely to reach?

7 Newton and the Cyclical Cosmos: Providence and the Mechanical Philosophy*

David Kubrin

The important debate between Newton and Leibniz in 1715 over metaphysical principles served to bring out many fundamental differences in the way the two conceived of physical reality. At the heart of the debate were several basic tenets of Newtonian science which Leibniz objected to, one of which was Newton's 1706 statement of the world's decay. Newton had said that though the system of the sun and planets would continue for 'many Ages', over the course of years irregularities arising from the mutual attraction of the planets and the comets '... will be apt to increase, till this System wants a Reformation...'[1]

Leibniz objected to such a conception of an imperfect system of the world: to him it implied an imperfect Creator, lacking either the foresight or the ability to fashion a cosmic machinery able to last without His constant meddling. A truly perfect Creator, Leibniz insisted, would have fashioned a world which would last forever unless He were to intervene purposely to destroy it. This contrasted with Newton's belief that God would wisely fashion His creation in such a way that '... nothing is done without his continual government and inspection ...'[2] so

---

* David Kubrin, 'Newton and the Cyclical Cosmos: Providence and the Mechanical Philosophy', *Journal of the History of Ideas*, 1967, 28, 325–46. This paper is a revision of a public lecture delivered on 22 April 1966 at the Johns Hopkins University.

[1] The quotation is from Newton's 23rd Query to the 1706 Latin *Opticks*, but the 23rd Query became the 31st Query for the 1717 edition. I quote from the Dover reprint (New York, 1952) of the fourth edition (London, 1730), 402.

[2] H. G. Alexander (ed.), *The Leibniz–Clarke Correspondence* (Manchester, 1956), 14. The quotation is from Samuel Clarke, Newton's spokesman in the debate with Leibniz. I am using Clarke's statements in this debate to represent the ideas of Newton. For the very active rôle that Newton took in the formulation of Clarke's statements, see Marie Boas and A. R. Hall, 'Clarke and Newton', *Isis* lii (1961), 583–5, and I. B. Cohen and A. Koyré, 'Newton and the Leibniz–Clarke Correspondence', *Archives internationales d'histoire des sciences*, xv (1962), no. 58–9: 63–127. As Professor Henry Guerlac has pointed out to me, Newton's desire to preserve God's Providence is reflected also in his General Scholium to the *Principia*.

that God had to act merely to allow the world to continue. Left by itself, an imperfect system made of mere dead matter, the world would tend over the course of centuries to become so unwound that a new creation – or reformation, as Newton put it – would be necessary.[3]

This aspect of Newton's thought is, of course, well known. But I do not believe its real significance and meaning have been fathomed. In this paper, I would like to show why Newton was led to believe the world was unwinding and to relate this opinion to Newton's cosmogony, a cosmogony which indicated how the world would eventually be corrected or reset by its Creator.[3a] I shall treat first the reasons for Newton's believing in the unwinding cosmos, follow this by a brief description of Newton's cosmogony in its mature form, and then give an account of the development of these views. To understand the context of this aspect of Newton's thought, we must consider first the reaction of most English philosophers to the mechanical philosophy which was the world-view of the late scientific revolution. Many Englishmen while initially seeing in the mechanism offered by Descartes a support both for natural philosophy and for religious orthodoxy, had by the late 1660s severe misgivings that Cartesianism would usher out of the world all notions of Providence. Henry More, the Cambridge Platonist, Robert Boyle, the natural philosopher, and Walter Charleton, the physician, for example, all saw that the mechanical philosophy, to be acceptable, had to make God more than a mere Creator;[4] for a mere Creator, once His task was done, might become a mere absentee deity, and such a view of God was dangerously similar to the teachings of the deists.

To avoid such an implication, many of the English adopted

(*Mathematical Principles of Natural Philosophy* ... translated by Andrew Motte and revised by Florian Cajori [Berkeley, 1960], 544.)

[3] *The Leibniz–Clarke Correspondence, passim.*

[3a] By cosmogony I mean not only a theory accounting for the creation of the cosmos, but one which also sought to explain its subsequent development.

[4] It is convenient for my purposes to use Descartes's system as the epitome of the mechanical philosophy. See on More, Marjorie Nicolson, 'The Early Stage of Cartesianism in England', *Studies in Philology*, xxvi (1929), 3:356–74; Sterling Lamprecht, 'The Role of Descartes in Seventeenth-Century England', *Studies in the History of Ideas* (New York, 1935), III, 181–243; J. E. Saveson, 'Differing Reactions to Descartes Among the Cambridge Platonists', *JHI*, XXI (1960), 560–7; Danton Sailor, 'Cudworth and Descartes', *ibid.*, XXIII (1962), 133–40; and Robert A. Greene, 'Henry More and Robert Boyle: 'On the Spirit of Nature', *ibid.*, XXIII (1962), 451–74. On Boyle and Charleton, see Robert Kargon, 'Walter Charleton, Robert Boyle, and the Acceptance of Epicurean Atomism in England', *Isis*, LV (1964), 184–93. Newton's place in this tradition is discussed in Henry Guerlac, *Newton et Epicure, Conférence donnée au Palais de la Découverte le 2 Mars 1963* (Paris, 1963).

an interpretation of the mechanical philosophy which made God responsible not only for initially creating matter and motion – the two principles responsible for all phenomena according to the mechanical philosophy – but also for preserving motion in bodies. Merely to persist in their movements, bodies needed constant Providential care by God; in this sense, He was the cause of motion.[5] Worried by the dangers inherent in a thoroughly mechanized world, many English philosophers would allow neither their growing knowledge of the laws of motion[6] nor the concept of inertia (claiming that a body in motion will stay in that state unless disturbed) to persuade them that motion could persist without God's care. Among English divines and natural philosophers, there was a further fear: unless it could be shown that God's Providence acted at the *present* time, some would doubt whether it had *ever* been a force in the world. Criticizing the attempt in George Cheyne's *Philosophical Principles of Natural Religion* (1705) to make motion dependent upon God's will, the English mathematician Brook Taylor – illustrating this danger – wrote:

> As we can conceive a portion of Matter, which now is, to continue its being without the operation of a Cause, to all Eternity (for it seems rather to require a Cause to make it cease to be, than to continue it) so we may as easily conceive it to have been from all Eternity, or to have had no cause of its existence, that is to be Self-Existen[t].[7]

Taylor extended his argument to the motion of the planets, seeing no reason why this could not have gone on from all eternity.[8] Earlier arguments, similar to Taylor's, had led Richard Bentley to attack in his sermons those who 'have asserted, that the same quantity of motion is always kept up in the world; which may seem to favour the opinion of its infinite duration . . .'.[9]

This central problem, that of the relation of God's Providence to the mechanisms at the foundation of the new philosophy, thus

[5] See, for example, Harry Hynne to Henry More (19 August 1671), Christ's College Cambridge MS BB. 6. 7, no. 19, and More's answer to him (21 August 1671), Cambridge University Library MS Gg. VI. 11, fol. 3[r]. More and others misinterpreted Descartes on the extent of God's concurrence in the phenomena of nature.

[6] For this reason, Robert Boyle objected to the very term 'law of nature'. (Boyle, *Christian Virtuoso*, quoted in John Ray, *The Wisdom of God Manifested in the Works of the Creation* [London, 4th edn, 1704], 56.)

[7] [Brook Taylor], Royal Society MS [82], ff. 13[r]–13[v]. Written March 1713/14. I am grateful to the Royal Society for permission to use and quote this manuscript and those mentioned below in notes 46 and 52.

[8] *Ibid.*, fol. 13[r].

[9] Richard Bentley, *A Confutation of Atheism* (1693), in *Works* (ed.) Rev. Alexander Dyce (London, 1838), III, 144.

arose, in part, from a general concern that the banishment of Providence from the present world would lead men to believe that the world had always been without Providence, indeed, had been without Creator or Creation, lasting from all eternity. Bentley, co-editor of the second edition of Newton's *Principia* (1713), changed certain lines in Edmund Halley's Ode to Newton, which had appeared at the beginning of the first edition, because Bentley thought these lines were open to the interpretation that the world had always existed.[10] Although Halley obtained a promise from Newton that the Ode would appear in its original form for the third edition of 1726, the editor of the third edition, Henry Pemberton, again struck out the offending lines and left them in the form of Bentley's innocuous emendation.[11]

Bentley's and Pemberton's concern about the belief in the world's eternity reflected several decades of argument by the English hierarchy against this particular challenge to orthodoxy.[12] These arguments had been implicitly directed against a few atheists and deists who *were* – in conversation, in manuscripts, and even in printed pamphlets – proclaiming the eternity of the world.[13] Two years after his edition of the *Principia*, in which he

[10] The various Latin versions of the Ode are given in Appendix V of Eugene MacPike (ed.), *Correspondence and Papers of Edmund Halley* (London, 1937), reprinted from Sir David Brewster, *Memoirs of the Life, Writings and Discoveries of Sir Isaac Newton* (Edinburgh, 1855). Neither Halley's nor Newton's permission had been obtained for the changes. Halley had written these lines as follows: '... until, the origin of things / He established, the omnipresent Creator, unwilling the laws / To violate, He fixed the *eternal* [my emphasis] foundations of His work'. Bentley changed them to '... until, the origin of things / He put together, the all-powerful Creator Himself, His laws, / Named; and indeed set the foundations of His works'.

[11] *Ibid.* See also Conduitt's memoir of Newton's promise to Halley, Kings College Cambridge, MS Keynes 30, no. 7, cited in part in Appendix V of *Correspondence and Papers.*

[12] See especially the jurist Sir Matthew Hale, *The Primitive Origination of Mankind, Considered and Examined According to the Light of Nature* (London, 1677); the Bishop of Worchester, Edward Stillingfleet, *Origines Sacrae, or a Rational Account of the Grounds of Christian Faith ...* (London, 1662); the Archbishop of Canterbury, John Tillotson, 'The Wisdom of Being Religious', *Works* (London, 9th edn, 1728), Vol. I, 10. Their arguments were repeated by dozens of less eminent writers.

[13] One of these is the anonymous manuscript in what appears to be a mid-seventeenth-century script and style, *Whey^{re}* [whether] *there were any men before Adam? Answ^{re}*, BM Sloane MS 1115, ff. 15–16. See also the early work by Henry More, written prior to his disillusionment with Cartesian mechanism, *Democritus Platonissans: or an Essay on the Infinitie of Worlds out of Platonick Principles* (Cambridge, 1646). The idea also is found in [Isaac de la Peyrère], *Men before Adam*, translated from the Latin (London, 1656) and *A Theological Systeme Upon that Presupposition That Men were before Adam*, translated from the Latin (London, 1655). See also Lady Anne Conway, *The Principles of the Most Ancient and Modern Philosophy, Concerning God, Christ and the Creatures ...* (Lon-

persisted in emending Halley's Ode to Newton, Pemberton wrote an exposition of Newtonian philosophy in which he made the logical connection between Newton's belief that the world was unwinding and the orthodox position that the world could not be eternal:

> I think it not improper to mention a reflection made by our excellent author [Newton] upon these small inequalities in the planets motions; which contains under it a very strong philosophical argument against the eternity of the world. It is thus, that these inequalities must continually increase by slow degree, till they render at length the present frame of nature unfit for the purposes it now serves. And a more convincing proof cannot be desired against the present constitutions having existed from eternity than this, that a certain number of years will bring it to an end.

Chiding Leibniz for his pretension of knowing 'all the omniscient Creator's purposes in making this world ...', Pemberton argued that the Leibnizian position cast 'a reflection upon the wisdom of the author of nature, for framing a perishable work'.[14]

Newton and Samuel Clarke, in their debate with Leibniz, made this same point in a more pointed way:

> by the same reason that a philosopher can represent all things going on from the beginning of the creation, without any government or interposition of providence; a sceptic will easily argue still farther backwards, and suppose that things have from eternity gone on ... without any true creation or author at all, but only what such arguers call all-wise and eternal nature.[15]

In his fifth and last letter to Leibniz, Clarke asked rhetorically,

> [w]hether my inference from this learned author's [Leibniz] affirming that the universe cannot diminish in perfection ... [that] the world must needs have been ... eternal, be a just inference or no, I am willing to leave to the learned ... to judge.[16]

---

don, 1692), and the work of the deist Charles Blount, *Oracles of Reason* ... (London, 1693). In another paper on Halley, I discuss these assertions of the world's eternity at greater length.

[14] Henry Pemberton, *A View of Sir Isaac Newton's Philosophy* (London, 1728), 180–1. Leibniz's opinions are attacked, but he is not named.

[15] Clarke's first reply to Leibniz (26 November 1715), *Leibniz–Clarke Correspondence*, 14.

[16] 29 October 1716, *ibid.*, 113. Compare Newton's draft number 10 of his letter to the Abate Antonio Conti (26 February 1716) reprinted in Cohen and Koyré, *op. cit.* in note 2, 114: 'And by the same Argument any man may affirm ... that God created the world from all Eternity. ...'

To maintain a rôle for Providence meant providing essential chores for God to perform, so that He did not rule over a universe able to exist without Him:

> And as those men [said Clarke], who pretend that in an earthly government things may go on perfectly well without the king himself ordering or disposing of any thing, may reasonably be suspected that they would like very well to set the king aside...

so too those who think that the universe does not constantly need 'God's actual government' but that the laws of mechanism alone would allow phenomena to continue, 'in effect tend to exclude God out of the world'.[17]

Now, in order to include God *in* the world, Newton declared, in the 1706 Latin *Opticks*, that the world by itself tended to dissolution, and consequently needed periodic reformation by the Creator. Newton, however, not only felt the need for these periodic acts of reformation, he later hit upon a possible mechanism by which they could be performed. This mechanism, ultimately controlled by the Providential God, used the recently discovered periodicity of comets to accomplish the acts of reformation and, in Newton's view, was part of a complex cosmogony, involving the creation and subsequent development of stars, planets, moons, and comets, a cosmogony to which we now turn.

It is a commonplace that the Newtonian world-picture consisted of a cosmos which since its Creation *ex nihilo*, had remained substantially the same through the course of time, changing, if at all, only insignificantly. It is, however, a commonplace well worth challenging. There is, to be sure, some evidence to support a static interpretation of the Newtonian cosmos. Did not Newton even discourage speculation about the creation, writing in the 31st Query of the *Opticks* that God at the creation set the material universe in order, and that 'if he did so, it's unphilosophical to seek for any other Origin of the World, or to pretend that it might arise out of a Chaos by the mere Laws of Nature'?[18] And did not Newton in his letters to Richard Bentley seek to reassure him that '[t]he Hypothesis of deriving the Frame of the World by mechanical Principles from Matter evenly spread through the Heavens ... [is] inconsistent with my System ...'?[19] Newton also seemingly discouraged treatments of

[17] Clarke's first and fifth replies, *Leibniz–Clarke Correspondence*, *14*, 117.
[18] *Opticks*, 402.
[19] Written 11 February 1692/93, and reprinted in Isaac Newton, *Papers & Letters on Natural Philosophy*, ed. I. B. Cohen (Cambridge, Mass., 1958), 310.

the development of the planetary system. He explicitly rejected as erroneous and inconsistent with his system 'the Cartesian Hypothesis of Suns losing their Light, and then turning into Comets, and Comets [turning] into Planets ...'.[20] And Newton similarly dismissed as absurd the belief in 'the Growth of new Systems [of the sun and planets] out of old ones, without the Mediation of a divine Power ...'.[21]

It is important, however, to note carefully Newton's qualifications in the above admonitions against cosmogonies: what appeared absurd to Newton was the attempt to show how the system of sun and planets could have arisen by mechanical principles 'without the Mediation of a divine Power'. If accomplished by the will of such a power, either directly or indirectly, such attempts were allowable. Similar treatments of the development of the already created cosmos were also acceptable. When Thomas Burnet in 1680 sent Newton an attempt to show how God could have accomplished the creation of the Earth by mechanical principles, Newton was in general sympathy with the treatise.[22] He suggested to Burnet several alternative mechanisms by which the surface of the Earth could have been put into its present uneven form, with its numerous caverns, mountains, seas, and rivers. He also discussed with Burnet the possibility of mechanisms by which the rotation of the Earth could gradually have been increased during the six days of the Mosaic Creation, so that Creation could have taken longer than what are now six days.[23] In addition, Newton later encouraged his disciple, William Whiston, to write a treatise on the Creation of the Earth.[24]

We must turn elsewhere to find the development of Newton's cosmogony, for he nowhere followed up his early suggestions to Burnet, and he did not enter later into the controversy surrounding the treatises by Burnet and Whiston. We turn to the seemingly

---

[20] Newton to Bentley (10 December 1692), ibid., 283. Descartes held that after stars lost their light, they wandered as comets through the heavens. Citation to Descartes, Les Principes de la Philosophie ... Oeuvres de Descartes, ed. Adam et Tannery (Paris, 1904), tome 9, article 119, 172–3.

[21] Newton to Bentley (25 February 1692/93), ibid., 302. Professor Maurice Mandelbaum has suggested to me that many of these statements of Newton were possibly expressions more of his hostility to Cartesianism than to cosmogony.

[22] Sir David Brewster, Memoirs of the Life, Writings and Discoveries of Sir Isaac Newton, Vol. II, 99–101. Two letters from Newton, of which one has been lost, and one from Burnet, quoting part of the lost letter, were exchanged. See Isaac Newton, The Correspondence, (ed.) H. W. Turnbull (Cambridge, 1959–), Vol. II, 319–35.

[23] Ibid., 322, 329–31, 333–4. In the case of the slow increase of the Earth's rotation, Newton did not think a mechanism to accomplish this could be found.

[24] William Whiston, Memoirs of the Life and Writings of William Whiston ... (London, 2nd end, 1753), I, 38–9.

unrelated concern which Newton had for the problem of renewing the sources, whatever they were, of heat, motion, and other forms of activity found in nature. At various times Newton suggested that this renewal was accomplished by certain aethereal spirits. At other times, he suggested that it was performed by what he called 'active principles', an agency Newton insisted was necessary in order to reintroduce some principle of activity into nature to act on the matter which the Cartesian mechanical philosophy had made dead and passive. Newton first introduced this concept in the Queries to the 1706 Latin *Opticks*, insisting that from the *vis inertiae*, a mere passive principle of bodies, there could be no motion in the world;[25] for both the beginnings and the conservation of motion, some other, active, principles were necessary. Newton saw such active principles in the causes of gravity, fermentation, light, heat, cohesion, and life.

If the amount of motion and activity decreased without being renewed, there would be an eventual cessation of the various phenomena they generated, and all bodies would become cold, life would cease, and 'the Planets and Comets would not remain in their Orbs'.[26] Newton thus apparently associated the loss of the amount of motion with the increasing irregularities arising from the mutual attractions of the planets. When he later suggested a mechanism by which the planetary orbs could be reformed, that mechanism was also associated with replenishing the motion and activity in the cosmos.

This reformation, however, was to be of more than physical significance; not only would it reform the planetary orbs and replenish the amount of motion in the cosmos, but it was meant to provide, as promised in the Apocalyptic tradition, for the new Earth to arise after the Millennium. As a student at Cambridge in the 1660s, in the concluding part of his earliest surviving notebook, Newton had written of the Earth, 'Its conflagration testified 2 Peter 3^d [chapter], vers 6, 7, 10, 11, 12.... The succession of worlds, probable from Pet 3^c. 13^v....'[27] But how was this succes-

---

[25] *Opticks*, 397.

[26] *Ibid.*, 399–401. This was added to the 1717 second English edition. Newton's concept of active principles changed sometime after 1706. When in 1717 he revived his earlier aethereal speculations in order to suggest a possible cause for gravity, he tended to use the concept of the aether and that of active principles interchangeably. In effect what had earlier been metaphysical, now had a material basis in the aether. Throughout his life, however, it was both the aether and the active principles, and the later marriage of the two, which fulfilled the important task of replenishing the sources of activity.

[27] Isaac Newton, 'Of Earth', in *Qu[a]estiones quaedam Philosophiae*, Cambridge Add. MS 3996, fol. 101^r. Richard S. Westfall, 'The Foundations of Newton's Philosophy of Nature' (*British Journal for the History of Science*, i [1962], part II, no. 2, 171–82), suggests that this early notebook of Newton's was begun in early 1664. Newton's interests in the Apocalyptic tradition

sion to be carried out? Newton wrote to Burnet in 1680 that probably 'all ye [the] Planets about our Sun were created together, there being in no history any mention of new ones appearing or old ones ceasing'.[28] By 1694, Newton had conceived of a possible source for new planets, and he told his disciple David Gregory that '[t]he Satellites of Jupiter and Saturn can take the places of the Earth, Venus, Mars if they are destroyed, and be held in reserve for a new Creation'.[29] Some thirty years later, Newton greatly elaborated the suggestion he had made to Gregory. As John Conduitt related, Newton told him at the end of 1724, that

> it was his [Newton's] *conjecture* ... that there was a sort of revolution in the heavenly bodies ... that the vapours & light emitted by the sun ... gathered themselves by degrees, into a body ... & at last made a secondary planett [that is, a moon] ... & then by gathering ... more matter became a primary planet; & then by increasing still became a comet w[ch] [eventually] ... became a matter set to recruit & replenish the Sun....[30]

Such a 'revolution in the heavenly bodies' could account for the succession of worlds, and guided by 'the direction of the supreme being',[31] the system would undergo a reformation and have its quantity of motion restored.

This was the cosmogony that Newton held in his final years. It is instructive to see the development of these ideas, for the younger Newton had neither perceived this same solution, nor indeed recognized the problems which would engender this solution. Though a skeletal outline of his final ideas had been formulated relatively early, it was not until the second edition of the *Principia* in 1713 that the flesh of these ideas appeared in something approaching their final form. In Newton's hypothesis of an aethereal mechanism to account for gravity – a mechanism tried and then rejected in his private manuscripts and letters, only to be revived by him at last in the 1717 edition of his *Opticks*[32] –

---

continued; for example, 'De Millenio ac Die Judicij', *A Com[n] Place Book of S[r] Is: Newton*, King's College, Cambridge MS, Keynes 2, 21.

[28] *The Correspondence*, II, 332.

[29] Memorandum by Gregory (5–7 May 1694), *ibid.*, III, 336. Gregory's visits to Newton, after which he made numerous memoranda relating what Newton had told him, form an invaluable source for Newton's ideas, since Newton himself was loath to publish anything that might bring on controversy.

[30] Memorandum by Conduitt, King's College, Cambridge MS, Keynes 130, no. 11. The memorandum will be discussed at length below.

[31] *Ibid.*

[32] See the papers of Henry Guerlac, *Newton et Epicure*; 'Sir Isaac and the Ingenious Mr Hauksbee', *Mélanges Alexandre Koyré* (Paris, 1964); 'Francis

this skeletal outline can be found. But when he first proposed this aethereal hypothesis for gravity about 1664, Newton did not believe that the amount of motion in the world tended to decrease. On the contrary, throughout the manuscript *Qu[a]estiones quaedam Philosophiae* in which his aethereal hypothesis first appeared, Newton went so far as to suggest various ways in which one could obtain perpetual motion.[33]

Later in his career, however, as we have seen, Newton came to hold that the amount of motion in the world does tend to decrease. The first clear reference to this appeared only in the Latin *Opticks* of 1706, but some related forms of 'decay' in nature had appeared earlier in the 1687 *Principia*. He was led to this concept of decay, at least in part, by his growing realization that a mechanical universe in which the amount of motion remained the same could be used by atheists to argue against the existence of a Deity.[34] Once he had decided that the amount of motion did decrease, Newton turned to his earlier aethereal hypothesis for an indication of a mechanism by which the amount of motion in the world could be renewed. Newton was able to indicate such a mechanism only after the writing of the second edition of the *Principia*. The remainder of this paper will be concerned with the development of Newton's ideas on this renewal of the cosmos; I shall try to show how he became aware of the problems and in what ways he was led to the solutions which make up his cosmogony.

Newton's aethereal hypothesis for gravity, in one of its forms, pictured the Earth like a sponge, drinking up the constant stream of fine aethereal matter falling from the heavens, this stream by its impact on bodies above the Earth causing them to descend.[35] To prevent the Earth from becoming larger and larger as the aether accumulated, Newton suggested that the aether, having fallen on the Earth, changed its form, and then ascended again into the heavens.[36] As Newton suggested

---

Hauksbee: expérimentateur au profit de Newton', *Arch. int. d'hist. des sciences*, XVI (1963), 119–28. I am very much indebted to Professor Guerlac for allowing me to use his copies of manuscript drafts by Newton for the Queries to the *Opticks*, for bringing to my attention the numerous important changes between the various editions of the *Opticks*, and, in general, for introducing me as a student in his seminar at Cornell University to Newton's problems regarding gravitation and the aether.

[33] Newton, *Qu[a]estiones quaedam Philosophia*, ff. 97ʳ, 102ʳ, 121ᵛ.

[34] As a student at Cambridge, Newton had read Henry More, who warned against this tendency; Newton referred to More in his *Qu[a]estiones quaedam Philosophia*. In addition, see Newton's and Clarke's statements above, n. 15.

[35] Newton, 'Questiones ... Of Gravity & Levity', *Qu[a]estiones quaedam Philosophiae*, Cambridge Add. MS 3996, ff. 97ʳ, 121ʳ. Newton to Oldenburg (7 December 1675), *The Correspondence*, I, 336.

[36] Cambridge Add. MS 3996, fol. 97ʳ; *The Correspondence*, I, 366.

in an hypothesis concerning the properties of light which he sent to Henry Oldenburg in 1675, nature seemed to have its origin in the transmutations of certain aethereal spirits into different forms:

> Perhaps the whole frame of Nature [Newton wrote to Oldenburg] may be nothing but various Contextures of some certaine aethereall Spirits or vapours condens'd as it were by praecipitation, much after the manner that vapours are condensed into water or exhalations into grosser Substances ...; and after condensation wrought into various formes.... Thus perhaps may all things be originated from aether.[37]

Newton indicated how there followed from this the possibility of transformations back and forth between these various states, so that spiritous matter in space would be absorbed by the thirsty Earth, while gross matter in the bowels of the Earth would be changed to an aereal and then to an aethereal form as it rose first into the atmosphere and then into the heavens:

> nature makeing a circulation by the slow ascent of as much matter out of the bowells of the Earth in an aereall forme wch for a time constitutes the Atmosphere, but being continually boyed up by the new Air, Exhalations, & Vapours riseing underneath, at length ... vanishes againe into the aethereall Spaces, & there perhaps in time ... is attenuated into its first principle....[38]

From the functions given by Newton to the aethereal matter, it is clear that it served, as would later what he came to call 'active principles', as the source of motion and activity in the cosmos. This aethereal source of activity was perpetually being circulated.

> For nature is a perpetuall circulatory worker, generating fluids out of solids, and solids out of fluids, fixed things out of volatile, & volatile out of fixed, subtile out of gross, & gross out of subtile, Some things to ascend, & make the upper terrestriall juices, Rivers, and the Atmosphere; & by consequence others to descend for a Requitall to the former. And as the Earth, so perhaps may the Sun imbibe this Spirit copiously to conserve his Shineing, & keep the Planets from recedeing further from him. And they that will, may also suppose, *that this Spirit affords or carryes with it thither*

---

[37] Newton's paper was entitled 'An Hypothesis explaining the Properties of Light'. Newton to Oldenburg, *The Correspondence*, I, 364.
[38] *Ibid.*, 366.

*the solary fewell & materiall Principle of Light; And that the
vast aethereall Spaces between us, & the stars are for a sufficient repository for this food of the Sunn & Planets.*[39] [my
italics]

The paper to Oldenburg was written in late 1675; by 1687
when he wrote his *Principia*, Newton was evidently less convinced of the existence of aethereal mechanisms in nature, for
nothing was said of either the aether or these mechanisms in the
Principia. Newton, in avoiding this spiritous aether dispersed
through space, turned his attention instead to another possible
means of achieving a circulation of the sources of motion. This
means he found in comets, a new member of the celestial
machinery, using them as causal instruments.

As late as the early 1680s, Newton had not been convinced of
the periodic nature of comets. In 1680/81 he argued against the
astronomer John Flamsteed's contention that the two appearances
of comets in that year on either side of the sun were from one
and the same body.[40] By the time of his *Principia*, however,
Newton believed that comets, like other bodies of the sun's
system, moved around the sun in orbits corresponding to the
conic sections.[41] Perhaps the most striking aspect of the appearances of the comets was their tails; these were able to grow in the
short time that comets were visible from a mere two or three
degrees to fifty or sixty degrees in angular length. Indeed, whatever made up these tails must be a rare and subtle form of matter.
There is a tendency, Newton noted in the first edition of the
Principia, for the matter of these tails slowly to dissipate into
space, so that it was

scattered through the whole heavens, and by little and little . . .
attracted towards the planets by its gravity, and mixed with
their atmosphere; . . . for the conservation of the seas, and
fluids of the planets, comets seem to be required, that, from
their exhalations and vapors condensed, the wastes of the
planetary fluids spent upon vegetation and putrefaction, and
converted into dry earth, may be continually supplied and
made up; . . . and *hence it is that the bulk of the solid earth
is continually increased;* [my italics] and the fluids, if they
are not supplied from without, must be in continual decrease,
and quite fail at last. I suspect, moreover, that it is chiefly

[39] *Ibid.*
[40] See his correspondence with Flamsteed (28 February 1680/81, *The
Correspondence*, II, 340–7, and (18 September 1685), *ibid.*, 419–21. At the
time of the latter letter, Newton was writing the *Principia*. See in addition
the notes to Flamsteed's letter to Newton (15 December 1680), *ibid.*, 315–17.
[41] At first Newton thought these would be parabolas, but by the second
edition of the *Principia* he believed that they were elongated ellipses.

from the comets that spirit comes, which is indeed the smallest but most subtle and useful part of our air, and so much required to sustain the life of all things with us.[42]

Rather than abandon his earlier conjectures to Oldenburg, which were based on the aether, Newton simply altered the conjectures slightly. In the 1675 paper the circulation throughout the heavens of aethereal matter was the mechanism which renewed motion and activity in the cosmos; but in 1687 Newton suggested that the circulation of the tails of comets performed this function.

Two significant changes in Newton's outlook had taken place, however. In his paper to Oldenburg, Newton had suggested a mechanism to recruit new fuel for the sun and stars as well as for the Earth, but no such mechanism was described in the first edition of the *Principia*; only the Earth was replenished. Since the tails of comets at their longest when near the sun, were always found pointing *away* from the sun, Newton inferred that there was a force overcoming the gravitational attraction of the sun and stars for these rare vapors. Such a force prevented the vapors from replenishing the sun and stars.[43] There was another change in the *Principia* from his 1675 letter, in which the Earth had been pictured as absorbing aether from the heavens and giving up aereal matter to the heavens, 'Some things to ascend ... and by consequence others to descend for a Requitall to the former'.[44] But this balance claimed to exist between the matter being lost and that being gained no longer was accepted in the *Principia* of 1687, where Newton now claimed that 'the bulk of the solid earth is continually increased ...'.[45]

By these changes, Newton for the first time suggested that the cosmos was a machine that was unwinding. Nature in 1675 had been a 'perpetual worker'. In 1687, by implication, nature would have its period: at a certain time the sun and stars, not being replenished, would lose their fuel; at a certain time also the Earth would have so increased in size that she would no longer fit harmoniously in the present system with the sun and moon. It is not certain that Newton noticed these implications of his *Principia* immediately. But by 1694, he realized that the Earth's system would change dynamically in the course of time:

Halley say'd that Mr Newton had lately told him, That there was reason to Conclude That the bulk of the Earth did grow

[42] Newton, *Philosophiae naturalis principia mathematica* (London, 1687), 506. I have used the Motte–Cajori translation in *Mathematical Principles of Natural Philosophy* ... (Berkeley, 1960), 529–30.
[43] Newton, *Mathematical Principles of Natural Philosophy*, 522–9.
[44] Newton, *The Correspondence*, I, 366.
[45] Newton, *Principia* (1687), 506; *Mathematical Principles of Natural Philosophy*, 530.

and increase ... by the perpetuall Accession of New particles attracted out of the Ether by its Gravitating power, and he [Halley] Supposed ... That this Encrese of the Moles of the Earth would occasion an Acceleration of the Moons Motion, she being at this time Attracted by a Stronger Vis Centripeta than in remote Ages.[46]

It was twelve years later, in the 1706 Queries to the Latin *Opticks*, that the various ways in which Newton believed nature to run down were, for the first time, made explicit and developed at length. For the first time Newton emphasized the increasing irregularities in motions of the planets, which he thought would lead to an end of things if not reformed.[47] For the first time also, he mentioned the tendency for the amount of motion in the world to diminish, which he thought would lead to an end of things if not replenished:

> ... Motion is more apt to be lost than got, and is always upon the Decay.... Seeing therefore the variety of Motion which we find in the world is always decreasing, there is a necessity of conserving and recruiting it by active Principles....[48]

To Bentley Newton had written in 1692 that the frame of nature implied God and His Providence.[49] In 1706 he made explicit the ways God and His Providence were indeed essential. Without His Providence, Newton emphasized, the world could not long continue.

But the question still remained how God was to accomplish this renewal of motion and this reformation of the planetary orbits. Was this to be done by a direct *fiat* or was it to be by God's using secondary mechanisms? 'Where natural causes are at hand God uses them as instruments in his works, but I doe not think them alone sufficient for ye creation ...' Newton had written Burnet in 1680.[50] Nor did natural causes alone seem sufficient for the reformation, for that would seemingly defeat the whole purpose of requiring a reformation.

From 1692 to 1706 Newton was uncertain about the extent of God's rôle in natural phenomena. To Bentley he had written

---

[46] *Journal Book* of the Royal Society, 31 October 1694. Newton mentioned this idea in the 2nd edn of the *Principia*, 481, but omitted it in the 3rd edn.
[47] *Opticks*, 402.
[48] *Ibid.*, 398–9.
[49] Letters to Bentley in Isaac Newton, *Papers & Letters on Natural Philosophy*, 284–7, 298, 306, 311.
[50] Newton, *The Correspondence*, II, 334.

Gravity must be caused by an Agent acting constantly according to certain Laws; but whether this Agent be material or immaterial, I have left to the Consideration of my Readers.[51]

The attempt by Newton's friend Fatio de Duillier to provide a mechanical explanation for gravity based on the aether met neither with Newton's outright approval nor with his clear disapproval; while interested in the possibilities of such an explanation, he was more attracted to the supposition that gravity was implanted in matter by God.[52] Newton was also ambiguous about the means by which motion was initiated. In 1706, he suggested that all motion in the world arose either through the effects of the active principles or by 'the dictates of a will';[53] the latter in Newton's sense could be either the will of an individual influencing the movements of his own body or the will of the Deity who has power over the world of matter.[54]

In the decade following 1706, Newton changed his mind about God's rôle, and, resolving his ambiguity, began to commit himself to seemingly mechanical means. At the beginning of the 1717 edition of the *Opticks*, Newton wrote that he had added some indications of how gravity might be the result of an aethereal mechanism '. . . to shew that I do not take Gravity for an essential Property of Bodies . . .'.[55] Similarly, he now attributed motion only to the effects of an active principle, now in effect materialized, instead of to a metaphysical active principle, or dictates of a will, as he had in 1706.[56]

[51] 25 February 1692/93, *Papers & Letters on Natural Philosophy*, 303.
[52] Fatio's hypothesis has been reprinted along with a commentary by Bernard Gagnebin in *Notes and Records of the Royal Society*, VI (1949), 106–60. It is described by Gregory in a memorandum (28 December 1691), *The Correspondence*, III, 191. Gregory's last line in this memorandum, telling of Newton's amusement at Fatio's hypothesis, was added at some date later than the original entry, for it is in a different ink and is written off to one side. (Royal Society MS Gregory, fol. 71ᵛ.) See also the letter of Fatio to De Beyrie to be forwarded to Leibniz (30 March 1694), *The Correspondence*, III, 309. Newton came more and more to believe, in this period, that gravity was probably caused by the will of God. See Gregory's memorandum of 21 December 1705, Walter Hiscock (ed.), *David Gregory, Isaac Newton and their Circle; Extracts from David Gregory's memoranda 1677–1708* (Oxford, 1937), 29–30, and the quotation from Fatio given in *The Correspondence*, III, 70 n. l. While Newton was tempted to think that God *might* be the direct cause of gravity, his disciples Clarke, Whiston, Bentley, and John Freind all explicitly committed themselves to an immaterial cause for gravity. See in addition to their works the excellent book by Hélène Metzger, *Attraction Universelle et Religion Naturelle chez quelques commentateurs anglais de Newton* (Paris, 1938).
[53] H. G. Alexander, 'Introduction', *Leibniz–Clarke Correspondence*, xviii.
[54] Cambridge University Library Add. MS 3970, fol. 619ʳ. I wish to thank Professor Henry Guerlac for drawing my attention to this MS, and allowing me to consult his copy of it.
[55] *Opticks*, cxv.   [56] *Ibid.*, 399.

Not only were the underlying causes of gravity and motion in general seemingly mechanical in his opinion, but sometime in the same period he similarly conceived a natural mechanism by which God could reform the system of sun and planets and renew the active principles in the cosmos. Whatever the reasons for his change of mind regarding gravity and motion,[57] his discovery of a mechanism to renew and reform the cosmos seems to have arisen from his work in preparing the second edition of the *Principia*. There he extended his theory of the motion of heavenly bodies to show more precisely how comets moved, using, he wrote, 'more examples of the calculation of their orbits, done also with greater accuracy'.[58] In the first edition of the *Principia*, Newton had indicated a cometary mechanism which served to replenish the vapors and spirits lost by the planets, but the same mechanism could not have worked for the sun or stars. In the new work on comets for the second edition, he was struck by how close some comets came to the sun, and by the possibility that such comets, if disturbed slightly in their orbits, might fall from their regular orbits into the body of the sun. The regularity and permanence of comets' orbits, so recently established, had turned out to be somewhat dubious. To the second edition of the *Principia* Newton added a new paragraph:

> The comet which appeared in the year 1680 was in its perihelion less distant from the sun than by a sixth part of the sun's diameter; and because of its extreme velocity in that proximity ... and some density of the sun's atmosphere, it must have suffered some resistance and retardation; and therefore, being attracted somewhat nearer to the sun in every revolution, will at last fall down upon the body of the sun. Nay, in its aphelion, where it moves the slowest, it may sometimes happen to be yet further retarded by the attractions of other comets, and in consequence of this retardation descend to the sun. *So fixed stars, that have been gradually wasted by the light and vapors emitted from them for a long time, may be recruited by comets that fall upon them....*[59] [my italics]

Such recruiting of the fuel of stars, Newton suggested, might enable the stars to shine suddenly with new brilliance, explaining the puzzling occasional sudden appearances of new stars in the heavens.[60]

With comets now apt to fall occasionally into stars, the stars'

[57] Reasons have been suggested by Henry Guerlac; cf. above note 32.
[58] *Mathematical Principles of Natural Philosophy*, xix.
[59] *Philosophiae naturalis principia mathematica* (Cambridge, 1713), 481; *Mathematical Principles of Natural Philosophy*, 540–1.
[60] *Ibid.*

and planets' sources of motion and activity might well be replenished. And thus once more, as in his 1675 paper to Oldenburg, there was a continuous circulation of spiritous matter reaching to *all* parts of the cosmos, and nature once more was a 'perpetual circulatory worker'. Newton went further, working out a complete theory of the cycles of the cosmos. The cycles of his theory turned upside down the Cartesian hypothesis – which Newton had rejected in his letter to Bentley[61] – of suns turning into comets, and comets, in turn, becoming planets. Newton's cosmogony now accounted both for the creation of the cosmos and for the cyclical development of the already created cosmos. He was able to account for both the periodic recruiting of motion and activity for the sun and planets and the 'reformations' necessary to reset the system from time to time.

In a conversation with John Conduitt in March 1724/25, some six years after the second edition of the *Principia*, Newton made Conduitt privy to his ideas:

> [Newton repeated] what he had often hinted to me before, viz that it was his *conjecture* (he would affirm nothing) that there was a sort of revolution in the heavenly bodies that the vapours & light[62] emitted by the sun which had their sediment in water and other matter, had gathered themselves by degrees in to a body & attracted more matter from the planets & at last made a secondary planett (viz one of those that go round another planet) & then by gathering to them & attracting more matter became a primary planet, & then by increasing still became a comet wch after certain revolutions by coming nearer & nearer the sun had all its volatile parts condensed & became a matter set to recruit & replenish the Sun ... & that would probably be the effect of the comet in 1680 sooner or later....[63]

Newton had told David Gregory in 1694 how the satellites of Jupiter and Saturn 'can take the places of the Earth, Venus, Mars if they are destroyed, and be held in reserve for a new Creation'.[64] Gregory probably later learned from Newton how his cometary mechanism could accomplish this celestial transmigration, for in Gregory's *Elements of Physical & Geometrical Astronomy*, he told how comets could cause such a change of a moon into a planet:

[61] See above, note 20.
[62] Conduitt crossed out 'gathered'.
[63] Memorandum by Conduitt, King's College, Cambridge MS, Keynes 130, no. 11. This memorandum has been printed with some changes in Edmund Turnor, *Collections for the History of the Town and Soke of Grantham containing Authentic Memoirs of Sir Isaac Newton* (London, 1806), 172–3.
[64] See above, note 29.

There may also be another Effect or Use of a Comet. Namely, if a Comet passes near a Planet ... it will so attract it that its Orbit will be chang'd ... whence the Planet's Period will also be chang'd. But the Comet may also by its Attraction so disturb the Satellite, as to make it leave its Primary Planet and itself become a Primary Planet about the Sun....[65]

In a similar manner, one imagines a planet could be so disturbed in its orbit as to become a comet, as Newton had also indicated to Conduitt. Newton also told Conduitt of the eventual replenishment of the sun by the comet of 1680,

that he could not say when this comet would drop in to the sun it might perhaps have 5 to 6 revolutions more first, but whenever it did it would[66] so much encrease the heat of the Sun that this earth would be burnt & no animals in *this earth* could live....[67]

Newton added that it was his belief that the new stars seen by Hipparchus, Tycho, and Kepler were really the effects of the increase of light of regular stars occasioned by such a comet.[68]

Such revolutions in the heavens, replenishing stars and providing a cycle among the heavenly bodies, were accomplished by mechanical means, but Newton believed that they were under divine supervision.

[65] David Gregory, *The Elements of Physical & Geometrical Astronomy* (London, 1726²), II, 853. Gregory might also have obtained this suggested mechanism from Whiston, *A New Theory of the Earth* (London, 1696). It is not clear who first decided that comets could serve to recruit the active principles lost by the sun, as well as those lost by the planets. Gregory's *Astronomiae Physicae & Geometricae Elementa* (Oxford, 1702), 481, from which the above was translated, expressed the idea before Newton did in the second edition of his *Principia*. It is possible that Newton got the idea from Gregory. It is also possible that Newton, who was planning from the early 1690s to put out a new edition of the *Principia*, found, well before 1713, the supposed tendency of comets to fall into the sun, and told Gregory about it. Gregory's book was in fact used by Newton to publish his own short discourse on how the ancients agreed that gravity existed. This discourse was inserted into the Preface under Gregory's name, although it had been written by Newton. (James Gregory, 'Notice concerning an Autograph Manuscript by Sir Isaac Newton ...', *Transactions of the Royal Society of Edinburgh*, XII [1830] 1, 64–77.) The issue of priority is of small matter, however, for the idea was picked up by Newton's various commentators and disciples and attributed to him, and his contemporaries knew it as his idea not Gregory's.
[66] Conduitt crossed out 'occasion'.
[67] King's College, Cambridge MS, Keynes 130, no. 11.
[68] *Ibid.* He later included this in the third edition of the *Principia* (1726), (*Mathematical Principles of Natural Philosophy*, 541–2).

He[69] seemed to[70] doubt [whether?] there were not intelligent beings superior to us who superintended these revolutions of the[71] heavenly bodies by the direction of the supreme being. . . .[72]

Of course, such a complex machinery as Newton was describing could not be without divine guidance. For the comets to pass by the moons or planets only after this size had so increased that they were fit to be changed into another type of body (planet or comet, as the case may be) and for this, in turn, to occur at the times when new creations were needed to take the place of an earth or a Venus destroyed in the Apocalypse – all this would require the utmost attention to coordinate.

Such coordination by the Creator would indeed require that He be, as Newton had described Him in a letter to Bentley, 'very well skilled in Mechanicks and Geometry'.[73] And we can understand Newton's insistence that comets, moving in orbits quite different from those of planets, have uses quite different from those of planets in the scheme of things.[74] For to Newton, as to his friends Halley[75] and Whiston,[76] comets were instruments of the divine will. For Newton the comets were instruments which God used to reconstitute the cosmos; for Halley, comets were instruments used to bring about the Noachian deluge, and for Whiston, the fundamental basis for the Creation, deluge, and conflagration as well as for the various changes to the Earth which took place after Adam's Fall. Newton believed that such a reconstitution by comets had occurred in the past and was likely to occur in the future.

He seemed to be very clearly of the opinion that the inhabitants of this earth were of a short date & alledged as one reason for that opinion that all arts as letters ... printing needle &c were discoverd within the memory of History wch could not have happened if the world had been eternal: &

[69] Conduitt crossed out 'said he di'.
[70] Conduitt crossed out 'think'.
[71] Conduitt crossed out 'planet'.
[72] King's College, Cambridge MS, Keynes 130, no. 11.
[73] 10 December 1692, in Papers & Letters on Natural Philosophy, 287.
[74] Opticks, 369. Memorandum by Gregory, 5–7 May 1694; The Correspondence, III, 336.
[75] Halley, 'The Obliquity of the Ecliptick and Elevation of the Pole continue unaltered', Philosophical Transactions ... Abridged ... ed. John Lowthorp, I (London, 5th edn, 1749), *263–5; Halley, 'Of the cause of the universal deluge. . . .' Ibid., ed. Reid and Gray, vol. VI, part 2 (London, 1st edn, 1733), 38–41. Halley had begun to suggest his ideas on comets as early as 1686/87.
[76] William Whiston, A New Theory of the Earth ... (London, 5th edn, 1737) Book II, passim. The first edition appeared in 1696.

that there were visible marks of ruin upon it wch could not be effected by a flood only, when I asked him how this earth could have been repeopled if ever it had undergone the same fate it was threatened with hereafter by the Comet of 1680, he answered that required the power of a Creator....[77]

When Conduitt asked Newton why he did not make these ideas public, Newton answered somewhat characteristically that he would not, because, 'I do not deal in conjectures ...'.[78] Conduitt mentioned, however, the passage in the second edition of the *Principia* where, after noting the close approach to the sun by the comet of 1680, Newton had suggested that the fixed stars could be replenished by comets falling into them.[79] Conduitt relates:

I observing that he [Newton] said there of that comet [of 1680] incident in corpus solis, & in the next paragraph adds stellae fixae refici poss[unt] & c told him I thought he owned there what wee had been talking about – viz that the Comet would drop into the sun, & that fixed stars were recruited & replenished by Comets when they dropt in to them, & consequently the sun would be recruited too & asked him, why he would not own as freely what he thought of the Sun as well as what he thought of the fixed stars – he said that concerned us more, & laughing added he had said enough for people to know his meaning....[80]

'That concerned us more ...' – Newton felt free to express his ideas as they applied to a system of stars and planets far removed from us, but felt that to speak openly of the system of *our* sun and planets was not advisable. For Newton's ideas implied the existence of Earths before this one, with the presence of races of man before Adam, and it was probable that the creation of the Earth described in *Genesis* was only one in a series of creations. Carrying the implications even further, an orthodox divine might have seen in Newton's conjectures the belief that the world in one form or another had existed from all eternity.[81]

This, indeed, was the danger in the attempt by Newton – and by certain of his contemporaries – to enforce the belief in God's Providence by showing how, at regular intervals, He must intervene in the mechanisms of the world: such an assertion of intervention, or re-creation from time to time, tended to lead to the

[77] King's College, Cambridge MS, Keynes 130, no. 11.
[78] *Ibid.*
[79] See above.
[80] King's College, Cambridge MS, Keynes 130, no. 11. This ended the conversation.
[81] For example, Bentley, *Confutation of Atheism* in *Works*, III, 65.

inference that a series of Earths have existed from eternity, each one arising out of the ruins of its predecessor. Paradoxically, it had been the fear of this very notion of an eternal Earth which had prompted the English philosopher's concern to demonstrate that God's Providence acted continuously. Such, it seems, was the almost inevitable conflict between natural philosophy and religion in the seventeenth- and early eighteenth-century England, a conflict not between reason and revelation so much as between a mechanistic philosophy and a Providential God.

To be sure, each new Earth, according to Newton, arose out of a past Earth only through 'the Mediation of a divine Power'.[82] But the necessity for that mediation could and would be overlooked by those deists, sceptics, and atheists who wished to use the mechanical means provided by Newton and certain of his contemporaries to show that no other divine means were at all necessary. In fact, some among Newton's friends were thought to have so negated Providence. Edmund Halley, whose lines in the Ode at the beginning of the *Principia* had been changed because they seemed to imply such an eternity of the world, had failed in 1694 to obtain the position of Savilian Professor of Astronomy at Oxford because the ecclesiastical authorities thought Halley 'guilty of asserting the eternity of the world'.[83] Newton, who had kept his own unorthodox questioning of the divinity of Christ secret in order not to lose his position at Cambridge, would not jeopardize that position by disclosing his unorthodox cosmogony.

Conclusion

Although Newton was unwilling explicitly to indicate his cosmogonic speculations, I think it clear that he did entertain such ideas. He was led to these ideas as a result of his belief that the cosmos declined in its powers and regularity, a belief he shared with many other Englishmen. Thus he hoped to avoid the doctrine of the world's eternity. Once having decided that the cosmos declined, Newton sought a mechanism by which the Creator at times could renew the amount of motion and the regularity of the motions of the heavenly bodies. He found such a mechanism in comets. Having shown how comets could account for the circulation of the sources of motion, he then showed how they could account for changes in the bodies of the sun's system. This vision of the cosmos explained not merely the renewal of the amount

---

[82] See above, note 21.
[83] Halley to Abraham Hill (22 June 1691), *Correspondence and Papers of Edmund Halley*, 88. Halley's belief in this unorthodox idea of the eternity of the world, the way in which it influenced his astronomical researches, and his controversies with the ecclesiastical authorities because of these beliefs will be the subject of a later paper.

of motion but also the continual cyclical re-creation of the system and its subsequent development in time until the moment of the next creation.

This being so, two widespread interpretations of seventeenth-century scientific thought seem open to reconsideration. The first is that given by the late R. F. Jones in his *Ancients and Moderns, A Study of the Rise of the Scientific Movement in Seventeenth-Century England*; here he characterized the scientific revolution as proceeding from the energy released by man's new-found confidence in his powers of reason once the notion of the world's decay had been abandoned.[84] Such an interpretation ignores the fact that in seventeenth-century England the idea of the decline of the world meant not that the world would end in an ignoble dissolution, but rather, that the Millennium and second coming of Christ was at hand.[85] Even at the end of the seventeenth century, millennial thought was still quite widespread in England. The various treatises on world-making written near the end of the century by Burnet, John Ray, and Whiston were all concerned not only with the creation, but also with the future conflagration of the world and the millennium associated with it. In addition to the millennial aspects of his cosmogony, Newton dealt with the future millennium in his theological writings.[86] Those who anticipated the millennium did so with optimism rather than pessimism. This optimistic millennialism is associated, no doubt, with primitivism in seventeenth and eighteenth-century English thought, a subject which cannot be explored in this paper. A revealing statement by Newton's disciple Whiston, however, reveals the extent to which the notion of decay was associated with a joyous expectation of the dissolution and subsequent reconstitution of the world. Whiston wrote of Newton's discovery of the gravitational principles of the world :

> Which noble discovery proved the happy occasion of the invention of the wonderful Newtonian philosophy : which indeed, I look upon in a higher light than others, and as an eminent prelude and preparation to those happy times of the restitution of all things, which God has spoken of ... since the world began, Acts, iii, 21.[87]

---

[84] Berkeley, second edition, 1965. The first edition was published in 1936. This is the central thesis of the work, but see particularly page 22.

[85] There were doctrinal disagreements among millennialists as to the order of occurrence of the dissolution of the world, the second coming, and the millennium, but the three were associated.

[86] 'De Millennio ac Die Judicij', *A Com^n Place Book of S^r Is: Newton*, King's College, Cambridge MS, Keynes 2, p. 21.

[87] Whiston, *Memoirs of the Life and Writings of Whiston*, (London, 1753), I, 34. Acts, iii, 20–1 : 'And he shall send Jesus Christ ... [w]hom the heaven must receive until the times of restitution of all things ...'.

Whiston's point is clear: with the writing of Newton's *Principia*, man had attained such insight that it brought him to a state of near perfection. And this, in turn, made the Millennium all the more imminent.

The second interpretation of the seventeenth century which I think warrants reconsideration is the idea that the world-view of Newton, and by inference that of the century in general, was a static one. If Newton did have ideas regarding cosmogeny, then it is wrong to claim that 'the formation of the world ... was seen during the seventeenth and eighteenth centuries as a single creative event, which once accomplished [the world] was eternally enduring and finished for all time'.[88]

This is not to say that I think we should look to Newton for ideas which 'anticipated' those of the late eighteenth, still more of the nineteenth century, in which the development of animals, societies, Earth, and cosmos alike were widely treated. Rather, Newton and many of his English contemporaries seem, like the Stoics, to view the cosmos as going through successive cycles. The destroyed Earth of one cycle would serve as the chaos out of which the Earth of the next cycle would emerge. Illustrative of this outlook is the frontispiece of Burnet's *Sacred Theory of the Earth*[89] in which the progress of the Earth is pictured as it goes from primitive chaos to mature Earth and on to final dissolution. The Earth after its dissolution does not fade into nothingness or into a permanent oblivion; instead, Burnet portrays the states of the Earth in cyclical series, and the skeleton of the Earth, after its destruction, remains to develop later into a new Earth. Newton, I think, would have agreed.

[88] Among many such interpretations, this one is from Stephen F. Mason, *A History of the Sciences* (New York, 2nd edn, 1962), 318.
[89] As mentioned above, Burnet sent Newton a copy of this work for his criticism.

8   The Apologetic Defence of Christianity*

John Dillenberger

THE NEW SCIENCE BECOMES A PHILOSOPHY

Prior to the time of Newton, the philosophical premises of the scientists were consciously related to their scientific theories. There was no attempt to hide such presuppositions. But Newton, on the other hand, had consciously laid metaphysial principles aside. This basic distinction is valid, in spite of the fact that the predecessors of Newton had philosophical assumptions of which they were unaware and that Newton did not really succeed in laying all metaphysical assumptions aside. But in the last quarter of the seventeenth century, a very different movement came into being. It made a philosophy out of the new science. This does not mean that the scientists necessarily believed in this development. Nevertheless, many saw implications in the new science which lent themselves to the popular philosophical movement.

The new philosophy had its roots in France. But it was quickly taken up in England. The achievement of the movement was that of bringing the ideas associated with the new science into a coherent world view and of popularizing the results. Its task was that of organization and of interpretation. The new ideas were brought into the orbit of a shared culture, and thereby indirectly into the orbit of the common man. This is what Locke characterized in his statement that no one read Newton, but everyone talked about him.

One of the books which widely disseminated and defended the new ideas, though written shortly before Newton published his *Principia*, was Fontenelle's *The Plurality of Worlds*. Originally published in French in 1686, it was already in English translation two years later. It went through at least a dozen editions in the ensuing century.[1] Fontenelle was not so much interested in the

---

* John Dillenberger, 'The Apologetic Defence of Christianity', in *Protestant Thought and Natural Science*, Collins, 1961.
[1] A. O. Lovejoy, *The Great Chain of Being* (Cambridge: Harvard University Press, 1953), p. 131; Butterfield, *Origins of Modern Science* (New York, 1953), p. 123.

details of the new science, as in the vistas which it opened. No longer, he declared, was the centre of attention upon the earth and its puny drama; that was much too provincial. Fontenelle went so far as to admit that the vista of many worlds was a depressing thought to man, revealing to him his own insignificance. But if one contemplated the vastness of the universe and remembered that it was man who did the contemplating, it was a bearable thought.

Fontenelle was thrilled by the prospect of the plurality of worlds. He was aware that he could not prove the existence of life on other planets. But on the basis of analogy, he believed that is was highly probable. Had not the apparent difference between the earth and the other planets been discarded as a result of the repudiation of Aristotle and the discoveries of the new science? Was it not therefore logical to assume that what was true on earth, was applicable to other planets as well? Was not science itself, when properly understood, a kind of theology?

Fontenelle was not alone in using this argument. Thomas Burnet argued that just as the knowledge gained in surgery on one man was applicable to other men, so knowledge gained in the exploration of our planet gave reliable knowledge of other planets. He went on to contend that the world of Aristotle was far too small to exhibit the wisdom of God in His creation.[2] God is made too small by thinking of life only on this planet. He said:

> We must not ... admit or imagine, that all Nature, and this great universe, was made only for the sake of man, the meanest of all intelligent creatures that we know of; nor that this little planet, when we sojourn for a few days, is the only habitable part of the universe: these are thoughts so groundless and unreasonable in themselves, and also so derogatory to the infinite power, wisdom and goodness of the first cause, that as they are absurd in reason, so they deserve far better to be marked and censured for heresies in religion, than many opinions that have been censured for such in former ages.[3]

Likewise Charles Blount, in *The Oracles of Reason*, published in 1693, argued that the plurality of inhabited worlds was more agreeable to the greatness and goodness of God than the notion of but one world.

Fontenelle, Burnet, and Blount no longer emphasized or acutely understood the Christian account of redemption. By contrast, Robert Jenkin, a more traditional theologian who was not adverse to the new science, was instructive if not altogether satisfactory. He tried to relate the concept of the plurality of worlds to the Christian view of redemption.

[2] T. Burnet, *The Sacred Theory of the Earth* (London, 1816), pp. 359–60.
[3] Burnet, *op. cit.*, pp. 352–3.

I observe, that though it should be granted, that some Planets be habitable, it doth not therefore follow, that they must be actually inhabited, or that they ever have been. For they might be designed, if mankind had continued in innocency, as places for colonies to remove men to, as the world should have increased, either in reward to those that had excelled in virtue and piety, to entertain them with the prospect of new and better worlds; and so by degrees, to advance them in proportion to their deserts, to the height of bliss and glory in heaven; or as a necessary reception for men (who would then have been immortal) after the earth had been full of inhabitants. And since the fall and mortality of mankind, they may be either for mansions of the righteous, or places of punishment for the wicked, after the resurrection, according as it shall please God, at the end of the world to new modify and transform them. And in the meantime, being placed at their respective distances, they do by their several motions contribute to keep the world at a poise, and the several parts of it at an equilibrium in their gravitation upon each other, by Mr Newton's principles.[4]

Jenkin had obviously related the notion of the plurality of worlds to the possibilities inherent in the total sweep of the Christian drama.

His views were pure conjecture. But so were the views of Fontenelle, Burnet, and Blount. While we have learned to keep the plurality of worlds as an open question, it was not so understood in the later seventeenth and eighteenth centuries. The debate hung on the assumption that human life existed on other planets. But while the externals of the debate were centred here, the fact of possible life on other planets was not as such the issue. The latter was neither affirmed nor denied in the Bible, and only those who believed that all truth had to be found in the Bible were theologically upset by the sheer fact of life on other planets. On this specific problem, as in most of those with which we have been concerned, the central issue was the question of natural knowledge, even a natural theology, versus the authority of the Biblical tradition. Specifically, the form which the problem took was that the plurality of worlds spoke more convincingly of God, the Creator, than did the Bible of God, the Creator and Redeemer.[5]

In the Bible, the redemptive work of God in Christ had ap-

---

[4] Robert Jenkin, *The Reasonableness and Certainty of the Christian Religion* (London, 1700) Book II, p. 222.
[5] Arthur Lovejoy and Marjorie Nicolson, who have made much of the threat to theology through the notion of the plurality of worlds, have not seen that the above was the real threat to Christians.

peared central. Creation was understood in the context of redemption. Now creation, interpreted as the wisdom of God in
His works, was more significant than redemption. For some the
concept of redemption itself was called into question. But even
those who still believed that redemption was paramount had to
admit that there was an entire realm where science was valid
and where the Biblical tradition had nothing to say. For some
time, a large group of writers had contended that the account of
God's creative wisdom could more adequately be given in science
than through Moses. But they still assumed a common realm of
reality concerning which the Biblical tradition and the new
science both spoke. When, by contrast, the notion of the plurality
of worlds was seriously entertained, it became apparent that a
whole area of reality had been opened concerning which the
Bible said nothing at all. All at once, God the Creator had come
into His own. Men were ecstatic concerning the wisdom and
marvels of God expressed in the perfections of such an infinite
world. Such a world staggered the imagination and no provincial interpretation sufficed. Depressed in part by the discovery of
such vastness, men were yet intoxicated by it, and saw their
place in the scheme of things in tracing out the marvels of the
Creator's world. In fact, this was their vocation as men. Nature
and Nature's laws were everywhere, testifying to the marvellous
wisdom of God. It was the task of everyone, and of the scientists
particularly, to exhibit it to plain view. In this development, the
concern with nature had become central for the knowledge of
God. Heretofore, history and particularly the Biblical history,
had been the central key to the knowledge of God. Natural knowledge of God had heretofore always been subservient to revelation, either as a first step or in integral relation to it. Now natural
theology was independent of revelation; it had come into its own.

This is not to say that the new independence of natural theology was the result only of the impact of the plurality of worlds
in the latter part of the seventeenth century. The general direction was reinforced by related though fairly independent factors.
The discontent of many with the confessional battles between
the Lutheran and Reformed churches was also a major item in
fostering disillusionment with a Biblically centred Christianity.
Later, too, the knowledge of other religious cultures entered the
picture. Nevertheless, the notion of the plurality of worlds, in
spite of the long history of the concept, only came into its own
in this period. It caught on as the natural expression of those who
believed that philosophy and science must be wrested from the
domination of those Christians who adhered so strictly to a
Biblical tradition. It was such a powerful symbol because it provided an area of knowledge which testified to God apart from
any strict Biblical dictation.

This new trend was firmly established by the early eighteenth century. It had an effect also on the more traditional theological circles. More and more natural theology became a first and independent section in theology with hardly any reference to the Biblical tradition. Those in the tradition of Derham, Burnet, and Ray, to Paley, maintained that natural theology was a prelude to revealed theology. The task of natural theology was to trace the marvels of God's works in nature. This, they believed, did not detract from revelation, though it must be pursued in independence of it. Among the deists, however, a truncated natural theology became a substitute for revelation. In all of these groups, the independence of natural theology was expressed. They were followed by a development in which natural theology was neither a first step in theology nor a substitute for revelation, but the avenue for understanding revelation. That development, which will concern us in the next chapter [omitted – Ed.] is classically expressed in the transition in the Continent from Protestant orthodoxy to the Enlightenment.

We shall not undertake to trace the history of the groups we have mentioned. The influence of natural theology upon the orthodox will be included in the next chapter, where the transition to the Enlightenment will be delineated. Neither the tradition from Derham to Paley nor that of the deists can be said to be central enough to a positive Protestant tradition to warrant separate elaboration here. For our purposes, it is more important to note the type of apologetics used in the defence of Christianity by the orthodox and by those sympathetic to Christianity. Such apologists had now to meet the new philosophy as it expressed itself so cogently in such notions as the plurality of worlds, the views of the deists, and the French equivalents to both.

THE EVIDENCES FOR CHRISTIANITY

It was in the eighteenth century, prepared in decisive form in the latter half of the seventeenth, that the self-evidence of the Christian outlook was first challenged in post-medieval history. Until then one could assume interest in and knowledge of Christianity among those who were at all concerned about religious issues. Now began the bid for a religious understanding which placed Christians under the necessity of defending their views. Previously in Protestant history, the debates had centred in the issues which divided the Protestant fold internally and in the relation of Protestantism to Roman Catholicism. Insofar as the Christian claim previously had to be defended at all, it was against so-called atheism. But this type of defence assumed the superiority and dominance of the Christian understanding. Christians were sufficiently secure to be condescending in debate. Now, however, a new situation had arisen. While Christianity was not a minority movement, its hold on the minds of men, particularly in the traditional sense, could no longer be assumed. A new juncture in history had come. At one and the same time, Christianity had to defend its own understanding against all the new forms of thought, as in extreme orthodoxy, or to show, on grounds similar to the new philosophy, that it should not be ruled out, but rather accepted all the more enthusiastically.

The apologetic for Christianity primarily took four forms; the evidences through miracle and prophecy (which we shall treat together), the delineation of the wisdom of God in creation, and the argument from the analogy between nature and Scripture. Of these, the first two, miracle and prophecy, were considered absolutely essential for the defence of Christian revelation. And the amazing fact was that these arguments were utilized even by those whose Christian understanding had been rationalized to the point where one wonders how much Christian substance was left.

Miracle and prophecy

In this period it was almost universally accepted that the truth or falsity of Christianity depended upon the credibility of the Biblical miracles. The defence was always buttressed by reference to the Biblical tradition and to the early Church. Since the argument from miracle and prophecy had always had its place in Christian history, all could assume its significance. But, as we shall note, it was doubtful that it even had the pre-eminent position in the early Church which was now accorded to it. While the argument had been repeated by the orthodox theologians, it was now singled out for particular attention by orthodox and less orthodox alike.

The general thesis was that the authenticity and confirmation of Christ came through the miracles which He performed, and which the early disciples performed in His name. In the history of Israel, miracles too had their place. But in the course of history, they had stopped occurring. It was said that the Spirit had departed from Israel. But it was affirmed that when the Messiah arrived, He would be known through the miracles which He performed, that is, through the power of the Spirit. It must be added, however, that interpreters in this period stressed the *fact* of the miracles more than their association with the work of the Spirit. Indeed, there was some suspicion of the Spirit. Something as tangible and factual as miracles was demanded. Talk about the Spirit laid one open to the charge that one paid attention to the work of God in a private and therefore unconfirmable sense. Robert Jenkin argued that prophecy and miracles were more dependable than any immediate revelation from God. Imposture and scorn were removed, he declared, for miracles, unlike revelation and the Spirit, were public property.[6]

Our contemporary vogue of considering miracles in a way which takes attention away from whether or not they occurred as recorded, had not arisen in the minds of those thinkers. For them, the occurrence or non-occurrence of miracles was the issue. This left only one basis for decision about them, namely, the credibility of the witnesses. On this point all were agreed; for example, Robert Jenkin, the most traditional of theologians; Ralph Cudworth, in a more Platonist tradition; John Locke, in an essentially rational mould; Joseph Butler, in his mediating position; or William Paley, in a tradition of natural theology as late as the beginning of the nineteenth century.

For Locke, the reasonableness of Christianity rested on the confirmation of the messiahship of Jesus through the miracles which He performed. Although miracles had ceased among the Jews, they were expected of the Messiah.[7] Jesus had performed miracles, according to eye witnesses; consequently what could be more rational than that He was the Messiah? Locke was aware that everything depended upon the opinion of the spectators and that questions could be raised about the reliability of the witnesses. But in good rational form, he met such questions by suggesting that anyone who raised doubts about the credibility of the opinion of the spectators was beset with the same difficulty with respect to his own views.[8] He therefore concluded that the truth of Christianity rested upon a proper and reasonable understanding of miracles.

The type of argument used to confirm the credibility of the witnesses is readily illustrated in the work of Charles Leslie, *A Short and Easy Method with the Deists*. Accepting the notion that the truth of the miracles would establish the truth of Him who performed them, Leslie proceeded to argue for the credibility of the witnesses to miracles on the basis of three related rules. In the first place, we have to do with matters which can be confirmed by the outward senses, things which are seen and heard. Hence, miracles must be substantiated by the senses in the same way in which anything else in nature is open to verification. In the second place, in order to be authentic, miracles must be public. Everyone must be able to see them; in fact, it is necessary that they be seen by many people. In the third place, some customs or observances must follow in the wake of miracles, testifying

---

[6] Jenkin, *op. cit.*, I, 29.
[7] Locke, *The Reasonableness of Christianity*, Works (12th edn, London, 1824), VI, 17, 18, 32.
[8] J. Locke, *A Discourse on Miracles*, Works (12th edn, London, 1824), VIII, 256.

to the impact which these events made upon subsequent history. The memory of Israel's miraculous delivery from Egypt was part of the observed and constant memory of the Church. Its impact upon the Church testified that it was an authentic event. It was not a freak event, as would be the case, Leslie points out hypothetically, if one made the claim that in the eighteenth century everyone cut off his middle finger. Since neither witness nor significant memories or actual cultic practices testify to it, such a claim can be called unauthentic. With respect to the first and second rules for the confirmation of miracles, Leslie gave himself to his descriptions with utter abandon. The Red Sea events, for example, are especially miraculous because the Sea was full and overflowing; moreover 600,000 men had witnessed the dividing of the waters. So many men could not be wrong. According to Leslie, those who interpreted the Red Sea story in the context of a Spring tide, or some such natural explanation, had capitulated to the point where Biblical truth was in doubt. He wrote:

> I say this for the sake of some Christians, who think it no prejudice to the truth of the Holy Bible, but rather an advantage, as rendering it more easy to be believed, if they can solve what ever seems miraculous in it by the power of second causes; and so to make all, as they speak, natural and easy: wherein, if they could prevail, the natural and easy result would be, not to believe one word in all those sacred-oracles. For if things be not as they are told in any relation, that relation must be false. And if false in part, we cannot trust to it, either in whole, or in part.[9]

Leslie obviously believed in the inerrancy of the Bible; but in respect to miracles, the argument was no different on the part of those who no longer held a literalistic view.

In addition to the three rules Leslie elaborated for the confirmation of miracles, many writers added a fourth, namely, that of the willingness of Christians to suffer for their faith. The early Christians, it was stated, were so convinced by what they had seen that they could not and did not shrink from the consequences. This argument was still used as late as Paley.[10] But it was a supplemental argument, and therefore did not carry the weight of the more direct arguments. It must be added, however, that the interest centred, not in the miracles as such, but in what they confirmed. They testified to the Messiah. Writers were quick to point out that miracles were not unique. Many claimed to have

[9] C. Leslie, *A Short and Easy Method with the Deists* in *The Theological Works* (Oxford, 1832), I, 23.
[10] W. Paley, 'The Evidences of Christianity', in *Miscellaneous Works* (London, 1820), I, Part 1.

performed them. Further, many individuals who had never performed miracles were considered as unique as those who had. The convincing point of the argument from miracles was that they confirmed the Messiahship. Things happened precisely as predicted; role and witness were conjoined, just as had been prophesied. Writer after writer pointed out that this was not the case of other religious figures. Mohammed was not confirmed by miracles performed or predicted.[11]

This line of argument was widely accepted, in spite of disagreement on whether miracles were still performed, occurred rarely, or had again entirely ceased. While there was no unanimity about such matters, there was unanimity that they had occurred in the past. Nevertheless, most theologians believed that miracles were now indeed rare or had ceased completely. In fact, the argument for their credibility partially depended upon the fact that they no longer occurred frequently. Bishop Butler maintained that miracles should be compared to rare events in nature, such as comets, rather than to the orderly course of nature.[12] Burnet suggested that one should stick to the level of secondary causation as long as possible and flee to miracles only as a last resort. Jenkin believed that miracles had entirely ceased; but that they were confirmed with reference to Christ and therefore were decisive in that setting.

> Faith in the miracles of Christ is required of men in all ages of the world, though miracles are ceased; and if this be reasonable now, it could not but be fitting then, that those who came to Christ, should believe in him for the sake of the miracles, which they had been certified that he had done upon others. For miracles, when they are fully attested, are as sufficient a ground of faith, as if we had seen them done; and to manifest that they are so, our Saviour might require belief in his former miracles, of those who expected any advantage from such as they desired him to do.[13]

By the middle of the eighteenth century, the role of miracles so understood was severely challenged. Men such as Christian Wolff suggested that Christians should concentrate on the order of nature as much as possible. He argued that God's power was more manifest in the orderly course of nature than through miracles. This way of thinking gained considerable support during the eighteenth century. The second major challenge came in Hume's criticism of miracles. After contending that all witnesses

---

[11] J. Butler, *Analogy of Religion* (New York, 1870), p. 276; W. Paley, *op. cit.*, p. 368.

[12] Butler, *op. cit.*, p. 219.

[13] Jenkin, *op. cit.*, II, 489–90.

are at best secondary, and asserting that many contradictory and bizarre things are said about miracles, he concluded that:

> upon the whole, then, it appears that no testimony for any kind of miracle has ever amounted to a probability, much less to a proof; and that, even supposing it amounted to a proof, it would be opposed by another proof; derived from the very nature of the fact, which it would endeavour to establish. It is experience only, which gives authority to human testimony; and it is the same experience, which assures us of the laws of nature. When, therefore, these two kinds of experiences are contrary, we have nothing to do but subtract the one from the other, and embrace an opinion, either on one side or the other, with that assurance which arises from the remainder. But according to the principle here explained, this subtraction, with regard to all popular religions, amounts to an entire annihilation; and therefore we may establish it as a maxim, that no human testimony can have such force as to prove a miracle, and make it a just foundation for any such system of religion.[14]

Hume's criticism was directed equally to miracles, to the laws of nature, and to a natural theology built upon design and the constancy of human nature. His own views were too radical to be taken seriously in his own time. Most theologians accepted both the laws of nature and the fact of miracles. The latter were but the expression of God's power over and above nature. Only the deists directly attacked miracles from the standpoint of the order of nature. The usual line of defence continued the old tradition, namely, whatever was above nature was as reasonable and certain as nature itself. In retrospect, the contention that miracles had occurred in the past but had ceased, only postponed facing the inevitable question of whether they could any longer be defined along traditional lines.

The traditional conception of miracle, as we have already indicated, was intertwined with the conception of prophecy. The miracles of Jesus and His near contemporaries were significant because they testified to the fulfilment of the Messianic prophecies. Hence, miracles in the restricted sense of the Messianic problems, pointed to the reality of fulfilled prophecy. In fact, the argument from prophecy had a distinct advantage over miracle. Irrespective of whether or not it was held that miracles had ceased or continued to happen, the miracles associated with the Messianic claim were past events. But prophecy had the

[14] Hume, *An Inquiry Concerning Human Understanding*, in *The English Philosophers from Bacon to Mill*, ed. Burtt (New York: Modern Library, 1939), pp. 664–5.

strength of past prediction and subsequent fulfilment. Its significance increased in proportion to the length of time which elapsed between the enunciation and fulfilment of a prophecy. Robert Jenkin wrote:

> Prophecies are generally of more concernment, and afford greater evidence and conviction in future ages, than when they were first delivered. For it is not the delivery, but the accomplishment of prophecies, which gives evidence of the truth of any doctrine: The events of things in the accomplishment of prophecies are a standing argument to all ages, and the length of time adds to its force and efficacy; and therefore when all that God saw requisite to be foretold, is delivered to us in the Scriptures, there can no longer be any need of new prophecies; which would be of less authority than the ancient ones, inasmuch as their antiquity is the thing chiefly to be regarded in prophecies.[15]

Ralph Cudworth from a different theological perspective also stressed the importance of prophecy. He suggested that prophecies were more valid than the recorded miracles.[16] The reason was that prophecies were written down and were fulfilled later. The Old Testament preceded the New Testament in time, and the latter fulfilled the former. By contrast, miracles were considered concurrent with the event to which they testified; prophecy included antecedent factors. The authority of the Bible finally rested upon the fact that what God had predicted in the old covenant had come true in the new.

On the basis of this assumption, theologians and non-theologians alike attempted to decipher the content of other predictions in the Bible which had not been fulfilled. Just as the prediction of the Messiah had been fulfilled, so too, the predictions of the end of the world would be fulfilled and were already recorded in the Biblical material. Just as God's thoughts were read after Him in nature, so he who knew the Bible could discern God's thoughts and perhaps His infallible knowledge of the future. Knowledge of the future, it was believed, was certainly hidden in the Bible and could perhaps be discovered. Hence, Newton and others of a similar spirit, as we indicated previously, read both nature and the Bible, particularly the sections on prophecy, with an eye to uncovering knowledge of the future.

The argument from prophecy was challenged when it was discovered, particularly by those of a more rational bent of mind, that the prophecies had not always been fulfilled as predicted,

---

[15] Jenkin, op. cit., II, 491.
[16] R. Cudworth, The True Intellectual System of the Universe (London, 1678), pp. 714–15.

that some were never fulfilled though the time for their fulfilment had passed, and that some predictions had been inaccurate. Those who were so minded could, of course, find explanations which saved the prophecies.

More important than the specific debates is the context for the arguments from miracle and prophecy. We have already indicated that the form of the apologetic stems from the ancient tradition of the Church. But it is doubtful that the seventeenth–eighteenth-century context was the same as that of the early Church. The early Church, convinced that He who had come was the Messiah, affirmed that the expectations and predictions had been fulfilled. Convinced that He was the Messiah, the miracles were positive signs and proof of the event. Prophecy meant that the concrete expectation had been fulfilled and miracles were corroborative testimony that the new age had dawned. But it is doubtful that in the early Church the truth of the Christian claim rested on the form of the argument. Greeks and Jews alike shared the assumption that all knowledge of the future had already been disclosed in the past, and that the validity of truth was proportional to its antiquity. This was as true for understanding the myths of Homer as it was for understanding the Bible, and it indicates why Genesis was even more significant than Isaiah. In that way of thinking, the New Testament use of Old Testament passages in a predictive sense is intelligible and partially convincing. The fulfilled expectations now provided the possibility of seeing predictive allusions where they had not been seen before. Prophecy thus had a very significant role to play in the understanding of the early Church, whereas the question of the credibility of miracles was raised very early in the history of the Church.[17]

In the post-Reformation developments, the form of the argument was more significant than it was in the early Church. Hence, the analogy between the two does not hold. In the seventeenth and eighteenth centuries, one believed because of the miracles which occurred, and because prophecies as predicted, had been fulfilled. As we have indicated, miracle and prophecy were considered as objective facts, no different from those in the domain of science. Confirmation for the revelation of God in Christ was of the same order as that in the natural sciences. The Messiah had Himself become an object of ordinary knowledge and demonstration. He was no longer in the first instance the source of that new life which transformed old relations.

The fateful consequences of such a position are all too obvious. The defence of Christianity through miracle and prophecy in the sevententh–eighteenth-century sense is an unfortunate

17 R. M. Grant, *Miracle and Natural Law in the Graeco-Roman and Early Christian Thought* (Amsterdam, 1952).

chapter in the history of Protestant theology. It was already a mistake to discuss theological questions as if they were on the same level as the knowledge of nature. It was but a short and fatal step from understanding the messianic claims in categories appropriate to nature to rejecting them because the knowledge of nature made them appear incredible. On the old path, no new directions were possible. The latter occurred as late as Friedrich Schleiermacher in the early nineteenth century.[18]

The wisdom of God in creation – the argument from design

Just as was the case with reference to the interpretation of miracle and prophecy, so too the argument for a deeper understanding of God through the marvels of nature rested upon a Biblical foundation and the situation in the early history of the Church. Anyone who has read the Psalms or Job or Second Isaiah knows something of the power of those Biblical passages in which the marvels and mystery of God's creation are confessed and declared. But the world into which Christianity entered had no uniform conception of nature. It was variously assumed that the world, including nature, was subject to the power of inexorable fate and that chance was operative on every level. Frequently, both fate and chance were affirmed by the same person. It should be said here that fate was not the equivalent of inexorable law. It was a meaningless sway of a dark power from which there was no escape. In a world of fate and/or chance, Christianity affirmed the meaningful and purposeful character of all the events of nature and history. The powers of fate and fortune were challenged in the light of a destiny for man under God, even when that destiny was expressed in the most deterministic terms.

Cudworth felt a conscious kinship to the early Church as he undertook his own apologetic labours. Throughout the *True Intellectual System of the Universe* he contended against a mechanical view of the world and the concept of chance. He considered both to be atheistic views, which in different forms had already been met in the early Church. He recalled that Anaxagoras had said that man chanced to have hands. Cudworth found such a statement devoid of all meaning. Hands obviously have purposes, as do all aspects of reality. The concept of purpose was, in fact, the main argument against chance; in the last analysis, it was the defence against atheism.[19]

The argument from purpose which we encountered in a previous chapter was not only revived in this time; it was re-

---

[18] In anticipation, it should be said that the less dogmatic character of contemporary science and the abandonment of a concept of rigid order are no bases for a return to miracle in the old sense, though this seems frequently to be the assumption.

[19] Cudworth, *op cit.*, p. 685.

vived with new power, that is, with the support of all the insights
and extensive knowledge which came from the science of nature.
The intoxicating effect of this new knowledge was apparent in
such a traditional theologian as Robert Jenkin.

> Indeed infidelity could never be more inexcusable than in the
> present age, when so many discoveries have been made in
> natural philosophy, which would have been thought incred-
> ible to former ages, as any thing perhaps that can be imagined,
> which is not a downright contradiction. That gravitating or
> attractive force, by which all bodies act one upon another, at
> never so great a distance, even through a vacuum of prodi-
> gious extent, lately demonstrated by Mr Newton; the Earth,
> together with the planets, and the sun and stars being placed
> at such distances, and disposed of in such order, and in such
> a manner, as to maintain a perpetual balance and poise
> throughout the universe, is such a discovery, as nothing less
> than a demonstration could have gained it any belief. And
> this system of nature being so lately discovered, and so won-
> derful, that no account can be given of it by a hypothesis in
> philosophy, but it must be resolved into the sole Power and
> good pleasure of Almighty God, may be a caution against all
> attempts of estimating the Divine works and dispensations by
> the Measures of humane reason. The vastness of the world's
> extent is found to be so prodigious, that it would exceed the
> belief not only of the vulgar, but of the greatest philosopher,
> if undoubted experiments did not assure us of the truth of
> it.[20]

Similar sentiments were elaborated by such men as John Ray
and William Derham. Ray, on the one hand, pointed to the
immense size of the world and on the other, to the species in
nature which are so small that they are unnoticed by most of us.
He found it difficult to believe that this panorama was made for
man alone.[21] The possibility of life on other planets intrigued
him and he believed that such life belonged to the purposes of
God. But even planets which have life, he declared, can be utilized by us to contemplate God's creative work. Likewise, the
multitude of species can be viewed in different ways. By observing them, we can contemplate the wisdom and power of God
and affirm that they have uses which we do not yet know.[22]
Derham, in a similar vein as John Ray, was impressed by the
immensity of the universe. But he was equally enamoured by

[20] Jenkin, op. cit., II, 18–19.
[21] J. Ray, The Wisdom of God Manifested in the Work of Creation (11th
edn, 1743), p. 177.
[22] Ibid., pp. 368–9.

its apparent suitableness for the enrichment and purposes of man.

> The motions the terraqueous Globe hath, are round its own axis, and round its fountain of light and heat, the Sun. That so vast a body as the earth and waters should be moved at all, that it should undergo two such different motions, as the diurnal and annual are, and that these motions should be so constantly and regularly performed for near 6000 years, without any the least alteration ever heard of (except some hours which we read of in Joshua x, 12, 13, and in Hezekiah's time, which, if they cannot be accounted for some other way, do greatly increase the wonder); these things, I say, do manifestly argue some divine infinite power to be contained therein. But especially, if to all this we add the wonderful convenience, yea absolute necessity of these circumvolutions to the inhabitants, yea all the products of the earth and waters. For to one of these we owe the comfortable changes of day and night; the one for business, the other for repose; the one for man, and most other animals to gather and provide Food, Habitation, and other necessities of life; the other to rest, refresh, and recruit their spirits, wasted away with the labours of the day. To the other of those motions we owe the seasons of summer and winter, spring and autumn, together with the beneficial instances and effects, which these have on the bodies and states of animals, vegetables, and all other things, in the torrid, temperate, and frigid zones.[23]

For Derham, the whole universe was still geared to the necessities and comforts of man. Approximately a century later, William Paley doubted the usefulness of astronomy in relation to natural theology.

> My opinion of astronomy has always been that it is not the best medium through which to prove the agency of an intelligent creator; but that, this being proved, it shows, beyond all other sciences, the magnificence of his operations. The mind which is once convinced, it raises to sublimer views of the Deity than any other subject affords; but it is not so well adapted as some other subjects are to the purpose of argument. We are destitute of the means of examining the constitution of the heavenly bodies ... We see nothing but bright points, luminous circles, or the phases of spheres reflecting the light which falls upon them. Now we deduce design from relation, aptitude, and correspondence of parts. Some degree, therefore, of *complexity*, is necessary to render a subject fit

[23] W. Derham, *Physico-Theology* (London, 1720), pp. 43–6.

for this species of argument. But the heavenly bodies do not, except perhaps in the instance of Saturn's ring, present themselves to our observation as compounded of parts at all.[24]

In spite of this difference between Derham and Paley, there was a remarkable similarity in the arguments which they employed. Derham saw in the astronomical realm precisely that degree of adaptation to purpose which made Paley more enamoured of biology. In fact, purpose was seen everywhere, and whatever was, was obviously meant to be as it was, in order to serve its purpose in the best way. Derham, contemplating the position of the eye, decided that it would have been more convenient to have the eye in one's hand because of the greater manoeuvrability of the hand; nevertheless, it was wiser to have it in one's head where it was not so susceptible to injury.[25] Writers continued to be intrigued by the marvellous workmanship and mystery of the eye. Paley suggested that if we had no other

> example in the world of contrivance except that of the eye, it would be alone sufficient to support the conclusion that we draw from it, as to the necessity of an intelligent Creator.[26]

On the whole, however, one is struck by the tedious obviousness and lack of imagination in this literature. Two passages from Ray will suffice:

> The great wisdom of the divine creator appears, in that there is pleasure annexed to those actions that are necessary for the support and preservation of the individual, and the continuation and propagation of the species; and not only so, but

---

[24] W. Paley, *Natural Theology* (London, 1836), II, 13–14.
Charles Raven makes much of the difference between the more organic and living biology of Ray and the more contrived, mechanical, and lifeless biological work of Paley. He believes that concentration upon the work of Ray provides a fruitful clue to a genuine partnership. Generally speaking, Raven believes that not enough attention has been given to the biological sciences in the science–religion question and that astronomy and physics have received disproportionate attention. Certainly the opposition is less prominent in the field of biology, and in this sense Raven is right in stating that corrections need to be made. But it seems to me that he too easily pushes aside the fact that it was precisely in astronomy and physics that the original issues did occur and that they did, as he himself indicates, create problems in the field of biology. See Charles Raven's *John Ray, Organic Design*, and his two volumes, *Natural Religion* and *Christian Theology*.
[25] Derham, *op. cit.*, p. 89.
[26] W. Paley, *Natural Theology*, I, 81. The conic structure of the eye is still one of the great mysteries of biology. But it is doubtful that the theological conclusions which such interpreters as du Noüy derive from it are valid.

pain to the neglect or forbearance of them. For the support of the person, it hath annexed pleasure to eating and drinking, which else, out of laziness or multiplicity of business, a man would be apt to neglect, or sometimes forget; indeed to be obliged to chew and swallow meat daily for two hours space, to find no relish or pleasure in it, would be one of the most burdensome and ungrateful tasks of a man's whole life; but because this action is absolutely necessary, for abundant Security Nature hath inserted in us a painful sense of hunger, to put us in mind of it; and to reward our performance hath enjoined pleasure to it; and as for the continuation of kind, I need not tell you that the enjoyments which attend those actions are the highest gratifications of sense.[27]

Or again,

That whereas the breast is encompassed with ribs, the belly is left free, that it might give way to the motion of the midriff in respiration, and to the necessary reception of meat and drink as also for the convenient bending of the body; and in females for that extraordinary extension that is requisite in the time of their pregnancy.[28]

Two books even appeared in the eighteenth century with the titles, *Insect-Theology*, and *Water Theology*.[29]

Whatever was, was obviously right. (Basil Willey calls it Cosmic Toryism.) Believing that this was the best possible of all worlds, these men spelled out precisely the sense in which that was true. Ray reminded his contemporaries that the most pernicious insects provided us with medicine, and that sometimes God was pleased to send us scourges through insects, as in the case of the Egyptians, in order to chastise us.[30] Paley contended that mortal diseases reconciled us to death and thus ended the horror of it.[31] Derham admitted the inconvenience of volcanic action, but affirmed that a volcano supplied a necessary chimney for the fire burning in the earth.[32] Ray and Paley were so busy ascribing purpose and usefulness to everything that the agony and disproportionate character of human suffering did not seriously enter their horizon; and Derham never raised the question of imperfections in nature. Assuming the wisdom of God in creation, they elaborated the obvious positive uses of all things and even ascribed purposes to the most embarrassing aspects of

[27] Ray, *op. cit.*, pp. 239–40.
[28] *Ibid.*, pp. 287–8.
[29] F. C. Lesser, *Insecto–Theologie*; and J. A. Fabricius, *Wasser–Theologie*.
[30] J. Ray, *op. cit.*, pp. 374–5.
[31] Paley, *Natural Theology*, II, 137.
[32] Derham, *op. cit.*, p. 69.

the universe and of existence generally. It is not surprising that this type of natural theology was unconvincing in the long run. And just as he had done in the case of miracles, Hume mercilessly attacked it.

These writers, just as those who defended Christianity through miracle and prophecy, claimed that they were following the tradition of the early Church. But they too did not see that their situation was not identical, and that they had inverted the original apologetic.

To believers, according to the Biblical tradition and the early Church, nature manifested the glories of God the Creator. It was however, a subsidiary theme. Missionaries preached the drama of creation as a part of the drama of redemption. But in the period under discussion, the domain of nature was divorced from its Christological centre. The heavens no longer declared the glory of God to the eyes of faith. Rather, the heavens were used to argue for the wisdom of a Creator. It is understandable that such an apologetic should appear persuasive to those who were trying to interpret the new science in a religious sense. It is also understandable that such astounding discoveries should have taken on religious dimensions.

But in the long run, two factors were definitely against the usefulness of such an apologetic. First, as the scientific tradition continued to develop, scientists saw no need for such an interpretation of their work. In fact, many of them opposed it. Second, those interested in the wisdom of God in creation were so enamoured with what they saw that they practically subsumed the concern with revelation. The originally dubious charge of the theologians that too much attention given to science would take attention away from revelation had become more than a suspicion; it had become a fact. Reflection on this period raises the question whether a conscious apologetic is not usually a boomerang. If theologians and scientists had been less interested in writing apologetics for each other, their relationship might have been more creative in the long run. They might have been able to distinguish and then relate their concerns. As it was, they met on grounds detrimental to both.

The analogy between nature and Scripture

The analogy between nature and Scripture, as we have noted before, meant that the affirmations and problems in each bore a proportionate relation to each other. The particular form of the usual analogy referred to the clarity and obscurity of nature and Scripture. Moreover, just as in the case of the arguments from miracle, prophecy, and design, it was maintained that the analogy was already used in the early Church. In setting forth his intention in the *Analogy*, Bishop Butler made this quite clear:

From analogical reasoning, Origen has with singular sagacity observed, that 'he who believes the Scripture to have proceeded from him who is the author of Nature, may well expect to find the same sort of difficulties in it, as are found in the constitution of Nature'. And in a like way of reflection, it may be added, that he who denies the Scripture to have been from God, upon account of these difficulties, may, for the very same reason, deny the world to have been formed by him.[33]

While this passage immediately shows how conscious Butler was of standing in the old apologetic tradition, it also indicates that here, as in the other instances, a great reversal had taken place. Origen argued against those who would not take Scripture seriously because of its obscurities, and he maintained that Scripture was just like nature, that is, full of obscurities. He who objected to Scripture on the ground of obscurity, he argued, must logically reject nature, for here one encountered the same difficulties. Butler, on the other hand, confronted an entirely new situation. No longer did men feel that nature was obscure. That had to be argued. Butler had to contend that there were many true and real aspects of nature which could not be discovered by our natural faculties.[34] Origen had argued that Scripture was like nature, that is, like a view of nature which all accepted; but Butler had to argue that nature was like Scripture, with the disadvantage that neither nature nor Scripture were understood as he desired. The analogy which Origen utilized proceeded from the accepted to the unaccepted, maintaining that there were similarities between the two. Butler put himself in the position of arguing that nature as generally accepted was not really as orderly as assumed; of maintaining that the analogy between nature and Scripture was valid; and of assuming that Scripture ought therefore to be accepted. Even if it were true, such an argument could hardly be convincing. Butler's *Analogy*, could not be the wave of the future. It was too widely held that nature was orderly and that its mysteries were being pushed aside by new discoveries. Butler was correct in sensing that the new science did not provide an adequate understanding of nature. But he attacked at the wrong point and was destined to fight a losing battle. In point of fact, the conception of analogy could more tellingly be used against him, particularly when, as in the case of Origen, one argued from the accepted to the unaccepted. Men were sure that nature had lost its obscurities. Obscurities remained only in Scripture. Hence, the inevitable hope was that they could be expunged from Scripture. And the obscurities of

[33] J. Butler, *op. cit.*, p. 86.
[34] *Ibid.*, p. 214.

Scripture were indeed set aside, so that Scripture corresponded to the simplicity of nature. But since the principles for deciding what was obscure were derived from reason and nature rather than from Scripture, it was inevitable that the understanding of Scripture was drastically transformed in the process. This resulted in that increasing rationalization of Christian revelation which led directly to the Enlightenment.[35]

As we indicated previously, the most devastating attack on the arguments from miracle and prophecy came from David Hume. In his *Essay Concerning Natural Religion*, he also repudiated the argument from design and the conception of a definite and stable human nature upon which natural theology depended. The degree to which Hume was actually open to considering revelation as an alternative to natural theology, in the closing section of the Essay, is a debatable point; our only concern here is to stress that the philosophical method which included the certainty of the evidences and of natural theology was not so self-authenticating and convincing in the long run as its protagonists thought. While Hume was not accepted in his own time or extensively thereafter, his basic point was taken up by others in a less radical way. Natural theology was rejected as the pillar which sustained the Christian enterprise. In fact, it can be maintained that natural theology was mainly responsible for the demise of Christianity in many areas.

SELECTED THEOLOGICAL FIGURES

Bishop Butler and John Wesley confronted the same problem within Anglicanism. They were deeply disturbed by the lack of a vibrant and living faith in the established Church. The contrast in the accomplishments of the two men suggests that the salvation of the Christian enterprise came not from the rearguard apologetics of Butler, but from the proclamation of the redeeming Word as preached by Wesley and his associates. Wesley's ideas were not held in opposition to the knowledge of his time; but the impact of the redeeming Christ upon the lives of men was its own apologetic. Wesley was so busy with his central mission of proclaiming Christ that many theological problems were lightly met rather than either carefully opposed or championed in new directions. The consequence is that we have a somewhat ambiguous picture of Wesley's relation to various forms of thought, including the natural sciences.

He shared the suspicion that science tended to take one's attention away from theological problems. In fact, he was not sure

[35] See next Chapter [omitted – *Ed.*]

that it was always a proper way to spend one's time. In his Journal, he wrote:

> At the desire of some of my friends, I accompanied them to the British Museum. What an immense field is here for curiosity to range in! One large room is filled from top to bottom with things brought from Otaheite; two or three more with things dug out of the ruins of Herculaneum! Seven huge apartments are filled with curious books, five with manuscripts, two with fossils of all sorts, and the rest with various animals. But what account will a man give to the Judge of the quick and dead for a life spent in collecting all these?[36]

And in the light of experiments which he carried out, Wesley reported that he could not study mathematics, arithmetic, or algebra to an appreciable extent without becoming a deist, if not an atheist.[37] On the other hand, he declared that the study of nature humbled man's pride, showed forth the wisdom of God, warmed men's hearts, and filled us all with wonder, love, and praise.[38]

Whatever his attitude toward theoretical science, Wesley did popularize scientific results. His first concern was to make practical and useful information available. Two of his books belong in this category: one on medicine, entitled, *Primitive Physic*, and a book on electricity called, *Desideratum: or Electricity made Plain and Useful*. The former is full of helpful remedies for various recognized illnesses of the time, and it even suggests that psychological states have a bearing on bodily health. But by and large, these books were not original; they consisted of compilations of useful information taken from others. Much of the material was already out of date at the time Wesley published the books.

Wesley also published a volume entitled, *A Survey of the Wisdom of God in the Creation; or a Compendium of Natural Philosophy*. In it he expounded the traditional arguments from design; he quoted Ray, Derham, and many others, including Cotton Mather. Wesley himself said that his work was largely translated from the Latin work of John Francis Buddeus,[39] though he retrenched, enlarged, altered, and corrected it.[40] Originally published in two volumes in 1763, it was immensely popular and

[36] *The Journal of the Reverend John Wesley*, Curnock edition (Epworth Press, 1938), VI, 301.
[37] Sermon, 'The Use of Money' in *Works of John Wesley* (1809), VIII, 384. (Incorrectly paginated as 284.)
[38] J. Wesley, *A Survey of the Wisdom of God in Creation; or, A Compendium of Natural Philosophy* (London, 1777), I, viii.
[39] *Elementa Philosophiae Practicae et Theoreticae*.
[40] Wesley, *op. cit.*, p. v.

frequently republished. In the process, it grew to five volumes. Excerpts from it were reprinted in the *Arminian* magazine.

While Wesley's scientific writings were not original, they were highly successful in terms of circulation and republication. The situation with reference to his views on Copernicus and Newton is ambiguous. Dorothy Stimson has written that Wesley was one of the last opponents of the Copernican system.[41] But the evidence seems to me to be that while Wesley believed that the Copernican view tended toward infidelity, he could not find Biblical reasons for denying it. He probably accepted Copernicus's views over against the Ptolemaic system. However, he was more sceptical of Newton than of Copernicus. This was due in part to his interest in the Hutchinsonians. In 1724, John Hutchinson published his *Moses's Principia*, obviously directed against the *Principia* of Newton. While Wesley did not fully accept the views of the Hutchinsonians, he was sympathetic to their charge that the Newtonian system tended toward atheism. Hence, Wesley's own position remained somewhat unclear. This was only natural. His interest in science was not genuinely theoretical in the sense of a concern for a true system of science. He was interested in the practical ways in which science assisted men in their pursuits and in the ways in which it disclosed the glory of God. On scientific matters, he felt dependent on the work of others and was not seriously perturbed by the competing claims; hence his own vacillation on theoretical issues. Nevertheless, through his publications and practical interest, he helped to create a favourable attitude toward the scientific enterprise.

On scientific matters, Cotton Mather was more consistent than John Wesley. But Mather was no more original in his scientific and philosophical writings than was Wesley. He freely admitted his debt to John Ray and William Derham.[42] His interest was clearly expressed in the full title of the volume, *The Christian Philosopher – a collection of the best discoveries in Nature with Religious Improvements*.[43] This meant that he wanted the best of contemporary science understood in a Christian context. He believed his writing to be philosophical, but also evangelical.[44] He accepted the general distinction between the book of nature (creatures) and the book of Scripture, quoted Chrysostom in support of it, and added that the distinction stemmed from the Church fathers.[45]

Mather held the Copernican position, particularly the basic affirmation of the 'stability of the Sun and the motion of the

---

[41] Stimson, *op. cit.*, pp. 93, 99.
[42] C. Mather, *The Christian Philosopher* (London, 1721), p. 3.
[43] The parallelism to Wesley is clear.
[44] *Ibid.*, p. 2.
[45] *Ibid.*, p. 8.

earth,' to be beyond dispute. Only a complete reversal of all the causes of celestial motions as they were known could challenge the Copernican position, he declared, and that appeared unlikely.[46] Mather, too, exhibited something of the quasi-religious awe in which Newton was held in this period.

> But then comes the admirable Sir Isaac Newton, whom we now venture to call the *Perpetual Dictator* of the learned World, in the *Principles of Natural Philosophy*; and than whom, here has not yet shone among mankind a more sagacious reasoner upon the *Laws of Nature*.[47]

But Mather did not agree with a matter of central concern to Newton. He refused to assume the existence and power of gravity without further evidence. Nor was he willing to accept more favourable views of gravity. He agreed with Clarke that what passed for gravity was not to be understood as 'motion originally impressed upon Matter'.[48] And he agreed with the physician and quasi-theologian, Cheyne, that one should not resort to various principles of motion as propounded by the philosophers. Mather made his meaning clear when he wrote of Cheyne:

> He asserts, and with demonstration ... that there is no such thing as an *universal Soul*, animating the vast System of the World, according to Plato; nor any *substantial Forms*, according to *Aristotle*; nor any omniscient *radical Heat*, according to Hippocrates; nor any *plastick Virtue*, according to Scaliger; nor any *hylarchick Principle*, according to More. These are mere allegorical terms, coined on purpose to conceal the ignorance of the authors, and keep up their credit with the credulous part of mankind. These unintelligible Beings are derogatory from the Wisdom and Power of the great God, who can easily govern the Machine He could create, by more direct Methods than employing such subservient divinities; and indeed those beings will not serve the design for which we invent them, unless we endow them with faculties above the dignity of secondary agents. It is now plain from the most evident principles, that the great God not only has the springs of this immense machine, and all the several Parts of it, in his own Hand, and is the first Mover; but that without His continual Influence the whole Movement would soon fall to pieces. Yet, besides this, he has reserved to Himself the power of dispensing with these Laws, whenever He pleases.[49]

[46] *Ibid.*, pp. 75–6.
[47] *Ibid.*, p. 56.
[48] *Ibid.*, pp. 84–5.
[49] *Ibid.*, pp. 87–8.

Mather was afraid of any emphasis upon secondary causes, or upon principles of explanation and movement which inevitably take on the status and functions of lesser divinities. Mather was contending for the grounding of all causation directly in the omnipotent cause.[50] Neither rest nor the motion of anything depended upon itself, but upon God directly. Hence, the concept of gravity could not be introduced as if it were a solution to the problem of motion. Even the old criticism of the Copernican system, that the speed of the earth in its path around the sun would result in the earth's disintegration, was still taken with seriousness. Mather contended that it did not fly to pieces because it was moved by God. While the laws of nature were real, Mather believed that they were anchored in the activity of God. They did not even have a semi-autonomous status.

Since Mather's aim was to provide a proper Christian interpretation of the new science, it is understandable that he wished thoroughly to ground causation in the pervasive activity of God, without the quasi-independence of laws or independent forces of motion, such as gravity. But when the logic of such a position was later applied in the field of biology, it led to the defence of the fixity of species. The power of God in every phase of creation and created existence can be assumed or proclaimed in faith. But it is doubtful that it can be argued successfully or legitimately.

Mather also reiterated the dictum that a preoccupation with the scientific enterprise could easily lead to the neglect of the Christological centre of Christian understanding. Still during the time of Mather most scientists considered themselves to be Christian. Having declared that the works of God are exhibited to us through nature, Mather hastened to add that the Christ of God must not be forgotten. Certain minimal Christological motifs for understanding creation are then elaborated. Early in the book, he declared that a small part of the wisdom of God was revealed in creation; but he added that those who did not admire wisdom itself – and by this he meant revelation – must be stark blind. And toward the end of the book, he declared:

> This is not all we have to think upon; we see an incomparable Wisdom of God in his creatures; one cannot but presently infer, what an incomprehensible wisdom then in the methods and affairs of that redemption, whereof the glorious God has laid the plan in our Jesus.[51]

Mather distinguished between nature and Scripture; but he also interpreted events in the light of both. In his analysis of comets, he accepted the natural explanations of his time, includ-

[50] *Ibid.*, p. 88.
[51] *Ibid.*, p. 301.

ing the predictions of Halley, but then added that comets had a theological meaning also. He stated that when he saw a comet, he thought of a wicked world made into a fiery oven in the time of God's anger, of what it would be like if our world were so afflicted, and of how wonderful it was that we were saved from such a calamity.[52] Likewise, after giving a natural account of the rainbow in Newtonian terms, Mather added that Christians should remember that the rainbow had been a covenant sign.[53] Thunder, too, was understood in natural terms; but it should remind us how quickly God can destroy us and that we are in need of the Saviour.[54]

Mather's instincts were correct, namely, that the same phenomena can be understood in a natural and in a theological sense. But the theological meaning was forced; at every point it reflected an old heritage in which the theological meaning was outlined in terms analogous to the natural meaning. Once the natural order was accepted, theologians should have conceived of the theological meaning in quite different terms. Here, too, the form of theological understanding was under the domination of nature. A decisive theological transformation had not yet taken place in either Mather or his contemporaries.

It is well known that Locke's psychology and Newton's conception of nature had their impact on Jonathan Edwards. Like Mather, Edwards had a sense for the central Christological core in Christianity but also for the new science. Edwards particularly utilized Newton's concept of causation, in which sequences exist without knowing their mysterious connections, as a proper analogy to the complex of faith and regeneration.[55] He too believed that there was an analogy between the order of nature and of faith. But while Edwards related Christian insight to the currents of his time more astutely than most theologians, he did not determine the future in such matters. More creative than most, he did not slavishly reflect the past nor did he, as we have indicated, decisively influence the future at this level. For this reason, a fuller exposition will not be undertaken here.

[52] *Ibid.*, p. 45.
[53] *Ibid.*, pp. 57–8.
[54] *Ibid.*, p. 63.
[55] Perry Miller, *Jonathan Edwards* (New York: William Sloane Associates, Inc., 1949), p. 79.

9 Thomas Chalmers's Astronomical Discourses: A Study in Natural Theology*

David Cairns

A few years ago a leading Scottish theologian drew attention to the recent tendency among continental Protestant theologians to 'write off' natural theology. This, he suggested, had been accepted with undue complacency by certain Scottish writers, and he rightly drew attention to the fact that there was a great, indeed a predominant, tradition in the Christian Church, which accepted natural theology, and that among Scottish theologians, no less a man than Thomas Chalmers would have been shocked at the suggestion that natural theology was invalid.

This remark led the writer of this article to think again about natural theology, and also to study Chalmers's Astronomical Discourses, which up to that time had been familiar to him only through quotations from some of their more purple passages. The result of some of these reflections is offered here.

This article will not attempt to deal with the fascinating, important and difficult question of the legitimacy and validity of natural theology, but an attempt will be made to distinguish it from certain other types of apologetic, and the question will be raised whether and how far natural theology is to be found in the Astronomical Discourses, which are by common consent Dr Chalmers's most important apologetical work.

Natural theology may be defined as 'The attempt to find, outside the Christian revelation, arguments for the existence and certain attributes of God which are cogent for the reason of an honest sceptic.' If this definition be considered not too narrow, but generally acceptable, then there will be two marks characteristic of all natural theology. The first will be the conscious and explicit refusal, for the time being, to use specifically Christian presuppositions. The second mark will be the conviction that the proofs offered have demonstrative force, and that nothing but lack of intellectual acumen or a sinful and blinded will – with the possible addition of an element of invincible

* David Cairns, 'Thomas Chalmers's Astronomical Discourses: A Study in Natural Theology', *Scottish Journal of Theology*, 1956, 9, 410–21.

ignorance – can prevent our interlocutor from seeing the force of our argument.

If this definition be accepted, then natural theology will be merely one type of apologetic. There seem to be at least two other types.

In the first type the apologist will argue from the Christian position, thinking out the implications of Christian belief in various fields of thought, and stating them in such a way as to maintain a conversation with the unbeliever in the world, and the unbeliever in his own soul. His will be a *fides quaerens intellectum*. It is not always at once clear whether a certain piece of apologetic belongs to this type of apologetic, or to natural theology. For, while in the modern western world there are many unbelievers and it is not hard to find one, it is hard to find a man whose thought has not been deeply imbued by Christian concepts and ways of thought. Even men consciously opposed to Christianity may hold and value certain beliefs which they cannot logically stand by without accepting the full Christian revelation, or at least a theism tinged by Christianity. A legitimate, if dangerous, task of apologetic which would not be an incursion into natural theology, would be the attempt to demonstrate to such a man that those beliefs to which he eagerly clings, demand the full Christian faith. There is a cheap and specious kind of apologetic which tries to make the whole existence of morality depend upon the acceptance of the full Christian faith, and no attempt is here made to defend this. But even apart from such deformations, there is a danger in this type of argument. We intend to fan the smoking flax into a flame, but we may actually quench it. We may make the man with whom we are talking decide, not to accept the faith, but to scrap what remains to him. And yet this task of apologetic is a legitimate one, and it is not natural theology, for the argument does not imply that we are ignoring the positive basis of Christian faith on which we stand.

There is another situation somewhat similar to the one just described, where again the ambiguity may arise whether natural theology is being used or not. Here again both participants in the conversation are agreed upon certain Christian presuppositions as in the former case, but here both are clearly men of belief, though belief may be stronger in one than in the other. When the Psalmist wrote: 'The heavens declare the glory of God'; and Christ, to quote Chalmers's words, drew from the beauty of the lily 'the delightful argument of confidence in God', were they embarking on natural theology? It is rather a soulless dissection of these wonderful sayings to examine them in this way, but we might say that, in so far as the Psalmist and Christ were both speaking within the context of biblical revelation, to men who already believed that 'God is mindful', these two sayings should probably not be considered as natural theology. Of course, to the Psalmist, who believed in the God of the Covenant, the heavens really did declare the glory of God, and to Christ the beauty of the lilies really did reveal His providence. Both were justified in seeing there a confirmation of the faith which they already had, and both were justified in strengthening the faith of others by pointing out that revelation in nature to them.

A second type of apologetic which is distinct from natural theology, is the demonstration of the error of certain objections to Christian belief. Here the apologist sets out to show that these objections or difficulties rest on misunderstandings of Christian teaching, or confusions of thought. The misunderstandings of Christian teachings and their correction need no explanatory comment. But an example may be given of the clearing up of a confusion which has led to an objection to Christian faith. The apologetic answer to the old positivism would be an attempt to show that it was a confusion of thought which led to the conclusion that all who make the claim to truth must approximate to the procedure of the natural sciences, the procedure of theory and experiment. When he has cleared up this confusion, the apologist has shown that Christian faith is not necessarily illusion because it does not use experiment or hypothesis exactly as natural science does, and 'verification' cannot mean the same thing here as it does in the natural sciences. In such a discussion, the apologist is indeed arguing with his partner merely as one rational being with another, and his own Christian presuppositions are well in the background, and thus he is somewhat like the natural theologian. But he is different from him in this, that he is seeking, not so much to prove theism, as to remove difficulties in the way of belief.

Having thus defined the limits of natural theology, and distinguished it from two other types of apologetic, we may now go on to enquire how far natural theology is to be found in Dr Chalmers's Astronomical Discourses, and how far they contain arguments which are examples of the other kinds of apologetic.

The study of these lectures, confident in their splendid and flamboyant oratory, and occasionally almost toppling over into the absurd, does yet give the reader a vivid sense of the power and passion of Chalmers as an apologist and a preacher. It is said that while they were being delivered (on Thursday afternoons in 1816 in the Tron Church of Glasgow) shops and businesses were closed in order to give masters and employees a chance to hear them. Here we are in touch with a great mind, a man who makes us feel that the world is a grander place, and grace a more wonderful mystery than we had realised. There is in the discourses a repetitiveness which may indeed be an expression of Chalmers' skill in hammering home his points in the minds of his

hearers. It is not enough for him to say a thing twice, he often
says it in different words six times. Consequently each discourse
does not contain a great deal of logical material, and it is not
impossible to summarise the arguments of the seven discourses
within the limits of this article. My purpose in so doing will
be to ask how far his arguments still hold for today, and further
to inquire whether this is really natural theology at all.

The first discourse is called 'A Sketch of the Modern Astronomy', and in it Chalmers attempts to disarm beforehand those
narrow-minded Christians who may feel that the whole project
is useless and unworthy. St Paul, he argues, made himself all
things to all men, if by any means he might win some. And if
Gentile Christians had not understood what was the drift of his
reasoning against the Jews, it would have been seemly for them,
not to despise and condemn Paul, but to be glad that their common faith was being commended to others, even if it were in
terms that were above their own comprehension. Chalmers asks
for a like considerate treatment at the hands of 'declared professors of the truth'.

The first discourse introduces the main theme of the lectures.
After a description of the solar system, in which he achieves the
feat of not mentioning any planet save the earth by name, Chalmers sketches in the background of the vast stellar universe
which lies in the outer darkness beyond. From the littleness and
insecurity of man's estate he draws the Christian conclusion that
we should be humble and grateful to God because 'He is mindful
of us'. But – and now we come to the main theme of the discourses – 'this very reflection of the Psalmist has been appropriated to the use of infidelity, and the very language of the text
has been made to bear an application of hostility to the faith.
'What is man that God should be mindful of him or the son of
man, that he should deign to visit him?' Is it likely, says the
Infidel, that God would send His eternal Son, to die for the puny
occupiers of so insignificant a province in the mighty field of His
creation?' (p. 53).

In some respects, times have not changed since Chalmers's
day. The psalmist, on seeing the glory of the universe, was
astonished at God's grace. For, on the strength of God's covenant
and revelation of Himself to his people, he knew that God *was*
mindful of man; the size and splendour of the Universe made him
realise afresh the condescension of such an act, and he gave God
the praise. Today Fred Hoyle takes the same text and misunder-
stands and misreads it in the same negative sense as did the
infidels of Thomas Chalmers's day.

Chalmers conclues the first discourse with the statement that
it is right that every such sceptical argument 'should be met and
manfully confounded, nor do we know a more discreditable

surrender of our religion than to act as if she had anything to fear from the ingenuity of her most accomplished adversaries'. Surely there are few Christians who would not feel their hearts thrill when they read this sentence. If this be natural theology, then the more of it we have, the better. But is it natural theology? Surely it is rather that type of apologetic which sets forth to point out the misunderstandings and false presuppositions on which these apparently so formidable arguments against the Christian faith rest. It is content with demolishing the foundation of error and misunderstanding on which they are erected.

The second discourse is called 'The Modesty of True Science' and it is built round the figure of Isaac Newton. All men today, says Chalmers, agree in praising Newton, but the greater part of them have no true understanding where his greatness lay. It lay in his use of scientific method. All his wonderful discoveries had their origin in this, that he accepted nothing without evidence, and this principle limited the scope of his assertions also, so that where clear evidence was not available, he would never venture, but in 'the humble form of a doubt, a conjecture, or a question' (p. 72).

Now, part of the argument of the infidels against Christianity rests on the assumption that God's plan of salvation is assumed to have reference only to this tiny world among vast universes. And here, Chalmers continues, they all, from Voltaire downwards, are resting on pure speculation, for which there is not the slightest shred of positive evidence. 'For all they know, many a visit has been paid to each of them (the other worlds) on the subject of our common Christianity, by commissioned messengers from the throne of the Eternal' (p. 79). Newton composed a commentary on the Book of the Revelation, and therefore Voltaire made him the butt of his gibes, saying that this commentary was a proof of the dotage of the human understanding. But Newton was really more scientific than Voltaire, not only because he avoided unverifiable speculations about other worlds, but because of his outlook on the Christian faith, an outlook displayed in the commentary so frivolously derided by his critic. For in this commentary, says Chalmers, 'we see the very same principle which carried him through all the profoundest and the most successful of his investigations ... the tenacious adherence to every one doctrine that had such valid proof to uphold it as could be gathered from the field of human experience', and the rejection of all merely plausible arguments which had no solid foundation in evidence.

For Newton accepted the Bible as the record of an actual communication from God to the inhabitants of this world, seeing in the miracles a proof that Christ was the approved ambassador of God. He further relied on the trustworthiness of the human testimony paid to Christ by the apostles, and he trusted the confirmatory evidence of fulfilled prophecy. 'These formed the solid materials of the basis on which our experimental philosopher stood' (p. 89).

It is not necessary to defend, as Chalmers does, the commentary of Newton, nor is it necessary to accept in detail the partially outmoded apologetic with which he buttresses the trustworthiness of Christ's claim to be the vehicle of a divine revelation. But is there not here in Chalmers's argument something of permanent value, not only in the rebuke to Voltaire for his baseless and unverifiable assertions, but also in the acknowledgment that in different fields of inquiry, different types of evidence are relevant, and different types of verification are to be sought for? All this is not natural theology, nor is there any disguise made of the fact that Chalmers is all the while basing himself on the faith that a revelation has been made in Christ.

The third discourse treats of the 'Extent of the Divine Condescension'. Here, for the sake of argument, Chalmers is willing to accept the unprovable hypothesis that the divine plan of salvation has been put in operation on our earth alone. Is there any thing here, he asks, which is really incredible to the intellect? Surely to hazard a doubt here is to be guilty of a foolish anthropomorphism. If a *man* has a great deal of business to attend to, doubtless the detail of his work will be in danger of neglect. But God is not man, and all the evidence we have goes to show that He is as able to attend to all the details of the life of each man's body, and 'the vegetation of each blade of grass', as to the control of the stellar systems. Chalmers defies his opponents to point to a single mark of God's being oppressed by the multitude of the detail of His creation.

Thus far Chalmers has been refuting the argument that if the universe be as large as astronomy has in fact shown it to be, God, if there be a God, could not be interested in, or capable of, dealing with the destiny and government of the earth and all its inhabitants. Now he turns his own reasoning in a slightly different direction, from the natural to the moral attributes of God. With the evidence before him which nature supplies of the omniscience and power of God, Chalmers finds himself by no means disposed to reject as imposture the claim of a message professing to come from God, and informing him of God's mighty doings for the happiness of our species. Filled with confidence in this God, 'I will not be afraid, for I am of more value than many sparrows.' He then goes on to point out that while the telescope has given us news about the vastness of the universe, which the infidels have misinterpreted as undermining the Christian faith, so the microscope has given us information about the marvellous

skill and construction of the minutest parts of nature, information which goes far to refute the false anthropomorphism of
the sceptical argument from the knowledge supplied by the
telescope.

At this point we might again pause, and ask: 'Is this at last
natural theology?' I would suggest that it does not appear from
any of the arguments given here that at any point Chalmers has
departed from the ground given him by the special revelation.
All the while he stands confessedly as a believer on this ground,
and traces in the world of nature certain facts which confirm
him in this belief. This implies the conviction that there is such
a relevance between the knowledge which the sciences present
to us on the one hand, and faith on the other, that the believer
may find both confirmation of his faith and difficulties for it in
this field. But it would seem again that the most that Chalmers
believes himself able to do vis-à-vis his sceptical opponent, is to
prove the invalidity of the arguments brought forward against
belief and the possibility of revelation. If this be natural theology,
then the writer of this essay is an unashamed exponent and
defender of it, and is prepared to accept the broad lines of Chalmers's argument.

There is, however, a criticism of the detail of Chalmers's position which must be made here. He does at one point seem to stress
his argument beyond what is legitimate. This occurs in those
sentences (too long for quotation) where, on p. 108 he defies his
opponent to point to a single mark of God's being oppressed by
the detail of His universe, or some traces of neglect or of carelessness in His management of our world. There are, indeed, wonderful adaptations in the world such as Chalmers points out, and
the over-subtle arguments of David Hume against giving weight
to these are unconvincing. But there are also puzzling signs of
ill-adaptation to ends which might well be fairly adduced by the
sceptic as precisely such arguments against God as Chalmers defies
him to give. For in the eyes of the sceptic these really are arguments against *the existence* of God. For when he says that the
world is so vast that God could not be interested in our tiny
lives, or that there are puzzling maladaptations which show that
He could not care about us, he is not really arguing that God is
indifferent or heedless, though he puts his objection in this way
to his Christian opponent. He is arguing that there is no God at
all. It is at this point in the discussion, where Chalmers defies
his sceptical interlocutor to point to a single mark of God's
being oppressed by the detail of His universe, or to indicate some
traces of neglect or carelessness in His management of our
world, that he does appear to verge upon natural theology, as
defined in the earlier part of this article. And it is precisely
here that his argument seems weakest. He continues himself

indeed to speak as a Christian believer, from the insight which faith gives him. But he comes very near to arguing that the argument from design is conclusive, and that there is no evidence against it at all.

The fourth discourse treats of 'The Knowledge of Man's Moral History in the Distant Places of Creation'.

In this discourse, Chalmers states that the principal purpose of revelation is not to give us information about far distant places in God's creation, but to inform us of our fearful guilt and danger, and to lay before us God's overtures of reconciliation. So that we should not expect from it detailed and full information about other parts of God's universe and their inhabitants and destiny. Nevertheless, the Bible does give us some knowledge, enough to tell us that the history of the redemption of our race is known in other and distant parts of the creation, and enough to hint to us that the redemption itself may stretch beyond the limits of our world.

But even though redemption were only happening in our world, there is something in its character to draw the eye of the universe to it. The objection from the narrowness of the theatre is grossly materialistic. In the eye of spiritual beings the redemption of a sinful world derives its chief interest from the way in which it reveals God's mind and purposes and glorifies Him. So, even on earth, a great king and conqueror might, by one act of mercy to a single enemy, draw such a lustre round him as would eclipse the renown of his public achievements. A further objection is brought forward by the infidel on the score of the length of time taken to redeem one single world. Chalmers retorts, the argument is utterly absurd. Has not God all eternity at His disposal? And some day the whole story of human redemption will be seen as a mere short episode in the eternal ages.

The fifth discourse is entitled 'On the Sympathy that is felt for Man in the Distant Places of Creation', and, with the sixth, 'On the Contest for Ascendancy over Man among the Higher Orders of Intelligence', it merely continues the argument of the fourth, underlining and developing it. The fifth discourse starts with a contrast of infidels with angels, to the detriment of the former, who think that, because the universe is wide, God cannot care for men. But the angels, Scripture tells us, are intensely interested in us, and 'desire to look into' the mystery of our salvation. On which of these two characters do we see the impress of heaven? Chalmers has hitherto been appealing to our reason; now he will appeal to our hearts. Surely, as men grow in benevolence, they approximate to the angels. This benevolence comes from heaven; is it surprising that the denizens of heaven feel it too? Think what happens in a human family when one member is in peril or sick, and his destiny undecided! Wonder not, if all in your destiny being in the balance and uncertain, the angels look on you, and pray!

In the sixth discourse Chalmers brings to his aid the powerful illustration that in warfare some small and even insignificant piece of land may become a symbol of honour and prestige to contending empires such that immense treasure and life are expended to ensure its conquest from the enemy. May it not be that our earth, tiny and insignificant as it is, has such a value in the vast struggle between the powers of light and the powers of darkness? Such a battle, the Bible tells us, is in progress on the earth. It is not finished yet, though Christ has overthrown Satan in single combat. To infidels this will sound wild and visionary, but is it not in harmony with our own human experience? How much the temptations of the world are with us! Whence comes its power? Does our own heart not tell us something of the allurement and desperation of the devil? But the day hastens when the struggle will be over, and on that last great day, how vain will appear the presumptions of infidel astronomy!

The last discourse is entitled 'On the Slender Influence of Mere Taste and Sensibility in Matters of Religion'. This discourse has perhaps not very much to do with the main theme of the course, but it is none the less very significant. Chalmers begins by picturing the impression made on a sensitive person by the splendour of religious music or oratorio. Feelings are here awakened, which bear a very close resemblance to those of religious devotion, and yet the hearer may leave the place where this has happened as dead in trespasses and sins as when he entered. It is not the emotion, but the will, which counts in such a situation. And Chalmers goes on to consider the splendour of the theme which he has been expounding, and the wide vistas in the universe of nature and the universe of grace which have been opened up. Though modesty makes him talk slightingly of his own reasoning and eloquence, he cannot but have been conscious of the power of the latter and its dangers. So he closes with an appeal that his hearers will not remain in the sphere of delighted aesthetic appreciation, but asks them what progress they are making in the modest work of prayer and study of God's word and in Christian living. Without the power of eloquence, but full of trust in God's power and saving word, men like the Moravians have been the channels of saving divine power to whole benighted communities. While men of quick aesthetic sensibilities and lively reason in the affairs of this world, have shown themselves utterly blind in the understanding of God's word and the province of His grace. 'With a religion so argumentable as ours, it may be easy to gather out of it a feast for the human understanding. With a religion so magnificent as ours, it may be easy to gather out of it a feast for the human imagination.

But with a religion so humbling and so strict, and so spiritual, it is not easy to mortify the pride, or to quell the strong enmity, of nature ... or to invest faith with a practical supremacy, or to give its objects such a vivacity of influence as shall overpower the near and hourly impressions, that are ever emanating upon man from a seducing world. It is here that man feels himself treading upon the limit of his helplessness. It is here that he sees where the strength of nature ends; and the power of grace must either be put forth, or leave him to grope his darkling way without one inch of progress towards the life and the substance of Christianity' (p. 249).

On reading this, one feels that only a man who is thus aware of the limitations of apologetic should venture to undertake it. It is probably the instinctive feeling that the apologist is trying, by virtue of his superior skill and knowledge, to *reason* another man into the faith, that makes so many people doubtful altogether of the legitimacy of the apologetic task.

But that task is essential for the Church, for there are genuine difficulties in the way of believing, and some of them are due to intellectual errors and confusions. Perhaps the most that apologetic can directly do, is to remove some of these difficulties. But when they have been removed, then we must not assume that the man with whom we have been reasoning has been made, by this process, a Christian. All that we can say is that certain difficulties and misunderstandings in the way of his faith and our own, have been removed. Here then are the limits of apologetic. It is not only that the wills of men are stubborn and sinful, even when their minds have been freed of misunderstandings. The further and more important limitation is, that God has reserved it within His own power to give faith to men. Just as the preacher must remember this and can only preach with power when he does so, so also the apologist must remember it, if he is to do his own task effectively. The remembrance will awaken in him a due humility, and this will make his reason and his person a tool fit for the work to which God has called him. Then God may bless the work of the apologist by doing His own work of grace in and through, but also beyond it.

10 The Principle of Uniformity*

M. J. S. Rudwick

Geology has been strangely neglected in the current revival of interest in the history of science. It is generally acknowledged that geology provided an essential background to evolutionary theory, and that the enormously lengthened time-scale which it postulated has had a profound effect on thought in general. Yet most books on the history of science give it the most perfunctory treatment, and are content with facile generalisations copied faithfully and uncritically from earlier books of the same kind. For example, in the spate of hagiographical works occasioned by the Darwin centenary, most writers continued to repeat the traditional judgment that Darwin's evolutionary theory was a logical extension of Lyell's 'uniformitarian' geology.

Professor Hooykaas's book should go far to remedy this situation. Its subtitle indicates, more clearly than the title, the scope of the book – 'A historical–critical study of the principle of uniformity in geology, biology and theology'. Its aim is to analyse the philosophical structure of geological and palaeontological theory, chiefly by referring to nineteenth-century work but also pointing out the continuation of the same debates in modern geology. Even at the opening of its 'heroic age', geology was recognised as belonging to an altogether new kind of science, which posed problems of a kind that had never arisen before. It was the first science to be concerned with the reconstruction of the past development of the natural world, rather than the description and analysis of its present condition. The tools of other sciences were therefore inadequate. The processes that shaped the world in the past were beyond either experiment or simple observation. Observation revealed only their end-products; experimental results could only be applied to them analogically. Somehow the past had to be interpreted in terms of the present. The main conceptual tool in that task was, and is, the principle of uniformity.

* M. J. S. Rudwick, 'The Principle of Uniformity', a review of R. Hooykaas, *Natural Law and Divine Miracle* (Brill, Leiden, 1959), in *History of Science*, 1962, 1, 82–6.

This is the point at which too many accounts divide the *dramatis personae* into those who were 'for' and those who were 'against' uniformity. Hooykaas shows, from a wide study of the primary sources, that such a conclusion is grossly oversimplified. For 'uniformity' was, and is, understood in several different senses. Some of the more polemical uniformitarians tried to suggest that their opponents believed the physical 'laws of nature' to have been different in former times. But in fact all geologists, from the late eighteenth century onwards, accepted as axiomatic the uniformity of *physical* 'causes': indeed this was one of the grounds for their emphatic rejection of the 'phantastical theories' of the earlier 'cosmogonists'. Uniformity in this sense was never in dispute. Hooykaas distinguishes two other senses by introducing the term 'actualism' (from the continental term for uniformitarianism) for one of them. Actualism is the belief that all agencies responsible for geological events in the past are to be found among those that can be observed in operation at the present (*causes actuelles*). To quote the subtitle of Lyell's *Principles of geology*, it is the 'attempt to explain the former changes of the earth's surface, by reference to causes now in operation'. But Lyell, like Hutton before him, went beyond actualism to assert something very different: that these geological 'causes' or processes had always operated with the same 'intensity' or at the same 'tempo' as at present. Hooykaas terms this strict uniformitarianism. Catastrophism (to which many of the best nineteenth-century geologists adhered) was opposed not to actualism so much as to strict uniformitarianism. They rejected it because it assumed *a priori* what the facts themselves ought to be allowed to prove or disprove. To assume that the tempo of geological processes has always been constant seemed to them arbitrary and unjustified: they felt themselves impelled by the facts to recognise the signs of periodic intensifications of these processes (i.e. 'catastrophes'). Lyell, on the other hand, believed the facts could be 'reconciled' with strict uniformity: by postulating great lengths of time, the appearance of violence became an illusion, and all phenomena could be attributed to the gradual action of gentle processes. It is impossible to say, even with the advantage of hindsight, that either catastrophism or uniformitarianism was 'right', or even that one aided the progress of the science more than the other. For example, the 'violence' of the events that were interpreted as catastrophes has largely disappeared from modern geology; but on the other hand it was the catastrophists who were most readily converted to the theory of a widespread Ice Age, for such an event was too radical a change in the 'intensity' of glaciation to appeal to uniformitarians. The reason for this ambivalence, in Hooykaas's view, is that uniformity should be regarded merely as a methodological principle and not as a 'law of nature'. This was admitted in theory by both Hutton and Lyell, but in practice their advocacy of the principle was so dogmatic that they became blind to the facts that could not be reconciled with it. In fact, as Whewell pointed out, there is no hard-and-fast line between catastrophism and uniformitarianism: Lyell was satisfied if the *average* tempo of geological processes had remained constant, but did not specify what period of time he demanded as the standard by which to judge this constancy.

In the second part of the book Hooykaas turns to the biological application of the principle of uniformity. He points out that Huxley was incorrect in asserting that 'consistent uniformitarianism postulates evolution as much in the organic as in the inorganic world'. Consistency demands that if the average state of the inorganic world has remained constant, so has that of the organic world. Then there can have been no true evolution of life – no appearance of genuinely novel forms of existence. This is what Lyell asserted in the *Principles*, postulating that species have been continually replaced, as they became extinct, by others of a similar kind. This position forced him to deny the evidence (by that time really overwhelming) of a true 'progression' in life – at least as measured by the appearance of new groups of vertebrates. The only other consistent position is that adopted by Chambers, in postulating that the evolution of life had been matched by a parallel 'development' in the inorganic world. All other positions, whether the theory of progressive creation or the evolutionary theories of Lamarck and Darwin, were necessarily 'inconsistent', in that they abandoned any strict parallel between the organic and the inorganic worlds. This explains how Lyell could support Cuvier's uniformitarian biology while opposing his catastrophist geology. It also explains the complexity of Darwin's relation to Lyell. Darwin did not simply borrow geological uniformitarianism from Lyell and apply it to biology – for unlike Lyell he accepted the evidence for a 'progression' of life. Nor did he borrow actualism – for he was unable to demonstrate evolution as a present process visibly producing new species (Cuvier had earlier rejected Lamarck's evolution on precisely these actualistic grounds). Indeed Darwin, and all other evolutionists until this century, inverted actualism by using the evidence of the past – the evidence for large changes of fauna and flora – to interpret that of the present, i.e. to interpret variants as incipient species. What he did derive from Lyell was the concept of slow and imperceptibly gradual change: Huxley's remark is true only if uniformity is understood as the belief that *natura non facit saltum*.

The final section of the book is concerned with the philosophical and theological factors involved in the principle of uniformity. These, like the scientific factors, turn out to be much more complex than is generally assumed. Although uniformity has often been acknowledged as a purely methodological principle, attitudes towards it have almost always been influenced to some extent by metaphysical factors. Here Hooykaas's analysis of Hutton's work is particularly interesting, for it becomes clear how far Hutton was from being (as he has often been depicted) a positivist bravely banishing theology from geology. In fact his work is deeply influenced throughout by deism – which probably accounts for the tradition that his theory is unreadable and best tackled in Playfair's exposition (which cut out the metaphysics). Rather surprisingly, Hooykaas classes Buckland, Sedgwick and others, who are usually regarded as the orthodox opposition to uniformitarianism and evolution, as 'semi-deists'. But this seems justified, for they divided the world into two compartments: a virtually deistic part in which physical law reigned supreme, and an 'interventionist' part which was the sphere of action of the God of theism. They took over Cuvier's strictly scientific catastrophism and re-interpreted the catastrophes and the sudden new faunas as signs of the 'immediate exercise of divine power'. Feeling that Newtonian science had eliminated the Christian God of action from all but the personal sphere, they welcomed the geological evidence that His action had had wider scope. But by this solution they implicitly accepted a deistic interpretation for all other events, and exposed their vestigial theism to gradual annihilation by the progress of the science. The true theists in Hooykaas's classification are those (e.g. Hugh Miller) for whom any division between nature and supernature was simply unreal, for whom a phenomenon became no less a sign (though not a proof) of God's action when it could be 'explained' in scientific terms. This he characterises as the biblical view of nature (though it has not always been the dominant view among Christians); and he does not conceal his own sympathy with it. His general conclusion is that although particular methodological and metaphysical attitudes to uniformity have often been linked, the relation has been highly complex, and in no way supports a positivist view of the history of the science.

This book is perhaps the first major attempt to analyse the philosophical structure of geological science, using the historical evidence of the period during which its methodology was still a matter for open debate. It should be read by all who are concerned with the development of science in the nineteenth century. For its analysis of the great geological controversies pays equal attention to the strictly scientific and the metaphysical factors, and shows how they were related. In this respect it should be a valuable corrective to accounts which underestimate the scientific problems and treat the controversies as purely metaphysical. It is to be hoped that it will stimulate further detailed work on primary sources, much more of which is needed if the history of geological science is to take its rightful place beside the history of physical and biological sciences.

It is a pity that such interesting and important material should be concealed beneath so uninformative, indeed misleading, a title. The theological aspect is an important part of the work; but it is only a part. What Hooykaas has to say on it receives its value from its dependence on his analysis of uniformity in its scientific context – and it is that which constitutes the bulk of the work. As it is, anyone who merely glances at the title might be forgiven for assigning it to that class of ill-informed apologetical works from which Professor Hooykaas would, I believe, emphatically wish it to be dissociated.

11   Diluvialism and Its Critics*

Leroy E. Page

In my opinion, the influence of religious preconceptions on the thinking of geologists in Great Britain in the early nineteenth century has been overemphasized. There has been perpetuated the old, but erroneous, idea that the Wernerian theory was strongly influenced by the Bible and that it regarded the flood as a great geological event.[1] This error probably arose because (1) some of Werner's British disciples did introduce the flood into their geological writings,[2] and (2) Charles Lyell misrepresented the subject in his *Principles of Geology*.[3]

Werner's geological views seem to have been no more affected by a desire to confirm the Bible than were Hutton's. Werner, like Hutton, was apparently a Deist.[4] The appeal of the Wernerian geognosy to many was that, unlike previous 'theories of the earth', it invoked neither catastrophes nor unfamiliar agents and refused to speculate about the origins of the earth. It seemed to be based, not on imagination nor on the Bible, but on an induction from the facts.[5]

The Wernerians distinguished between the hard strata laid down by the universal ocean and the alluvial or loose beds above

* Leroy E. Page, 'Diluvialism and Its Critics', in *Towards a History of Geology*, ed. Cecil J. Schneer, MIT Press, 1969, 259–71.
[1] See Stephen Toulmin and June Goodfield, *The Discovery of Time* (New York: Harper & Row, 1966), pp. 152–3.
[2] Notably Richard Kirwan, *Geological Essays* (London: D. Bremner, 1799), pp. 54–86, and Robert Jameson (see notes 9 and 10).
[3] Charles Lyell, *Principles of Geology, Being an Attempt to Explain the Former Changes of the Earth's Surface, by Reference to Causes Now in Operation* (3 vols.; London: John Murray, 1830–3), Vol. I, p. 69. Lyell's purpose was to free geology from theological influence by emphasizing the harm it had done geology in the past.
[4] Personal communication from Professor Alexander M. Ospovat, Department of History, Oklahoma State University, Stillwater, Oklahoma, 20 March 1967.
[5] Robert Jameson, *System of Mineralogy, Comprehending Oryctognosy, Geognosy, Mineralogical Chemistry, Mineralogical Geography, and Economical Mineralogy* (Edinburgh: William Blackwood, 1808), Vol. III, pp. 41–2. See, also, a review of William Brande's *Outline of Geology, British Critic*, VII (1817), 553.

the hard strata formed by the breaking up of the latter that occurred either during the retreat of the universal ocean or since then under the action of local causes. They, as well as some Huttonians, tended to ignore the evidence that was to convince many geologists that the alluvial beds were in large part the product of a geologically recent, catastrophic deluge that had seemingly covered much, if not all, of the earth.[6] This evidence was the existence in the alluvial beds of many poorly assorted deposits of gravel and clay that had evidently been transported great distances before being dumped. Also found in association with these were very large erratic blocks that had clearly been carried from distant sources as well as the bones of large animals, such as the mammoth, whose extinction was held not to be explicable by ordinary causes. It was felt, also, that only such a deluge could have formed the larger valleys.[7]

The most popular and influential book on this subject in Great Britain was a work by Georges Cuvier, which in 1813 was published in English under the title *Theory of the Earth*, with a preface and notes by Robert Jameson, professor of natural history at the University of Edinburgh and the leading Wernerian geognost in Great Britain.[8] In his work on geognosy in 1808, Jameson had stated that the rising of the universal ocean that had produced the Newest Floetz Trap strata could be called 'a Deluge'. He had otherwise ignored the flood and had referred the overlying alluvial beds to local causes.[9] In his preface to Cuvier's work, however, Jameson made much of the close coincidence of geology and the Mosaic history. He supported the interpretation of the six days as periods of indefinite length, and he approved Cuvier's view that the alluvial beds were in large part the product of a deluge.[10] By the time of the third edition, in 1817, Jameson had had second thoughts, and he omitted all reference to Moses. This change was probably caused by the criticism that his interpretation had received.[11]

---

[6] Jameson, *System of Mineralogy*, pp. 26–36, 97, 206–11. See also, Sir George Mackenzie, 'Deluge, or Debacle, in Geology', in David Brewster (ed.), *The Edinburgh Encyclopaedia* (18 vols; Edinburgh: William Blackwood, 1830), Vol. VII, p. 604, for a statement that the Wernerians ignored the geological deluge (written about 1815).

[7] This evidence was summarized by William Buckland, *Vindiciae Geologicae; or the Connexion of Geology with Religion Explained, in an Inaugural Lecture Delivered Before the University of Oxford, May 15, 1819, on the Endowment of a Readership in Geology by His Royal Highness the Prince Regent* (Oxford: the Author, 1820), pp. 35–8.

[8] Georges Cuvier, *Essay on the Theory of the Earth ... with Mineralogical Notes, and an Account of Cuvier's Geological Discoveries, by Professor Jameson*, trans. Robert Kerr (Edinburgh: William Blackwood, 1813).

[9] Jameson, *System of Mineralogy*, pp. 203, 206, 349.

[10] Cuvier, *Essay*, pp. v–vi, viii–ix.

[11] Cuvier, *Essay* (3rd edn; 1817), pp. v–ix. For the controversy started by

Cuvier's diluvial theory maintained that the sea had shifted its location during the flood, overwhelming the previous land and evacuating its former bed, which became the present land. Cuvier also assumed that there had been at least one previous revolution, before the creation of man, in which the sea had deserted its bed in order to occupy the continents. The effect of the flood, therefore, was the return of the sea to the bed it had occupied prior to the first revolution.[12] Another theory, held by William Buckland, maintained that the present continents had existed immediately before the flood. This theory regarded the flood as a temporary incursion upon the land and rejected Cuvier's first revolution.

At this time, both theories were about equally consistent (or inconsistent) with the known phenomena; however, each had its own theological merits. Cuvier's was in agreement with his idea of successive creations: the first revolution destroyed the old forms of life, man and the present species being created afterward (in six days) and inhabiting the present sea bed until the second revolution (the flood). The theory was thus consistent with the biblical statement that every species was rescued from the flood. It also explained why man's remains had not been found in the diluvial deposits, which in this theory were produced, not by the flood, but by the first deluge or by the sea between the two revolutions. The flood itself would have produced few visible deposits, as it was essentially a retreat from the continents. Its main effects would have been the carving of some valleys and the removal of material into the sea. The mammoths and other extinct species would have been overwhelmed by the first revolution. This theory was complicated by an additional deluge; and it assumed that the antediluvian land was not the same as the present land, which seemed to contradict certain statements in Genesis.[13]

The publication of Cuvier's *Theory of the Earth* had been a hopeful sign to those, especially of the clergy, who had been

---

Jameson's preface, see the *Philosophical Magazine*, September 1815 to October 1816, especially vol. XLVI (1815), pp. 225–9.

[12] Cuvier, *Essay* (1st edn), pp. 171–2.

[13] Buckland, *Vindiciae Geologicae*, p. 31. Cuvier's theory was similar to that of Jean André De Luc of Geneva, tutor to Queen Charlotte of England. De Luc's first revolution was caused by the collapse of a portion of the bottom of the universal ocean, into which all of the ocean rushed, uncovering the first continents. Then, at the time of the flood, caverns under these first lands collapsed, and the sea occupied the resulting basin, leaving dry its former bed, which became the present continents. See De Luc's *Lettres sur l'Histoire Physique de la Terre, Adressées a M. le Professor Blumenbach, Renfermant de nouvelles Preuves géologiques et historiques de la Mission divine de Moyse* (Paris: Nyon, ainé, rue du Jardinet, 1798), pp. 227–9 (Lettre V). These letters were originally published in the *British Critic*, 1793–5.

disturbed by the lack of correspondence between geology and Moses, and it suggested to Thomas Chalmers a way of reconciling the two. As Chalmers expressed it:

> Moses may be supposed to give us not a history of the first formation of things, but of the formation of the present system; and as we have already proved the necessity of direct exercises of creative power to keep up the generations of living creatures; so Moses may, for anything we know, be giving us the full history of the last great interposition, and be describing the successive steps by which the mischiefs of the last catastrophe were repaired.[14]

This interpretation was also adopted by John Sumner, later Archbishop of Canterbury:

> We are bound to admit, that only one general destruction or revolution of the globe has taken place since the period of that creation which Moses records, and of which Adam and Eve were the first inhabitants. ... *But we are not called upon to deny the possible existence of previous worlds, from the wreck of which our globe was organized, and the ruins of which are now furnishing matter to our curiosity.*[15]

William Buckland was appointed reader in mineralogy at Oxford in 1813, succeeding John Kidd; in 1814 he began to lecture annually on geology as Kidd had done before him. Buckland's correspondence with his friend, William D. Conybeare, indicates that in the spring of 1814 both of them were very interested in the relationship between Moses and geology, presumably because Buckland would need to lecture on this subject. In 1815, in order to illustrate his lectures, Buckland published a table comparing the English strata with those on the continent, as arranged by Werner. In this table, which was widely circulated, he introduced the term *diluvian detritus* to refer to that part of the alluvium produced by the flood and distinguished it from the postdiluvian detritus attributable to wind and rivers.[16] Cuvier had previously

---

[14] Thomas Chalmers, 'Remarks on Cuvier's *Theory of the Earth,*' in Extracts from a Review of That Theory Which was Contributed to *The Christian Instructor* in 1814', in *Miscellanies; Embracing Reviews, Essays, and Addresses* (4 vols; New York: Robert Carter, 1848), Vol. I, p. 191.

[15] John Bird Sumner, *A Treatise on the Records of the Creation, and on the Moral Attributes of the Creator; with Particular Reference to the Jewish History, and to the Consistency of the Principle of Population with the Wisdom and Goodness of the Deity* (2 vols; London: J. Hatchard, 1816), Vol. I, pp. 284-5.

[16] Mrs Elizabeth Oke (Buckland) Gordon, *The Life and Correspondence of William Buckland, D.D. F.R.S., Sometime Dean of Westminister, Twice*

distinguished between two kinds of aluvium, belonging to two different geological epochs. The older deposit, which contained only extinct species, had been produced by a great marine inundation, while the more recent deposit contained only existing species and was attributable to the ordinary processes of erosion and deposition.[17] Buckland's diluvian detritus contained both extinct and existing species.

In his inaugural lecture, after his appointment as reader in geology at Oxford in 1819, Buckland asserted that geology supported the Bible and religion, citing Cuvier and Sumner among his authorities, but insisting, in opposition to the former, that 'the antediluvian continents were the same with the present'.[18] The chair in geology seems to have been created as the result of a compromise, like that proposed by Sumner, in which the Church would encourage geology if geologists, in turn, would support the Bible with respect to the flood. In the summer of 1819, Buckland began field investigations in order to substantiate his theory of the flood; out of these came a paper, which he presented to the Geological Society in December.[19] His best new evidence was that from the Kirkdale cavern, discovered in 1821, on which he published his *Reliquiae Diluvianae* in 1823.[20]

It is a misconception that there was virtually no opposition

President of the Geological Society, and First President of the British Association (New York: D. Appleton and Company, 1894), pp. 14–18. Buckland's table, entitled 'Order of Superposition of Strata in the British Island', is appended at the back of William Phillips, *A Selection of Facts From the Best Authorities, Arranged so as to Form an Outline of the Geology of England and Wales* (London: William Phillips, 1818). Joseph Townsend had earlier (1812) divided the alluvial deposits into 'ancient alluvial, which may be called Diluvian', and recent alluvial; see his *Geological and Mineralogical Researches, During a Period of More than Fifty Years, in England, Scotland, Ireland, Switzerland, Holland, France, Flanders, and Spain: Wherein the Effects of the Deluge are Traced, and the Veracity of the Mosaic Account is Established* (Bath: Samuel Bagster, 1824), p. 252 (first published in 1812).

[17] Georges Cuvier, 'Sur les os fossiles de ruminans trouvés dans les terrains meubles', *Journal de Physique*, LXVIII (1809), 377.

[18] Buckland, *Vindiciae Geologicae*, pp. 5, 24, 29.

[19] William Buckland, 'Description of the Quartz Rock of the Lickey Hill in Worcestershire, and of the Strata Immediately Surrounding It; with Considerations on the Evidences of a Recent Deluge Afforded by the Gravel Beds of Warwickshire and Oxfordshire, and the Valley of the Thames from Oxford downwards to London; and an Appendix, Containing Analogous Proofs of Diluvian Action. Collected from Various Authorities', *Transactions of the Geological Society*, V (1821), 506–44. This was read on 3 December 1819.

[20] William Buckland, *Reliquiae Diluvianae; or, Observations on the Organic Remains Contained in Caves, Fissures, and Diluvial Gravel, and on Other Geological Phenomena, Attesting the Action of an Universal Deluge* (London: John Murray, 1823).

by geologists in Great Britain to Buckland's diluvial theory in the years immediately following its promulgation.[21] Although most geologists at this time accepted the evidence for a geologically recent and widespread deluge, only a minority, mostly clergymen, such as Buckland, Conybeare, Sedgwick, and Kidd, identified this deluge with the flood.[22] Geologists had a far more liberal attitude toward the Bible than most laymen, some of whom attacked the current geology (and Buckland in particular) because they believed that the flood was responsible for much more than geologists would allow.[23]

The interpretation of the flood as a quiet rising of the waters that left no distinctive traces was stronger among geologists at this time than has been recognized. Jameson, in 1827, while naming Cuvier and Buckland as authorities for the violent theory of the flood, stated that 'numerous writers' had advocated the nonviolent theory.[24] Buffon had argued this view, and many of his arguments were repeated at this time by opponents of the violent theory.[25] It is well known that the Huttonian theory made no use of deluges.[26] Although it is questionable whether Hutton himself believed in the flood,[27] his follower, Playfair, certainly did, and he held to the nonviolent interpretation.[28] The catastrophist Huttonians, Sir James Hall and Sir George Mac-

---

[21] See Charles C. Gillispie, *Genesis and Geology: A Study in the Relations of Scientific Thought, Natural Theology, and Social Opinion in Great Britain, 1790–1850* (New York: Harper & Brothers, 1959), pp. 108, 111. This view was also criticized by Walter Cannon in *Victorian Studies*, December 1961, p. 126 and note 34.

[22] John Kidd, *Outlines of Mineralogy* (Oxford: J. Parker, 1809), Vol. I, pp. vi, xxi. Kidd was not so positive in his second work: *A Geological Essay on the Imperfect Evidence in Support of a Theory of the Earth, Deducible Either from its General Structure or from the Changes Produced on its Surface by the Operation of Existing Causes* (Oxford: the Author, 1815), p. 163. For Adam Sedgwick, see his 'On Diluvial Formations', *Annals of Philosophy*, X (1825), 34–5. See, also, Rev. Joseph Townsend (see note 16).

[23] See, for example, Granville Penn, *A Comparative Estimate of the Mineral and Mosaical Geologies: Revised, and Enlarged with Relation to the Latest Publications on Geology* (2 vols; 2nd edn; London: James Duncan, 1825).

[24] See Georges Cuvier, *Essay on the Theory of the Earth, ... with Geological Illustrations, by Professor Jameson* (5th edn; Edinburgh: William Blackwood, 1827), p. 437.

[25] Count de Buffon, *Natural History, General and Particular ... The History of Man and Quadrupeds*, trans. by William Smellie, edited by William Wood (20 vols; London: T. Cadell and W. Davies, 1812), Vol. I, pp. 128–32. This is in the 'Proofs of the Theory of the Earth, Article V'.

[26] John Playfair, *Illustrations of the Huttonian Theory of the Earth* (Edinburgh: William Creech, 1802), p. 400.

[27] Hutton seems to deny that God would act so as to destroy life; see his *Theory of the Earth, with Proofs and Illustrations. In Four Parts* (2 vols; Edinburgh: William Creech, 1795), Vol. I, p. 273.

[28] [John Playfair], Review of Cuvier's *Essay on the Theory of the Earth*. *Edinburgh Review*, XXII (1814), 469.

kenzie, regarded their deluge as having occurred long before the flood.[29]

Many non-Huttonians also refused to identify the geological deluge with the flood. Chalmers objected to Cuvier's violent flood.[30] The geologist Robert Bakewell accepted Cuvier's evidence for 'the last grand revolution of the globe before the formation of man', but said nothing about the flood, the Bible being ignored in his work.[31] William Smith believed in the geological deluge, but did not relate it to the Bible.[32] Thomas Whitaker, an English clergyman, stated in 1819 that current geological opinion supported the nonviolent view of the flood and cited Linnaeus and Cuvier in his support:

> How little reason there is, from the account of Moses himself, for believing that the general surface of the globe underwent any material change in consequence of that catastrophe. The annihilation of the human race, with a few exceptions, was the object of God, and for that purpose an inundation, without these supposed convulsions, otherwise than as required for producing that inundation, was quite sufficient.[33]

The nonviolent interpretation of the flood was particularly commendable to scientists because of the tradition of not mixing science and religion, for the good of both. William Knight, in 1818, after quoting Francis Bacon on the folly of mixing science and the Scriptures, added:

> This is a passage which cannot be too often remembered, and which, like many others in the same immortal work, is pregnant with the spirit of true wisdom. It seems, as Professor Playfair justly remarks, to have been prophetically addressed to De Luc, Kirwan, and the other cosmogonists of the present day, who have done all in their power to degrade the Sacred

---

[29] See Sir James Hall, 'Experiments on Whinstone and Lava', *Transactions of the Royal Society of Edinburgh*, V (1805), 68, and Mackenzie, *Edinburgh Encyclopaedia*, Vol. VII, p. 605.

[30] Chalmers, 'Remarks', p. 187.

[31] Robert Bakewell, *An Introduction to Geology, Illustrative of the Structure of the Earth; Comprising the Elements of the Science, and an Outline of the Geology and Mineral Geography of England* (2nd edn; London: J. Harding, 1815), pp. 430–1. Bakewell does state that natural appearances confirm the Mosaic history with respect to the recent creation of man.

[32] William Smith, *Strata Identified by Organized Fossils, Containing Prints on Colored Paper of the Most Characteristic Specimens in Each Stratum* (London: the Author, 1816), Introduction (second unnumbered page).

[33] [Thomas Dunham Whitaker], Review of Thomas Gisborne's *The Testimony of Natural Theology to Christianity*, *Quarterly Review*, XXI (1819), 53.

Writings by the arguments which they have brought forward in their defence.[34]

John Farey, the pupil and spokesman of William Smith, wrote a letter to the *Philosophical Magazine* criticizing Buckland's inaugural lecture in the following way:

> I remember having seen Mr Bakewell commended in your Work, for having in the year 1813 abstained, from introducing the Deluge of Moses into his *Introduction to Geology*, as the previous Writers had almost invariably done, to the manifest injury of Geology on the one hand, and of Religion on the other: since which, the practice has almost entirely grown into disuse, while the number of writers on Geological subjects, have been greatly on the increase; and I regret therefore to see, the new Geological Professor at Oxford, attempting now to revive the exploded notion, that any of the phaenomena at this time *visible*, on or within the Earth, are, with any proper regard to probability, referable to the Deluge of which Moses writes.[35]

Farey believed that universal and violent floods had occurred on the earth, but long before the deluge of Noah, which had been nonviolent. James Smithson, in what is probably a veiled attack on Buckland, wrote in 1824 that, although it had been natural for believers to refer many geological phenomena to the flood, 'the success ... was not such as to obtain the general assent of the learned; and the attempt fell into neglect and oblivion'. He then proceeded to attack the latest 'revival of this system'.[36]

The Baconian tradition of eschewing speculation also reinforced the tendency to ignore the Bible in geological writing. Thomas Thomson, who had been introduced to the Wernerian geognosy by Jameson, criticized in 1819 the reasoning of George B. Greenough on the deluge:

> It possesses considerable plausibility as he has placed the arguments. But I have no doubt that Deluc, were he now alive, and in the vigour of his understanding, could write an equally plausible refutation of the whole essay; that Sir James Hall could give an air of plausibility to his doctrine of eleva-

---

[34] William Knight, *Facts and Observations towards Forming a New Theory of the Earth* (Edinburgh: Archibald Constable & Co., 1818), p. 325.

[35] [John Farey], 'Reflections on the Noachian Deluge, and on the Attempt Lately Made at Oxford, for Connecting the Same with Present Geological Appearances', *Philosophical Magazine*, LVI (1820), 10–14.

[36] James Smithson, 'Some Observations on Mr Penn's Theory Concerning the Formation of the Kirkdale Cave', *Annals of Philosophy*, VIII (1824), 50–1 (dated June 10).

tions; and that Mr Jameson could state very plausible reasons for supposing that the mountains and valleys either existed originally, or have been produced by the gradual action of the weather. The subject does not admit of precise reasoning. I consider it as but of second-rate importance, and am of opinion that those persons who confine the science of geology to such speculations mistake its true nature, and rather injure than promote its progress by calling off the attention of its cultivators from the investigation of facts to loose discussions which are not susceptible of accurate demonstration.[37]

There is evidence that even the geological deluge was not considered as well accepted before Buckland. Benjamin Silliman, a Wernerian, although favorably inclined, considered the theory in 1820 as unproved; and Edward Hitchcock stated in 1824 that

> ... the general belief is, that existing streams, avalanches and lakes, bursting their barriers, are sufficient to account for all their phenomena, and not a few geologists, especially those of the Huttonian school, at whose head is Professor Playfair, have till recently been of this opinion.[38]

William Fitton's review of Buckland's *Reliquiae Diluvianae* was critical, despite Fitton's desire not to offend his friend. He accepted much of Buckland's theory, but he concluded that there was not 'sufficient data from which to reason with safety, upon any general question touching the comparison of the antediluvian population, with the actual inhabitants of the globe'. He also objected to arbitrary assumptions whose purpose was to make the geological deluge more closely resemble the flood:

> That there has been a deluge, affecting universally all parts of the Earth's surface, and producing every where the same or similar effects, no person who has duly examined the evidence can deny.... The only question is, whether that great event ... is proved by *physical evidence*, to have been *recent*, transient, and *simultaneous*; and upon these points ... the facts appear to us to afford but imperfect evidence as to *the*

[37] [Thomas Thomson], Review of George B. Greenough's *Critical Examination of the First Principles of Geology*, *Annals of Philosophy*, XIV (1819), 373. The growth and extent of the reaction in geology against speculation was noted by W. H. Fitton in his review of the *Transactions of the Geological Society*, vol. II, *Edinburgh Review*, XXVIII (1817), 175–7.
[38] [Benjamin Silliman], Review of Horace H. Hayden's *Geological Essays*, *American Journal of Science*, III (1821), 48. [Edward Hitchcock], 'Review of Buckland's *Reliquiae Diluvianae*', *American Journal of Science*, VIII (1824), 332.

date, and still less as to *the duration*, of the submersion. . . . For to speak of the support to the Sacred narrative afforded by extrinsic inquiry, *if the narrative itself be made to form a part of the evidence*, is a mode of reasoning that appears to us to be altogether inadmissible.[39]

Buckland's nemesis was the Reverend John Fleming, of Fifeshire, Scotland. In 1824, at Jameson's request, Fleming began the controversy with Buckland that resulted in the downfall of his theory.[40] Although this controversy is pertinent and interesting, this paper will be concerned only with Fleming's earlier and lesser known writings, which reveal more clearly the connection between the uniformitarianism and Wernerianism.[41]

Fleming studied for the ministry at the University of Edinburgh, where he was exposed to both Wernerian and Huttonian influences. He found the former doctrine more congenial, and through his friendship with the chemist Thomas Thomson, he acquired a love for mineralogy. He also, from an early age, had a strong interest in natural history. After leaving the university in 1805, he joined the Wernerian Natural History Society of Edinburgh, whose founder and president was his friend Jameson. He became a fellow of the Royal Society of Edinburgh in 1814, having been proposed by Jameson, Playfair, and David Brewster.[42]

Fleming opposed the Huttonian theory because of its plutonism and because he regarded it as a speculation constructed without examination or knowledge of the rocks. His earliest writings reveal a uniformitarian approach to geology. He be-

[39] [William H. Fitton], Review of Buckland's *Reliquiae Diluvianae*, *Edinburgh Review*, XXXIX (1823), 229–32.
[40] John Fleming, 'Remarks Illustrative of the Influence of Society on the Distribution of British Animals', *Edinburgh Philosophical Journal*, XI (1824), 287–305 (dated July 19). Jameson was the editor of this journal; for hints of his devious role in the controversy, see John Duns's memoir in John Fleming, *The Lithology of Edinburgh. . . . Edited, with a Memoir, by the Rev. John Duns* (Edinburgh: William P. Kennedy, 1859), pp. xxxvii–xl. Fleming wrote in 1829 that his friends had assured him that his articles had given 'the death-blow to the diluvian hypothesis. Certain at least it is, that, since that time, with the exception of a very few individuals who may still be found on stilts, amidst the "retiring waters", the opponents of the hypothesis have become as numerous as were formerly its supporters, and the period is probably not far distant, when the "Reliquiae diluvianae" of the Oxonian geologist will be quoted as an example of the *idola specus*.' See John Fleming, 'Additional Remarks on the Climate of the Arctic Regions, in Answer to Mr Conybeare', *Edinburgh New Philosophical Journal*, VIII (1829), 68.
[41] For a discussion of this controversy, see my unpublished dissertation, *The Rise of the Diluvial Theory in British Geological Thought*, University of Oklahoma, 1963, pp. 133–50.
[42] The best published sources for Fleming's life are the memoirs by John Duns (see note 40) and Alexander Bryson, *Transactions of the Royal Society of Edinburgh*, XXII (1861), 655–80.

lieved that 'many of the inequalities of the earth's surface owe their existence to the long-continued action of air and water', which is good Wernerian as well as Huttonian doctrine;[43] and he recommended the study of the laws regulating the distribution of recent shells as the best preparation for studying their distribution in the past.[44] He consistently opposed catastrophist explanations, such as 'deluging the earth by a comet'.[45] Fleming criticized Knight's theory of the earth because it was mostly plutonist hypothesis, but he agreed with Knight (and Playfair) that the scientist must be free to inquire without regard for the Scriptures.[46] While critical of the Wernerian theory in some respects, he defended most of its principles before the 1820s.[47]

During the years 1819 to 1823, Fleming's geological opinions were in a state of flux. By nature he was conservative, always reluctant to alter views once they were firmly established. Yet his writings reveal two opposing tendencies. He tended to favor the Wernerian explanations, and yet he indicated how little faith he put in these and other speculations. His old convictions were shaken by the defection of Wernerians to the vulcanist camp.[48]

Despite his distrust of theory, Fleming was appalled and disgusted by the skepticism of Greenough's *Critical Examination*, which he felt would only injure geology. Since his attitude to Greenough's work was shared by other geologists, his comments are worth quoting:

Before taking our leave of Mr Greenough, we feel disposed to state candidly, that his performance is one by no means calculated to advance his own reputation, or promote the interests of geology.... He appears to be totally unacquainted with the laws of evidence. With him the testimony of every mineralogist is of equal value; all are supposed to have been equally well informed, and to have studied the subject with equal care....

[43] John Fleming, 'On the Mineralogy of the Redhead in Angusshire', *Memoirs of the Wernerian Natural History Society*, Vol. II (1811–16), pp. 343–5, 349, 352. This was read on 4 February 1815. For criticisms of Hutton, see also in the same volume, 'Observations on the Mineralogy of the Neighbourhood of St Andrew's in Fife', pp. 153–4 (read 5 February 1813).

[44] [John Fleming], 'Conchology', *Supplement to the Fourth, Fifth, and Sixth Editions of the Encyclopaedia Britannica* (6 vols; Edinburgh: Archibald Constable and Company, 1824), Vol. III, p. 316 (written before 1818).

[45] John Fleming, 'Observations on the Orthoceratites of Scotland', *Annals of Philosophy*, V (1815), 200.

[46] [John Fleming], Review of Knight's *Theory of the Earth*, *Edinburgh Monthly Review*, I (1819), 356.

[47] Fleming, *Mem. Wern. Nat. Hist. Soc.*, Vol. II, p. 365.

[48] [John Fleming], Review of A. Boué's *Essai Geologique sur l'Ecosse*, *New Edinburgh Review*, III (1822), 372.

There has resulted from all this a kind of geological scepticism, which we regard in this instance as the index of a mind unaccustomed to philosophical induction, but which others may consider as the mark of free and independent thinking. It is calculated to disgust the adept, and to perplex the tyro. It has been publicly intimated, that the author is a gentleman of independent fortune, and that he has expended large sums in furnishing an extensive collection of minerals. These circumstances, while they aggravate his errors, and render him more dangerous as an authority, recall an expression of the late illustrious Playfair in reference to De Luc, 'to *reason* and to *arrange*, are very different occupations of the mind; and a man may deserve praise as a mineralogist, who is but ill qualified for the researches of geology'.[49]

Fleming was also dissatisfied with Cuvier as a geologist, and with Jameson for approving his views:

Now here we are left to choose between Dr Hutton and M. De Luc; as the former elevates and the latter depresses the strata. Not a hint of Werner all this time; although we did believe that Cuvier's works were to confirm those of the philosopher of Freyburg. Must we understand that the editor of this preface has read it with approbation, and sanctioned it with his name and his preface too; or are we mistaken in supposing that he is teaching and publishing doctrines the reverse of these? We are ourselves indifferent good Wernerians, but are always ready for conviction; and as we are also lovers of peace, shall be most delighted to find that there is some chance of agreement among the several belligerent powers on these subjects. Werner says decidedly, if we have not misapprehended what we learnt at college, that there have not been any subversions of strata, either by depression or elevation, but that all rocks were deposited as we now see them, having been crystallized, compound and simple, veins, conglomerates and all, from solutions in the waters of the sea. For our parts, we are ready to believe any thing, provided we are told what it is to be; Werner, or Hutton, or Whiston, it is all one; but we cannot believe one thing one day, and the reverse the next.

With reference to Cuvier's claim to priority in the recognition of the value of fossils in geology, Fleming commented:

We have a notion that M. Cuvier is better acquainted with his own writings than with those of other geologists. He could

[49] [John Fleming], Review of Greenough's *Critical Examination*, *Edinburgh Monthly Review*, IV (1820), 571.

not else have imagined that he was among the first to point out the importance of organic remains. . . .

After pointing out that many geologists, including Smith, had recognized this, he took up Jameson's claim that Werner deserved credit:

> We must pardon M. Cuvier in this particular case at least. But for Professor Jameson's friendship, we might have made the same mistake ourselves, and imagined that Werner was entirely ignorant of the organic department of geology. If a man will 'die and make no sign', how can we know his meaning?

However, he did not agree with Cuvier's estimate of the importance of organic remains in geology in which, Fleming believed, mineralogy was the foundation 'and bulding too'. He was also unconvinced by Cuvier's revolutions:

> Surely M. Cuvier does not mean to say that, if animals are not found in any particular alluvial strata, it is because their races were destroyed by irruptions of the sea, and that such an absense is a proof in itself of the revolutions and deluges in question. He must know better than we do, that a race of animals may disappear from a particular tract in consequence of many causes, dependent, not on geology, but on their own habits or natures. . . . [He mentions the destruction of forests, disease, famine, enemies, and man.] . . . We do not happen to know what the opinion of Werner was on this subject, or whether, indeed, he had ever considered it. We may possibly have misapprehended his general views, as it is not easy to get at those doctrines of his which have never been properly before the public; but our general impression is, that he does not admit of such interminable revolutions of the sea and land after the deposition of the latest rocks, whatever these may be. As all his opinions must be considered valuable, we rather regret that Professor Jameson has not informed us what the fact is, and we shall be thankful for that information at some future day.

Fleming questioned Cuvier's belief that the genera change with the strata, claiming that the latter was refuted by the evidence in his own book, which showed that the greater part of the genera in the transition limestone 'are found all the way up . . . through the greywacke, and through all the secondary strata, up to the chalk – nay, to the very living ocean itself'.

Cuvier's stand against the evolution of man and in favor of his recent origin met Fleming's approval, although he could see none but a sinister purpose in bringing up subjects on which there was such universal agreement:

> He argues like a sound naturalist, and well, against the philosophers, who, like Darwin, De Maillet, and others, chose to imagine that man had volunteered from the condition of an oyster into his present service. These personages do not deserve so much attention.
>
> Among all the wildest theories of geologists, there is not one who has ever thought of giving to the human race a higher antiquity than that which is assigned by Scripture, and which is amply confirmed by every thing that we know of the progress of human society, arts, and languages. These were matters fully admitted before Cuvier undertook to prove them; and we can see no purpose in bringing them forward again, unless it be to excite doubts in the minds of those who never examined the question.[50]

This attitude was undoubtedly a common one among scientists, which perhaps explains the conspiracy of silence that existed until Lyell with respect to Lamarck's views in Great Britain.

As late as 1822, Fleming was willing to allow that the flood had produced great changes in life on the earth, although he attributed changes in the earth's surface to nonviolent causes. At the same time, however, he argued that many changes in life were explainable by natural causes, and he soon would question whether any detectable change could be referred to the flood.[51]

It is not necessary here to go into Fleming's subsequent history. Enough has been shown, I think, to suggest that there were strong uniformitarian tendencies in Wernerianism that may have facilitated the later acceptance of Lyell's more comprehensive uniformitarian views. Lyell's work would also express the feelings of the majority of geologists that their science should be kept free from involvement with religion. On this subject, Lyell was to get much more support than on his uniformitarian thesis.

[50] [John Fleming], Review of Cuvier's *Essay on the Theory of the Earth* (4th edn), *New Edinburgh Review*, IV (1823), 383-4, 387-5. Jameson later admitted that Werner had not advocated 'the geological diluvian hypothesis', *Edinburgh Philosophical Journal*, XI (1824), 299.
[51] John Fleming, *The Philosophy of Zoology; or a General View of the Structure, Functions, and Classification of Animals* (2 vols.; Edinburgh: Archibald Constable & Co., 1822), Vol. II, p. 104.

12 Cuvier and Evolution*

William Coleman

> Order is the selection of one set of appearances rather
> than another because it gives a better sense of the
> reality behind the appearances. Science is an orderly
> language for describing some events and predicting
> others like them. The order is a selection of appearances.
> And any selection itself implies, and imposes, an inter-
> pretation.
>
> J. BRONOWSKI[1]

Cuvier now stands revealed as the defender of the integrity of
the individual animal and of the species and as the eloquent advocate of a wholesale return to the principles of teleological zoology.
Of species transmutation he could speak only in negative terms.
These zoological arguments were one motive and, it appears, by
far the most important motive lying behind his rejection of the
transformist doctrine. There existed a second possible motive for
his opposition. Many naturalists were strongly influenced by the
seeming necessity of finding in nature the literal realization of the
events catalogued in Divine Scripture. On many issues of natural
history, and particularly that of the nature of biological species, it
was commonly believed that the Bible was to be either the final
authority or at least a repository of general truths of which none
could be safely or legitimately disregarded by a truly philosophical naturalist. Cuvier was fully aware of these views and, as a
good Christian, he was not entirely unsympathetic toward them.
He was not, however, a doctrinaire Biblical zoologist. As a basis
for intelligent discussion of the problems of natural history he
preferred nature and the animals to ancient nonzoological authority. Cuvier saw presented in Scripture instructions for increasing
the happiness and moral well-being of mankind and not texts for

* William Coleman, 'Cuvier and Evolution', in *Georges Cuvier, Zoologist*,
Harvard University Press, 1964, 170–86.
[1] J. Bronowski, *The common sense of science* (Cambridge, Mass.: Harvard
University Press, 1953), 48.

the exact study of natural history; this study was the province of science and not of theology.

THE CORRELATION PRINCIPLE EXCLUDES SPECIES TRANSMUTATION

Reduced to its simplest terms, Cuvier's zoological system was based upon a philosophy of stability. Immutability was the essence of his doctrine. Transformism demanded the major transformation of the biological species during both the present period and the extensive past history of the earth. It was to this consequence of the transformist doctrine that Cuvier most vigorously objected. Application of the principle of the correlation of parts to the over-all pattern of the animal kingdom had convinced him that the various zoological groups were the result of a harmonious assemblage of the constituent parts of each organism. The principle was, in this sense, a direct statement determining inevitably the structures of each creature. The principle was also a powerful negative tool which disclosed with equal facility which structural combinations were impossible or, in Cuvier's terms, 'incompatible'. 'The truth remains [evident]', he declared, even

> ... after so much writing and discourse, just as we established it in an article thirty-two years ago [Introduction, *Leçons d'anatomie comparée*, edition 1] and therefore before all of these so-called philosophical excursions: Nature, inexhaustible in fecundity and omnipotent in its works, if this does not imply a contradiction, has been settled [*arretée*] in the innumerable combinations of organic forms and functions which compose the animal kingdom by physiological incompatibilities alone. It has realized all those combinations which are not repugnant [*incoherent*] and it is these repugnancies, these incompatibilities, this impossibility of the coexistence of one modification with another which establish between the diverse groups of organisms those separations, those gaps, which mark their necessary limits and which create the natural *embranchements*, classes, orders, and families.[2]

The gaps between species as well as these groups themselves were the direct and necessary consequence of the principle of the correlation of parts. The organism, being a functionally integrated whole each part of which stood in close relation to every other part, could not, under pain of almost immediate extinction, depart significantly from the norms established for the species by the first anatomical rule. Just as it would be a geometrical contradic-

[2] Cuvier, *Leçons d'anatomie comparée* (Paris, edn 2, 1835), I, 64.

tion for the three angles of a triangle to exceed 180°, so it would be a physiological contradiction for a bird whose length is increased 4 times to be suspended in air by wings extended only 4 times. The correct factor would be 8 times because of the additional volume and weight. The ruminant could not have a short, straight digestive tube; the eagle was forbidden webbed feet; the serpent had no external limbs; the cave-dwelling crustacean lacked acute eyesight. The correlation of parts dictated that, in sum, any combination of organs was possible which was not in itself contradictory and that all incompatible combinations remained unrealized. Cuvier's principle almost seemed to say that whatever can exist does exist, and that whatever does not exist cannot exist.

Zoologists today also believe in a correlation of parts, without which an organism would literally disintegrate, and yet they believe in evolution too. Obviously, the modern view and Cuvier's principle are not the same. What, then, is peculiar to Cuvier's correlation principle which excludes the possibility of transmutation of species?

The answer again lies in the limitation of variation by the correlation principle. It is the degree of permitted variation which now becomes crucial. Cuvier freely admitted almost unlimited intraspecific variation. The surest proof of this is the fact that he believed that no two members of a given species were morphologically alike. The correlation principle was therefore not so rigid as to prevent variation altogether. Cuvier was careful, however, to insist that variation could not extend beyond well-demarcated limits, limits which coincided with those of the species.

These small intraspecific variations were considered to be of minor zoological importance. They affected only parts of unimportant peripheral and superficial organs. There was no question about the stability of the essential organs, of the nervous system, heart, lungs, and viscera. Here one observes the two apparent levels of variation which concerned Cuvier. Intraspecific variation was structurally insignificant and aimless in direction. It also seemed to have no basic effect on the functional integrity of the organism. In contrast, variation of gross structure, of the major organs, if it occurred, would have had disastrous consequences. A major change, for example, a sharp increase in the heart beat or the diminution by half of the kidney and thus a reduction in renal secretion, would by itself have wrought havoc with the general constitution of the animal. In order that an animal might persist after a change of this magnitude it would be necessary that the other organs of the body be also proportionately modified. In other words, an organism must change en bloc or not at all. Only saltatory modification could occur, and this idea was to Cuvier, as it is to most modern zoologists, but for very different reasons, unverified and basically absurd. Transmutation by the accumulation of alterations, great or small, would thus be impossible. This would be especially true if no adequate mechanism were available to 'direct' the accumulative process.

The correlation principle, as understood by Cuvier, so restricted variation as to make it 'evolutionarily' insignificant. To ridicule macromutational trends was an easy task. Consequently, the principle of the correlation of parts was an elegant means of stating and demonstrating the impossibility of significant variation, that is, variation providing the basic material for the subsequent transmutation of species. Cuvier's efforts to limit the amplitude of species (and individual) variability, even under severe environmental stress, were, in the final analysis, promoted by his desire to reduce the presumed potential raw material for transmutation.

The impracticality of reproductive isolation as a readily verifiable species criterion reinforced this conclusion by compelling Cuvier the systematist to enunciate definite and unvarying structural characteristics for each species. Other taxonomic units were defined in the same manner. The species was thereby morphologically 'defined', and the principle of the correlation of parts was called in to 'explain' the definition. To create a sound taxonomic representation of the animal kingdom, Cuvier required more or less invariable criteria. Cuvier is perhaps the most distinguished figure in a long succession of naturalists after Linnaeus who insisted that only a clearly defined, morphologically similar group of individuals was taxonomically real, and who failed to recognize that a dynamic, variable population could also be classified.[3]

Cuvier moreover seems to have been constitutionally unable to support or to appreciate the basic idea of change. This introduces a possible third factor into the question of motives or predispositions against the transformist viewpoint. Was Cuvier's opposition determined wholly or in part by ingrained traits of character, by long-entrenched and unshakable patterns of thought? Was it really a phenomenon on the psychological level? The answer must of course be affirmative, but such a response has really little obvious additional usefulness. It explains too much, for no one would deny that the design argument of the more eager natural theologians or even Cuvier's own correlation principle were not in part and perhaps to a very great degree conditioned by their advocates' over-all intellectual attitudes. This can be

[3] E. Mayr, 'Species concepts and definitions', *The species problem*, ed. E. Mayr (Washington, D.C.: American Association for the Advancement of Science, 1957), 2.

illustrated by the fact that the bold thoughts of Cuvier's colleagues, Lamarck and Geoffroy, were so totally repugnant to his whole manner of thinking that it was only by great effort that he was able to form a tolerably clear idea of what these naturalists were attempting to create. His counter-argumentation, when it came, was a purely scientific affair. The ever-present psychological predispositions, if they had any major influence upon Cuvier's scientific studies, were expressed not in general and indistinct terms but always within the context of the relevant zoological issue. Cuvier's unadventurous and authoritarian spirit was unreceptive to new ideas and reluctant to alter old and accepted views. His range of vision was great, embracing all of the sciences, but his sphere of active thought was confined and was not further cultivated. He was always the legislator or universal mind, extraordinarily well informed, industrious, lucid in thought and exposition – anything, indeed, but an innovator.

If it is true that in forming a scientific system (a task which occupied Cuvier as it did his contemporaries) each researcher is compelled to select between numerous possible hypotheses to explain given phenomena, then it may be concluded that the very nature of Cuvier's intellect had already seriously reduced the number of alternatives available. Cuvier failed even to see the problem posed by the occurrence of vestigial organs. He was unable to consider seriously the possibility that the recognized sequence of fossil vertebrate animals might tell something more about the earth's history than the mere fact of organic extinction. Many other individuals, of course, suffer parallel limitations. Lamarck, for example, was so obsessed by transmutation that he denied the demonstrable occurrence of extinction. Cuvier's limited vision, however, joined to his deliberate rejection or reinterpretation of evidence favoring species transmutations, reemphasizes the absence from his zoological investigations of proper consideration for the possibility and problems of organic change.

Specific change and the Cuvierian zoological *type* were contradictory concepts. Cuvier the taxonomist demanded precise definition and long-term stability, classificatory criteria which the current transformist schemes could not provide. He found factual evidence in his zoological observations which convinced him that the biological species were unvarying and he supported his practical discoveries with physiological generalizations taken ultimately from Aristotle. The historian faces in Cuvier that extraordinary situation in which a man discovers and interprets after his own opinions data which will soon undermine his entire system. Comparative anatomy, for example, and, to a lesser extent, paleontology were among the principal disciplines which ultimately provided the factual foundations for the theory of evolution. Cuvier's conservative scientific temperament helped determine which phenomena were to be regarded as valid facts and which facts were to be considered as significant, and not one of the vast store of the then available zoological data was believed to support the idea of species transmutation.[4] Demonstration of such transmutation Cuvier knew would have struck at the heart of his system and the labor and thought concentrated in the principle of the correlation of parts would have then served no end. With consistency and genuine conviction of the validity of his own system, he opposed with zoological arguments the new and disruptive doctrines. There was no other alternative before him.

THE RELIGIOUS MOTIVE A SECONDARY FACTOR

The Bible was not, in Cuvier's opinion, a scientific text. Cuvier's conception of Christianity and of the teachings of the Bible stressed unquestioning faith and correct conduct and did not seek in Scripture an authoritative description of the past history and present processes of the physical world. The long and tendentious struggle between science and religion was a subject which failed entirely to please him. Religion, being essentially a question of the relation between the individual and his Creator, he regarded as unsuited for acrimonious public dispute. Cuvier was so confident in his own religious convictions that he had no need to seek their confirmation in external, scientific discoveries.[5] He was aware, furthermore, that theology, like any other discipline, could be damaged by indiscriminate meddling in affairs not wholly relevant to its purposes.

A classic problem in Protestant theology had long been the relative conceptual merits regarding the existing world of nature (or reason) and divine Scripture. In Cuvier's own and other Protestant churches a crisis had been reached by the end of the seventeenth century. Luther had been especially concerned not to identify God with nature or to remove Him from effective control of His creation. God was wholly apart from the world, but still everywhere and at all times omnipotent. The successes of the Counter Reformation and the hardening of a new Lutheran scholasticism which met Roman traditionalism with Scriptural inerrancy and the elevation of Aristotle to philosophical primacy forced Protestant thought into narrow literalistic interpretations of Biblical texts. At the same time science and geographical dis-

[4] Cf. S. Toulmin, *Foresight and understanding* (Bloomington: Indiana University Press, 1961), 91–2.
[5] R. Hooykaas, *Natural law and divine miracle* (Leiden: E. J. Brill, 1959), 198.

covery were demonstrating in a vital, tangible manner the existence and fascination of the physical world. There came to certain of the pious the idea of seeking God not in the historical, ecclesiastical context but in nature. God to these believers became above all a Creator God.[6] The stage was now set for the prolonged battle throughout the eighteenth and nineteenth centuries, within and without the churches and fought by believers, deists, and atheists, over the various means of demonstrating God's existence and His attributes. Science, especially biology and geology, became, for better or worse, one of the principal armaments of Christian apologetics.

Those whose faith was secure might nevertheless be bothered by possible consequences of Christian doctrine for scientific belief, or vice versa. Certainly the questions of the origin and nature of man, of the creation of the world and of living things, and the scientific meaning or explanation of the Noachian Deluge were issues with which any sensitive or literalistically inclined Christian thinker would have to deal. Cuvier, it has been seen, considered the scientific evidence bearing on each of these issues. He found no evidence for the great antiquity of man, but also did not demand recent human origins. The nature of man was a psychophilosophical or even a religious problem; zoology could only discuss man's physical state. There was, futhermore, no scientific evidence telling of the presumed creation of the world or of life on the earth. Creation was a mystery still untouched by science. Memories of a great Deluge were known to exist in the records of ancient societies. It was already clear, however, that this Deluge had not caused all mankind to perish and Cuvier was careful to admit the possibility that antediluvian man had existed.

Cuvier was concerned with demonstrating the noncontradiction between science and religion. He was not seeking a positive concordance between them. He believed that the spirit of the sciences and that of religion could exist together. Although science provided the only uncontested truths to which man could aspire, it was no less true that the greatest natural philosophers were also deeply religious men. Newton, Leibniz, and Pascal were cited by Cuvier as examples showing that 'geometers' and 'physicists' may also be men devoted to Christianity. This does not mean, of course, that Cuvier's popular scientific expositions, the two geological *Discours*, were devoid of religious presuppositions and implications. The tone of these treatises is clear. Throughout the *Discours* are poorly concealed attempts to show the simul-

---

[6] J. Dillenberger, *Protestant thought and natural science* (Garden City, N.Y.: Doubleday, 1960), 136–7. See C. C. Gillispie, *Genesis and geology* (Cambridge, Mass.: Harvard University Press, 1951); C. E. Raven, *Science and religion* (Cambridge: Cambridge University Press, 1953).

taneity of the most recent catastrophe and the Noachian Deluge, to emphasize the recent appearance of civilized man, and to prove that destruction and migration, and not successive creations, were responsible for the history of life on the earth. Cuvier's treatises were strikingly different from those written by naturalists who were also natural theologians. Cuvier had great admiration for the intricacies of the parts of the organic world, but he never used these latter to demonstrate, by analogy or design, the existence and action of the Creator. Even less does one find in Cuvier's works the overt application of the results of zoology and geology to the specifically theologically conditioned interpretations of the earth's history of the kind which appeared from the hands of William Buckland or Adam Sedgwick. Here is one of the notable characteristics of Cuvier's writings: a deliberate attempt not to mix science and religion. The *Discours* are, even with their numerous errors, scientific treatises. They are not noisy, apologetic religious tracts.

An author, especially an author as familiar with the achievements of his science as Cuvier, in 1812 or even in 1830 still enjoyed the great 'benefit of a doubt' conferred by unavoidable ignorance. Fossil man was yet so poorly known that he became no hindrance to a literalistic interpretation of Scripture. And Cuvier, as has been shown above, was not committed to proving a priori man's lack of antiquity. He was also secure when disallowing all appeals to investigate or to describe the creation(s). Scepticism, meaning 'no grounds for discussion', on this subject was among his most valuable contributions to the investigation of earth history. Lamarck, for example, had vainly devoted innumerable pages of his wildest fancies to developing an almost completely worthless hypothesis for the origin of life. Cuvier's advocacy of geological catastrophism was perhaps his greatest violation of contemporary scientific knowledge. Here he confined his attention to a limited and special geological system. He was unable to escape his early studies of Wernerian geology and was, ironically, perhaps somewhat influenced by the prevailing mood of great and forceful change which was current in a revolutionary age. Cuvier was therefore able to accept, on the grounds of non-contradiction, both a not too literal reading of the Mosaic narrative and the results of modern science. Areas of conflict were still ill-defined and some sciences, particularly historical zoology, were still in a rude state.

Perhaps Cuvier saw that the real danger of science for religion was not in specific problems such as the nature and date of the Deluge or the origin of man. On all of these points Cuvier and a growing number of his contemporaries were content to use the Mosaic texts as a definitive source only for the period following the Noachian Deluge and the subsequent resurgence of humanity at this time, that is, the formation and perpetuation after this disastrous event of civilized societies with oral or written records.[7] When, in passing comment, Cuvier criticized Descartes and the *Philosophes*, praised Newton and Aristotle, and attacked the *Idéologues* and the *Naturphilosophen*, he was not always guided by purely scientific considerations. Cartesianism and the Enlightenment philosophy were dangerous because they had not confined their critical enquiry to proper limits and, while criticism was useful in the sciences, authority must prevail in other areas of human endeavor, including religion. By emphasizing scientific methods and achievements, which would permit science to encroach upon the unique elements of the religious experience, he feared that only crass materialism could result. Materialism could only mean the illegitimate divorce of the Creator from His universe, a situation which Cuvier would not tolerate.

The *Naturphilosophen* and the emerging French philosophical school of eclecticism, centered about German philosophy, were guilty of another crime. This was pantheism, wherein God and His universe and all spiritual and existing things merged to become only One. Cuvier's distaste for the *Naturphilosophen* has already been noted. There exists a transcript of his marginal notes to V. Cousin's *Fragments philosophiques*, a basic manual of eclecticism, in which he alternately shouts 'pantheist' and 'hypocritical piety' at Cousin's profession of faith and accuses him of dissimulating his true 'Spinozism' (IFFC 316(5)). Materialism and pantheism were terms of bitterest reproach for Cuvier. Pantheism he employed more frequently, but perhaps only because this was a prevailing doctrine after the decline of Enlightenment materialism and also during his own lifetime. Both doctrines attempted to solicit support from the sciences and it was these pseudoscientific pretensions which most annoyed Cuvier, since they gave the appearance that science was not nonreligious but antireligious. God's existence and the certainty of His benevolent concern for all mankind were never questioned by Cuvier. He admitted freely that nature was a 'happy allegory which plainly teaches us that one of our first duties is to fill our minds with the goodness and wisdom of the Author of Nature by a continued study of the products of His power'.[8] It should be noted that this passage, of a tone rare in Cuvier's works, mentions only the attributes of the Creator; His existence was assumed and was considered beyond question. The sciences might stimulate our re-

---

[7] Cuvier, *Discours sur les révolutions de la surface du globe et sur les changemens qu'elles ont produits dans le règne animal* (Paris, edn 3, 1830), 82–3. Cf. A. Houtin, *La question biblique chez les catholiques de France au XIXe siècle* (Paris, 1902), 136–7.
[8] Cuvier, *Recueil des éloges historiques lus dans les séances publiques de l'Institut de France* (Paris, 1861) III, 272.

ligious sensibility or initiate us into the more profound riches of the Christian tradition, but they had nothing to say concerning the personal faith of the believer.

A further word is necessary upon the role of religious motives in Cuvier's thought. To argue that his religious convictions were not directly involved in the refutation of the transformist doctrine does not entirely remove them from the historian's attention. It was perfectly obvious, although unstated, that the principle of the correlation of parts was understood by the naturalist to have been decreed by God Himself. The correlation principle was the prime example in natural history of the presumed fundamental lawfulness of nature. Hence, the question arises, is the fact that religious considerations lay behind an essentially zoological generalization an appropriate index of the possible influence of these views on Cuvier's rejection of the idea of the transmutation of species?

This question may perhaps best be answered by distinguishing between religious motives and religious arguments. The former are never absent from Cuvier's thought and no one should or can attempt to minimize their importance. As has been seen above, demonstration of the noncontradiction of science and religion was a central feature of Cuvier's task. But the use or justification of individual theological arguments in their literal form was not a part of his study. Without considerable exegesis, Genesis does not insist upon the absolute stability of biological species. Genesis tells of the creation of the original pairs of organized beings and it is understood that these are the direct predecessors of those kinds of animals and plants still living. On this point, certainly, Cuvier is in complete agreement with Scripture. It is clear, however, that he considered reproductive continuity to be also a primary biological fact, a fact made inescapable by the studies and writings of Harvey, Linnaeus, and many others. It was not on inflexible religious dogma but on scientific authority that he based his argument. If Moses recorded the extinction of great numbers of creatures during the Deluge, he did not have in mind a series of disasters which, over a long span of centuries, destroyed various kinds of animals and plants. Cuvier adopted a system of geobiological catastrophes, and this without hesitation or with any concern that these events were unrecorded in Scripture.

It would be interesting to know how Cuvier would have reacted had it not been possible that scientific belief and religious dogma might then still exist in reasonably harmonious accord. As to all historical questions of this kind, no answer can be given. The significant fact is that Cuvier believed, rightly or wrongly, that they were in accord. Further interrogation was considered unnecessary. It was Cuvier's peculiar conception of zoology which provided his arguments against transformism. Moses and

Scripture did not speak to scientists *qua* scientists. The problem of the possible transmutation of species Cuvier regarded as a scientific affair and not a theological issue. Theology, trespassing without warrant on forbidden grounds, often had lost more than it had stood to gain.

AFTER CUVIER AND TOWARD EVOLUTION

There have already been frequent occasions to call attention to the paradox that, whereas Cuvier himself vigorously opposed the transmutation idea, his studies in comparative anatomy and paleontology helped to prepare the climate in which the theory of organic evolution later developed. Certain elements of Cuvier's antitransformism were perhaps indispensable to the formulation of evolutionary theory. At the same time his direct spiritual disciples, naturalists and zoologists of the caliber of Louis Agassiz, Richard Owen, P. M. Flourens, and many others, were altogether too subservient to their master's philosophy to wish or to be able to break away from his intellectual dominion. The development of evolutionary ideas in the half-century prior to the *Origin of Species* is an enormously complex and still inadequately explored subject. The following review attempts only to suggest the possible influence of Cuvier's ideas on this development.

Cuvier passed along to later biologists a heightened realization of the functional integrity of the individual organism. Without recognizing the significance of his own achievement, Cuvier was in great part responsible for focusing the attention of botanists and zoologists upon the problems of biological adaptation. Adaptation, the close adjustment of over-all organic structure and functions to one another and to long-term external conditions, is a phenomenon of greatest importance for evolutionary theory and is also among the phenomena which this theory has accounted for most successfully. Cuvier was able to see that the organism maintained and reproduced itself under often highly unfavorable conditions. This circumstance, according to his system, was a necessary consequence of the conditions of existence. Each kind of animal was provided by the Creator with whatever structures, behavior patterns, and so on would best maintain the individual or group in the varying organic economy of the world. The world was populated by many and different kinds of creatures, and organic diversity was one of the best-established lessons of natural history. But this diversity was not unlimited, even in theory, and herein lay the burden of Cuvier's argument. In all instances the correlation principle 'explained' the occurrence of different creatures and also denied existence to any important divergences from the *type*. Applying his laws of organic correlation, he saw animal organization submitted to morphological demands expressed in the rules governing the vital processes of the organism, but he failed to recognize that these correlations, that the adaptations of the parts of the organism to one another and of the whole creature to prolonged external conditions, could be due to exclusively 'natural' forces. Hindsight must be denied the critic: it was not until Darwin's clarification of the effectiveness of natural selection acting upon small variations that a plausible mechanism for the production of observed adaptations was enunciated. It has been seen that Cuvier was thoroughly dissatisfied with the one serious contemporary proposal of a 'natural' adaptive mechanism and that he rejected Lamarck's suggestion of environmental influences as much for its dangerous materialistic tendencies as for its strictly scientific inadequacies. But, beyond these several qualifications, one basic fact is seen to pervade Cuvier's entire zoological system, and this is the fact of adaptive diversity itself. The *type* concept destroyed the possibility of a simplistic representation of organic nature. As Lamarck demonstrated in his later works and as all subsequent advocates of the doctrine of descent with modification understood, it was clearly impossible that all kinds of organisms had arisen serially from one or even a few primitive forms. Descent had to be sought elsewhere than in a unique zoological *série*. The recognition that organic nature was orderly yet diverse was surely one of Cuvier's greatest contributions to science, and it detracts little from his accomplishment that the order of nature is accounted for today by the operation of forces peculiar to nature herself and not by conservative rules imposed upon nature by her Creator.

Cuvier's destruction of the zoological *série* had been accompanied by the demonstration of an indisputable faunal succession. In general, the remains of structurally more complex organisms characterized the more superficial geological deposits, while deeper strata preserved the impressions of lesser creatures. This statement is essentially ambiguous and must necessarily be so. There was, in Cuvier's opinion, no single criterion or set of criteria which would permit a naturalist to assign degrees of perfection to any organism whatsoever. For Cuvier the geopaleontological sequence was merely a record of organic succession and not of organic progression, of an advancing replacement of faunas culminating, as stated by the classic progressionists, in the appearance of man. His system was based on the simple fact of faunal replacement. He deliberately avoided the temptation to place all of these creatures in a single or even a partially ramified line reaching from the simplest to the most complex organism. Progressionism was in part an ill-disguised return to the old unique *série*. The *série* this time was based more on paleontological than on taxonomic evidence. Cuvier's paleontological studies had shown, however, that the fossil record failed to support zoological progression just as morphological and taxonomic evidence had failed to support the ordinal *série*. This is an historically complex situation, for the special feature of progressionism was its denial of the possibility that the various kinds of organisms found in the fossil series really represented the historical development of life. The progressionists, and Cuvier, refused categorically to admit that the different fossil groups were genetically related to one another and to modern forms. Neither the progressionists nor Cuvier could accept descent with modification. An era of intense paleontological activity followed Cuvier's pioneering studies and there were indeed few of these paleontologists who were transmutationists. Owen and other English geologists, Agassiz, Elie de Beaumont, and Adolfe Brongniart all agreed with the main teachings of Cuvier. Flourens, Cuvier's self-appointed interpreter but no paleontologist, and A. D. d'Orbigny were the principal proponents of the successive catastrophe doctrine. D'Orbigny in 1849 had already identified at least 27 distinct geological and faunal periods and thus revealed 27 pairs of catastrophe and creation. That the known fossil record in 1830, or in 1859, could not compel naturalists to acknowledge a sequential development of even a single species or genus is seen from the fact that T. H. Huxley, in 1870, was embarrassed by the difficulty of finding a suitable example to illustrate the contribution of paleontology to evolution.[9] Nevertheless, Cuvier's successionism and the progessionist doctrine which arose from it were among the first truly scientific indications of the long and confused faunal history of the earth. Zoology and geology would henceforth work together in reconstructing this history.

From the revelations of comparative anatomy and paleontology, two sciences whose development is due more to Cuvier than to perhaps any other individual, came the surprising conclusion that the surface of the earth had in the past been inhabited by a succession of different and well-defined populations of animals. Here was a fact which accorded well with the transformist view of nature, a view which Cuvier had wholly failed to appreciate. He chose to interpret this evidence in precisely the opposite manner and his opposition to the transmutation idea can be traced to the teleological sources of the *type* concept. Cuvier's most brilliant achievement and his greatest failure are joined in the *type* concept and the philosophical principles with which it was associated. Cuvier linked the reality and the immutability of

[9] A. D. d'Orbigny, *Cours élémentaire de paléontologie et de géologie stratigraphique* (Paris, 1849), I, *passim*; T. H. Huxley, 'Paleontology and the doctrine of evolution', *Discourses biological and geological* (New York, 1897), 354–5.

the biological species, and justified both with the principle of the correlation of parts. By applying one of the oldest of all biological generalizations, Aristotle's functional conception of the organism, Cuvier rejected the early and perhaps premature statement of another and yet still more fruitful and exciting doctrine, the idea of the transformation of species.

13   Buffon, Lamarck and Darwin: The Originality of Darwin's Theory of Evolution*

J. S. Wilkie

Empedocles, as is well known, produced an odd theory of the origin of living things. He suggested that, in the beginning, there were limbs and parts of limbs, heads and trunks of various kinds lying about loose; that these came together by chance, and that, of the combinations so produced, only the workable ones survived. It would be possible to attempt an account of the origin of the theory of evolution along the same lines: taking Maupertuis's brain, Buffon's hands and eyes, Lamarck's trunk and legs, and filling up with smaller parts of lesser-known authors, we might produce something having a certain resemblance to Darwin, and thus suggest that there was nothing original about him, and that the *Origin of Species* is not the original and epoch-making work it is commonly supposed to be.

That the publication of the *Origin of Species* did mark an epoch seems to be an indisputable matter of history, and it is not easy to see how this could be, if the book had not been in some important way original; but it is not at once clear wherein its originality lay, for certainly all its major theoretical positions had been advocated by one writer or another before it was printed. It would be possible to devote the rest of this essay to a consideration of the nature of originality in scientific work in general, and to ask whether Darwin's work on evolution had any claim to be considered original in any of the senses discovered in our discussion: I shall, indeed, attempt to state in a very summary manner what I suppose the nature of his originality to have been, but my principal task will be to examine the work done by his two great predecessors in the field of evolutionary theory, and I hope that the importance and originality of his own work will then appear in as clear a light as historical study can give. I say 'his two great predecessors' because I feel very strongly that the theory of evolution must be considered as a scientific theory, a theory, that is, proposed to explain or systematize a set of facts, and that

* J. S. Wilkie, 'Buffon, Lamarck and Darwin: The Originality of Darwin's Theory of Evolution', in *Darwin's Biological Work*, ed. P. R. Bell, Wiley, 1965, 262–307, 340–3.

no one has any claim to be considered as a serious rival to Darwin in the 'discovery' of this theory who did not conduct his evolutionary studies upon a reasonably wide basis of fact. To have ideas, *aperçus*, is not enough, and it is the overvaluation of such clever but uncontrolled guesses which is apt to produce the ludicrous situation to which I have referred in my opening paragraph: a fallacy of combination, in which fragments of the final theory are collected from widely scattered sources and are combined in such a way as to impugn the originality of him who was the first to see how such a synthesis was possible. I shall not, therefore, consider here all those authors, including Darwin's own grandfather, who may be considered to have anticipated Darwin on some particular point or points of theory.

Originality in scientific work may be of different kinds. Seeking for terms of comparison within the history of the biological sciences I am tempted to consider Darwin's work on evolution in comparison with the principal discoveries of Harvey, on the one hand, and of Mendel, on the other. What Harvey successfully attempted, was to establish an essentially synthetic theory, of which the two major terms had already been propounded by others, with, however, most inadequate empirical verification. These terms were: the notion of the circulation of the blood through the lungs, and the notion of its circulation through the body generally. In advocating the first of these, Harvey freely acknowledged his debt to Colombo,[1] and pointed out that even Galen [2, 3, 4] had suggested something of the kind: namely, that at least some of the blood might pass from one ventricle of the heart to the other through the lungs. Harvey either did not know, or had forgotten, that the existence of a general circulation had been suggested by Cesalpino;[5] but anyone who will read without prejudice the appropriate passage in Cesalpino's writings will, I think, readily admit that we have here the merest hint, and that the evidence given to substantiate the notion is grossly inadequate. Indeed, I cannot convince myself that Cesalpino had in mind a constant and rapid circulation; it seems to me that what he writes is consistent with the supposition that he imagined the blood to pass outwards from the heart during the day, and to return to it at night. But one may readily concede that both the major theoretical terms of Harvey's theory had in fact been sug-

[1] Willis, R. (1847), *The Works of William Harvey M.D.*, p. 41. London.
[2] Willis, R. (1847), *ibid.* pp. 42-5.
[3] Galen, C., *De Usu partium*, lib. vi, cap. 10.
[4] Kühn, C. G. (1822), *Medicorum Graecorum Opera.* Lipsiae. *Claudii Galeni Opera omnia*, III, pp. 455-7.
[5] Cesalpino, A. (1593), *Andreae Caesalpini Aretini Quaestionum Peripateticarum Lib. V, Q. Medicarum Lib. II, De Medicament. facultatibus Lib. II.* Venetiis. *Q. Med. Liber Second. Q.* 17, pp. 234-5; *Q. Peripat. Liber Quint., Q.* 3, pp. 115 *et seq.*

gested before Harvey's time. Most of the facts which he used in his verification were also common knowledge, and some had received partial theoretical explanation : Galen, for example, understood the valves of the heart as valves,[3, 4] though his explanations of their functions were imperfect. All these anticipations, however, do not in any way invalidate the claim of originality made for Harvey. What he did was to assemble the existing evidence, to add to it, and to use it to establish a clearly formulated theory.[6] The simple historical fact is that the general acceptance of the theory was due to Harvey's work.

Mendel's discovery,[7] however, is of a different kind. His extremely bold theoretical simplification had not, I believe, been anticipated by anyone, and he certainly did not find a large body of well-established and generally accepted facts to challenge the application of his theory. Whereas it is possible to assert that all the important empirical evidence for Harvey's theory was either ready to his hand or was collected by him, the validity of Mendel's theory and its extremely wide powers could only be seen in comparatively recent times, many years after the theory was propounded. What is impressive in Mendel's papers is not the handling of great masses of varied evidence, but the extent to which he had developed the theoretical consequences of his hypothesis. It is on account of this development that we are so ready to consider Mendel as unquestionably deserving the title of originator; the originality of Harvey has to be judged by other criteria. One of these is the placing of Harvey's publications in the historical development of physiology. Where there is a high degree of internal development of a theory, itself essentially novel, we can assert originality even though, as in the case of Mendel, the work had no immediate effect upon contemporaries; but where the novelty of the theory is more questionable, or the development slight or absent, it is reasonable to deny the title of founder where no influence upon contemporaries can be shown. Thus it is justifiable to assert that Harvey's title rests partly upon the abundant evidence for the wide and immediate influence of his work, and to ask those who may wish to establish the rival claims of Cesalpino why it was that the Italian schools were so long accepting the theory,[8] if in fact Cesalpino, and not Harvey, was its discoverer?

Darwin's theory clearly resembles Harvey's rather than Men-

[6] Woodger, J. H. (1952), *Biology and Language*, Cambridge, Appendix A, pp. 75–92. An analysis of Harvey's *De Motu cordis et sanguinis*.

[7] Sinnott, E. W., Dunn, L. C. and Dobzhansky, Th. (1952), *Principles of Genetics*, New York, Appendix, pp. 463–93. *Experiments in Plant-Hybridization*, by Gregor Mendel.

[8] Bayon, H. P. (1938, 1939), William Harvey, physician and biologist: his precursors, opponents and successors, *Ann. Sci.*, 3, 59–118, 435–56; ibid., 4, 65–106, 329–89.

del's, and by the test of rapid and widespread influence and, indeed, acceptance it unquestionably demonstrates its superiority to the theory proposed by Lamarck. Whatever may be the relative merits of the two theories, it is clear that Darwin contrived to make his presentation cogent, whereas Lamarck did not.

Consider the status of the general theory of evolution in 1859, when Darwin published the *Origin of Species*.[8a] It seems certain that Darwin himself underestimated the popularity of the general theory among biologists,[9] but by no legitimate use of language could this theory be described as well-established at that time. Yet Lamarck's principal work upon the subject, the *Philosophie Zoologique*,[10] had been published just fifty years before, in 1809. If, now, we consider the state of affairs in 1909, fifty years after the appearance of Darwin's book, we see that it would be difficult to find any responsible biologist who would have questioned the validity of the general theory.

A test of the degree of cogency of Lamarck's argument is supplied by the reception accorded to the general theory by the positivist philosopher Comte. In his *Cours de Philosophie Positive*,[11] published in 1838, Comte discusses the general theory of evolution and, surprisingly as it now seems, rejects it as without positive foundation. His rejection of the theory is based, it is true, partly upon his judgment that the causal mechanism suggested by Lamarck is totally inadequate, so that it is the Lamarckian theory which he rejects. But it would obviously have been open to him to reject the causal explanation as inadequate, while accepting the general theory; that he did not do so seems to me to be a measure of Lamarck's failure to provide the general theory with a convincing basis of fact. Comte was writing more that twenty-five years after the appearance of Lamarck's book; it is difficult to believe that he would have rejected the general theory of evolution had he been writing twenty-five years after the publication of Darwin's.

[8a] By 'the general theory of evolution' I mean the theory which states that all living species have arisen by the modification of pre-existing species, and which generalizes this notion of the origin of species to include fossil forms, so as to postulate that all species, past or present, have arisen from one or a few primitive types. This theory says nothing about the causes of evolution.

[9] Lyell, Sir Charles (1851), Anniversary address of the President, *Quart. J. Geol. Soc. Lond.*, 7, xxv–lxxvi.

[10] Lamarck, J. B. P. A. (1809), *Philosophie Zoologique, ou Exposition des Considérations relatives à l'histoire naturelle des Animaux, etc., etc.*, Paris. (This work is subsequently referred to as *Philosophie Zoologique*.)

[11] Comte, A. I. (1838), *Cours de philosophie positive*, vol. III, Leçon 42, pp. 554–5, Paris.

EVOLUTION AND THEOLOGY IN THE EIGHTEENTH CENTURY

Before commencing any study of the development of the theory of evolution in the eighteenth century, it is necessary to consider briefly the relationship of that theory to some of the theological ideas of the time.

Apart from certain traces of earlier theories, there is little in the *Origin of Species* which has any close relation to theology, and for the understanding of Darwin's ideas little or no knowledge of contemporary theology is required. In the *Origin of Species* itself, theology only intrudes in Darwin's unfortunate habit of contrasting evolution with 'special creation', as though 'special creation' were an alternative scientific theory. It is interesting to speculate on what might have been the reception of the *Origin of Species* had Darwin taken the supposition of spontaneous generation as the only scientific explanation of the origin of living forms which could be considered as an alternative to the theory of evolution. Open warfare with the theologians was by no means necessitated by the *Origin of Species*, though Darwin's later writings on the origin of man were bound to conflict with Christian theology.

It is clear, however, that in general, theology appears as something extraneous to Darwin's thought, not as a directing influence within it. With regard to Buffon, the position is somewhat similar, though he was necessarily more closely involved with theology than was Darwin, and this for two reasons. In the first place, orthodox theology wielded temporal power in France during the whole of Buffon's life, and the theologians of the Sorbonne, who exercised a form of censorship over books, caused him to issue, in 1753,[12] a recantation of some of his published opinions, which recantation he later characterized as 'sotte et absurde'.[13]

Secondly, although all the evidence inclines us to believe that he endeavoured to purge his mind of all influences from the side of theology, it was scarcely possible for a man of his time to do so completely. He, like all other intellectuals among his contemporaries, was to some extent infected with ideas originating in the heterodox theology of Deism. Though these influences were, in his case, neither powerful nor numerous, they can be more or less clearly observed, as will later be more fully explained, both in his early prejudice against schemes of classification, and in the

---

[12] Buffon, G. L. L. Comte de (1753), *Histoire naturelle, générale et particulière, avec la description du Cubinet du Roi*, v, pp. xii–xv, Paris. (This author is subsequently referred to as 'Buffon' and this work as *Hist. nat.*)

[13] Buffon, H. N. de (1860), *Correspondance inédite de Buffon*, vol. II, p. 68, Paris.

traces of systematic optimism which prevented him from forming any clear idea of the struggle for existence.

In Lamarck, however, we encounter a theorist deeply and consciously imbued with the notions of Deism, and without some reference to the more influential of these notions it is really impossible to give an intelligent account of the structure and sources of his theory of evolution. That Lamarck seriously believed in the theological principles which he enunciated, there is no reason to doubt. All those of his works which we shall here examine were published before the final return of the Bourbons to power, so that we may suppose him free, when he was writing, from any external pressure: nor is there, in what we know of him, any indication of undue subservience to authority.

The central tenet of Deism is that the relation of God to the created world is essentially 'rational', that is, that the ways of God in dealing with his creatures are comprehensible to the un-aided human reason. With this central notion were associated a number of subordinate propositions which could follow logically from the basic assumption only if it were also supposed that all God's purposes were known, and that to achieve them he would use only the means which recommended themselves to the common sense of the average enlightened man of the time.

One of the assumptions as to the purposes of God was that he must be supposed to create anything which is of its nature possible, or, in Leibniz's treatment of the subject, anything which is *compossible*[14, 15] with the existence of the other candidates for creation. Buffon, in an early essay, accepts this position,[15a] which he expresses in the words, 'Il semble que tout ce qui peut être est'.[16] The idea was commonly linked with the old axiom that 'nature makes no jumps', and when applied to taxonomy it suggested the existence of an infinity of forms and of infinite gradations between forms.

Why this principle should be supposed to result in the creation of a specifically linear series of forms, a Chain of Being, is not easy to understand. One would expect a Plenum of Being, rather than a Chain, and we do indeed find in the eighteenth century suggestions of other possibilities. These suggestions appear in connection with the search for a natural classification of plants and animals. Thus Linnaeus speaks of specific forms of plants being related taxonomically as the points on a two-dimensional sur-

[14] Russell, Bertrand (1951), *A Critical Exposition of the Philosophy of Leibniz*, 4th impr., 2nd edn, pp. 20 (note), 66, 67, 223, London.
[15] Latta, R. (1898), *Leibniz. The Monadology and other Philosophical Writings*, p. 64, Oxford.
[15a] Characteristically, however, he sees in it an argument against the deistic supposition that we can see the world as God sees it.
[16] Buffon (1749), *Hist. nat.*, vol. I, p. 11.

face, a map,[17] are related; and at least one writer[18] seems to have flirted with the idea that the relationships of species to one another could be expressed only by the use of all three dimensions. The linear scheme appears to have been suggested by rough empirical schemes of classification, for if the classes are sufficiently broad and sufficiently vague it is possible to arrange them in a descending scale, with man at the top, without doing too much violence to the facts. The easy and uncritical acceptance of this descending scale and of the general principle of linearity must be attributed to the extreme looseness of deistic thought. But, loose as it undoubtedly was, deistic thought was remarkably influential, and its influence was curiously tenacious. Among its tenets that of the Chain of Being[19, 20] was of cardinal importance in the development of biological thought in the eighteenth century. On the one hand, the transition from the notion of an infinitely graded series of separately created forms to that of a gradually developing temporal, or evolutionary series was extremely easy to those who, like the Deists, were not concerned with revelation, and consequently had not to fit their ideas to the Book of Genesis. On the other hand, the *a priori* assumption that the only natural classification of living forms must be a linear one was a considerable obstacle to the development of systems of classification, and it gave to Lamarck's evolutionary speculations an archaic framework which made inevitable a clean break between the Lamarckian and the Darwinian theories. The insistence upon a linear tendency in evolution, a kind of vector of development, was to the last a central feature of Lamarck's theory, long after he had realized that a linear scheme of classification was untenable. Historically, this insistence upon linearity had the piquant consequence of constraining the development of the theory of evolution itself to become non-linear and discontinuous.

So tenacious was the influence of the Chain of Being that it was accepted as axiomatic by Comte,[21] and as late as 1851 Sir Charles Lyell thought it necessary to deny the existence of a linear scale of plant forms and to discuss that of a 'progressive chain' of animals.[9]

The idea of a Chain of Being, much as it was favoured by the Deists, did not originate with them: its roots can be traced far back into antiquity.[19] The same can be said of another axiom

---

[17] Linnaeus, C. (1751). *Philosophia Botanica*, Sectio 77, Stockholm.

[18] Hermann, J. (1783). *Tabula affinitatum animalium, etc.*, Argentorati.

[19] Lovejoy, A. O. (1936). *The Great Chain of Being, A Study of the History of an Idea*, Cambridge, Mass.

[20] Daudin, H. (1926). *Les Méthodes de classification et l'idée de série en botanique et en zoologie de Linné à Lamarck, 1740–1790*, Paris.

[21] Comte, A. I. (1838), *Cours de philosophie positive*, Leçons 40–2.

which they found well suited for incorporation into their system, the axiom that 'nature does nothing in vain'.[22] God, they supposed, could do nothing useless in creating the world, and since the main purpose of creation was commonly supposed to be the preparation of a convenient dwelling for man, the existence of anything not directly useful to man was apt to cause difficulties. Thus the possibility of any species becoming extinct, except through the destructive tendencies of ill-conditioned men, was frequently denied. Lamarck, who took his natural theology seriously, was much more hampered by this difficulty than was Buffon.

The relationship of Deism to the prevailing optimism of the first half of the eighteenth century is a subtle one. If God had made the world in accordance with human common sense and directed to human convenience, the expectation would certainly appear to be that the world would be a pleasant enough place to live in. If, however, we are to consider Leibniz's theology as a form of Deism, we have to admit that a facile optimism was not a necessary ingredient of deistic systems. There can, I think, be no doubt that Voltaire misunderstood the doctrine of Leibniz which is summarized in the expression 'the best of all possible worlds'. Voltaire supposed the stress to fall on the 'best', whereas for Leibniz the stress fell heavily upon the 'possible', the implication being that the best of all possible worlds was still far from the most desirable of worlds.[23]

But though truth obliges us to be cautious in attributing optimism to this particular version of Deism, there is no doubt that the general climate of opinion tended to optimism in the early part of the eighteenth century, and that traces of optimism survived the shock of the Lisbon earthquake in 1755. To this optimism and to the closely related expectation of good housekeeping in the affairs of nature must be attributed, I believe, the almost total absence of any reference, in the works of Buffon and of Lamarck, to the struggle for existence.

THE THEORY OF EVOLUTION IN THE WORKS OF BUFFON

Introduction

Though it is, of course, impossible to give any precise date to the first stirrings of the embryo which was to develop into the theory of evolution as we now know it, yet it is possible to begin a description of its development with events occurring in 1749.

In this year Diderot published in London his *Lettre sur les*

---

[22] Aristotle, *De Anima*, Book III, 9; 432 b 20.
[23] Barber, W. H. (1955), *Leibniz in France from Arnauld to Voltaire*, Oxford.

Aveugles,[24] in which, in a scandalously mendacious account of the death of Saunderson, the blind mathematician of Cambridge, he makes use of the ancient Empedoclean idea of the origin of living things. In the same year Scheidt printed, for the first time, the *Protogaea*[25],[26] of Leibniz, in which Leibniz at least hints at the possibility of the transformation of species.

Finally, it was in the same year that Buffon brought out the first three volumes of his great *Histoire Naturelle*,[27] the further publication of which was to occupy the whole of the rest of his life, and to be continued for some years after his death by a collaborator, La Cépède. Thirty-five quarto volumes were published during Buffon's life, and nine volumes were added to the series after his death in 1788.

It would be impossible, I believe, to exaggerate the influence of this work on European thought during the second half of the eighteenth century, during the whole of the nineteenth century, and even up to the present time. But to claim that Buffon was *un des fondateurs du transformisme*[28] seems to me to be completely wrong-headed and to do justice neither to Darwin nor to Buffon himself. His place in the history of the development of the theory of evolution is of the highest importance, for he was the first to subject the theory to extensive criticism based upon a wide range of empirical evidence, but he cannot be said to have elaborated any theory of his own. There is no Buffonian theory of evolution, in the sense that there is a Lamarckian theory. The reasons for this failure, if indeed it is a failure, are not difficult to discover.

In the first place, the alternative of either special creation or evolution did not appear to him as an inescapable dilemma, for he had, as has well been pointed out by Jean Rostand,[29] a third explanation of the origin of species: that they arose by spontaneous generation. It may seem to us an outrageous suggestion that a man, or even a mouse, could arise directly from inorganic matter, but when Buffon was young (he was born in 1707) it was commonly believed that 'worms' often arose by spontaneous generation, and at that time the class of 'worms' was most imperfectly delimited, and, at least for many naturalists, included animals as highly organized as insects. Moreover, those who to-day take an entirely 'mechanistic' view of all living things must believe that the synthesis of even the highest animal from in-

---

[24] Assezat, J. (ed.) (1875), *Œuvres complètes de Diderot*, vol. I, pp. 275–342, Paris.
[25] Ravier, E. (1937), *Bibliographie des Œuvres de Leibniz*, p. 264, Paris.
[26] Leibniz, G. W. (1749), *Summi polyhistoris Godefridi Guilielmi Leibnitii Protogaea etc.*, p. 41, Goettingae.
[27] Buffon (1749), *Hist. nat.* I, II and III.
[28] Guyenot, E. (1941), *Les Sciences de la Vie aux XVIIe et XVIIIe Siècles, l'Idée d'Evolution*, p. 394, Paris.
[29] Rostand, J. (1932), *L'Evolution des Epèces*, pp. 57–8, Paris.

organic matter is in principle possible, though in practice the difficulties of such a synthesis may be insuperable.

It is clear, as I shall show by citation from his works, that Buffon was prevented from giving whole-hearted support to the theory of evolution, not only by the possession of an alternative theory of the origin of species, but also by the inadequacy of the causal mechanisms which he could understand. It is simply not the case that he had 'a very clear appreciation of the struggle for existence';[30] such a notion was extremely difficult for a man of the eighteenth century to entertain, especially for one whose formative years were passed in the first half of the century, with its general tendency to optimism and its belief in a rational and economical ordering of the world.

I do not mean that Buffon was incapable of thinking that, on occasion, some one species might exterminate some other. But he did not think of the competition between species as an element in the causal processes underlying evolution. Passages in his writings which seem to suggest an appreciation of the struggle for existence commonly belong, in fact, to a system of thought which is far removed from that of Darwin: for example, one such passage terminates in nothing more than a reference to the ancient maxim, 'The corruption of one is the generation of another'.[31]

Buffon, it is true, calculated that, by the tendency to a geometrical ratio of reproduction, 'in one hundred and fifty years the whole terrestrial globe might be entirely converted into one single kind of organic matter';[32] but to quote this in support of the thesis that he understood natural selection is to neglect not only the general tendency of his works, but also the particular context of the calculation; for he is arguing in this place that it is a mistake to suppose that there is any special difficulty in accounting for the origin of living beings. 'Reflecting upon this kind of calculation,' he writes, 'we become familiar with the curious idea that the organic is the most ordinary work of nature, and apparently that which costs her the least.'[33]

Near the beginning of the chapter in which the calculation appears, Buffon argues that we cannot be sure what is simple and what is complex in the real world of nature; plants seem more complex than stones, and animals than plants.

> This notion is correct in relation to us [that is, from our point of view], but we do not know whether in reality the one kind

---

[30] Zirkle, C. (1941), 'Natural Selection before the *Origin of Species*', *Proc. Amer. Phil. Soc.*, 84, 71–123.
[31] Buffon (1749), *Hist. nat.*, vol. II, pp. 40–1.
[32] Buffon (1749), *ibid.*, p. 38.
[33] Buffon (1749), *ibid.*, p. 39.

may not be as simple or as complex as the other, and we cannot tell whether a sphere or a cube comes more difficultly to nature (coûte plus ou moins à la nature) than a germ or some particular organic part.[34]

In fact, the whole of the immediate context of the calculation, so far from being an argument in favour of evolution by natural selection, is an attempt to make plausible the existence of indestructible 'living molecules'. A belief in these made it particularly easy for Buffon to attribute the widest powers to spontaneous generation, which became for him merely the recombination of such molecules.

Finally, it seems that Buffon's reluctance to produce a general theory of evolution was due in large measure to the empirical tendency of his mind. He was fond of theorizing on the grand scale, but extensive acquaintance with his works suggests that he, unlike Lamarck, did not attach great importance to such exercises. Thus, having begun the biological section of his great work[34a] with an all-embracing theory of spontaneous generation, he seems to have adhered to this theory in later life rather because he thought it no worse than another, than because he thought it better. His mind was always open to evolutionary speculations, but he simply did not think the facts sufficiently known to justify a firm adherence to the evolutionary theory. We may, I think, take a sentence[34b] from a late volume of the *Histoire Naturelle*, the third volume of the *Suppléments*, published in 1776, as his last word on the subject: 'In general, the relationship between species is one of those profound mysteries of nature which man cannot investigate except by experiments which must be as prolonged as they will be difficult.'[35]

The article on the ass

The task which Buffon set himself in the *Histoire Naturelle* was in itself vast and diffuse, embracing not only the natural history of animals and plants, but also physical cosmology, geology, mineralogy and anthropology. From the first he displayed a marked disinclination for systematic presentation. In the *Premier Discours*, which opens the first volume, he examines the system of Linnaeus, as it then existed, and rejects it together with all other attempts at systematic classification of plants and animals. He proposes to treat of animals in the order of their interest for

[34] Buffon (1749), *ibid.*, p. 23.
[34a] The first volume is devoted to physical cosmology.
[34b] In the same place Buffon gives what is, I believe, his only reference to the struggle for existence. He asks whether it may not be the case that 'the weaker species have been destroyed by the stronger'.
[35] Buffon (1776), *Hist. nat.* (Suppl. III), p. 32.

man, beginning with man himself and taking next the domestic animals. As the great work proceeded he became aware of the necessity of some scheme of classification, and convinced himself that such a scheme could be at least largely 'natural', that is, based upon fundamental resemblances between the organisms themselves and not merely formed for the convenience of the naturalist; but from first to last the plan of the work, though it gradually became more orderly, lent itself to digressions and remarks which might almost be described as asides. The reader must not, then, be surprised to find Buffon's earliest remarks upon the subject of evolution introduced, as it were casually, into a chapter upon the natural history of the ass, and even the most conscientious study which falls short of reading the whole of the *Histoire Naturelle* from the first volume to the thirty-sixth will probably pass over one or more casual references to the subject. However, I have done my best in another place[36] to present a full study of Buffon's treatment of the theory of evolution, and since many authors have scrutinized his works precisely to find evidence for the claim that he was a founder of evolutionary studies, or to examine this claim critically,[28, 37, 38, 39, 40] it is improbable that anything of importance has been passed over.

I shall consider here only the two comparatively extensive passages in which Buffon considers the theory more or less systematically : the article on the ass, in which he appears to reject the theory altogether; and the essay 'On the Degeneration of Animals', in which he allows that evolution may have taken place to a very limited extent. The article on the ass has given rise to a great deal of controversy, several authors having supposed that Buffon did not intend his readers to take seriously the arguments it contains.[28, 40, 41] I shall later give my reasons for thinking this interpretation an entirely mistaken one.

At least one historian[42] of science has thought to find evidence of a revival of Buffon's interest in the subject in some of the latest of the volumes of his work, those concerned with the natural history of birds. This evidence, however, is extremely inconclusive. Buffon probably never entirely lost interest in the

---

[36] Wilkie, J. S. (1956), 'The idea of evolution in the writings of Buffon', I, *Ann. Sci.*, *12*, 48–62; II, *ibid.*, *12*, 212–27; III, *ibid.*, *12*, 256–66.

[37] Lanessan, J. L. de (1889), 'Buffon et Darwin', *Rev. Scient.*, *1*, 385–91; 2, 425–32.

[38] Perrier, E. (1886), *La Philosophie Zoologique avant Darwin*, 2nd edn, Paris.

[39] Rostand, J. (1931), *L'Etat présent du Transformisme*, Paris; (1932) *L'Evolution des Espèces*, Paris.

[40] Butler, Samuel (1911), *Evolution, Old and New*, 3rd edn, London.

[41] Ostoya, P. (1951), *Les Théories de l'Evolution*, p. 47, Paris. (Lists other French authors sharing this opinion.)

[42] Rostand, J. (1932), *L'Evolution des Espèces*, p. 54; but see also p. 60, footnote.

subject of evolution, but the passages in the articles on birds
which seem to show a substantial revival or increase of interest
were written at a time when he was becoming more and more
dependent upon the help of collaborators, and was beginning to
use whole passages written by them, contenting himself with, at
the most, emendations and alterations which were merely stylis-
tic.[43] All we can conclude from these passages is that Buffon did
not violently object to the scraps of evolutionary lore which they
contain.

The first three volumes of the *Histoire Naturelle*, which were
published together in 1749, contain no references to evolution.
The second volume contains the curious calculation already referred to, showing the effects which would result from the un-
checked multiplication of even one species, but these calculations,
as I have pointed out above, are shown by their context to have
nothing to do with the theory of evolution. The first volume contains a passage of some length of which the general theme is that
'it is possible to descend by almost imperceptible degrees from
the most perfect creature to the least informed matter, from the
best organized animal to the merest mineral'.[44] To take this for a
reference to an evolutionary series, however, would be most unwise, unless other passages could be found referring explicitly to
genetic links between the members of the series. In fact there is
no such reference in these first volumes, and the passage from
which a few lines have been quoted here is merely an allusion
to the Chain of Being, such as one would expect in any general
work on natural history written at that time. Indeed, the whole
passage might be, and perhaps is, a paraphrase of a similar one
in the works of John Locke.[45]

If it is true, as I believe, that there is no reference to evolution in the first three volumes, what had happened between the
publication of these volumes and that of the fourth volume, in
1753, to direct Buffon's attention to the idea? For it is in this
fourth volume that we discover the article on the ass.

The question is not difficult to answer, for we know that
Buffon was at this time in correspondence with Maupertuis,[46]
and the article with which we are concerned bears a footnote[47]
referring to a published letter of that author. This footnote gives
no precise indication as to which letter is intended, nor of where
it was published before 1753, but we may confidently identify
it with one printed in the collected works of Maupertuis. It is

[43] Flourens, P. (1860), *Des Manuscrits de Buffon avec des fac-similé de Buffon et de ses collaborateurs*, Paris.
[44] Buffon (1749), *Hist. nat.* vol. I, p. 12.
[45] Locke, John, *An Essay concerning Human Understanding*, book III, ch. 6, section 12.
[46] Buffon, H. N. de (1860), *Correspondance inédit de Buffon*, vol. I p. 46.
[47] Buffon, G. L. L. (1753), *Hist. nat.* vol. IV, p. 387.

clear that the letter contains information about a family of which several members had six digits on both hands and both feet. This is the Ruhe family about which Maupertuis was able to publish fairly complete information relating to four generations, and the letter describing this family appears in the collected works of Maupertuis published in Berlin in 1753.[48] It may have been published before that date, but it was probably also seen by Buffon before its publication.

In this letter Maupertuis makes only a very brief reference to evolution, but one which is entirely unambiguous. Having said that such characters as the polydactyly of the Ruhe family probably arose by chance in the first place, he adds, 'and it may be thus that all species have multiplied themselves', the context showing clearly that evolution and not merely reproduction is intended.

For the comprehension of the article on the ass, it is well to notice particularly two features of Maupertuis's letter. Although the genealogy of the Ruhe family shows a remarkable tenacity of the character in question, which appears to be a simple Mendelian dominant, yet, in the last of the recorded generations, the six digits appear only on one hand and one foot, at least in the case of one of the sibs. It was this, probably, which suggested to Maupertuis that the character 'becomes altered by alliance with those who have five digits, and by the repetition of such alliances would probably disappear, just as it would be perpetuated by the union of persons of the two sexes both showing it'.[49]

The second feature of importance in the letter is a most remarkable passage in which Maupertuis shows us a way of calculating the probability of parent and offspring both showing the character by chance, as opposed to causal inheritance.[50] When Buffon comes to consider the problem of evolution based upon chance variation, he seems to have this calculation in mind; for he objects that, if two persons having the character must be united in order to perpetuate it, and we must suppose that they came together by chance, then the probability of such chance characters being perpetuated so as to give rise to new species becomes vanishingly small.[51]

This letter, then, appears to be the one referred to by Buffon in his footnote. It must be admitted that the mention of evolution which it contains is of the briefest, but it is unlikely that Buffon had not also seen the curious tract, first published in 1751 in the form of a Latin *Dissertatio* and attributed to a fictitious

[48] Maupertuis, P. L. (1953), *Les Œuvres de Mr de Maupertuis*, vol II, pp. 378–92, Berlin.
[49] Maupertuis, ibid., p. 386.
[50] Maupertuis, ibid., p. 388.
[51] Buffon (1753), *Hist nat.* vol. IV, pp. 389–90.

Dr Baumann,[52] but already appearing (in a French translation) in the collected works of Maupertuis in 1756.[53] In this there is a longer and even more explicit reference to evolution by the accumulation of chance variations:

> There may be some arrangements so tenacious that, from the first generation they are prepotent over all previous arrangements, and efface their habits.[53a] Could we not explain in this way how, from only two individuals, the multiplication of the most various species could have resulted? Their first origin would have been due simply to some chance productions, in which the elementary particles would not have kept the order which they had in the paternal and maternal animals: each degree of error would have made a new species; and by repeated deviations the infinite diversity of animals which we know today would have been produced; and this diversity, it may be, will increase still further with time, though possibly the succession of centuries only results in imperceptible changes.[54]

This passage, and the letter already discussed, together contain all that is of importance in Maupertuis's theory of evolution. The anticipation is remarkable, but since it is almost certain that Buffon derived his first ideas on the subject from this source, it is necessary to be quite clear as to what Maupertuis has contributed in these passages. There is in them absolutely no reference to any form of selection, whether artificial or natural; and in the absence of any suggestion of how the ratio of new to old forms of animal or plant might be changed, Buffon was totally justified in treating the theory with considerable scepticism. Authors who have supposed that Buffon's arguments against the theory of evolution, in the article on the ass, are to be considered ironical have commonly been unaware of the form in which the theory was first presented to him.

To make the deficiencies of Maupertuis's theory the more apparent, let us consider a full anticipation of the idea of evolution by the selection of chance variations, an anticipation acknowledged by Darwin himself.[55] This occurs in an essay by Dr

[52] Baumann (1751), *Dissertatio inauguralis, de universali naturae systemate, pro gradu doctoris habita*. Erlangen.
[53] Maupertuis, P. L. (1756), *Œuvres de Mr de Maupertuis, à Lyons*, vol. II, pp. 137–68, Système de la Nature.
[53a] Maupertuis is referring to arrangements of hypothetical reproductive particles, resembling the pangenes of Darwin's theory of heredity. To account for their regular arrangement in the egg or in the sperm, Maupertuis supposed them to have something analogous to memory or habits of association.
[54] Maupertuis (1756), *ibid.*, pp. 150–1.
[55] Darwin, Charles (1880), *The Origin of Species*, 6th edn, p. xv, London.

W. C. Wells, a native of South Carolina who had come to live in England after the first rebellion of that restless colony, and who acquired a substantial reputation as a physician in the later years of the eighteenth century.

> Those who attend to the improvement of domestic animals, when they find individuals possessing, in a greater degree than common, the qualities they desire, couple a male and a female of these together, then take the best of their offspring as the new stock, and in this way proceed, till they approach as near the point in view, as the nature of the thing will permit.
>
> But what is there done by art, seems to be done, with equal efficacy, though more slowly, by nature, in the formation of varieties of mankind, fitted for the country which they inhabit. Of the accidental varieties of man, which would occur among the first few and scattered inhabitants of the middle regions of Africa, some would be better fitted than the others to bear the diseases of the country. This race would consequently multiply, while the others would decrease, not only from their inability to sustain the attacks of disease, but from their incapacity of contending with their more vigorous neighbours. The colour of this vigorous race I take for granted, from what has already been said, would be dark;[55a] *I do not however suppose, that their different susceptibility of disease depends, properly, on their difference of colour. On the contrary, I think it probable, that this is only a sign of some [other] difference in them.* But the same disposition to form varieties still existing, a darker and a darker race would in the course of time occur, and as the darkest would be the best fitted for the climate, this would at length become the most prevalent, if not the only race, in the particular country in which it had originated.[56]

Returning now to Buffon's article, I believe it can be asserted with some confidence that the part of it which discusses the origin of species by the accumulation of chance variations consists of an entirely just criticism of Maupertuis's theory; for this theory, lacking any reference to natural selection, deserves to be rejected as fundamentally incomplete. We may note, however, that though Buffon found the theory unconvincing in the

[55a] The passage between asterisks is inserted from another page of the same essay (p. 434), where Dr Wells also writes: 'Among men, as well as among other animals, varieties of greater or less magnitude are constantly occurring.'
[56] Wells, W. C. (1818), *Two Essays: one upon Single Vision with two eyes; the other on Dew; etc., etc.*, pp. 435-6, London.

form offered by Maupertuis, he was quite unable to supply what we should now consider the missing element. This is one of the passages in which Buffon can be observed in the act of not discovering the principle of natural selection.

The part of the article which deals explicitly[56a] with Maupertuis's ideas has not been much noticed by those who suppose that the whole article is nothing but an expression of Buffon's belief in the general theory of evolution, in the form of a sarcastic presentation of the arguments against the theory. It has been supposed, and the case has been persuasively argued by Samuel Butler,[57] that Buffon was obliged by his fear of the powerful theologians of the Sorbonne to express disbelief in the theory of evolution, but that he did so with irony and sarcasm so unmistakable as to leave no doubt of his wholehearted acceptance of the theory. Samuel Butler, however, as is often the way with rebels, was not as free from the all-pervading influences of his age as he supposed, and he argues as though there already existed in Buffon's time a fully elaborated theory of evolution which any enlightened person might be expected to accept; and this, of course, was not the case. However, it must be admitted that there are features of this article on the ass which at first sight are extremely puzzling, and which could be easily explained by the assumption that much or all of the article is to be taken as ironical.

Because the references to Maupertuis occur in the concluding section of the article, I have considered that part first. It will now be necessary to consider the opening section, which begins with the words:

> Considering this animal, even with attention and in detail, it appears to be no more than a degenerate horse ... we might attribute the slight differences which exist between the two animals to a long-standing influence of climate, of food, and to the chance succession of many generations of small wild horses half-degenerate, which little by little had degenerated still more, had then degenerated as much as is possible, and had finally produced for our contemplation a new and constant species.[58]

It would be unwise to attach too much importance to the word 'degenerate', and to what appears to us the inversion of the evolutionary sequence which we should expect. It is clear that the word 'degenerate' is for Buffon a technical term which had lost some of its original meaning, and elsewhere he writes 'degen-

---

[56a] We may say 'explicitly', because of Buffon's footnote referring to Maupertuis.
[57] Butler, Samuel (1911), *Evolution, Old and New*, 3rd edn, London.
[58] Buffon (1753), *Hist. nat.*, vol. IV, p. 377.

erated or perfected' in describing evolutionary change. Nevertheless, it has been correctly observed that, when choosing examples, he nearly always selects such as appear to common sense
to be examples of degeneration.[59] This choice is partly explained
by the historical circumstance that changes from one species
to another, which were thought to have been observed during
the previous century, clearly appeared to be degenerative; and
partly by the importance which Buffon attached to the heat of
the earth, which he believed to have cooled from a state of in-
candescence, in determining the degree of development of
species.[60] He tended to think that the more highly developed
organisms would be produced in the warmer conditions and
climates,[61] and this, coupled with his conviction that the earth
was and always had been growing colder, undoubtedly made it
difficult to think of the temporal sequence of organisms as progressive. Though it would be unwise to attach too much importance to all this, yet it probably would be true to say that the
use of the word 'degeneration' does express a certain tendency
to think of changes of faunas with time as being on the whole
changes for the worse, and that this tendency was a factor, if
only a minor one, in the production of Buffon's scepticism regarding progressive evolution.

Having started his article with a statement of some of the
arguments in favour of a genetic relationship between the horse
and the ass, Buffon immediately begins to suggest doubts and
difficulties; among others, 'the impossibility of uniting them [the
horse and the ass] to form a common species, or even an intermediate species capable of reproducing itself'. This was for him
an argument of very great power and one to which he attached
the greatest importance during the whole of his life. I have quoted
above a sentence which I have suggested might be Buffon's last
word on the subject of evolution: 'In general, the relationship
between species is one of those profound mysteries of nature
which man can only investigate by experiments which must be
as prolonged as they will be difficult.' Among the experiments
which he regarded as necessary to establish or to refute the
theory, he attached the highest importance to experiments in
hybridization, a kind of experiment which he himself early
began to make.[62] During the whole of his life he believed that
different species of animals which had descended from some
common ancestral species would always show an ability to produce interspecific and fertile hybrids. It is absolutely indispensable to an understanding of Buffon's evaluation of the general

[59] Ostoya, P. (1951), *Les Théories de l'Evolution*, Paris, p. 52.
[60] Buffon (1778), *Hist. nat.* (Suppl. V), pp. 1–254, Epoques de la Nature.
[61] Buffon (1761), *ibid.*, vol. IX, pp. 106–9.
[62] Buffon (1776), *ibid.* (Suppl. III), pp. 3, 5.

theory of evolution to appreciate the importance which he attributed to this test of common ancestry: to understand this will render clear what has appeared most obscure, and will show to be consistent views which might otherwise seem at variance with one another. Thus, in the article on the ass, he denied the possibility of the horse and the ass having a common ancestor, because, when he wrote the article, he believed mules to be sterile. Later, in the essay 'On the Degeneration of Animals', he allowed that these two species might have descended from a common stock, because, in the years intervening between writing the article and writing the essay, he had convinced himself not only that the mule is not entirely sterile, but that other forms which appear to be entirely distinct species, such as the sheep and the goat, can also produce together fertile hybrids.[63] Finally, the fact that he was never willing to accept as established any theory of evolution of wide application, however probable he might think such a theory to be, is readily explained by the difficulty or impossibility of obtaining evidence based upon the hybridization of widely dissimilar forms.

Up to this point, it might be thought that the article on the ass presents no very difficult problems of interpretation. But Buffon, having considered the problem of common ancestry in the particular case of the horse and the ass, passes immediately to a consideration of the theory of evolution in its most general form. He says that, if the horse and the ass are to be considered as belonging to the same family, because they resemble one another, we might, by the same argument, conclude that 'not only the ass and the horse, but even man, the ape, the quadrupeds and all animals might be regarded as making only one family'. He then asserts that to establish one case of common descent of diverse species would be enough to establish the possibility of common descent for all organisms:

> If it were true that the ass were merely a degenerate horse, there would be no limits to the power of nature, and we should be justified in supposing that, from a single being, she had been able to produce in the course of time all organized beings. But no! It is certain, from revelation, that all animals have participated equally in the grace[63a] of creation.[64]

This certainly presents a major problem. Nowhere else does Buffon assert that one case of common descent would be enough to establish the general theory of evolution. The assertion is obviously nonsense, and Buffon was perfectly capable of ap-

[63] Buffon (1766), *ibid.*, vol. XIV, pp. 342–3.
[63a] This odd expression is Buffon's own.
[64] Buffon (1749), *ibid.*, vol. IV, p. 382.

preciating this. Moreover, the appeal to revelation is certainly not sincere: even if nothing were known about Buffon's life and thought outside his works, it would still be certain, from the works themselves, that he did not care two pence for revelation.

It is true that when he wrote the article on the ass, or at least when he published it, he had been irritated by a condemnation launched by the theologians of the Sorbonne against certain propositions in the first three volumes of his work; and it is certain that he submitted to ecclesiastical authority only for the sake of peace. The supposition that all the arguments against the theory of evolution which Buffon has set forth in this particular place are to be regarded as ironical in intention is therefore extremely persuasive, particularly if no other explanation can be found for his sudden appeal to revelation. However, the thesis that he is saying in effect, 'Obviously all species have originated by evolution, and only those blinded by theological prejudice could fail to appreciate the fact', is somewhat anachronistic, because it could not have been obvious, in 1753, that the theory of evolution was the correct explanation of the origin of species. Then again, as I have tried to show, the article contains the expression of doubts and difficulties which are reasonable in themselves, and which, there is evidence to show, Buffon intended to be taken seriously.

We seem to be faced with an insoluble conundrum, but there is, I believe, a perfectly natural and satisfactory solution. If we turn to the very first essay in the *Histoire Naturelle*, the essay entitled 'Premier Discours de la Manière d'Étudier et de Traiter l'Histoire Naturelle', we find a long dissertation, written before Buffon had been irritated by the theologians and therefore, presumably, not to be suspected of irony due to this particular source at least. This essay or dissertation is largely an attack upon systematists in general, and upon Linnaeus in particular. Now, it can be shown[65] that Buffon's prejudice against systematists, or *nomenclateurs* as he calls them, was so violent as to result in a kind of feud, which constantly recurs, and so irrational as to persist even when he himself had adopted a scheme of classification which did not differ essentially from that used by Linnaeus.

If the *Premier Discours* is read immediately before the article on the ass, many points of similarity are discovered, even in detail, and the article appears as another incident in the recurrent feud. The mysterious passage ending in the appeal to revelation, for example, is introduced by the words, 'Do the ass and the horse come originally from the same stock? Are they, as the *nomenclateurs* say, of the same family?'

Then, after what seems a long digression on the subject of classification, Buffon concludes,

[65] Wilkie, J. S. (1956), *Ann. Sci.*, *12*, 48–62.

> Each species, each series of individuals capable of reproducing their kind and incapable of mixing with other species will be considered apart and treated separately, and we shall make no use of families, genera, orders and classes, any more than nature makes use of them.[66]

I have said that the central part of the article, which lies between these two references to systematists and to their devices, might seem to be a digression, because I believe it is in fact a mistake to regard the whole article as being principally concerned with the theory of evolution. It is easy for us, interested in the theory and in its origins, to misunderstand the intentions of any author who refers to the theory. Whereas for us the centre of interest in this article lies in the discussion of evolution, for Buffon, I suggest, this discussion is a digression and the centre of interest is in the problem of classification.

The explanation which I offer, then, for the paradoxical aspects of the article on the ass is that Buffon, concerned primarily with problems of systematics and with his feud against Linnaeus, is using what appeared to his contemporaries, especially to the more pious among them, to be an odd and even dangerous idea, as a means of discrediting his opponents. Immediately after the assertion that, if the ass and the horse are of the same stock all animals whatever might be considered to have arisen from a single species, *en se perfectionnant et en dégénérant*, he adds:

> Those naturalists who establish so lightly families among animals and plants do not appear to have been sufficiently sensible of these consequences, which would reduce the immediate productions of creation to any desired small number of individuals. . . . [And it is after this that we find the passage already quoted:] If it were true that the ass were merely a degenerate horse, there would be no limits to the power of nature, and we should be justified in supposing that, from a single being, she has been able to produce in the course of time all organized beings. But no! It is certain, from revelation that all animals have participated equally in the grace of creation.[64]

The thunderbolt, intended to make the reader's flesh creep though the author thought it but stage-fire, is aimed at the systematists.

It is, of course, at this late date, impossible to prove exactly what was Buffon's full intention in writing the article we have been examining, but I think we can assert with confidence that it cannot be used as unimpeachable evidence that Buffon, when he

[66] Buffon (1749), *Hist. nat.*, vol IV, p. 386.

wrote it, was convinced of and wished to advocate the validity of the general theory of evolution. This is important, because in other passages of his great work, where he examines the theory and rejects it as unproven, there is nothing like the same colorable suggestion of irony as there is in the article on the ass. Of the other passages which make any reference to evolution, by far the most important is the essay 'On the Degeneration of Animals', which I shall now discuss.

The Essay on the 'Degeneration of Animals'

The essay 'De la Dégénération des Animaux', appears in the fourteenth volume of the *Histoire Naturelle*, in the volume, that is, published in 1766. By the time he wrote this essay, both the facts of geographical distribution of animals and his studies of hybridization had led Buffon to take a slightly more favourable view of the theory of evolution than that expressed, at least overtly, in the article published in 1753. Buffon tells us that he began to make experiments in hybridization with goats and sheep in 1751.[67] What the results of these were it is not easy to say. Buffon certainly believed that he had obtained hybrids of these two species, and that these hybrids were fertile; but authorities with whom I have discussed this question have expressed themselves as extremely sceptical of the possibility of even the first-generation hybrids. However, there seems no reason to doubt that Buffon honestly believed that he had obtained fertile hybrids from two animals which common sense would regard as belonging to different species. Whether he was deceived by dishonest assistants or really did obtain the hybrids must remain uncertain, but clearly some animals supposed to be hybrids were produced and were coupled and found to be fertile. All this would take at least two, and probably three or four years, so that the crucial result – the fertility of the hybrids – would not have been available to Buffon when he wrote for the volume of 1753.

His studies of geographical distribution concern the mammals of the Old and New Worlds, and he thus sums up his results:

> Thus, of ten genera and four isolated species,[67a] to which we have tried to reduce all the animals belonging particularly to the New World, there are only two, the genus containing jaguars, ocelots and so on, and the species of the pecari, with its varieties, which one can refer with any certainty (avec quelque fondement) to the animals of the old continent. The jaguars and ocelots can be regarded as species of leopard or of

[67] Buffon (1776), *ibid*. (Suppl. III), p. 3.
[67a] Isolated species, he explains elsewhere, are those which are the only species of their genus.

panther, and the pecari as a kind of pig. Then there are five genera and one isolated species, the species llama, and the genera of monkeys with, and those without prehensile tails, the genera of skunks, of agoutis and of ant-eaters, which can be compared, but in a most uncertain and distant manner, with the camel, with those monkeys of the Old World which have tails, with the polecats, with the hare and with the scaly ant-eaters; and, finally, there remain four genera and two isolated species, the opossums, the coatis, the armadillos, the sloths, the tapir and the capybara, which cannot be referred to, nor even compared with genera or species of the Old World. This seems to prove sufficiently that the origin of these animals peculiar to the New World cannot be attributed simply to degeneration; however great, however powerful might be its effects, we could never persuade ourselves, with any appearance of reason, that these animals had originally been the same as those of the old continent; it is more reasonable to suppose that, at one time, the two continents were continuous or contiguous, and that the species which had taken up their abode in the New World, because they found the climate more suitable to their nature, were shut off and separated by the irruption of the sea.[68]

I have quoted this passage in full because it shows Buffon at his best as a conscientious naturalist, and seems to dispose completely of the supposition that any hesitation he had in accepting a wholehearted theory of evolution arose merely from fear of further trouble with the theologians. But why, it is natural to ask, did he draw the line where he did? Why accept a common origin for the pig and the pecari, and not for the camel and the llama? The answer to these questions is, I think, that he did not believe that the causal mechanisms which his mind had assimilated were adequate to the production of more than the most trivial differences. He writes:

It would be very difficult to see how the tailed monkeys of the Old World could have taken on in America a differently shaped face, a muscular and prehensile tail, a long partition between the nostrils, and the other characters, both generic and specific, by which we have distinguished them from the monkeys of the New World.... With regard to the agoutis and pacas ... they can only be compared with the hare and the rabbit ... but what makes it doubtful that there can have been anything common in their origins, is that the hare has spread in nearly all the climates of the old continent, without its nature having changed, and without any other

[68] Buffon (1766), *ibid.*, vol. XIV, pp. 372–3.

alteration than that of the colour of its coat; one cannot, therefore, imagine with any justification that the climate of America was able to do what no other climate could, and that it could change the nature of our hares so far as to turn them into *tapetis* [*Lepus americanus*] and *aperea* [wild guinea-pig or restless cavy] which have no tail, or agoutis, with their pointed snouts, with short rounded ears, or pacas with thick heads, short ears, short rough hair and white bands.[69]

I have spoken of the causal mechanisms which Buffon's mind had been able to assimilate, because he does indeed mention artificial selection, and even a kind of 'Lamarckian' mechanism; but he nowhere even suggests natural selection, and he makes no use of the 'Lamarckian' mechanism when, as in the example just quoted, climate does not seem adequate to explain the production of the observed differences. The particular case he mentions of the inheritance of an acquired character is that of the callosities on the legs or chests of camel and llama,[70] but these he regards as merely the effects of 'servitude or domestication'; it does not seem to occur to him that anything of the kind could be an important cause of evolutionary change in wild animals.

Even artificial selection appears not to have received from him the attention it deserves. For example, in his article on the dog, which is in the fifth volume of the *Histoire Naturelle*, published in 1755, he mentions artificial selection as one of the causes of new breeds, but entirely forgets it (though the whole article is of only a few pages) in summarizing at the end of the article. In the course of his summary, he says that, of the thirty known breeds, seventeen are due to the influences of climate and the other thirteen are mongrels produced from these seventeen climatic races.[71] Having just stated that the twisted legs of the basset are due to the inherited effects of rickets, he concludes:

All these races with their varieties have only been produced by the influence of the climate, joined to the comforts of shelter, the effects of food and the results of careful training (une éducation soignée); the other dogs are not of pure race, and come of mixtures of the other races.[72]

Again, in the essay 'On the Degeneration of Animals'; 'Climatic temperature, the quality of food, and the evils of servitude, these are the three causes of change, alteration and degeneration of animals.'[73]

[69] Buffon (1766), *ibid.*, pp. 371–2.
[70] Buffon (1766), *ibid.*, p. 325.
[71] Buffon (1755), *ibid.*, vol. V, p. 217.
[72] Buffon (1755), *ibid.*, pp. 226–7.
[73] Buffon (1766), *ibid.*, vol. XIV, p. 317.

Here, then, we have three causes, of which only two are said to be operative in the wild state. Later in the same essay he makes an obscure reference to a cause of change linked with the number of individuals in the race, which should clearly constitute a fourth cause, but later still he speaks of 'the three causes of change'.[74] This looks like another lapse of the kind which occurs in the article on the dog. It may be, however, that, in the final reference to three causes Buffon means, though he does not say so, the three causes acting in the wild state. But, in any case, the mention of a cause of variation linked with the number of individuals is no more than a memory of Maupertuis's theory, which Buffon entirely fails to complete by any reference to natural selection. Had he possessed even an imperfect grasp of this concept, he surely would have spoken of it in this context.

I have tried in these pages, which are too few to do full justice to so voluminous an author, to give as clear an idea as possible of Buffon's treatment of the idea of evolution. I do not think he can be called an originator or founder of the idea, and on the whole there seems to be small reason to suppose that he even subscribed to it. He seems to have regarded it as an interesting speculation of which a lot might be made some day, but which certainly could not be established upon the basis of such facts as were known to him. This seems to me to be exactly the position which a competent naturalist should have adopted during the eighteenth century, and to say that Buffon did adopt it is, I think, in no way to detract from his stature, rather, indeed, to enhance it. But the relation of Buffon to the theory of evolution is by no means merely that of a prudent judge who regarded it as non-proven. His services to the cause of the theory were not unimportant. He attempted a natural explanation of the origin of the earth in general, and of sedimentary rocks in particular, and thus did for Lamarck much what Lyell did for Darwin: he fostered the idea of a gradual temporal development due to natural causes. He directed attention to the problems associated with the theory of evolution, and he was, as far as I am aware, the first to appreciate that the geographical distribution of animals contained an essential part of the evidence relating to the origin of species. Finally, he recognized that many species of animals had become extinct before the appearance of man on earth, and that there were, consequently, causes of extinction which owed nothing to human agencies. This is a not unimportant element in the case for evolution, and it is one which Lamarck failed to understand.

[74] Buffon (1766), *ibid.*, p. 334.

BUFFON AND LAMARCK

Buffon and Lamarck belonged to two successive generations which might, perhaps, be expected to differ profoundly. Buffon was born in 1707, and belonged to the time of Louis XV; Lamarck, who was born in 1744, was of the generation of Robespierre and Jefferson. It is, however, difficult to convince oneself that the two men would not have shown much the same differences of taste and temperament had they been born in the same year.

Buffon appears to have been expansive, avid, sensual and energetic. He was not of noble birth, and we feel no surprise on learning that he inherited his fortune from a fermier général, and that he himself greatly added to what he had inherited.

The impression one has of Lamarck is that he was restrained, perhaps a trifle prim, and conscientious even to a fault: a poor aristocrat worried by the incomprehensible difficulties of practical life.

In praising the naturalists of antiquity, Buffon has left us more than a hint of what, we may suppose, he would like said of himself:

> The ancient authors who wrote on natural history were men of parts, who had not confined themselves to this study alone; their minds were elevated, their knowledge was various and profound; they had broad views, and if it appears to us that they lacked exactitude in certain details, it is not difficult to see that they did not suppose it necessary to give to trifles the attention which they have received in recent times.[75]

But though Buffon left the accumulation of detailed knowledge to others, he had a great respect for any facts which he had convinced himself were well established; and though he loved a 'broad view', as his two little essays called 'Vue de la Nature'[76, 77] testify, he did not mistake such pieces of bravura for contributions to natural science. It is no anomaly, but entirely characteristic of him, that his contribution to evolutionary thinking is fragmentary; when he wrote as a scientist, if he saw only fragments he described only fragments.

Lamarck was certainly not less conscientious, but he distinguished less clearly between what he could prove and what he should have recognized as speculation with only the flimsiest basis of fact. He was thus able to elaborate a complete and, apart from one fundamental flaw, a consistent theory of evolution, un-

---

[75] Buffon (1749), *ibid.*, vol. I, p. 43.
[76] Buffon (1764), *ibid.*, vol. XII, pp. iii–xvi.
[77] Buffon (1765), *ibid.*, vol. XIII, pp. i–xx.

hampered by any too nice an attention to evidence. It is a great deal easier to expound his theory of evolution than to sift the fragments which make up Buffon's contribution to the subject. But an exposition of Lamarck's theory cannot be entirely simple, because, as I have hinted, the theory was in one important respect not simple.

To explain this complexity, we must return for a moment to consider yet another contrast between the two great naturalists. Buffon never seems to have had any sympathy for any mono-theistic religion, though he might, perhaps, have had some in-tuitive understanding of some more ancient and more naturalistic religion; the relationships of his writings to theology are entirely external. Scepticism was Buffon's natural atmosphere, but it was one in which Lamarck's mind, essentially serious and orderly, could not breathe. In his works he shows himself a convinced Deist, and he even allowed that some truths might be known, and that man might approach the Supreme Being by means other than reason and observation.[78] In so far as he was a Deist, Lamarck belonged to an earlier age than did Buffon, and we find his theorizing hampered by elements of eighteenth-century, or even seventeenth-century thought which gave Buffon little trouble.

Buffon, it is true, began by accepting the Chain of Being, but the notion had no greater hold upon his mind than any other piece of metaphysics; the traditions which influenced his thought were rather those of the ancient world, especially Aris-totelian and Epicurean traditions, than those of the seventeenth century. But the Chain of Being haunted Lamarck's thoughts like an inexorcizable ghost.

LAMARCK'S THEORY OF EVOLUTION

The general structure of the theory

Lamarck gave three versions of his theory of evolution. In the first, published in 1801, which is a brief exposition originally given as a lecture, the whole of evolution seems to be attributed to the agency of the 'Lamarckian' mechanism, the inheritance of acquired characters. There is only the merest hint that Lamarck is concerned in any way with the Chain of Being, and the influence of the idea seems to be limited to the production of a scalar system of classification of animals, which one might easily

[78] Lamarck, J. B. P. A. (1815), *Histoire Naturelle des Animaux sans Vertèbres*, vol. I, p. 296, Paris. (The title page bears 'Par M. le Chevalier de Lamarck'.) (This author is subsequently referred to as 'Lamarck' and this work as *Animaux sans Vertèbres*.)

suppose to be merely a convenient artificial device, having no relation to the animals' mode of origin.

In the second treatment of the subject, contained in the first eight chapters of the *Philosophie Zoologique*,[79] first published in 1809, the central and principal evolutionary process is one which cannot be analysed causally: a natural tendency to increased complexity in organisms. This unexplained tendency, which is described as 'a law of nature', is supposed to result in a linear development on which is based the linear arrangement of the main groups of animals in Lamarck's classification. This linear scheme running from the least to the most complex animals is often described by Lamarck as a 'chain', and it is in fact a part of the Chain of Being, differing from the whole Chain, as described for example by Locke, only in being confined to animals (including man). Lamarck, who was an excellent botanist, constructed a second linear series for plants, since he saw clearly that the old notion of 'zoophytes' was untenable. In the *Philosophie Zoologique* the inheritance of acquired characters is relegated to an entirely secondary role: this process is now used to explain the obvious deviations from a linear order. It is thus true to say that the 'Lamarckian' mechanism, so far from being used to account for evolution, is here only called in to explain deviations from an ideal evolutionary progression.

It must be admitted that when Lamarck discusses, in a chapter specially devoted to the subject, the results of the inheritance of acquired characters, he does to some extent give the impression that the process is central to his theory; but it is easy to show that this impression is a mistaken one, and even in this chapter, devoted particularly to the 'Lamarckian' mechanism, he is at pains to point out its subordinate character. He does so briefly, but then he had made the position abundantly clear in the earlier chapters of his book.

The first version of Lamarck's theory, to which I have referred above, was printed as an introduction to his *Système des Animaux sans Vertèbres*, which bears the date *An IX 1801*, and the introductory passage bears the superscription *Discours d'Ouverture, prononcé le 21 Floréal An 8*. In 1815 Lamarck published a much enlarged treatise on the invertebrates, *Histoire Naturelle des Animaux sans Vertèbres*,[80] which he describes as 'susceptible d'être considéré comme une seconde édition de mon *Système des animaux sans vertèbres*'. The first volume of this second edition is devoted to a restatement of his biological principles, and here we find the third exposition of his theory of evolution. This third treatment of the subject appears unaltered in the posthumous edition of the *Animaux sans Vertèbres*, of

[79] Lamarck (1809), *Philosophie Zoologique*, Paris.
[80] Lamarck (1815), *Animaux sans Vertèbres*, Paris.

1835,[81] so that, especially as the general doctrine is the same as that expounded in the *Philosophie Zoologique*, we may consider this third treatment as definitive. It is also, I think, the most stylish of the three, so that I may begin my account of Lamarck's theory by a brief consideration of this final exposition.

Lamarck has been vexed by the accusation that he has merely refurbished the old Chain of Being, and he rejects with some asperity the notion of a single *chaîne graduée* linking 'the different bodies which nature has produced'; he does not believe that there can be any gradation between living and non-living things, and he reaffirms that there are no such things as zoophytes.[82] He attempts to remain consistently mechanistic, and attributes the sharp break between the living and the non-living to a difference in level of organization: 'The individuality of the species [consists] in the union, the disposition and the state of the constituent molecules of various kinds which compose their bodies, and never in any of these molecules considered separately.'[83] Animals and plants do not form parts of a single chain of beings, but constitute two independent lines; the differences between these two being due to differences in the chemicals initially used by nature in the synthesis of the primordial plant and the primordial animal respectively.

> I shall prove [he writes] that there is no real chain, linking together the productions of nature in general, and that such a thing can only be found in certain branches of the series which they form; and even there it only appears in a general way, and not in details (encore ne s'y montre-t-elle que sous certains rapports généraux).[84]

In spite of these disclaimers, however, Lamarck was, as we shall see, very far from having freed himself from the influence of the Chain of Being. It is true that he did not attempt to force all living things into a single linear scheme, but he constantly supposed that such a scheme underlay the relationships of animals, and he constantly speaks of branching in the systematic arrangement as a deviation or even an 'anomaly'. Moreover, he often uses the word *échelle*[85] in describing the basic classificatory series, and even slips into the use of *chaîne*[86] here and there, though perhaps less often than in the *Philosophie Zoologique*.

---

[81] Lamarck (1835), *Histoire Naturelle des Animaux sans Vertèbres*, Paris. (The title-page bears 'Par J. B. P. A. de Lamarck'. There are notes by G. P. Deshayes and H. Milne Edwards.)

[82] Lamarck (1815), *Animaux sans Vertèbres*, vol. I, pp. 8, 80.

[83] Lamarck (1815), *ibid.*, p. 53.

[84] Lamarck (1815), *ibid.*, p. 52.

[85] Lamarck (1815), *ibid.*, p. 131, for example.

[86] Lamarck (1815), *ibid.*, p. 153, for example.

In a *Supplément* at the end of the first volume of the *Animaux sans Vertèbres* of 1815, which appears unchanged in the edition of 1835, we find what must be almost if not quite literally Lamarck's last word on the subject of evolution. Here he allows two animal series, as though this were a new idea to him, though he had admitted in the *Philosophie Zoologique* the possibility of a short second chain or series,[87] and writes:

> After the spontaneous generations which began each series in particular, the later animals arose from one another. Now, though the laws which directed this production are always and everywhere the same, yet the diverse circumstances in which nature has worked, during the course of her labour, have necessarily produced anomalies in the simplicity of the scale (échelle) resulting from her operations. We should therefore try to form and to perfect two different tables:
>
> One giving the simple series, which we should use in our publications and lectures, to characterize, to distinguish and to describe the animals which have been observed; a series which we should in general model on the progression which occurs in the complexity of the various animal organisms, considering each in the totality of its parts, and making use of the directives which I have suggested.
>
> The other giving the particular series, with their simple branches, which nature seems to have formed in the production of the actually existing animals.[88]

The idea of two schemata, separable in thought but combined in nature, that is, in the actual process of evolution, both equally real because based upon two distinct 'causal' processes,[88a] run through Lamarck's writings with remarkable tenacity and consistency. Only in one place that I have been able to find does he seem to say explicitly that there is but one underlying process in evolution: the causal process usually called 'Lamarckian', the inheritance of acquired characters formed in the first place by reaction to environmental changes or as a result of the spontaneous formation of new habits. But even this apparent deviation from his usual doctrine disappears on careful examination. The difficult passage is as follows:

> By the four laws which I have just mentioned, all the facts of organization appear to me to be easily explicable; the progression in the complexity of organization of animals, and

---

[87] Lamarck (1809), *Philosophie Zoologique*, vol. II, pp. 462–3.
[88] Lamarck (1815), *Animaux sans Vertèbres*, vol. I, p. 461; and, in the edition of 1835, vol. I, p. 323.
[88a] One of the underlying processes is 'lawlike' rather than causal.

in their faculties, seems to me easy to comprehend (concevoir); finally, the means used by nature to diversify animals, and to bring them to the state in which we see them, become easily determinable.[89]

Now, the four laws which Lamarck has listed immediately before this passage are these: [89a]

1. Nature tends to increase the size of living individuals to a predetermined limit.
2. The production of a new organ results from a new need.
3. The development reached by organs is directly proportional to the extent to which they are used.
4. Everything acquired by the individual is transmitted to its offspring.[90]

Here, then, there seems to be no reference to the tendency to increasing complexity, and the whole of the evolutionary process appears to be attributed to the single causal factor of inheritance of acquired characters. This, however, turns out to be merely a piece of carelessness. In formulating the first of the four laws, Lamarck speaks of 'increase of size', but in commenting on the law he makes it clear that the phrasing of the law is defective. For he writes: 'This first law of nature, which gives to life the power of increasing the size of a body and of stretching out its parts ... enables this power gradually to increase its forces in the complexity of the animal organization.'[91] And he describes a process of increase of complexity due entirely to the movement of internal fluids, in no way guided by reactions to environmental changes or by the imprint of new habits upon the nervous system.

This, as I have said, is the only passage I have found in which Lamarck even seems to depart from his characteristic two-factor theory.

The zoological philosophy

Lamarck sets out his two-factor theory very clearly in the fourth chapter of his *Philosophie Zoologique*. The chapter begins:

Among the considerations of interest to Zoological Philosophy, one of the most important is that concerning the *degradation* and simplification observable in the organization of

[89] Lamarck (1815), *ibid.*, p. 201.
[89a] Paraphrased, for the sake of brevity, but nothing essential has been omitted.
[90] Lamarck (1815), *ibid.*, pp. 181–2.
[91] Lamarck (1815), *ibid.*, p. 185.

animals when we follow the animal series (la chaîne animale) from one end to the other, from the most perfect animals to those which are of the simplest organization.

Now, we have to find out whether this can really be established as a fact; for if so, it will throw a strong light on the plan which nature has followed, and will start us off on the way to the discovery of many of those of her laws which are the most important for us to know. I have here taken as my task to prove that what we are discussing is a positive fact, and that it is the consequence of a general law of nature, always acting in the same manner; to prove also, however, that a particular cause, which is easily recognizable, produces irregularities in one point or another within the whole extent of the animal series, disturbing the regularity which this law would otherwise have produced.

If the cause which is always tending to make organization more complex were the only one affecting the form and the organs of animals, the increasing complexity of organization would everywhere follow an extremely regular progression. But this is not the case. Nature is under the necessity of submitting her activities to the influences of circumstances which act upon them and everywhere (de toutes parts) these circumstances produce variety in her productions. This is the particular cause which gives rise here and there to the often bizarre deviations which the *degradation*, which we shall exhibit, shows us in its course. Let us try to make perfectly clear both the progressive *degradation* in the organization of animals, and the cause of the anomalies suffered by the path of this degradation within the animal series. Clearly, had nature produced only aquatic animals, and had all these animals always lived in the same conditions of temperature, the same kind of water, the same depth and so on, there can be no doubt that we should have found a regular and even a very fine (nuancée) *gradation* in the organization of these animals.

After having produced aquatic animals of all grades, and having varied them strikingly by the agency of the diverse conditions offered by the water,[91a] those which she [that is, nature] has induced little by little to live in air, first on the shore and then on the dry land, found themselves in time in conditions so different from the original ones and so powerfully affecting their habits and organs, that the regular *gradation* which they should exhibit, in the complexity of their organization, was greatly disturbed thereby, so that it is hardly to be perceived in many points.

These suppositions which I have turned over in my mind,

[91a] There is here an unconformity in the syntax of the French.

and which I shall establish by positive proofs, suggest to me the presentation of the following *zoological principles*, which seem to me incontestable.

The progression in the complexity of organization suffers, here and there, in the general series of animals, anomalies produced by the influence of the circumstances of the environment (circonstances d'habitation), *and by those of the habits contracted.*[92]

Now, although we no longer think in terms of a 'scale of perfection', the idea of advance in evolution is, of course, not totally to be rejected. An increase in complexity is indisputably present; but, more than that, one can also recognize certain well-defined advances which give to the animals possessing them an undoubted advantage over species less advanced. Some animals, for example, are at the mercy of comparatively small changes in the concentration of salts in their environment, while in others the concentration of salts in the body-fluids is independent, within wide limits, of changes in the environmental concentration. Again, the ability to preserve a constant body-temperature, while the external temperature varies widely, gives those animals which possess it a clear advantage over those which do not.

Where such clearly comprehensible advantages are concerned, it is reasonable to think of one group of animals as 'higher' than another. But Lamarck's desire to construct a linear scale of perfection carries him far beyond any such justifiable comparisons. Consider, for example, the following 'Observations on the Vertebrates', which occur later in the chapter from which I have just quoted:

Vertebrate animals, although they show among themselves great differences in their organs, appear to be all constructed upon a common plan. Passing from the fishes up to the mammals, we see that this plan becomes more perfect from class to class, and that it only reaches its final form in the most perfect mammals; but we also observe that, in the course of reaching its perfection, this plan has suffered numerous modifications, and even very striking ones, on account of the places in which the animals live and the habits which each race has been forced to acquire according to its circumstances.

Thus we see, on the one hand, that if vertebrate animals differ greatly from one another in the state of their organization, it is because nature only began to realize her plan for them in the fishes, that she improved it in the reptiles, that she carried it nearer to its perfection in birds, and that at last she

[92] Lamarck (1809), *Philosophie Zoologique*, pp. 130–4.

only contrived to bring it to its final state in the most perfect of the mammals; on the other hand, we cannot fail to perceive that, if the process of perfecting the plan of vertebrate organization does not show everywhere, from the least perfect fishes to the most perfect mammals, a regular and fine *gradation*, it is because nature's work has been often modified, impeded, and even changed in its direction, by the influences which strikingly different, and even contrary conditions have exercised upon the animals exposed to them for very many generations.[93]

Again, in the same chapter, we find the following, under the heading 'Molluscs':

If the molluscs, in their general organization, which is inferior in perfection to that of the fishes, also prove, for their part, the progressive *degradation* which we are studying in the animal series (chaîne), the same degradation is not so easily perceived among the molluscs themselves; because, among the very numerous and diverse animals of this class, it is difficult to separate what belongs to the *degradation* in question from what is the result of the habitats and habits of these animals.[94]

At least three times during the next few pages we find references to 'anomalies due to environment'.[95]

The next chapter, the seventh of the *Philosophie Zoologique*, is entitled 'On the influence of conditions upon the activities and habits of animals, and of that of the actions and habits of these living bodies, considered as causes modifying their organization and their parts'. This chapter, therefore, is devoted to an exposition of the 'Lamarckian mechanism'; but even in this chapter which deals particularly with only one of the underlying processes postulated by Lamarck's theory, there is an explicit and unambiguous reference to the other:

In the preceding section we have seen that it is now an incontestable fact that, considering the animal series (échelle) in the direction opposed to the natural one, we find that there is, in the groups (masses) which make up this series, a sustained but irregular *degradation* in the organization of the animals of the groups; an increasing simplification in the organization of these living bodies; finally, a proportional diminution of the faculties of these beings.

[93] Lamarck (1809), *ibid.*, p. 159.
[94] Lamarck (1809), *ibid.*, p. 169.
[95] Lamarck (1809), *ibid.*, pp. 185, 212, 217.

This well-known fact can throw the clearest light upon the actual order followed by nature in the production of all the animals she has made; but it does not show us why it is that the organization of animals, in its growing complexity, from the least to the most perfect, presents only an *irregular gradation* of which the whole extent displays a large number of anomalies or deviations which have no apparent order in their diversity.

Now, looking for the reason for this peculiar irregularity of the increasing complexity of the organization of animals, if we bear in mind the cumulative sum of the influences which infinitely diversified conditions all over the earth exercise upon the general form, the parts and the organization itself of these animals, all will then be clearly explained.

In fact, it will become clear that the actual state of animals is, on the one hand, the result of the increasing *complexity* of organization, which tends towards the production of a *regular gradation*, and, on the other, that it is the result of the influences of a multiplicity of circumstances very different one from another, which tend continually to destroy the regularity in the gradation of the increasing complexity of organization.[96]

THE TWO-FACTOR THEORY AND THE IMPORTANCE OF DEISTIC ELEMENTS IN LAMARCK'S THOUGHT

To show how seriously Lamarck took his two-factor theory, it is necessary to return, even at the risk of some tedium, to his treatment of it in the 'Introduction' of the *Animaux sans Vertèbres*. Cuvier had objected that it would not be possible to establish 'une série unique', because 'if each particular organ is considered, we shall have as many different series as we have taken for our guidance different organs ... to construct a general scale of perfection, we should have to calculate the resultant of each combination, which is hardly possible'.[97]

Answering this criticism, Lamarck writes:

This is the troublesome consequence of considering the data of observation as though there were but one cause responsible for the progression we are talking about. ... In fact all this has been looked at as though it were the product of one single cause ... but it is easy to see that we are dealing here with the results of two very different causes, of which the

[96] Lamarck (1809), *ibid.*, pp. 220–1.
[97] Cuvier, G. (1800), *Leçons d'Anatomie Comparée, de G. Cuvier*, An VIII, i, pp. 59–60, Paris.

one, although unable to destroy the predominance of the other, nevertheless frequently diversifies its consequences.

Nature's plan of campaign in the production of animals is clearly marked out by this primal and predominant cause, which endows animal life with the ability to complicate organization progressively, and to complicate and perfect gradually, not only the total organization, but also each system of organs in particular, as this cause has been able to establish each one. Now, this plan, that is, this progressive complication of organization, has really been effected by this primal cause among the various animals which exist.

But a quite separate cause, an accidental and consequently variable one, has here and there cut across the execution of this plan, without however destroying it, as I shall prove. This cause, in fact, has given rise to whatever real discontinuities there may be in the series, and to the terminated branches (rameaux finis) which depart from it, at various points, and diminish its simplicity, and finally to the anomalies to be seen in the various organ-systems of the different organizations.[98]

Lamarck then offers the 'proof', which he has promised, of the real existence of a scale of perfection. This 'proof' consists of an exhibition of animals arranged in a series so as to illustrate their gradual departure from the perfection of man. Lamarck also offers four 'facts on which are based the proofs of the existence of a progression of complexity of the organization of animals'; these add nothing material to the series he has exhibited, but they are of interest as illustrating his way of thinking about animals and about their scalar arrangement. The 'four facts' are: the general resemblance of animals one to another; the resemblances between man and other animals; the perfection of human organization; the fact that some animals resemble man more and some less.

The third 'fact' is stated thus:

One can present as a positive fact, as a truth susceptible of demonstration, that, of all types of organization, that of man is the most complex and the most perfect, considered as a whole, and from the point of view of the abilities which it procures for him. ...[99] [This is further explained in a footnote:] Many animals present, in some of their organs, a perfection and a wealth of abilities of which some organs in man are devoid. Nevertheless, his organization is more perfect in its totality than that of any animal whatever; a thing

[98] Lamarck (1815), *Animaux sans Vertèbres*, vol. I, pp. 132–3.
[99] Lamarck (1815), *ibid.*, pp. 136–7.

which cannot be denied. ... [Having established this to his own satisfaction, he continues] The organization of man being the most complex and the most perfect of all those which nature has been able to produce, it can be asserted that the nearer an animal organization approaches that of man, the more complex it is, and the more advanced towards its perfection (son perfectionnement); and, similarly, the further it is away, the more it is simple and imperfect.[99]

This, again, has a long footnote in which Lamarck writes that 'many zoologists' have found the expression 'perfect animals' and 'imperfect animals' ridiculous; as though, he says, they could not see that he means these expressions to be taken as implying a comparison with human perfection.

Who does not know that, in its actual state of organization, each living body of what kind so ever is a really perfect being, that is, a being which lacks nothing of that which is necessary for it! But nature having complicated animal organization more and more, and thereby having been enabled to endow the animals having the most complex organization with more and more advanced abilities, it is possible to see in the last term of her efforts a perfection from which those animals which have not attained it can be seen to recede by stages.

This passage seems to me to be important in showing how firmly Lamarck's thought was rooted in that of the eighteenth, and of preceding centuries; how seriously he took his scale of perfection; and, in his observations on the 'real perfection' of all animals, how generally his mind was imbued with the notion of a planned, and neatly planned, universe. This tendency to suppose that it must be relatively easy for any intelligent man to understand the intentions of nature appears again in Lamarck's slips into a teleology which really is vicious, and which can only be partly excused as a metaphor. Discussing the molluscs, he writes,

If these soft and jointless animals make only slow and weak movements, it is because nature, preparing to form the skeleton,[99a] has abandoned in them the use of horny teguments and the joints which she employed from the insects upwards,[99b] so that their muscles have, under the skin, only very feeble points of attachment (points d'appui).[100]

[99a] 'Skeleton' is used by Lamarck only for the skeleton of vertebrates.
[99b] His scale is: Insects, Arachnids, Crustacea, Annelids, Cirripedes, Molluscs; the insects being the lowest.
[100] Lamarck (1815), ibid., p. 147.

He had used the same kind of language in the *Philosophie Zoologique*:

> Nature, on the point of beginning the plan of organization
> of vertebrates, was obliged, in the molluscs, to give up the
> device of an encrusted or horny skin as supports for muscular
> action, and getting herself ready (se préparant) to carry these
> supports into the animal's interior,[100a] molluscs happened to
> be, as it were, in the path of this change.[101]

The metaphorical element in these statements is limited to the
personification of nature. Lamarck is elsewhere careful to assert
that nature is not a conscious agent:

> The general power which holds in its domain all the things we
> can perceive ... is truly a limited power, and in a manner
> blind; a power which has neither intention, nor end in view,
> nor choice; a power which, great as it may be, can do nothing
> but what in fact it does; in a word, a power which only exists
> by the will of a higher and limitless power, which, having
> founded it, is in truth the author of all that it produces, that
> is, of all that exists. ...
> And *nature* ... is only an instrument, only the particular
> means which it has pleased the *supreme power* to employ in
> the production of the various bodies, in their diversification;
> to give them properties, or even abilities. ... She is, in a way,
> only an intermediary between GOD and the parts of the
> physical universe, for the execution of the divine will.[102]

From the point of view of natural science, however, it matters
little whether we attribute conscious designs to nature, or consider her as an unconscious agent, if we too lightly assume that
the designs themselves will be easily comprehensible to us. What
is heterodox is not the supposition that the universe is planned,
but that the plan was made by a mind not essentially different
from our own. From the whole tone of Lamarck's writings it
seems certain that his appeals to the notion of a divine plan are
entirely sincere. It seems most improbable that, at the time he
was writing, such expressions were required, as they were in the
time of Buffon. There is internal evidence that they were no
longer *de rigueur*, for Lamarck himself tells us that the spirit of
his times was in general frankly naturalistic or atheistic: 'It has
been thought that nature is GOD, indeed, it is the opinion of the
majority. ... An odd thing! To confuse the watch with the

[100a] There is another syntactical unconformity here in the French. The
reading is guaranteed by a parallel passage in the *Animaux sans Vertèbres*.
[101] Lamarck (1809), *Philosophie Zoologique*, p. 172.
[102] Lamarck (1815), *Animaux sans Vertèbres*, vol. I, pp. 311, 331.

watchmaker, the work with its author!'[103] The effects of his Deism are nowhere more obvious than in his treatment of the problem of extinction. There is one passage in which he makes use of the concept of the struggle for existence as a contributory factor in the causal explanation of evolution:

> Another cause of change of activity which has contributed to the diversification of the parts of animals and to the multiplication of races is the following: As animals, by partial emigrations (par des émigrations partielles) changed the place of their abode and spread to different points on the earth's surface, they were exposed, on arriving in new situations, to new dangers which required new activities, if they were to be avoided; because most of them devour one another to conserve their existence.[104]

But this is an isolated flash of insight. In general, Lamarck shows that the notion of wastage of species was profoundly foreign to his mind. Thus in the *Philosophie Zoologique*, which was published only four years before the passage just quoted, he discusses only one cause of extinction, and only one class of extinct animals: the extinction of large animals such as Megatherium and Mastodon by human agencies.[105] In the same place he also proposes his own peculiar explanation of remains which appear to belong to extinct forms. He says that few, if any, species have ceased to exist except by changing into other species. He considers it most probable that no fossil form is extinct even in this sense, but that all species which appear to have been lost may one day be found living in out-of-the-way places on the earth, or in the depths of the sea. Somewhat later in the same work he mentions the checks on the numbers of one species provided by the activities of other species, but on this his comment is:

> By these wise precautions, everything remains in the established order; the perpetual changes and returns (renouvellements) which are to be seen in this order are maintained within limits which they cannot transcend: the races of living bodies all continue to exist, in spite of their variations, the elements of progress in the perfecting of organization are not lost; all which appears to be disorder, anomaly, returns endlessly into the general order, and even enhances it: and everywhere and always the will of the sublime Author of nature and of all that exists is done without exception.[106]

[103] Lamarck (1815), *ibid.*, p. 322.
[104] Lamarck (1815), *ibid.*, p. 194.
[105] Lamarck (1809), *Philosophie Zoologique*, pp. 75–81.
[106] Lamarck (1809), *ibid.*, pp. 100–1.

There is, I believe, a defect in Lamarck's theory of which he seems to have been unaware. If there is an implanted tendency in some living form to evolve into some more complex form, one can see no reason why this tendency should not be universally present in the less complex form. Were this the case, no living representative of the less complex form is to be expected; and since Lamarck undoubtedly supposes this state of affairs to be the rule, we should expect that the only living representative of the animal series would be the most complex. Yet he supposes that most, if not all links in the chain, or members of the series, are in fact still to be found alive. He does indeed suggest a mechanism which would result in some descendants of a given form differing from others, the mechanism of the inheritance of acquired characters, but this is supposed by him to explain deviations from the direct line of advance, and consequently could not be used to explain the persistence of ancestral forms within the direct line. It may be that he believed living forms which are in the direct line, but not at the summit, to be the products of other lines which originated independently of the line which produced man, by separate spontaneous generations at different times;[106a] but this clearly robs the theory of all its apparent simplicity and elegance.

CONCLUSION

Any satisfactory theory of evolution must be able to assimilate three great sets of data: the actual geographical distribution of plants and animals, the real similarities of structure which must form the basis of any system of classification of organisms, and, finally, the fossil record.

Buffon's most significant contribution in this field was his attempt to grapple with the problem of the distribution of mammals in the Old and in the New World. Not only does he approach the solution which Darwin gave for this problem, but even his methods are curiously like those of Darwin. No book of travels or memoirs is too remote; if it but contain some crumbs of information which appear significant and reliable, Buffon will find them. However, as we have seen, Buffon could not satisfy himself that the causal theory of evolution, as he understood it, was adequate to explain the differences he observed between the animals of the one World and those of the other.

It seems probable that Buffon suspected that it would one day be possible to elaborate a theory of evolution which would systematize, not only the facts of geographical distribution, but

[106a] I owe this suggestion to Mr H. G. Ll. Bevan.

also those of comparative anatomy and palaeontology; but it is certain that he did not produce, or even attempt to produce, such a theory. What we have in his work is a fragment towards the construction of a theory of evolution; it is no more than a fragment, but it is one of considerable brilliance, and what gives it its peculiar merit is that it is no mere essay in uncontrolled theorizing, but a piece of inductive science which scrupulously respects the facts.

Lamarck's methods were, as we have seen, the obverse of those of Buffon. The theory which he produced had every appearance of completeness and consistency, though in fact, as I have endeavoured to show, it had not that internal simplicity which we look for in a good theory. But whether it was good or bad, considered in isolation as a theory, it certainly produced insuperable difficulties when applied even to the one set of facts upon which Lamarck attempted to base its justification. For the theory required a classification of animals which should be in principle linear, and such a system is at variance with the facts. Thus, although Lamarck had already produced a branching scheme in 1809, he still adhered to a linear one in 1815, and he found himself obliged to produce two conflicting arrangements, one to satisfy the basic assumption of an ascending scale of perfection, and another to accommodate the obvious deviations from this order.

Lamarck was not unaware of the important evidence to be derived from the geographical distribution of organisms, but he nowhere, I think, sets forth this evidence in detail. A brief reference to this subject occurs in the *Animaux sans Vertèbres*:

> Let anyone pass slowly over the surface of the earth, especially in the north–south direction, stopping from time to time to give himself leisure to observe; he will invariably see the *species* varying little by little, and more and more as he is farther from his starting point. He will see them follow, in some sense, the variations of the localities themselves, the conditions, exposed or sheltered, and so on. Sometimes he will even see varieties produced, not by habits required by the conditions, but by habits contracted accidentally, or in some other way. Thus man, who is subject by his organization to the laws of nature, himself shows remarkable varieties within his species, and among these some which seem to be due to the causes last mentioned.[107]

In general, Lamarck appears to have had little appreciation of the nature and amount of evidence required to establish any

[107] Lamarck (1815), *Animaux sans Vertèbres*, vol. I, p. 198.

major theoretical position. Thus, in discussing the inheritance of acquired characters, he writes:

> Indeed, this law of nature, by which all that has been acquired by their progenitors during their life is transmitted to new individuals, is so true, so striking, so well attested by the facts, that there is no observer who has not been able to convince himself of its reality.[108]

Considering the three sets of facts given above which any theory of evolution must be able to systematize, we find that Lamarck gave full attention to the facts of comparative anatomy, that he considered those of geographical distribution only in a summary manner, and that he found nothing but difficulties in the fossil record. Indeed, the facts of palaeontology are particularly suited to throw into relief all the defects of his theory. These defects appear to me to be directly due to the fact that the theory was everywhere infected with bad theology. I think it can be asserted with confidence that Deism is bad theology, because it cannot sustain examination by its own canons. It affects to be greatly superior in rationality to orthodox Christian theology, but it suffers, itself, from a basic inconsistency. In common with all theologies of our era, Deism asserts that the mind of God is infinite, yet supposes that we can see things from God's point of view, and can easily discover what he would do in particular sets of circumstances. It is well enough to say that God would adopt the best means for achieving his purposes, and that he would avoid wanton waste: but even supposing us to know what his purposes are, how can we believe ourselves in a position to assign the best means for attaining them? And how are we to know what would appear wasteful to infinite power combined with infinite intelligence? It is, however, deistic assumptions of this kind which give Lamarck's theory its peculiar structure. He supposes that God, in directing the process of evolution, was aiming directly at the production of man, and that this must appear in an empirically discoverable linearity in the evolutionary series. Further, he cannot tolerate the idea that any species should be wasted on the way, so that he is unwilling to admit the possibility of extinction, in the simple sense of the word.

It was these presuppositions and their consequences which made the Lamarckian theory unable to adapt itself readily to the data of comparative anatomy; but they made it even less suitable to the assimilation of the fossil record, which shows no simple upward trend of organization. It is everywhere marked by

[108] Lamarck (1815), *ibid.*, p. 200.

evidences of the extinction of species, few of which can have been the direct ancestors of living forms.

These considerations help to explain a puzzling feature of Darwin's presentation of his theory. It must have struck many readers of the *Origin of Species* that Darwin seems to give unnecessary prominence to the causal part of his theory. Would it not have been possible, it might be asked, to assemble and sift the three main types of evidence, and to establish upon them the general theory, without necessarily propounding a causal theory at all? Yet it is clear that Darwin thought of his causal theory as an indispensable element in the establishment of the general theory, as, indeed, the full title of his book makes clear: *The Origin of Species by means of Natural Selection, or the Preservation of Favoured Races in the Struggle for Life.*

Though it is, I believe, correct from the point of view of analysis to separate the general theory of evolution from the causal theory, nevertheless, from the psychological and historical point of view the two are separated only with difficulty.

As I have tried to show, a major factor among those which prevented Buffon from elaborating a general theory was his inability to produce a causal theory satisfactory to himself. It is clear also that the common reaction to the suggestion that animals had been produced by evolution would be to ask, 'But how could that be?'

Plainly, Darwin thought it essential to answer this question before setting out the general theory, and this is reflected even in the arrangement of the *Origin of Species*, for the discussions of the Geological Succession, of Geographical Distribution and of the Mutual Affinities of Organic Beings are relegated to the last chapters of the book. But in one sense at least the general and the causal theories are really inseparably united within Darwin's theory, for it was necessary to present the general theory in a form capable of 'saving the appearances' of the geological record. This could only be done by stressing the element of chance in the actual course of the evolutionary process.

Thus at least a negative statement relating to the underlying processes was necessary. It had to be made clear that the theory offered by Darwin did not involve the postulation of any empirically verifiable directional tendency in evolution. Though Darwin did not view the matter in this way, we might say that only by stressing the element of chance could he finally exorcize the spectre of Deism, and present a theory consonant with facts as they undoubtedly appear to the human observer.

The indirect and meandering course of evolution, as presented in the fossil record; the starting and stopping; the bizarre experimentation; the long periods in which forms of life predominated which proved to be far from the directions of advance; the preservation, here and there, of archaic species; above all, what must strike the tidy mind as the intolerable wastage; none of these things could be reconciled with the delusion that the human mind can directly and fully comprehend the plan of the divine mind in the production of living things.

I hope that the originality and peculiar merits of Darwin's presentation of the arguments in favour of the general theory of evolution will be clearly revealed by this consideration of the work of his two great predecessors.

I offer no summary of the *Origin of Species*, for no summary could do justice to a work of which the principal value lies in the ordering of great masses of varied data to build up a cogent argument. In such a work the argument and the facts upon which it is based are inseparable; and the reader acquainted with the accidental circumstances which caused Darwin to write the *Origin of Species* when he did will remember that he himself regarded the book as the shortest account which could usefully be given of his theory.

It is very far from my intention to minimize the achievements of Buffon and of Lamarck. If Darwin himself appears to have done less than justice to his predecessors, we must remember that the labours he undertook as a naturalist might well have exhausted a more powerful constitution than that which he possessed: it is unreasonable to blame him for not having added to these labours those of an historian of science.

Although Darwin was little conscious of the preliminary work done by Buffon and by Lamarck, he must have profited by it, if only indirectly. Viewing the historical development of the theory of evolution dispassionately we can now see that there really was a development, though a discontinuous one. The merit of being Buffon in the eighteenth century, or Lamarck between centuries, is not necessarily less than that of being Darwin in the nineteenth, and anyone who likes to do so can say that Darwin only completed the building which others, under greater difficulties, had begun.

The fact remains that it was he who completed it.

14   Evolution and the Churches*

Owen Chadwick

In the year 1896 Frederick Temple became Archbishop of Canterbury. Twelve years earlier he delivered the Bampton lectures at Oxford, on *The Relations between Religion and Science*. These lectures assumed evolution as an axiom. It was not therefore surprising that his elevation to the most senior see should cause a protest. But the protest came from an unusual quarter. A clergyman named Brownjohn had resigned his parish because he accepted evolution and held it an impossible belief for a clergyman of the Church of England. Brownjohn appeared at Temple's confirmation in Bow church to lodge a protest against the faith of him who was nominated to be archbishop. The vicar-general overruled the protest.

This trivial little incident may be taken to mark the final acceptance of the doctrine of evolution among the divines, clergy and leading laity of the established church, at least as a doctrine permissible and respectable in an eminent clergyman. For no one who disbelieved evolution, and thought it incompatible with the faith of a Christian bishop, lodged a protest. For a decade or two after 1896 some members of the Church of England, especially among the evangelicals, and nearly all official members of the Roman Catholic Church, and most of the simple worshippers among the chapels of the poor, continued to know nothing of evolution or to refuse to accept it on religious grounds, that is, on their faith in the inspired truth of the Old Testament. To the end of his life (1900) the evangelical Bishop Ryle of Liverpool believed in the physical information of the Old Testament. But for two decades before 1896 the acceptance of the doctrine among educated Christians, while far from universal, was both permissible and respectable. Some more conservative divines sought to distinguish an acceptance of the evolution of animal species, which they regarded as permissible for a Christian, from an acceptance that man was part of the process of evolution. In 1885 Bishop Ellicott of Gloucester

* Owen Chadwick, 'Evolution and the Churches', in *The Victorian Church* Part II, Black, 1966, 23–35.

and Bristol, who was a good theologian, issued a charge to his diocese in which he condemned the doctrine that man was part of the evolutionary series. Even then the charge was regarded in many quarters as old-fashioned, and when in the year before Bishop Frederick Temple of Exeter delivered his Bampton lectures and took evolution for granted, no one commented. And yet in 1884–5 a bishop who allowed evolution in his pulpit was still just worthy of mention in the newspapers. In December 1885 Bishop Magee of Peterborough accepted evolution in a sermon at St Mark's in Peterborough, and the occasion was considered news by the press. Two years before Charles Gore, the first principal of Pusey House, heir to the ideals of the lately dead Pusey, accepted evolution in a sermon at Oxford and only one or two correspondents complained in the newspapers. As late as 1888 J. W. Burgon was writing of the *absurdity* of the Darwinian theory of the origins of man, but his advocacy was not able to commend his argument. Therefore the reception of the view, among more educated Christians, that evolution and Christian doctrine were compatible, can be dated to the twenty-five years from 1860 to 1885. We can mark its stages.

During the sixties, and especially after the publication in 1871 of Darwin's *Descent of Man*, which tried to explain the evolutionary growth of man's higher qualities, a large number of religious men probably regarded Darwinism as a menace both to Christian faith and to the social order. It is easy to find comments of this nature in the press, from the most famous of newspapers to the denominational magazines.[1] It is easy to find famous clergymen who at the Church Congresses of the sixties took up in their speeches positions that in a few years would be derided as obscurantist.[2] Archdeacon Denison rose at the Church Congress of 1867 to denounce the claim of science to equality with the Bible as a road to truth, saying, 'Those who accept the Bible do not investigate truth, they receive it',[3] and though he got cries of *no! no!* he was also greeted with loud cheers. In 1865 churchmen founded the Victoria Institute, 'to investigate fully and impartially the most important questions of philosophy and science, but more especially those that bear upon the great truths revealed in Holy Scripture, with the view of defending these truths against the opposition of science falsely so-called'. Though some of the founders were warm

[1] Many instances in Alvar Ellegård, *Darwin and the General Reader*, 99 ff.
[2] E. B. Birks and Dr Baylee at Norwich in 1865, CCR, 1865, 190 ff.; Archdeacon Freeman in the Anthropology section at British Association, Exeter, 1869, G, 69, 961, an astounding paper.
[3] G, 67, 1115; CCR, 1867, 206.

against Darwin, the institute gathered support and began to do good work.

To understand the conservatism of the sixties, which would later be called by many Christians and which was then called by Huxley obscurantism, it must never be forgotten that at the same time men were arguing over the historical evidence for the truth of the Bible. They were afraid of losing the Bible, and with it the evidence for the future life, the motive for right conduct, the ethical standards of civilised society. The Darwinians were on the side of those who attacked the truth of the Bible; and so at the extreme the *Family Herald* (20 May 1871)[4] asserted 'Society must fall to pieces if Darwinism be true'. Nor at that date did the scientific evidence for the truth of the Darwinian theory look so probable as it later came to look. The conservatives afterwards appeared more obscurantist than they were because the theory became more established as a scientific theory. They defended the Bible against a hypothesis which they could still with reason call 'speculative'.

Nevertheless, the speech of Archdeacon Freeman at the British Association of 1869 can hardly be defended. And the height of the conflict was marked by some strong antipathies. Hooker kept denouncing the ignorance of the clergy. In the choice of applicants for a lectureship in botany at St Bartholomew's hospital (1866) a clergyman turned out to be the best candidate, but some of the governors of the hospital were averse to the choice of a clergyman and preferred him not to be recommended to them.[5] Such illiberal opposition would have been unthinkable only ten years before. It is a sign of the widening gap, or of the sensation that the gap was widening.

At the other extreme stood the few who welcomed Darwin on religious grounds; some, like Asa Gray or Charles Kingsley, because Darwin reduced the number of inexplicable things in the universe and therefore pointed towards a design; others, like R. W. Church or Frederick Denison Maurice, because it was proper to welcome this evident search for truth and they saw nothing incompatible with God's goodness; and still others because they were pained by the gymnastics of those who in the name of religion sought to reconcile geology with Genesis, and saw evolution as a liberation from intolerable divinity. In *Omphalos* (1857) Philip Gosse, who was quite a good scientist and a devout Pymouth Brother, posed the question whether at the creation of the world that which came to exist came to exist bearing in itself the signs of growth, or birth. Adam had not been born – did he have a navel? The trees in the garden of Eden had not grown, did they when cut down show rings

[4] Ellegård, 101.
[5] *Life of Hooker*, ii, 57; *Memoirs and Letters of Sir James Paget*, 233.

which displayed growth? He suggested that the course of nature is circular and that God in creating must have created at some point by breaking into the circle and therefore there were indeed trees with rings though they had not grown and man and woman with the signs of birth though they had not been born. This kind of speculation displeased some who thought about their doctrine of God, and Darwin came among them like a preserver of Christian doctrine from what was unintentionally blasphemous. If they disbelieved evolution, they were left with more difficult problems about God-in-nature than if they believed it.

The liberal divines found it easy to welcome Darwin, and the new science generally, because they did not need to defend the literal inspiration of the Bible. Darwin's theory favoured those historians who did not believe all the historical information of the Bible, and this was the chief reason why conservatives shrank away. But as the liberal divines did not themselves believe all the history in the Bible, they had no need to fear on this score. On the personal plane Kingsley and Arthur Stanley did good work in keeping in touch with the leading scientists, and Stanley became the private pastor of that hammer of orthodoxy Professor Tyndall.

Meanwhile the great school of moderate theologians held their judgement in suspense; welcoming scientific advance if it could be shown to be well-founded, too cautious to hail every new theory as a revelation, perceiving a present disharmony between their faith and the tendencies of physical knowledge, not yet discerning how to reconcile that disharmony, but confident in the God of truth and therefore content that the way of reconciliation would one day appear. Bishop Tait of London was eminent among them. Dr Pusey and his disciple Liddon were both moderates in the field of physical science, unexpectedly, for they led the resistance to the new history of the Bible. A majority of the Anglican clergymen who thought about these matters awaited further light hesitantly, neither denouncing the Darwinians nor throwing themselves into the belief that evolution was a new revelation.

The *Guardian* newspaper recorded the advancing opinions of intelligent and moderate high churchmen. During 1867 it began to defend the clergy from an imputation, first made by F. W. Farrar,[6] that the clergy as a class were the enemies of science. They were entitled to be critical when scientists stepped outside their field and pronounced on ethics or metaphysics where they had no special qualifications. In 1868 the *Guardian* talked of Darwin's 'brilliant genius and patient research'. A few months

[6] *On some Defects in Public School Education*, 1867; answered by John Hannah, *Contemporary Review*, 1867, vi, 1 ff.

later it commended the tenth edition of Lyell's *Principles* where
he declared (at last) his adherence to Darwin. In 1871 it printed
a letter from Archdeacon Freeman in which he called Darwinism the most easily refuted sophism of the day and then printed
a reply from T. G. Bonney, the Cambridge geologist, that though
Darwinism was only a hypothesis it was a more probable hypothesis than Freeman's. Its reviewer was critical of Darwin's
Descent of Man, but believed that evolution would soon be
as axiomatic as the law of gravity, and accepted the necessity
that man was part of the evolutionary process. 'Nor is there any
reason why a man may not be an evolutionist and yet a
Christian. That is all that we desire to establish.... Evolution
is not yet proved, and never may be. But ... there is no occasion
for being frightened out of our wits for fear it should be.'[7]

Henceforth there could be only one solution. Two other in-
cidents marked the way towards the year 1885, when the question looked to be settled finally.

In 1874 T. G. Bonney published a book called *A Manual of
Geology*. The book's importance consisted in the publisher, the
S.P.C.K., an official publishing house of the Church of England.
It was not without protest. An attempt to unseat two members
of the publishing committee failed and S.P.C.K. continued to
publish Bonney's book.

Darwin died in 1882 and expected to be buried at Down.
Huxley considered briefly the possibility of burial in Westminster Abbey and dismissed it, confident that the request would
be refused. Canon F. W. Farrar said to him, 'we clergy are not all
so bigoted as you suppose', and elicited an application.[8] So
Darwin was buried in Westminster Abbey with Christian rites,
Huxley and Hooker and Wallace among the pallbearers, Dr
Bridge's anthem *Happy is the man that findeth wisdom*, and an
excellent sermon on the following Sunday from that most
humane of bishops Harvey Goodwin of Carlisle. A few pro-
testers complained that the funeral was unfitting, a Roman
Catholic writer talked of 'the giving of that which is holy
to the dogs'. But the churches generally took a national pride
in the decision, and were thankful that they could honour, and
be grateful for, such a quest for truth even though it cast them
into disarray. The general committee of the memorial fund[9] included not only Galton, Hooker, Romanes, Tyndall and Herbert
Spencer, but the Archbishops of Canterbury and York and the
Bishop of London. The Tractarian leader Liddon was invited to
serve on the committee but refused. His reason was interesting:
that his master, Dr Pusey, would not like it.

[7] G, 68, 952; 71, 681, 714, 937.
[8] *Life of Farrar*, 109.
[9] Darwin Papers, 140/5.

Towards the end of the century Darwin's friend Asa Gray told the Bishop of Rochester that looking back on the progress of thought in England and America, 'he could not say that there had been any undue or improper delay on the part of the Christian mind and conscience in accepting, in such sense as he deemed they ought to be accepted, Mr Darwin's doctrines'. But some leaders in the churches, including Cardinal Manning, still denounced those doctrines as false and unscientific.[10]

Six years later the school for the blind at Liverpool applied for a faculty for mosaic glass in its chapel; with the light of the world in the centre, and men or women deriving inspiration from him. Among the men appeared Charles Darwin. In granting the faculty, the chancellor commented that some might doubt whether Darwin should be there; but 'we have long ago satisfied ourselves that natural science, as represented by Darwin, is not contrariant to revealed religion; and it is a wholesome thing to be reminded that "every good and perfect gift cometh from above, from the father of lights". Darwin's remains were honoured with a funeral in Westminster Abbey, and I am not prepared to say his name is out of place.'[11]

The phrases of evolutionary biology could be made to sound religious.

Henry Drummond was of the Free Church of Scotland and devoted his life to evangelistic preaching of a revivalist type. But it was revivalism of a rare language. He became professor of natural science at the Free Church College in Glasgow. Already as a student (1870-1) he welcomed natural selection as 'a real and beautiful acquisition to natural theology' and The Origin of Species as 'perhaps the most important contribution to the literature of apologetics' to have appeared in the nineteenth century. Teaching science to students on weekdays and religion to working men on Sundays, he found that the one overflowed into the other. Applying the idea of laws of nature on weekdays, he began to apply them on Sundays, and published in 1883 Natural Law in the Spiritual World. If Herbert Spencer could use the laws of nature to order social theory, why should they not be used to order the equally intangible realm of the spirit? The book was a series of parables between the natural world used to show forth the world of the spirit. As Drummond did not think of them as parables, but real applications of the same law to the realm of nature and to the realm of grace, he alienated all philosophical readers by confusion of language. (Hort to Ludlow, 22 February 1886: 'a quite singularly

---

[10] Talbot of Rochester in CCR, 1896, 152. For Manning, cf. his letter of 14 April 1889, in Do we Believe?, 1905, 153-4.
[11] G, 03, 4.

muddle-headed book'.)[12] It is a sign of the Victorian state of mind, under the impact of the natural sciences, that the book was enormously successful. Its success was partly due to its purely religious side, to Drummond's ability to write movingly about the realm of grace. But its success was also due, at least a little, to its use of scientific jargon like biogenesis, and to its illustrations drawn from Darwin or Spencer, and its manifest assurance that science aided the religious understanding of man's predicament. His readers were 'not now concerned whether Drummond made out a case.... It was enough for them that they encountered a teacher who expounded, defended and enforced their deepest religious experiences upon what appeared to be the dominant intellectual methods of their generation.'[13] When ten years later Drummond published a similar book, The Ascent of Man, it won nothing like the same applause, and partly for the reason that the Victorians, having passed the worst battles of their conflict between science and religion, no longer needed this kind of devotional writing.

The theologians were busier with the consequences of Biblical criticism than the consequences of the natural sciences. But the acceptance of evolution affected their fundamental attitudes.

Unless they were Roman Catholics committed to a form of Thomism they slowly dropped natural theology, that is, they ceased to argue towards the existence or qualities of God from a contemplation of nature. The old arguments continued for a time, and for a time were still respectable.[14] But whether Darwin strengthened or demolished the argument from design, that argument became impossible to use in the old form of Christian apologetic. If they used the argument from design, they used it in some form hard to recognise, as in Henry Drummond's notion of natural law. They looked out upon the world and saw pattern, or providence, or a beauty which was not merely the wildness caused by an infinite succession of accidents. But they were no longer quite sure – or, even if they were sure, their public was no longer sure – that they perceived this pattern or beauty unless their soul or conscience was already in a state capable of perceiving it. Though men who matriculated at Cambridge university still needed to pass an examination on Paley's Evidences, Paley's argument from design became irrelevant to any late Victorian theology that mattered. The first shadow of the knowledge of God seemed to lie in the

---

[12] Life of Hort, ii, 340; Criticism of Drummond, especially by T. C. Finlayson, Biological Religion, 1885; and A. T. Lyttelton in CQR, Jan. 1885, 392–410; cf. John Kent, From Darwin to Blatchford, 20 ff.

[13] G. A. Smith, Drummond, 44–5, 214.

[14] Buckland's Bridgewater treatise was reprinted in 1869 with applause.

heart or the conscience, not in nature; and only after God was apprehended through feeling or through moral judgment did nature become evidently sacramental of his being.

On this matter the great divide came after the Bampton lectures (1865) of J. B. Mozley entitled *On Miracles*. The book is the last statement, by a great English Protestant theologian, of a world of divinity which henceforth vanished except in the scholastic manuals. Mozley's fundamental axiom was the need to 'prove' Christianity, as Paley once proved it; and the internal evidence of heart and conscience can supply no 'proof' to the reason. Miracles are needed to 'prove' the truth of the revelation which they accompany. They are the form of external evidence that is left now that it is no longer safe to use the external evidence of nature.

It is a watershed in Christian thought. Though Mozley's book reached a fifth edition in 1880, no divine of the first rank could ever again argue the case as Mozley argued. For their new historical knowledge made them shrink from basing the revelation of God upon documents which without doubt contained historical truth but no one could yet say how much truth; and secondly, the acceptance of evolution made them shrink from singling out special acts of God as alone worthy of the epithet *supernatural*. In throwing away the idea of a sequence of special creations, they looked rather to see God in the process, God not only as the creator but as the sustainer, not only as transcendent above and detached from his world but as immanent within the world and within its development. Therefore they did not wish to base revelation upon miracle, but saw the miraculous as part of, a consequence of, the revelation. How do we know that the revelation is indeed a revelation of God? Not, as Mozley said, by its miracles, but by the character of Christ and his effect upon mankind, by its correspondence with the highest moral aspirations of the soul, by the direct apprehension of the divine in so many members of the human race. Nearly all the English theology of the later nineteenth century was 'immanentist'; talked as often of God within the world as of God above the world; dwelt more upon the incarnation of the word in Christ and less upon the atonement wrought by Christ; and (like Coleridge and Maurice) based its ultimate claim upon the religious experiences of men. History contributed as much as science to this change of thought. But we cannot doubt that the enormous impulse which Darwinism gave to ideas of process helped to turn the Christian divines towards these characteristic attitudes of liberal divinity.

For a century and a half the civilised world had not expected miracles to happen. Historical knowledge separated the miracles of the New Testament as a special case, warranted by an overwhelming event, from the subsequent miracles of saints or the miracles alleged in heathen religions. When Newman wrote of the scriptural miracles (1826) he wrote assuredly and was read with respect, when he defended ecclesiastical miracles (1842) he wrote tortuously and was read with opprobrium. But after historical criticism began to treat the Biblical documents like other documents, the evidence of scriptural miracles began to lose its unique quality. The doubtful expectation began to apply as sceptically to Biblical miracles as to ecclesiastical. And meanwhile scientists talked much of the 'uniformity of nature', and regarded every physical breach in a generally observed law as a doubtful event which required further physical explanation. 'The declining sense of the miraculous', as Lecky called it in 1863, was pushed further into decline by Darwin and the public acceptance of evolution. By removing special creation of species, Darwin removed the need for very numerous interferences with physical laws.

Huxley was far too able to claim that science could disprove any miracle. He confessed the contrary. The evidence for miracle was historical, and rested upon witnesses to whom science, which worked by induction, had nothing to say. Yet 'the laws of nature' of which the scientists so often talked, looked like unalterable parts of the design of the universe. Some philosophers tended to convert 'hitherto unvarying' into 'invariable'. The liberal theologian Baden Powell gave up miracles, so far as they could be said to be violations of 'the laws of nature', during the fifties. Though 'science' could not disprove a single miracle, men who talked of the miraculous began during the sixties to look anti-scientific. Extraordinary and unaccountable things were confessed to happen. The incurably ill were cured. But the scientist preferred to call such events inexplicable rather than to call them supernatural. Liberal theologians slowly accepted the old doctrine of Hume, republished by Mill, that no evidence could prove a miracle to a man who did not already believe in God. Retaining all the belief that God acted in the world, they slowly became agnostic on whether some acts were breaches in 'the laws of nature', and refused to follow James Mozley in basing faith upon the evidence for miracle. All that the evidence could do was to prove the event to be wonderful, and it was faith which saw through wonder to the hand of the divine.

One other consequence of evolution was the rise of scientific anthropology. As soon as it was accepted that man had a prehistory before Genesis, the study of primitive man began. Since the pre-historians could hardly study civilised man in his primitive condition, they needed to study the primitive tribes in various parts of the earth, on the axiom that the development of these cruder societies might be found in part parallel to what could be postulated of an earlier development of civilised society. The acceptance of evolution coincided with, and was helped by, the sudden development of sea-transport and empire which enabled travellers to reach more remote peoples and to bring back a mass of new evidence. Their conclusions sometimes outran the evidence, for they partly depended on narratives by amateurs, and scientific work in the field did not begin until almost the end of the century. And in that flood-tide of evolutionary theory they rested upon two axioms that were not, and could not be, verified; that all societies develop through parallel stages, and that the developments are in general for the better, so that if a society is more primitive it is earlier. Upon these axioms they produced many fertile ideas and some misleading speculations.

In the middle-sixties the anthropologists confronted religious men with a new kind of conflict – the fall of man versus the rise of man. Members of the churches who abandoned the story of Adam and Eve as legendary were already engaged in freeing the doctrine of original sin from its reference to an alleged event of history and in seeing it more as bias towards evil by heredity and social environment. The anthropologists did no more to Christian thinking than to stimulate or hasten this work of turning history into parable. After 1875 Victorian churchmen showed little sign of being perturbed by researches into primitive cultures, and were more likely to welcome than to repudiate E. B. Tylor's speculative search for the origins of religion in primitive animism. Tylor was a humane scholar. But the *Anthropological Journal* of the middle sixties contained strange matter. If all societies developed in parallel, did all pass through a stage of cannibalism? A succession of orthodox writers, from Archbishop Whately downwards, seized upon the inconsistencies and unverifiable nature of the axiom that societies always developed upward and drew attention to societies which developed downward. They contended that civilisation was primitive and that barbarism was the consequence of fall. Their strongest argument observed that no society was known to raise itself in the scale of civilisation except by coming into touch with a higher society; and therefore the higher society must be original. They adduced the retrospective yearnings after an earlier golden age to be found among many savage societies, and the opinion of African travellers that some backward peoples were then growing more backward. The theory was attacked by many students from Lubbock downwards, but gave way less to new evidence or new arguments than to the general acceptance of evolution among educated men. By 1875 it became a piece of litter from the past of science.[15]

The early science of psychology had little effect, if any, upon religion in England. Troubled souls do not seem to have consulted their pastors after learning that the functions of the brain *might* be brought under laws of empirical observation. They were disturbed neither by the mental philosophy of Bain nor by Herbert Spencer's *Principles of Psychology* (1855, much extended 1870–2). Boyd Carpenter's Hulsean lectures of 1878 proclaimed that psychological enquiries were useful to religion. New work in this field first touched the theologians when William James studied the psychology of conversion in his Gifford lectures of 1901–2, *The Varieties of Religious Experience*.

Science contributed to the unsettlement of the educated English mind by its pushing men towards more scepticism over evidence for the miraculous; by giving the ordinary man the uncomfortable feeling that somehow, he knew not how, science favoured a materialistic philosophy of life, though no scientist known to fame was a materialist; by giving the historians their chance to treat the documents of the Bible as historical texts; and by first proving that parts of the Bible were myth. In the private papers of Henry Drummond on the Christian side, or Huxley on the agnostic side, perturbed correspondents lamented their loss of faith and attributed its loss to *science*. We need, however, to be sure that when they refer to *science* they mean natural sciences. Some of those who attributed loss of faith to *science* meant that *history* deprived them of their confidence in the inspiration of the Bible.

In the pews, no doubt, continued to sit large numbers of worshippers who never heard of Tylor, were indifferent to Darwin, mildly regretted what they heard of Huxley and, if they thought about it at all, knew that their faith rested upon moral considerations inaccessible to the physical sciences.

In 1900 men talked as though the conflict was over. The difficulties in the minds of the young were not scientific. A nonconformist of 1900 testified that his questioning young no longer assumed a conflict between science and religion, and that if they asked him about intellectual difficulties they often asked him about the textual criticism or the authority of the Bible.[16] Some sighed that the conflict no longer raged, for peace was established because religion had abandoned, or was abandoning, an ancient claim to give truths about the physical world.

[15] Whately, *On the Origin of Civilisation*, 1854; reprinted 1861 in *Misc. Lectures*, 26–59; J. Lubbock, 'On the Origin of Civilizations' in *Proc. Brit. Association*, 1867, ii, 118–25; Argyll, *Primeval Man*, 1869; *Contemporary Review*, 1869, xi, 164; *Journal of the Victoria Institute*, i, 1867, 189–96, etc.
[16] Charles Booth, vii, 118–19.

Those who sighed, preferred a territory where two sides competed for a no-man's-land, to a territory where each side was left in possession of its own domain without influence upon the other. Some philosophical divines were left with a sense of dissatisfaction, at this division of the world into compartments, which they bequeathed to the twentieth century.

15   The Christian Doctrine of Creation and the Rise of Modern Natural Science[*][1]

M. B. Foster

For the convenience of this article I shall use the term 'modern science' in a restricted sense, so as to exclude from consideration its most recent developments. Thus by 'modern physics' I mean what is now sometimes called 'the classical physics'. I do this not because I wish to imply that what I say of it is not true also of the most recent developments of science, but because I do not wish to raise the question here whether it is or not.

I approach my subject by way of a consideration of modern philosophy, and I apply the term 'modern' to philosophy with a similar restriction, meaning by 'modern philosophy' the philosophy which arose at the end of the Middle Ages and developed along the two main lines of Empiricism and Rationalism from Hobbes to Hume and from Descartes to Leibniz. About this philosophy as a whole I shall make two assumptions which I think will not be disputed. The first is that it was devoted (in so far as it was concerned with a theory of nature) mainly to establishing the possibility or justifying the presuppositions of the modern science of nature. It is necessary to use these two alternative descriptions because the relation of philosophy to science varied according to the degree of development which the latter had achieved at the time. By the later centuries of the modern era the sciences of nature had become so firmly established that they formed a datum from which philosophical speculation could start. This does not of course mean that the philosopher dogmatically accepted the truth of any scientific hypothesis. He assumed only that a science of nature was possible (because it was actual), enquired into the presuppositions

* M. B. Foster, 'The Christian Doctrine of Creation and the Rise of Modern Natural Science', *Mind*, 1934, 43, 446–68.

[1] I have anticipated something of what is said in this article in a paper entitled 'The opposition between Hegel and the philosophy of Empiricism' which was read at the third Congress of the International Hegel Society at Rome, Easter 1933, and published among the proceedings of the Congress. The subjects of the two papers are different enough to be largely complementary, but where they overlap I have not hesitated to repeat my arguments.

of its possibility, and tested his conclusions by their compatibility with it. This procedure is what Kant first named the Critical Method, but it was to some extent unconsciously anticipated by his predecessors in the later portion of the period which we are considering. But the assertions made about nature by the earlier philosophers of this period, while the sciences of nature were still in the founding, could not be grounded by such a method. Obviously the argument that nature must be such and such because otherwise the science of nature would not be possible, is cogent only when it is granted that the science of nature is actual. What I wish admitted is simply that these pioneers of modern philosophy, writing before the modern science of nature was fully established and not grounding their conclusions on its existence, did yet ascribe to the world of nature those very characteristics which the modern science of nature must presuppose in it as the condition of its own possibility. Thus Descartes, for example, denied that final causes are operative in nature; and modern physics was based upon the presupposition that final causes are not operative in nature. Locke declared that the Real Essence of natural objects was unknowable: and the modern empirical sciences of nature presupposed that the real essence of their objects was unknowable.[2] In a word: the early modern philosophers ascribed to nature the character which constituted it a possible object of modern natural science in advance of the actual establishment of that science.

I wish it admitted, secondly, that, these modern doctrines of nature being, as they were felt by their authors to be, incompatible with the Aristotelian doctrine of nature maintained in the Scholastic philosophy, precisely the element in them which is alien to Aristotle is the ground of the peculiar characteristics by which modern natural science is distinguished from the science of the Greeks or the Scholastics. Thus, to take the same two examples, when Locke asserts that the real essence of natural objects is unknowable, he is both contradicting Aristotle and by the same assertion ascribing to nature the characteristic which necessitates in the science of it that empirical quality by which the modern inductive sciences are distinguished from any science which had preceded them. When Descartes declares that only efficient causes operate in nature, he is substituting for the Aristotelian conception of nature another incompatible with it; and the difference between the Cartesian and the Aristotelian conceptions of nature is the ground of the difference between the modern science of physics and its ancient counterpart.

[2] Because if it were knowable, properties of the object would be deducible from it, not established by the evidence of experience.

The general question arises: What is the source of the un-Greek elements which were imported into philosophy by the post-Reformation philosophers, and which constitute the modernity of modern philosophy? And the particular question – which is merely part of the general question repeated: What is the source of those un-Greek elements in the modern theory of nature by which the peculiar character of the modern science of nature was to be determined? The answer to the first question is: The Christian revelation, and the answer to the second: The Christian doctrine of creation. The main object of this article is limited to establishing the answer to the particular question, but I will preface the attempt by a few remarks upon the general one.

Opposition to Greek philosophy in general, and to that of Aristotle in particular, was not raised for the first time in history when the post-Reformation philosophers rejected Scholasticism. On the contrary, the opposition between Christian revelation and Greek philosophy was as old as Christianity itself, and the endeavour to overcome it through the progressive assimilation of Christian dogmas by the philosophical understanding was the spring of the whole development of medieval philosophy.[3] Scholasticism itself is much more than a re-edition of Aristotle. If we ask from what source this *plus* is derived, there can be only one answer: it is clearly and obviously derived from the Christian revelation. My contention is that the conflict waged against Aristotle after the Reformation was only a continuation of the conflict waged against him before it; that as the one party in this opposition (Greek philosophy) remained the same after as before the Reformation, so also the other remained the same; and that the un-Greek element in modern has the same source as the un-Greek element in medieval philosophy: namely the Christian revelation. There is hardly a stronger argument for the truth of this contention than to draw the consequences of denying it. If we deny it we must suppose both that the un-Greek (i.e. specifically modern) element in modern philosophy was without a source, and that the un-Greek (i.e. specifically medieval) element in medieval philosophy was without an issue. This supposition can hardly even be entertained by one who has not been hardened in the belief that the history of philosophy begins again *de novo* with Descartes.

[3] This is brought out with fine lucidity in É. Gilson's *L'esprit de la philosophie médiévale*. But my whole article is a protest against Gilson's further assumption, that we must look to a resurrection of Scholasticism for a continuation of this great task, and against his implied judgment that the work of the classical modern philosophers represents a declension from the path upon which medieval philosophy set out.

To say this is by no means to deny that there was a crisis
in the history of thought at the time of the Reformation or that
modern differs from medieval philosophy in vitally important
respects. The effect of the Reformation in the sphere of thought
was analogous in two ways to its effects in the sphere of conduct. In the latter sphere it had the effect, first, of extending
the Christian order of conduct from the religious (i.e. monastic)
to the secular life. This involved, of course, the disappearance of
the 'religious' life as such, but by no means therefore of the
principles by which it had been governed. They continued to
be applied, with a rigour only intensified by their diffusion, in
the Puritan asceticism of the economic life.[4] The Reformation
had the consequence, secondly, of transferring the direction of
conduct from the external authority of the priest to the internal
authority of conscience. But conscience only imposed from
within the same laws of conduct which the priest had imposed
from without. The Reformation marks a term in the education
of the Christian peoples analogous to that which Aristotle proposes as the end of the ethical training of the individual. The
first stage in the acquisition of virtue by the individual is his
submission to certain principles of conduct prescribed by another, but the end of this submission is his acquirement of a
disposition to act in accordance with these principles. When
this is achieved, he is emancipated from his tutelage, and his
actions are determined henceforth from within himself. But
this does not in the least imply that his actions are now liber-
ated from the control of the principles to which they were
formerly submitted. It means simply that they are now animated by these principles whereas previously they were conformed to them. Similarly, at the Reformation conduct was
emancipated not from direction by Christian principles, but
only from their external prescription. Conscience itself was an
'acquired disposition', informed by submission to that very
prescription, and if its possessors could mistake it for a
'natural' faculty, that was only because it had been acquired so
thoroughly.[5]

[4] I refer especially to Max Weber's great work, *Die protestantische Ethik
und der Geist des Kapitalismus.*
[5] 'Der gesunde Menschenverstand und das naturliche Gefühl roher Türken
zum Mass-stab genommen, gibt abscheuliche Grundsätze. Wenn *wir* aber
von gesundem Menschenverstand sprechen, von natürlichem Gefühl, so
hat man dabei immer im Sinn einen gebildeten Geist; und die, welche die
gesunde Menschenvernunft, das natürliche Wissen, die unmittelbaren
Gefühle und Offenbarungen in ihnen zur Regel und Mass-stab machen,
wissen nicht, dass, wenn Religion, das Sittliche, Rechtliche sich als Inhalt
in der Menschenbrust findet, dies der Bildung und Erziehung verdankt
wurde, die nur erst solche Grundsätze zu natürlichen Gefühlen gemacht
haben.' Hegel, *Geschichte der Philosophie*, III, ii., 2; *Werke*, 2nd edn, vol.
XV, p. 439.

In the sphere of thought the Reformation had effects analogous to both of these. In the first place (I am reversing the order), philosophers claimed for reason emancipation from the authority of faith, to which it had been so long submitted. They did not realise that the reason for which they claimed autonomy was a reason itself informed by this very submission, and that what they called 'common sense' or 'the natural light' was only an internal revelation of what had previously been revealed externally to faith. If the reason upon which they relied had been in fact what they took it for, a 'natural' faculty bereft of the enlightenment of the Christian revelation, it could have discovered no truths not discovered by reason to the Greeks, and could not therefore have laid down the foundations upon which modern science was raised.

The delusion of the early modern philosophers that their philosophy was based wholly on the evidence of reason[6] (if they were Rationalists) or of experience (if they were Empiricists) prevented them from looking further for the source of their doctrines, or from so much as entertaining the supposition that they were indebted to Christian revelation. But it has been open to no succeeding philosopher to share the delusion. The work of criticism very speedily showed that neither the Rationalist nor the Empiricist philosophy was really based upon the evidence upon which it pretended to rely. No experience, to take one example, could serve as evidence to Locke of the existence of material substances, nor any reasoning demonstrate to Descartes the existence of a material world. No doubt, the assurance of 'common sense' might suffice for the one, and of the 'natural light' for the other. But then it must be admitted that 'common sense' is something other than sense and the 'natural light' something other than reason; and the way is open for the enquiry: What is the source of that certainty which is derived neither from reason nor from sense?[7]

[6] When Raymond de Sebonde declares in the prologue to his *Theologia Naturalis sive Liber Creaturarum*, that the exercise of the natural reason upon the Book of Nature suffices a man to know without difficulty 'whatever is contained in Holy Scripture' (C. C. J. Webb, *Studies in the History of Natural Theology*, p. 292 ff.), that is only an extreme form of the delusion shared in some degree by all the modern Rationalist philosophies.

[7] Mr A. K. Stout ('Descartes's Proof of the Existence of Matter', *Mind*, April 1932) has argued that Descartes's own doctrine is not that the existence of the material world is assured directly by the 'natural light', but that it is assured directly by something which Descartes distinguishes from the 'natural light' as the 'teaching of nature', and by the 'natural light' only indirectly, inasmuch as it is competent to establish the general veracity of the 'teaching of nature' (though not the truth of any particular one of its dictates).

Acceptance of Mr Stout's conclusions (which I am by no means disposed

It will not be enough to show that this certainty had its source in the Christian revelation; it has to be shown also that it had its issue in the establishment of the presuppositions of modern natural science. That these presuppositions are not themselves established by the evidence either of reason or of sense, any acquaintance with the 'problem of induction' or with Hume's difficulties about causation is sufficient to show. And in fact the criticism to which the Rationalist and Empiricist philosophies were subjected, in divesting them of all those conclusions to which they were not *upon their own premises* entitled, did divest them of every certainty which the procedure of modern natural science requires for its justification. If these philosophies had never laid themselves open to that criticism, if they had begun by resigning themselves to the scepticism to which they were ultimately reduced; or if, having laid themselves open to it, they had succumbed to it too soon – they would not have performed the function which in fact they performed in the establishment of modern science. What prevented them from succumbing sooner was their reliance upon the revelation which had raised them above scepticism in the first place. Regius and Malebranche, for example, being unable to defend against criticism Descartes' demonstration of the existence of the material world, do not therefore surrender the doctrine; they only recur overtly to the authority of revelation to establish a truth which Descartes had referred to the deliverance of the natural light. The very ease with which this transition is made is sufficient to indicate that Descartes' 'natural light' was informed by the same revelation.

The time came much later when the appeal to revelation lost the power of directing thought. Kant, who was perhaps the first to perceive quite clearly that the *whole* of the ontological doctrines of modern Rationalism were covertly dependent upon the authority of revelation, regarded this as a sufficient ground for dismissing them, and not as a confirmation of their truth. But by this time the 'dogmatic' philosophies had done their work. A body of natural sciences had arisen upon the presuppositions which they had laid down, and it was possible *now* for the philosopher to establish the presuppositions by the 'critical' method of working back to them from the sciences which were based upon them. During the whole period in which the modern natural sciences were in an early stage of growth the influence of re-

---

to question) would necessitate a certain revision of my terminology, but not any essential modification of my argument. However significant it may be that Descartes should have admitted the existence of a source of certainty other than reason, the admission is practically nullified by the proviso that the general veracity of the 'teaching of nature' must be demonstrable by reason. The proviso makes the certainty of the existence of matter to depend ultimately, if not immediately, upon the 'natural light'.

ligious authority upon philosophical thought was consistently exerted to preserve it from conclusions, whether sceptical or otherwise, which would have been incompatible with the possibility of these sciences; and religion surrendered this control only when the sciences were established firmly enough to serve in their turn as a datum for philosophical speculation. I will give an illustration at the risk of anticipating what belongs later. Descartes and Kant both reject final causation in nature, but their arguments differ significantly. Kant argues in effect from the absence of final reasoning in science to the absence of final causation in nature; nature must be without final causes because it is presupposed to be so by the science of mathematical physics. But Descartes proceeds in the reverse direction. The avoidance of final explanations by the physicist is not cited as a fact, but prescribed as a rule. The scientist, he says, *ought* to abjure the search for final explanations *because the purposes of God are inscrutable*. This argument is an enthymeme of which the premises to be supplied are that nature is *created* by God, and that the activity of creation is not directed by an intelligible purpose. So that Descartes's prescription to the physicist is based upon the metaphysical implications of Christian dogma.[8]

In the second place, as the Reformation in the practical sphere had the effect of extending the application of Christian principles of conduct beyond the religious to the secular life, so in the theoretical sphere it carried out the implications of Christian doctrines beyond the sacred into the profane sciences. The medieval philosopher had of course believed the Christian doctrine that nature is created. But the belief had been efficacious only in his theology. In his science of nature he had continued to seek for final causes, to define essences and to deduce properties: in a word – he had continued to employ the methods of Aristotelian science, entirely oblivious of the fact that Aristotle's science was based upon the presupposition that nature is not created. The modern investigators of nature were the first to take seriously *in their science* the Christian doctrine that nature is created, and the main differences between the methods of ancient and the

[8] The same connection may be illustrated by another example. Of Aquinas's presentation of the doctrine of the 'star-moving Intelligences' Prof. Webb remarks that 'the chief interest to us of these speculations ... lies in the fact that Thomas Aquinas is so thoroughly alive to the danger involved *to the religious principles of Christianity* in the acknowledgement of the divinity of the heavenly bodies' (*Studies in the History of Natural Theology*, p. 274. My italics). Acknowledgement of their divinity was the basis of the distinction between Celestial and Terrestrial physics, with the abolition of which modern physical science may almost be said to have begun. There could hardly be more striking evidence of the truth of my thesis than the fact that this criticism was first undertaken in the interest of the religious principles of Christianity.

methods of modern natural science may be reduced to this: that these are and those are not methods proper to the investigation of a created nature.

With this we may turn to a closer examination of the particular question. We have to determine, first, what the differences are which distinguish the methods of modern from those of Greek natural science; we have to show that these differences depend upon differences between the modern and the Greek philosophy of nature, and that these in their turn are derived from the differences between the Christian and the Greek conception of God and of God's relation to the world.

I have said what I shall mean by the term 'modern science of nature', but it might appear a difficulty to determine what is to be meant by the contrasted term 'Greek science of nature'. Greek science of nature was in most of its branches an attempt rather than an achievement, and an enquiry into its character might seem to be surrounded by all the difficulties which attend an investigation of the rudimentary and the embryonic. Even to determine what its methods were might seem to require an antiquarian learning which I am far from possessing and which could in any event hardly promise to yield results of philosophical importance.

I shall not embark on such an investigation and my purpose does not require that I should do so. We need not elicit the principles of Greek science from the vestiges of Greek sciences, because we possess a classical formulation of the principles in the Aristotelian Logic. By Greek science I shall mean such science, or attempted science, of nature as conformed to the canons of Aristotelian Logic; and I shall not be disturbed by the fact, if it be one, that the Greeks developed some sciences not so conformable; or that the systematic attempt to apply Aristotelian methods to the investigation of nature was characteristic rather of the medieval scholastics than of the Greek philosophers. The peculiar characteristics by which modern is to be distinguished from Greek natural science may consequently be determined simply as those which render the former unconformable to the canons of this logic.[9]

Judged by this criterion one of the most important and striking differences, though no doubt it is not the only difference, between the methods of modern and those of ancient natural science is the presence in the former of an empirical element lacking in the latter. Modern science describes natural substances instead of defining them, it discovers their properties by observation and experiment instead of by 'intuitive induction' and demonstration, it classifies their species instead of dividing their genera, it establishes between them the relation of cause and

[9] Cf. in this connection C. R. Morris, *Idealistic Logic*, chap. iv.

effect instead of the relation of ground and consequent. In each case the modern procedure will be found to differ from its ancient counterpart by the part which sensuous experience plays in it. This is not to say that sensuous experience played no part in ancient science, but that it played a different part: it supplied the illustration but not the evidence of the conclusions of science.[10]

All the peculiarities of Greek natural science are derived from the assumption that the essence of a natural object is definable, as the essence of a geometrical object is. Once let this be granted, and it follows that the properties must be deducible by reason from the essence, the species derivable by reasoning from the concept of the genus, the necessary connections between it and other objects such as can be perceived by reason to be involved in the essence; it follows, in a word, that empirical evidence must be inadmissible in the same degree and for the same reason in establishing the conclusions of natural science as it obviously is in establishing the conclusions of Euclidean geometry.

The methods of Greek natural science thus depend upon the assumption that the essences of natural objects are definable. What does this scientific assumption presuppose about the nature of the physical world?

Definition is an act of reason containing no element of sense, however necessary it may be that sensuous perception should precede it. No doubt I must have seen lines, or touched them, before I can define the line. But when I have reached a definition, then 'the line' which I have defined is intelligible only, neither visible nor tangible. That in objects which is intelligible as distinct from sensible is what the Greeks called their form as distinct from their matter. That the form of things is intelligible, and therefore definable, does not of itself constitute the whole of the assumption required to justify the procedure of Greek science, namely that the *essence* of things is intelligible, and therefore definable. It needs the complementary assumption, which the Greeks also made, that the form of things is their essence, i.e. that of the two elements, formal and material, of which every actual thing is composed, the form alone makes the thing to be what it is, whereas the matter contributes no positive element to its being. Matter is the correlative, in the object, of sense in the subject, as form is the correlative of reason; and thus the Greek assumption about science, that there can be no empirical evidence for scientific conclusions, depends upon the Greek assumption about nature which may be loosely designated the assumption of the 'unreality of matter'. The designation is loose,

[10] This is not, of course, the point at issue between Aristotle and Plato. They differ only in estimating differently the importance to be assigned to the sensible *as illustration*.

because it is not meant simply that matter is not actual except in union with form; for it is true equally, at least according to Aristotle, to say that form is not actual except in union with matter. What is meant is that the σύνολον of matter and form, which alone is actual, is determined to be what it is wholly by the one element of form. The object is *nothing more than* a realisation of form; its matter is the source of no being in it over and above that which it derives from its form, it is the source only of the imperfection with which the latter is realised. The method of Greek natural science thus involves a theory of nature according to which the actual world is distinguishable into the two elements of form and matter, the former intelligible, the latter sensible. Because the 'intelligible nature' is the ground both of all being and of all action in the actual world, whereas matter accounts only for diminution of being and impediment of action, it follows that intelligent comprehension of form is sufficient for the understanding both of what is and of what happens in the actual world, so far as this is capable of being understood, whereas sensuous experience represents no addition to, but only defect of, such understanding.

We have to ask finally what theory of God is presupposed in this theory of nature, and here I shall invert the natural order of investigation by stating my conclusion first. The theory of nature presupposes that neither of the two elements of which nature is composed is dependent for its being upon a power outside nature, i.e. that neither of them is created. If matter were created it would possess a positive being, if form were created it would not be intelligible. The twin Greek doctrines of the 'unreality' of matter and the intelligibility of form imply that matter and form are alike eternal. We may say in advance, then, that any development of Greek theology, if it is to remain consistent with the presuppositions of Greek natural science, must stop short of the attribution to God of an omnipotent power over nature. Nature may be conceived as dependent upon a supernatural power for the activity by which its two elements are conjoined, but not for the being of either element. I shall endeavour to show, in the briefest possible outline, how Greek theology observes this limitation even in its highest developments, and I shall make some remarks upon each in turn of the three following Greek theological conceptions: (i) the conception of God as identical with nature, or of nature as itself divine, (ii) the conception of God as subject of a purely theoretical activity, (iii) the conception of God as artificer or Demiurge of nature.

(i) The identification of God with Nature finds its earliest expression in the deification of natural powers which is characteristic of the Greek polytheistic religion. So long as this identification is both naïve and complete, so long, e.g. as the god is simply not distinguished at all from the natural object, it does not seem, indeed, that the religion founded upon it can give rise either to a theology or to a science of nature. But Greek[11] religion, though it may have begun with such a naïve identification, did not end with it. The withdrawal of the Gods to Olympus implies the recognition of *some* distinction between the natural and the divine. This is no absolute distinction; if it had been, Greek religion would have cast off at a stroke the character which distinguishes it as pagan from either the Jewish or the Christian; but it was sufficient to entail that the sensible object should be regarded henceforth not simply as the god, but as the *appearance* of the god, and its growth or motion rather as the *manifestation* of a divine activity, than as being itself divine.

This partial distinction between God and nature supplied the foundations of Greek science, for the Greek did not free himself from the teachings of his religion when he became a philosopher. The attitude of belief, no doubt, gave way in him to that of understanding, but what he now understood was only what he had previously believed. The great philosophical distinction which Socrates initiated and Plato worked out between the idea and the sensible object was only the explication of the distinction which had been already made in Greek religion between the God and the sensible object.

It will hardly be denied that this philosophical distinction was the foundation of the Greek science of nature, and if it be granted that the possibility of Greek natural science depended ultimately upon the distinction between God and nature achieved even by Greek religion, there may be a readier acceptance of the thesis that the far higher development of modern natural science depends upon the far deeper distinction between God and nature achieved by the Christian religion. The limitations of the pagan distinction are reflected in the peculiarities of Greek scientific

[11] I am using the term 'Greek' with an arbitrary limitation of meaning. By 'Greek religion' I mean the Greek Olympian religion, by 'Greek philosophy' the tradition of philosophy which began with Socrates and culminated in Aristotle, by 'Greek natural science' the science of nature based upon that philosophy, the actual pursuit of which was perhaps rather characteristic of Medieval Scholasticism than of the Greeks themselves. I need hardly say that I do not intend to deny the existence of what I ignore. There was, of course, a Greek religion other than the Olympian, a Greek philosophy before Socrates (there seems to have been a close connection between pre-Socratic philosophy and extra-Olympian religion), and there were at least the rudiments of a Greek natural science which was not a science of formal causes. Reaction against Aristotle in the early-modern philosophers was often enough accompanied by a renaissance of the theories of pre-Socratic philosophers. It remains none the less true that the reaction derived its force from Christian dogma, and only its watchwords from the pre-Socratics. These doctrines were revived and others discarded because these were more readily conformable to the doctrine of Creation.

procedure. If the gods are to be distinguished from nature, and yet not completely distinguished from it, they must be conceived as *appearing* in nature and as natural objects. The same difficulty concerning the relation of the sensible to the supersensible arises within the Platonic philosophy, and the solution of it is the same: the sensible is related to the idea as appearance to that which appears. The application of these categories to nature implies that the sensible (which is the material) is, *quâ* sensible and material, merely apparent, and this implication justifies the *a priori* methods of Greek natural science. But the doctrine of Creation implies that the material is real *quâ* material.

It is true that the doctrine of nature implicit in Greek polytheism is not of itself sufficient to supply the presuppositions even of Greek natural science. That the forms should be isolable in thought from the accidents of their material embodiment, is not sufficient to constitute them proper objects of a science. A scientific understanding (as distinct from a still quasi-aesthetic contemplation) demands that its objects be perceived to be inter-related one with another as members of a single system,[12] and this involves a view of the universe different from that involved in any mere polytheism. On the other hand, it does not involve any form of Theism, or belief in a God transcending nature. Nature must be conceived as a unity, but the principle which constitutes it one need not, for any of the considerations yet advanced, be held to possess an existence apart from nature, or to be related to the multiplicity of natural objects in any other wise than that, e.g., in which the principle of life in an organism is related to its bodily members. Though this principle of unity may be termed 'God', it is God only in the sense in which that term is compatible with Pantheism, or a God still imperfectly distinguished from nature. The Greek, in other words, in becoming a monotheist did not necessarily thereby cease to be a pagan; and Pantheism is no less incompatible than polytheism with the attribution of reality to sensible particulars.

(ii) There are Greek theological doctrines which transcend the limitations of Paganism. I shall content myself here with considering two of these, with pointing out in what respects they differ from the doctrine of God as Creator, and with trying to show that it is precisely in virtue of these points of difference that they are enabled to remain compatible with the Greek theory of nature, especially in the two crucial regards which I have mentioned.

The first of these is Aristotle's conception of God as First Mover. It is not without significance for my thesis that Aristotle's proof of the existence of a transcendent God is based upon the

[12] The possibility of syllogistic inference in especial depends upon the systematic interrelation of species.

necessity of accounting for the communication of motion by efficient causes in nature; in other words, that he approaches most
nearly to the Christian doctrine of God at the very point at which
his conception of nature approximates most closely to that of
modern physics. But Aristotle's God, though admitted to be
transcendent, is bereft of any power over nature except the single
power of originating motion. Neither the matter nor the form
of natural objects depends on him; and even of motion in nature
he is not himself the efficient but only the final cause. He is
not the source of energy in nature; that must be held to arise
within nature from the active potency of the form to realise
itself; but is only the end upon which all energy in nature is
directed. The only activity of which God is the source is his own
theoretical activity; and this activity terminates not upon the
world but upon himself.

It may well be questioned whether Aristotle's restriction of
God's operation upon the world is really consistent with his
argument for God's transcendence; whether, in other words, that
argument does not demand the conclusion that motion in nature
has a source as well as an end outside nature. However this may
be, it is certainly that restriction which enables Aristotle to retain
essentially unmodified the conception of nature already outlined.
Nature owes God nothing except that harmony of its operations one with another which they derive from their direction
upon a single end; and which might in fact be as well accounted
for by the Pantheistic hypothesis, that nature is animated by a
single soul.

The attribution to God of an activity of will sweeps away this
restriction, and with it the possibility of maintaining the Pagan
conception of nature as self-dependent.

(iii) There is one Greek doctrine of God which ascribes to him
a power of efficient causation in the constitution of the actual
world. This is Plato's doctrine of the Demiurge or Artificer, and
because this, of all Greek theological doctrines, bears the closest
superficial resemblance to the Christian doctrine of Creation it
will serve best to throw into relief the essential contrast which
still persists between the conception of God as Creator and any
conception of the divine activity which is consistent with the presuppositions of Greek natural science. The doctrine that God is
a Demiurge is perfectly consistent with them, because the activity
of a Demiurge (the activity which the Greeks called Techne)
is essentially both (i) *informative* and (ii) *purposive*, that is to say,
it is (i) confined to the information of a given matter, and (ii)
directed by the antecedent conception of an end. The activity
consists in the realisation in matter of the end, which becomes
by realisation the form or essence of the object produced, but
since the form must be conceived by the workman *before* he starts

his work it cannot derive its being, but only its embodiment, from his activity. The form must be 'given' to the Demiurge no less than the matter of his work; thus, if God is Demiurge of the actual world, his work is confined to the uniting of its two elements, form and matter, but cannot extend to the bringing into being of either element.

The ascription to God of the activity of a Demiurge is thus compatible with the fundamental assumption of Greek natural science, that form and matter are eternal. We may, indeed, see more vividly what is involved in this assumption if we reflect that to make it is to attribute to natural objects *a constitution identical with that of the products of a Techne*. Plato in the Timaeus may be unique in asserting that the natural world is the product of a Demiurge; but Aristotle asserts,[13] and all the methods of Aristotelian science presuppose, that natural objects *are as though they were* the work of a Demiurge.

We may illustrate the connection between this presupposition and those methods by an analogy. Any product of one of the useful arts is clearly and indisputably the work of an artificer. If we imagine an investigator (say an archaeologist who has uncovered the remains of an unknown civilisation) confronted with a collection of unfamiliar artefacts, it will be possible for him, provided only that he knows them to be artefacts, to institute an enquiry into them by an application of the very methods which Aristotle thought proper to a study of nature.

His first task will be to determine what the different objects are, or to define them; the initial assumption that they are products of an artificer involves the consequence that they are capable of definition. His method of determination will be that of intuitive, not of empirical induction, and what he determines will be the real, not the nominal essence of the objects. He will collect the greatest possible variety of examples of each kind, and will observe their sensible qualities, but his procedure will not be that of the empirical scientist as Locke, e.g., describes it in his doctrine of Abstraction. He will not tabulate the sensible qualities which all his examples have in common, assign a general name to such a complex of qualities, and determine to call by that name in future every object which shall be found to possess all of them. On the contrary, he will use his variety of sensible examples as the geometrician may use a variety of drawn figures, strictly as illustrations, and to facilitate his passage by an act of intuitive

---

[13] Cf. *Physics*, II, 8, 199a, 12. εἰ οἰκία τῶν φύσει γιγνομένων ἦν, οἵτως ἂν ἐγίνετο ὡς νῦν ἀπὸ τέχνης. εἰ δὲ τὰ φύσει μὴ μόνον φύσει ἀλλὰ καὶ τέχνῃ γίγνοιτο, ὡσαίτως ἂν γίνοιτο ᾗ πέφυκεν, and ib. 6, 30. Natural objects differ from products of art according to Aristotle only in the one respect, not relevant to the present issue, that they have their principle of action within them.

reason to a comprehension of something which is not itself sensible at all, but is the reason (λόγος) of the object.[14] What it comprehended will be at once the end which governed the design of the artificer, and at the same time the form of the products (since it is clearly that in the product which the artificer added to his materials, i.e. is that element in it which is to be distinguished from the material). It will be the real essence, because the end conceived by the artificer will in fact have caused the product to possess the qualities (its peculiar spatial configuration, e.g.), which it is found to have; and hence discovery of the essence will enable the investigator to understand the reason of what he had previously only observed to be a fact.[15]

The essence once defined can serve as the ground of demonstration of essential properties; if an object is to serve a given purpose, it must possess such properties as are evidently indispensable to its fulfilment.

Definition of the essence makes possible its subsumption under a genus and its differentiation into subordinate species by the method of Division : a method differing from that of empirical classification in that it proceeds *a priori* by an insight into the essential nature of a thing, not *a posteriori* by comparison of similar sensible qualities.[16]

That properties should be demonstrable *a priori* of the essence and that species should be subsumable *a priori* under genera, these are the two conditions necessary for the possibility of a Syllogistic inference which should be free from the fallacy of *Petitio Principii*. The investigator we have imagined could make a fruitful use of the syllogism in constructing a science of his manufactured articles.

In a word : their susceptibility of definition makes it possible to apply to manufactured articles all the other Aristotelian methods. The science of nature would conform similarly to the

[14] 'We found cuttings in the rocks which puzzled us for a long time, till I, who had seen the same in Syria, discovered that they were winepresses' (*Letters of Gertrude Bell*, I., p. 240). This discovery was not a detection by any of the senses of a sensible quality which had hitherto eluded them; what is discovered could not have been rendered *visible* by any microscope.

[15] Of a jug, e.g., the experience of his senses can inform him that it has a flat base and a projecting lip; but only a discovery of its purpose can enable him to understand why it has.

[16] Thus the unknown artefacts of our illustration could be classified empirically in any of a variety of ways according to similarity of sensible characteristics (colour, e.g., texture of surface or size) by one who did not know their purpose; or even if they had had none. But the discovery of the one true system of genera and species, according to which a given object is to be classed, e.g. as a kind of lamp, and not as a species coordinate with the sauce-dishes which it resembles in appearance : this presupposes knowledge of the purpose of the objects and is achieved by methods different from those of empirical classification.

canons of Aristotelian Logic *if nature were the work of Demiurge.*

For an object to be definable, two conditions must be satisfied: (i) its form must be intelligible, and (ii) its form must be its real essence. Both conditions are satisfied by the products of a Techne, and the possibility of an Aristotelian science of nature depends upon the assumption that both conditions are fulfilled by natural objects.

But the doctrine that nature is created involves the denial that natural objects can satisfy either condition.

(i) That the form of an object is intelligible, means that it is distinguishable in conception from the sensible material of its embodiment. The form of an artefact is thus distinguishable, because the activity of the Demiurge who made it was purposive, that is to say, was directed by conception of an end. What he conceived as end, we distinguish as form; and we are enabled to conceive in distinction from sensible accidents precisely so much as he conceived in advance of his execution.

But the work of creation is not purposive; and as there is no end distinctly conceived by the creator in advance of his execution, so there is no form distinguishable by us from the accidents of its embodiment. This may be most easily seen in the contrast of fine or creative art with the activity of a Demiurge or artificer. It is notorious that the creative artist, e.g. the painter, has no clear knowledge of what he is going to achieve before he has achieved it; and the critic on his side, when confronted with a work of creative art, is indeed aware that there is 'something more' in it than the sensible material – a great painting is more than a certain complexity of coloured surfaces – but this 'something more' (we may call it loosely 'the meaning') is *not* capable of being conceived in distinction from the sensible material in which it is expressed. The meaning of a painting is not intelligible in the sense in which the purpose of a wheelbarrow is.

The form of natural objects would be distinguishable (and the objects therefore definable) only if the activity of God were purposive, i.e. directed upon an end which is not itself the product of his activity. But if God is a Creator, natural objects can have no form distinguishable as the object of the intellect.

(ii) The doctrine of Creation attributes to God an autonomous activity of will. No doubt it is also implied in the conception of God as a Demiurge that he is the subject of some practical action. His work is not exhausted according to this doctrine in the theoretical contemplation of the forms, but he engages beyond that contemplation in the non-theoretical activity of embodying them. But it is characteristic of the work of a Demiurge that in it the practical is wholly subordinated to the theoretical activity. The entire activity of the craftsman, in so far as he is a craftsman, is dictated by the end or plan which is the object of his theoretical conception. No doubt the will of any human artificer may escape from this dictation by his reason; he may add details to his work which are not necessitated by the dictates of his craft (if he is a bad workman) or are even contrary to them (if he is a corrupt one). But this insubordination of will is a mere defect and simple failure to achieve the perfection of an artificer.

That in an artificial object which is not necessitated by its idea is the *contingent*, and just as the insubordination of will is nothing but an imperfection in the artificer, so the presence of the contingent is nothing but a defect in the artefact.

Bad workmanship is not the only cause of contingency in the product. This may arise also from recalcitrance of the material; and since bad workmanship cannot be argued in the divine Demiurge, contingency in the natural world must be attributed to this source. Natural objects are contingent, i.e. they fail to conform to their idea, precisely in so far as they are material.

Now if natural objects either are artefacts (according to the theory of the divine Demiurge) or are (according to the Aristotelian theory) in this respect analogous to artefacts that they *are* nothing but an embodiment of form, then the unavoidable element of contingency which they derive from their matter is nothing but a defect of their being. It does not make them something more than an embodiment of form, but makes them only a bad embodiment of form; just as two inches more on one leg of a table does not make it more than an artefact, but only a bad artefact.

Objects are intelligible in so far as they are informed, sensible in so far as they are material. The contingent, therefore, or that in them which is not derived from their form, is sensible only, without being intelligible. But since the contingent has been found to represent only a defect of being, it will follow that natural objects are sensible only in so far as they fail to achieve their being. That in them which constitutes them objects of sensation is no increment, but only a defect of their intelligible nature; and therefore sensation can contribute no evidence concerning the nature of the thing which should be additional to what is perceived by reason. As the being material is a defect and not an increment of being, sensation is an imperfection of knowledge,[17] not a way of knowing.

The absence of an empirical element in Greek natural science follows from this.

But the will of the maker can be subordinated to his reason, as the will of the Demiurge is, only so long as 'making' is identified with formation, because form alone can be the object of reason. In the creative act the will must exceed any regulations

[17] It is at the very most the *occasion* of knowledge.

which reason can prescribe. That is to say, the 'insubordination' of will to reason, which could be only a defect in God so long as God is conceived as Demiurge, becomes essential to his activity so soon as he is thought of as Creator. It is what constitutes him, not a bad Demiurge, but something altogether more than a Demiurge.

The *voluntary* activity of the Creator (i.e. that in his activity which exceeds determination by reason) terminates on the *contingent* being of the creature (i.e. on that element of its being which eludes determination by form, namely its matter and the characteristics which it possesses *quâ* material). If such voluntary activity is essential to God, it follows that the element of contingency is essential to what he creates. So soon as nature is conceived to be created by God, the contingent becomes more than an imperfection in the embodiment of form; it is precisely what constitutes a natural object more than an embodiment, namely a creature.[18]

But the contingent is knowable only by sensuous experience. If, therefore, the contingent is essential to nature, experience must be indispensable to the science of nature; and *not* indispensable merely as a stage through which the human scientist must pass on his way to attaining adequate knowledge by reason, but indispensable because knowledge by reason cannot be adequate to a nature which is essentially something more than an embodiment of form. This 'something more', the element in nature which depends upon the *voluntary* activity of God, is incapable of becoming an object to reason, and science therefore must depend, in regard to this element, upon the *evidence* of sensation. The reliance upon the sense for evidence, not merely for illustration, is what constitutes the empirical character peculiar to modern natural science; and the conclusion follows that only a created nature is proper object of an empirical science.

---

[18] I suggest that we use the term 'real' to attribute to a thing the being which is proper to a created object. Its meaning differs from that of the Greek ὄν precisely as created from uncreated being. That is why, for instance, reality is incapable of degrees, whereas οὐσία was capable of an indefinite number of them. What is created *ex nihilo* must be entirely present so soon as it has ceased to be wholly absent; but an object of which it is the whole being to be an embodiment of form, achieves a greater or less degree of being according to the degree of perfection with which form is realised in it. It is not without significance that the term 'real' in its modern sense passed into secular language only after the Reformation (see *O.E.D.*), i.e. at the period at which the concepts of Christianity began to revolutionise the sciences of nature.

Again, the terms 'nature' and 'natural' bear a different meaning from the Greek terms φύσις and φύσει. The difference is simply that we mean by nature '*created* nature', and call 'natural' what is proper to a created nature. We are generally conscious of the difference, but oblivious of its source.

What we have attempted to show is that the method of natural science depends upon the presuppositions which are held about nature, and the presuppositions about nature in turn upon the doctrine of God. Modern natural science could begin only when the modern presuppositions about nature displaced the Greek (this was, of course, a gradual process, but its crisis occurred at the date of the Reformation); but this displacement itself was possible only when the Christian[19] conception of God had displaced the Pagan, as the object (not merely of unreasoning belief, but) of systematic understanding. To achieve this primary displacement was the work of Medieval Theology, which thus laid the foundations both of much else in the modern world which is specifically modern, and of modern natural science.

Creative activity in God, material substance in nature, empirical methods in natural science – how closely each of these three involves the other is made clear by an examination of almost any of the great philosophies of the early modern period. A defect in the philosophical conception of God is reflected in corresponding defects both in the doctrine of nature and in the theory of natural science. Thus it is a mark of the philosophy of the Rationalist tradition that it is unable wholly[20] to digest that un-Greek element in the Christian theology according to which God is endowed with a *voluntary* activity in the creation of the world.

[19] I mean Christian, not Jewish. The Christian doctrine of God derived much from the Greek and thus included within itself, besides much from Jewish sources, much also from the very doctrine which it displaced. Cf. p. 468 *inf.*

[20] The qualification is to be emphasised. Modern Rationalism differs markedly from Greek Rationalism in its theories of God, nature and science, and the differences are due, as I have illustrated above, by the example of Final Causation, to its absorption of the truth of Christian doctrine. What I am maintaining here is that this absorption was still incomplete.

I must stress the fact that the limitation of the scope of this essay precludes me from doing justice to the philosophy of modern Rationalism. I have confined myself in the main to a single characteristic (the presence of an empirical element) by which modern differs from ancient natural science, and I have endeavoured to show its connection with a single Christian doctrine (that of the Creation). It is the essence of the *Empiricist* philosophy of nature to stress that element of natural objects which exceeds the grasp of the intellect, and it is easy therefore to give the impression that Empiricism alone is adequate either to exhaust the truth of Christian doctrine, or to supply the pre-suppositions of modern natural science; while modern Rationalism succeeds in doing either, if at all, only in so far as it has absorbed some of the truth of Empiricism. But modern differs from ancient natural science in other respects besides the part played in it by experience, and Christianity has other doctrines relevant to a philosophy of nature, besides that of Creation. My argument does not exclude either the possibility that modern Rationalism does justice to some features of modern natural science which Empiricism ignores or even that it has absorbed the truth of some Christian doctrines which Empiricism has neglected.

Descartes' 'clear and distinct idea' of God is the idea of an infinite *thinking* substance, and although the influence of Christian dogma is strong enough in many places to modify his language, so that, having proved the existence of God, he proceeds to attribute to him activities other than theoretical, what constitutes him Rationalist is precisely that this attribution is not more than verbal. Christian dogma works in him strongly enough to modify his language, but not strongly enough to transform his thought. The God of which he has *demonstrated* the existence is a God whose whole essence is to think. His Rationalist doctrine of nature corresponds with his Rationalist doctrine of God: as he cannot conceive a voluntary activity in God, so he cannot conceive the reality of a contingent element in nature,[21] and his identification of matter with extension is the inevitable consequence of his identification of the divine activity with thought. Spinoza carried the Rationalism of Descartes to its logical conclusion. He explicitly denied those elements both in the activity of God and in the being of nature, which Descartes had failed to conceive clearly, but which[22] the influence of Christian dogma had been powerful enough to prevent him from denying. It is obvious that the Rationalist doctrine of nature is incompatible in its turn with the presuppositions of empirical science. If the contingent in nature is condemned to the status of appearance, sensation can make no positive contribution to knowledge; and the only natural science possible upon the presuppositions of Spinoza's philosophy would be a science which should be, like Spinoza's 'Ethics', *more geometrico demonstrata*.

The Rationalist philosophy of nature had to be corrected if it was to be rendered consistent with the possibility of an empirical natural science. From what source could the correction come? The time had not yet arrived when it was possible to argue back from the existence of a body of natural science to the nature which it presupposed as its object. Neither could direct inspection of the natural world afford evidence either to support or to disprove any theory of its metaphysical constitution. There was no standard by which the Rationalist doctrine of nature could be corrected, there was a standard only for the correction of the Rationalist doctrine of God. That had to be remoulded so as to conform to the Christian doctrine that God is Creator, and this remoulding carried with it as an implicit consequence such a modification of the theory of nature as would have rendered it consistent with the presuppositions of empirical science.[23]

---

[21] Cf. e.g., *Princ.*, II, viii.: 'That quantity and number differ only in thought (*ratione*) from that which has quantity and is numbered'.
[22] At least the former of which.
[23] The essential connection which subsists between the doctrine that God has will on the one hand, and that a science of nature must be empirical

It may serve to obviate a misunderstanding, to which I have perhaps laid myself open, if I conclude with a remark on the philosophies of modern Empiricism. Berkeley, to take the example most apt to my purpose, stresses the share of sense in knowledge even to the denial of any share to reason, and he stresses the practical activity of God to such an extent that he would be forced, if he were consistent with himself, to deny to God any but a practical activity.[24] Must it not then be admitted, I imagine the objection, that Berkeley's philosophy has *wholly* assimilated the truth of the doctrine of Creation? And yet Berkeley's philosophy is incompatible with the belief in a material substance, and signally fails to justify the presuppositions of the modern science of nature. How is this to be reconciled with the thesis of an intimate connection between the doctrine of creation and the presuppositions of empirical science?

This supposed objection rests upon the mistaken identification of the Christian doctrine of Creation with the un-Greek element in the Christian doctrine. The failure of modern Rationalism

---

on the other, may be illustrated clearly by a reference to the Leibnizian distinction between the possible and the actual. Possible is whatever is object of God's understanding and of our 'clear and distinct' (i.e. intellectual, non-empirical) perception. The addition of existence to the possible Leibniz attributes to an activity distinguished from God's understanding as God's will. Existence is not intelligible; and since it is involved in the doctrine of God's will that existence is an addition to, not a diminution of, the being which belongs to the possible, the consequence cannot be avoided that intelligence is *inadequate* by itself to the knowledge of existent nature, and requires to be supplemented by sensation: i.e. that an empirical element is necessary to natural science.

Conversely the rationalist doctrine that sense is only defect of understanding may be seen to be incompatible with the attribution of will to God. According to this doctrine the sensible *is* the intelligible imperfectly known; i.e. it derives its sensible character from the imperfection of human perception, and therefore not from an activity of God.

Leibniz maintains a rationalist epistemology side by side with a voluntarist theology, in spite of their mutual incompatibility. Nothing short of the authority of Christianity could have prevailed upon him to admit the latter doctrine into his philosophy in the teeth of the opposition of the former. If he had but attached yet more weight to this authority, it would have led him to reform his rationalist presuppositions into consistency with his theology, and *thereby* into consistency with the procedure of empirical science.

[24] This implication of Berkeley's philosophy is clearly brought out in Mr J. D. Mabbott's admirable article 'The Place of God in Berkeley's Philosophy', in the *Journal of Philosophical Studies*, January 1931.

It is significant that Berkeley, like Descartes, is preserved from a consistency of error principally by the necessity of conforming to Christian doctrine in his theory of God. He does not shrink from the consequence that the science of mathematical physics is impossible, nor from outraging Common Sense by his denial of material substance, but he cannot allow himself to rest in the conclusion that the divine activity is one of blind will.

was its failure to do justice to this un-Greek element, the failure of modern Empiricism was its failure to do justice to anything else. The Christian doctrine on this, as on all other subjects, itself includes an element derived from Greek philosophy, and any doctrine from which all Greek elements are excluded is less than Christian. It is Christian to ascribe to God an activity of will, but it is not Christian to deny to God a theoretical activity or to ascribe to him a *blind* activity of will. It is a consequence of the Christian doctrine of Creation that the created world must contain an element of contingency, not that it must be nothing but contingent. It was because he drew this latter consequence, and was unable to attribute to matter the possession of any intelligible (as opposed to sensible) qualities that Berkeley was led to his denial of material substance, and to the conclusion, implicit in his philosophy if not admitted by himself, that a science of nature is not possible. Thus Berkeley falls short equally with Spinoza of expressing in his philosophy the whole of what is contained in the Christian doctrine of God. Spinoza had denied voluntary activity to God, Berekeley denies everything but voluntary activity. Similarly in their doctrines of nature, whereas Spinoza had denied contingency, Berkeley denies everything else; Spinoza's world is a nature, but is not created, Berkeley's is created but is not a nature, and so both are compelled, though for opposite reasons, to deny material substances, which can exist only in a created nature. This denial necessitates finally that both fail equally, again in opposite respects, of consistency with the presuppositions of modern natural science. Of Spinoza's world no science could be empirical, of Berkeley's no experience scientific.

Indexes

SUBJECT INDEX

INDEX OF PRIMARY SOURCES

INDEX OF SECONDARY SOURCES